Reading Jean-Luc Marion

INDIANA SERIES IN THE PHILOSOPHY OF RELIGION
MEROLD WESTPHAL, EDITOR

Reading Jean-Luc Marion

Exceeding Metaphysics

Christina M. Gschwandtner

INDIANA UNIVERSITY PRESS
BLOOMINGTON AND INDIANAPOLIS

This book is a publication of

Indiana University Press
601 North Morton Street
Bloomington, IN 47404-3797 USA

http://iupress.indiana.edu

Telephone orders   800-842-6796
Fax orders   812-855-7931
Orders by e-mail   iuporder@indiana.edu

The paper used in this publication meets the minimum require-
ments of American National Standard for Information Sciences —
Permanence of Paper for Printed Library Materials, ANSI
Z39.48-1984.

MANUFACTURED IN THE UNITED STATES OF AMERICA

Library of Congress Cataloging-in-Publication Data

Gschwandtner, Christina M., date
    Reading Jean-Luc Marion : exceeding metaphysics / Christina M.
Gschwandtner.
        p. cm. — (Indiana series in the philosophy of religion)
    Includes bibliographical references and index.
    ISBN-13: 978-0-253-34977-4 (cloth : alk. paper)
    ISBN-13: 978-0-253-21945-9 (pbk. : alk. paper) 1. Marion, Jean-Luc, 1946–
2. Metaphysics. 3. Descartes, René, 1596–1650. I. Title.
B2430.M284G73 2007
194 — dc22

                                                          2007017088

1 2 3 4 5   13 12 11 10 09 08

For Joanne

Der römische Brunnen

Aufsteigt der Strahl, und fallend gießt
Er voll der Marmorschale Rund,
Die, sich verschleiernd, überfließt
In einer zweiten Schale Grund;
Die zweite gibt, sie wird zu reich,
Der dritten wallend ihre Flut,
Und jede nimmt und gibt zugleich
    Und strömt und ruht.

            Conrad Ferdinand Meyer

The Roman Fountain

The stream wells up and falls below
To fill the marble basin's round,
And pours its veiling overflow
Into a second basin's ground;
The second gives in ceaseless reach
Into the third its wealth invests.
And each one takes and gives to each
    And flows and rests.

The gift cannot be received unless it is given, for otherwise it would cease to merit its name. The basin is not filled up by the cascade from above unless it ceaselessly empties itself into the basin below. Only the abandonment of that which fills it permits that the stream to come should fill it without cease.

    Jean-Luc Marion, Idol and Distance

Contents

Contents

PREFACE

Exceeding metaphysics. In reading Jean-Luc Marion, it is not particularly difficult to ascertain that his philosophical language is characterized by abundance, excess, and saturation. Nor is it hard to see that metaphysics and the possibility to engage in phenomenological and theological thought after its death are central to Marion's work. This desire to overcome metaphysics and to stretch the boundaries of phenomenology to their extremes are two of the most prominent features of Marion's writings, the ones for which he is also the most often criticized. In this work I do not seek merely to add another such critical voice to the group of Marion's theological and philosophical commentators. Rather I show why this need to exceed metaphysics is so central to Marion's work and why it leads him to articulate a theology of excess and a phenomenology of saturation.

It is difficult to pigeonhole Marion. Is he a philosopher profoundly interested in theological topics? Or is he a theologian employing philosophical categories and language? What is the ultimate concern of his work? Can one even speak of one "work" in Marion's corpus? Has he not rather been engaged in three very different projects that apparently have very little to do with each other, namely (1) primarily historical and exegetical work on Descartes, (2) theology, and (3) phenomenology? In each of these areas, Marion has produced a series (usually a trilogy) of significant works that upon first sight are wholly and exclusively devoted to one of these three disparate projects.[1] First, Marion has written extensively on the work of René Descartes, and much of his early career was characterized by careful, primarily historical, commentary on Descartes' writings and Descartes' late medieval and early modern context. To this day, Marion is head of the Descartes center [*Centre d'Études Cartésiennes*] at the University of the Sorbonne in Paris and is regarded as primarily a historian of philosophy — a Descartes scholar — in his native France.[2] He has written three major historical-exegetical treatments of Descartes that complement each other: one deals with Descartes' "gray" or "hidden" ontology [*Sur l'ontologie grise de Descartes*, 1975; English translation forthcoming 2007]; one, with his "white" or "blank" theology [*Sur la théologie blanche de Descartes*, 1981]; and a third examines his "metaphysical prism" [*On Descartes' Metaphysical Prism*, 1999/*Sur le prisme métaphysique de Descartes*, 1986]. Here Marion seeks to combine the results of the other two works, to locate them, and to carry them further. In all these early books, Marion reads Descartes very closely and puts forth arguments about Descartes' epistemology and metaphysics. He situates Descartes within the late medieval theological, philosophical, and scientific context and analyzes the historical significance of his work in light of later developments. The three works form a coherent unit. They are, however, supplemented by later books, mostly collections of papers published earlier — *Cartesian Questions* [*Questions cartésiennes*, 1991; English translation 1999] deals primarily with Descartes' metaphysical method, and *Cartesian Questions II* [*Questions cartésiennes II*, 1996; English translation, *On the Ego and on God: Further Cartesian Questions*, forthcoming in 2007] collects papers on the questions of God and the ego. He has also published a French translation of Descartes' *Regulae ad directionem Ingenii de René Descartes* [1977] and collaborated on an *Index* to that work [1976].

Second, Marion has written several significant works in theology. *Idol and Distance* [*L'idole et la distance*, 1977; English 2001] and *God without Being* [*Dieu sans l'être*, 1982] are maybe his two books best known to the English-speaking audience. *God without Being*, published in 1991, was for a long time the only one of Marion's works translated, and it introduced him to the English-speaking world as a theologian, or possibly a philosopher of religion. Both *God without Being* and *Idol and Distance* explore a kind of negative or mystical theology that dissipates the visual and conceptual idols of the past and present. Deeply influenced by the Roman Catholic theologians Hans Urs von Balthasar and Henri de Lubac, Marion articulates a theology that might be compared to that of Karl Barth in its emphasis on the transcendence and ineffability of God. These two books were later supplemented by *Prolegomena to Charity* [*Prolégomènes à la charité*, 1986; English 2002] and a work on aesthetics and theology, *The Crossing of the Visible* [*Le croisée du visible*, 1991; English 2005].

Finally, Marion has recently authored a further trilogy on phenomenology. A preparatory work, *Reduction and Givenness* [*Reduction et donation*, 1989; English 1998], closely explores several key texts and themes of Edmund Husserl and Martin Heidegger on the questions of ontology and of donation or givenness. This was followed by a significant and extensive study on phenomenology, *Being Given* [*Étant donné*, 1997; English 2002]. This book not only interacts with Husserl, Heidegger, and Jacques Derrida (especially on the question of the gift), but puts forth a radical phenomenology of givenness that culminates in a re-evaluation and dislocation of the Cartesian subject. Its major theses are carried further and elaborated in a third study, *In Excess* [*De Surcroît*, 2001; English 2002], which focuses especially on the "saturated phenomena" proposed in the earlier work. Most recently he has published a work on the erotic phenomenon [*Le phénomène érotique*, 2003; English translation, *The Erotic Phenomenon*, 2007] and a collection, entitled *Le visible et le révélé* [2005; English translation in progress], which brings together several of his articles concerning the relationship between philosophy and theology.

It may seem, then, as if Marion has three very different interests, in which he has engaged in a roughly linear and apparently disconnected fashion: his early work on Descartes (or strictly historical philosophy), a "middle period" on theology, and his most recent work in phenomenology, in the wake of Husserl, Heidegger, and Emmanuel Lévinas.

These extremely divergent interests are, however, much less incompatible than they might seem. In fact, all three apparently so disparate projects share certain commonalities. They are all characterized by a desire to overcome metaphysics: whether ascertaining the nature of metaphysics in Descartes, whether attempting to free the divine from the idolatry of being and onto-theo-logy, or whether extending phenomenology into new realms of possibility. All three projects are concerned with the divine: whether when outlining Descartes' "white/blank theology," when envisioning the distance of the divine icon, or when speculating about the possibility of a phenomenon of revelation. All three projects speak of the self: whether it is the Cartesian *ego cogito*, the person at prayer envisioned by the divine gaze, or the phenomenological self after the subject. Finally, all three projects point in the direction of love in an attempt to explore a new version of inter-subjectivity: in Pascal's "overcoming" of Descartes with a vision of charity, in theology's culmination in divine charity, and, most recently, in the erotic phenomenon. Furthermore, the boundary lines between the projects do not hold up, but the three emphases continually flow into each other and inform each other. Already Descartes is read through phenomenological eyes, in light of Husserlian and Heideggerian paradigms, and the reading is directed toward theological issues and questions. The theological works also draw heavily upon both phenomenological method and paradigms. The strictly phenomenological work, on the other hand, is infiltrated by examples from Scripture and Descartes' writings, and is many times directed toward and put in conversation with theological concerns. The boundary between philosophy and theology is thus far from clearly delineated in Marion's work, nor is their relationship easy to determine.

The parallels between Marion's theology and his phenomenology have often been recognized and at times heavily criticized. Thomas Carlson gives one of the most careful and generous accounts of these parallels by outlining what he calls the intense isomorphism of Marion's theological and phenomenological languages. In the introduction to his English translation of *Idol and Distance*, he argues that the language of the gift and of charity compromises Marion's work because it blurs the boundary lines between the two disciplines.[3] Because Marion's theology assumes a particular content for Christian faith, his philosophical structure in certain ways accommodates that content particularly well, even when it does not itself appear within it. The distinction between the two projects therefore is not clear for Carlson. Although he admits that Marion does not determine the content of his phenomenological phenomenon (it remains an "indeterminate excess of saturation"), his theological content can be inserted rather too easily into this phenomenological structure.

Other readers of Marion are less generous, condemning his phenomenology as a mere negative propaedeutic for his theology or seeing his theology as radically compromised by its phenomenological language. Dominique Janicaud, for example, finds that both Lévinas' and Marion's works "suppose a metaphysico-theological montage, prior to philosophical writing. The dice are loaded and choices are made; faith rises majestically in the background" (TT, 27). He insists that Marion's phenomenological work functions as a negative philosophy to supplement his negative theology and is therefore deeply unphenomenological. Marion's notion of givenness "is incompatible — for as much as it is utterable — with the astute detours by which Marion wants, at any price, to render phenomenological what cannot be" (TT, 62). Wayne Hankey, from the more theological perspective, objects to Marion's theology because it is too Heideggerian, "an opposed mirror of Heidegger's preoccupation with being."[4] He claims that Marion's work "changes theology's character" by "still working ever more deeply and completely within the fundamental Heideggerian narrative, framework and conceptions."[5] Kenneth Schmitz, similarly, wonders about *God without Being* "whether [Marion's] analysis has ever freed itself from the shaping hand of Heideggerian ontology, or has done so at too high a cost." He finds that although Marion seeks to overcome Heidegger, his conclusions "trail his ontology in their train."[6]

What is usually neglected in these critiques — and I would argue to their detriment — is Marion's work on Descartes. It is conspicuous in its absence from the secondary literature. One might almost say that there is both a shared excess and a shared deficiency in the commentary on Marion. On the one hand, most criticism meets in what it constantly emphasizes even when it does not seem to intend to do so: an excess of overlap, one might say, between philosophy and theology in Marion's work. This theme is excessively elaborated in almost all writing on Marion and is a constant in almost every criticism made of his work. On the other hand, almost all writings — with the exception of a few brief articles — display a common deficiency: hardly any critic ever deals with Marion's early work on Descartes. For whatever reason, Marion's writings on Descartes appear irrelevant to most people commenting on his later work in theology or phenomenology. (In a glaring example of this, Arthur Bradley calls Marion's *Idol and Distance* his *first* book, completely ignoring the publications on Descartes preceding it.[7]) Derek Morrow, one of the very few and relatively recent exceptions to this pattern, comments that much of the

> criticism suffers nonetheless from one glaring methodological omission: it fails to situate Marion's phenomenological concerns within the larger context of his extensive scholarship on Descartes. And insofar as this scholarship antedates and, to a large degree, sets the stage for Marion's phenomenological project, that this project is seen to be too "theological" for some and too "metaphysical" for others amounts to something of a nonsequitur. That is, from a methodological point of view, all such assessments of Marion's thought betray a certain impertinence in assuming, quite gratuitously, that

one can safely ignore a substantial portion of Marion's corpus and still arrive at an accurate understanding of his intention.[8]

Morrow is indeed correct that Marion's work in Descartes cannot be ignored if one wants to understand his project (or criticize it, for that matter).

These two constants (of excess and deficiency) in the commentary on Marion do not seem incidental to me. It is a central thesis of this book, instead, that they are intimately connected and that they provide the reason for much of the criticism made of Marion and indeed can illuminate or even alleviate some of it. This study seeks to show that what Marion develops in his early writings on Descartes and Descartes' late medieval/early modern context and interlocutors is absolutely essential for fully understanding and appreciating Marion's later arguments. Many of the later claims he makes regarding metaphysics, God, the self, the other, or love in his phenomenology and theology are deeply grounded and thoroughly prepared in his earlier writings. Marion's writings on Descartes still make up about half of the corpus of his published writings, and even in the most recent works he often refers back to these earlier ones. To disregard these comments, I would argue, is detrimental to a full comprehension of Marion's project. And at least some of the criticism — though certainly not all of it — regarding Marion's theology and phenomenology would evaporate or at least need to be rethought much more carefully, if more attention was paid to these early arguments and preparations. My purpose in this book is therefore twofold. On the one hand, I provide an introduction to Marion's work that shows the overall coherence of his project, despite its disparate foci, and seeks to explain his fundamental arguments: that we must overcome metaphysical constrictions and liberate God, self, and other from these traditional limits (and that "love" is the most successful way of doing so). On the other hand, I want to show how deeply Marion's later work is grounded in and prepared by his earlier study of Descartes.

The three parts of the book each treat one of the focal points of Marion's work: metaphysics (part 1), God (part 2), self and other (part 3). I begin each part with a short consideration of the secondary literature in order to examine the questions asked of Marion and the criticisms made of his claims. I then examine carefully his work in Descartes and show how this prepares Marion's argument (and maybe invalidates some of the critique). I go on to explicate how what he has worked out in Descartes impacts his theology, then how it is employed in his phenomenology. In each case I try to make clear especially how the later arguments are prepared and clarified by the earlier ones and how Marion's overall focus and argument is therefore sharpened.

In part 1, I show how Marion's desire to "overcome" metaphysics and get beyond its restrictions is deeply grounded in his examination of Descartes and the late medieval context. In the first chapter I explore his analysis of Descartes' "gray ontology," in which the Aristotelian language and its ontological concerns are subverted into epistemological paradigms. I argue that his outline of the doubled Cartesian metaphysical system — one centered on the ego, the other on God — determines significantly how Marion defines metaphysics and what about it he seeks to exceed in his theological and phenomenological work. I also argue that Marion's exploration of the Cartesian and Pascalian "exceptions" to the Cartesian metaphysics provides important pointers for his own attempts to play with the boundaries and limits of current metaphysical projects. In the following two chapters I go on to highlight how the insights Marion has gained from his study of Descartes guide and frame his theological (chapter 2) and phenomenological projects (chapter 3). I suggest that both the desire to describe a God "beyond" or "without" being and the need to postulate a "saturated" phenomenon that shows itself without the efficient causality of a transcendental subject arise from Marion's examination and critique of the Cartesian metaphysical system.

In part 2, I turn to Marion's writings about the divine. I begin by exploring the most significant objections made to Marion's talk about God in order to frame the fundamental concerns guiding this discussion. Although most of Marion's critics focus on his theological and phenomenological writings about God and revelation, I argue that this discussion especially must be read in light of Marion's writings on Descartes' "white/blank theology." In chapter 4, I explore Marion's analysis in detail, showing how his concern with the language of univocity in the early modern period, the demise of the traditional doctrines of analogy, and the failure of the theology of the divine names in the Cartesian discourse are presupposed in Marion's theological and phenomenological writings about the divine. In chapter 5 I substantiate this argument further by interpreting Marion's theological talk about God — especially the terminology of idol and icon, distance, and charity — as both a denial of univocity and a recovery of the medieval doctrines of analogy. I go on to explore (in chapter 6) Marion's phenomenological writings about the phenomenon of revelation, dealing especially with criticisms made of his writings by such thinkers as John Caputo, Thomas Carlson, Robyn Horner, Richard Kearney, and Bruce Benson. I conclude that when seen in light of the Cartesian and late medieval context, Marion's talk about God strikes a successful balance between the extremes of absolute transcendence and total immanence.

In part 3, I explore the implications of Marion's writings for a new account of the subject. Again I argue (in chapter 7) that his analysis of the Cartesian ego provides significant pointers both for the shortcomings of the traditional subject and for a more successful account of the self that might come "after" it. I show that Marion's consideration of the Cartesian subject leads him to criticize two aspects especially: on the one hand the ego's obsession with autonomy and self-sufficiency and on the other hand its solipsism. I interpret Marion's phenomenology as an attempt to deal with these insights gained from Descartes, first (chapter 8) in a new account of the self as radically dependent upon a prior claim, as laid out especially in *Being Given*, and second (chapter 9) in a reconsideration of inter-subjectivity, especially as a relationship of love. I conclude by employing a reconsideration of Marion's analysis of Pascal's response to Descartes as a way of bringing together the various aspects of Marion's proposal for exceeding metaphysics with new accounts of God, self, and other and in order to evaluate finally the relationship between Marion's theological and phenomenological ways of doing so. I contend that the division Marion outlines between Descartes and Pascal parallels and determines his own division between theology and phenomenology and that hence to disregard Marion's work on Descartes will make it difficult if not impossible to ascertain adequately this relationship among Marion's projects.

One caveat is in order at this point. As mentioned above, Marion engages throughout his various projects with numerous other thinkers and may be situated within several larger discussions. His work on Descartes interacts not only with a long history of interpretations of Descartes' writings (especially in France) but also considers the theological and philosophical context of Descartes' thought. In fact, it is precisely in a comparison of Descartes with various medieval and early modern thinkers (Thomas Aquinas, John Duns Scotus, Guillaume de Saint-Thierry, Pierre de Bérulle, Eustache de Saint-Paul, Francis Suarez, Gassendi, Gabriel Vasquez, Marin de Mersenne, Mothe le Vayer, Johannes Kepler, Galileo Galilei, Blaise Pascal, Baruch Spinoza) that Marion is able to show that Descartes responds to significant theological issues of the time and that this at once confines subsequent philosophical thought to a metaphysical system and renders impossible certain theological ways of articulating thought about God or transcendence. Furthermore, Marion's concern with the (im)possibility of talk about God, which defines much of his work, interacts with a discussion reaching all the way back to early Christian writings. It is exemplified especially in a thinker to whom Marion refers often: St. Dionysius the Areopagite.[9] Like Dionysius, Marion is often defined as a "negative theologian" (and thus also grouped with recent theologians such as Karl Barth and Hans Urs von Balthasar). Marion may therefore also be situated within a long discussion about the divine nature and the possibility of "naming" God and within a contemporary discussion regarding a revival of apophatic theological language. Even in his more theological writings, however, Marion usually approaches these questions with primarily phenomenological tools. He is not only profoundly influenced by but also actively explicates and criticizes Edmund Husserl and Martin Heidegger. Marion also often interacts with other contemporary or recent French thinkers, such as Michel Henry, Emmanuel Lévinas, Paul Ricœur, Dominique Janicaud, and Jacques Derrida.

All of these various fields and contexts, and specifically Marion's place within them, would suggest useful and important investigations. Marion's analysis of Descartes ought to be evaluated on its own terms. Marion's explications and criticisms of Husserl and Heidegger deserve their own treatment. The influence of von Balthasar or Henry on his thought would provide interesting explorations. His readings of Nietzsche, Hölderlin, and Kant should be evaluated separately. Since, however, one book cannot pursue all these avenues simultaneously and since no study so far has examined the coherence of Marion's project per se, I set aside most of these other questions in this project. While I deal with Marion's phenomenology, I neither trace Husserl's or Heidegger's influence on his thought, nor evaluate the coherence of his readings of these thinkers. I do not attempt to reiterate the history of negative theology or that of thinking about the divine names. Nor do I intend to rehearse the entire discussion comparing Marion's and Derrida's religious leanings or philosophies of the gift, although I certainly refer to it and take it into account. Instead I present Marion's project as a whole, showing its overall coherence and homogeneity, and focus especially on the grounding of this project in his early work on Descartes. Although I often disagree with Marion and have expressed criticism of his arguments in other places, I have in this book attempted to present his writings as generously as possible, since Marion's corpus at this point deserves a more comprehensive commentary and not merely critique of certain isolated aspects of his arguments. I hope that this will invite the reader to move from my reading of Marion to something much more important: reading Jean-Luc Marion himself.

Three concluding remarks regarding translation: First, I have followed the standard rendering of Heidegger's terminology into English, translating *Sein* [*être*] as "Being," *Seiendes* [*étant*] as "being," and leaving *Dasein* in the German. Second, throughout I have given references to both the original French and the English translations when available. If the translation is my own I have placed the French references first, followed by the English. If I have employed the English translation, I have given the English references first and then supplied the French page number. All translations from articles or monographs existing only in languages other than English are my own. Finally, Marion's talk about God and humans is always heavily masculine. While I have attempted to be as inclusive as possible in my own text, I have not amended direct quotations.

This book would not have been completed without the generous help of many people. I am very grateful to Dr. Timothy Casey and Dr. Patricia Gross, who read earlier drafts and made many helpful suggestions and corrections. Dr. Casey's careful reading, critical comments, and helpful explanations (especially in regard to the Heidegger material) were greatly appreciated. Our late secretary, Eleanore Harrington, assisted generously in tracking down references and procuring articles. My colleagues in the philosophy department and the librarians at the University of Scranton have aided the completion of this book in manifold ways. I am also grateful to Dee Mortensen and Laura MacLeod at Indiana University Press for patiently answering my many questions and for their sustained support of this project in all its facets.

The seeds for this book first germinated as a dissertation in philosophy at DePaul University. I want to thank the members of my committee for the energy invested in the project at the time that still reverberates to some extent in this later version. The assistance of my director, Professor David Pellauer, in particular was immeasurable. For his patient and thorough reading of several drafts of the original dissertation, for many conversations, and much encouragement along the way, I am most grateful. Professor Michael Naas was the first one to suggest I work on Marion, but he also taught me much about how to read and write philosophy. I want to thank Professor Peter Steeves for e-mails and explanations of Husserl sent from Venezuela, for his careful reading, and for raising Husserlian questions to Marion's project that I would not have been able to formulate. Professor Tina Chanter was especially involved in the parts on Lévinas that are no longer part of this book but have been published in other form. Her encouragement and advice throughout the original project was also much appreciated. I thank Professor Jean-Luc Marion for allowing me to attend three of his courses, two at the University of Chicago (Spring 2000 and 2001) and one at the Université de la Sorbonne (Winter 2000–2001), for his kindness in continuing the conversation beyond these courses, and of course above all for his rigorous and fruitful work that inspired the entire project in the first place. I am also very grateful to professors John Caputo and Merold Westphal, who have mentored me in more ways than they probably know. I'm not sure this book would ever have been written had Merold not reminded me repeatedly that he was still waiting for it. His support, probing questions, and insightful comments at conference discussions and other conversations are always greatly appreciated. And while I criticize Caputo's claims about Marion repeatedly (and at times sharply) in this book, his assistance in making Marion's work known in this country (in terms of conferences, translations, and various other projects) has been inestimable. His support of younger scholars always goes far beyond the call of duty. I am very grateful for his generosity and kindness at many a conference (and hope he will forgive me for disagreeing with his interpretation of Marion). He has also repeatedly permitted me to read and use unpublished versions of his papers. In that respect, I also want to thank Rebecca DeBoer at Notre Dame University Press and Kevin Hart for allowing me to read and use the proofs of Hart's edited volume on Marion that appeared only after this manuscript was already at the proof stage.

Finally I want to thank my family and friends for their continual support and encouragement throughout the various stages of writing and editing. I thank my sister Dorli for helping me with the translation of the German poem and for listening to my endless complaints about the project during many phone conversations across the Atlantic. Eric Severson contributed much to my thinking and writing (especially during the dissertation time) through conversation, comments, and helpful questions. I thank Lisa Gassin, friend and roommate for much of the time during which I wrote the original dissertation, for her patience and endurance of my fluctuating writing moods. Maria and Glen Johnson's friendship has sustained me through much of the past three years and I am very grateful indeed for their incredible generosity and unfailing support. Without the encouragement and friendship of all these and many other people, this project would not have seen completion.

I wish to dedicate this work to Joanne, whose friendship accompanied me both during the composing of the original dissertation and in the past couple of years (unfortunately more long-distance) during the writing and editing of the manuscript. Your penetrating insight, passion for the life of the mind, and equal dedication to its translation into practical action are incomparable. I have learned more from our conversations than any book or class could ever have taught me. Your kindness and generosity continually leave me humbled. Your faith in me is most undeserved but far more appreciated than I could possibly express. The gift of your friendship is a kind of "saturated phenomenon" of abundant givenness indeed. Thank you.

ABBREVIATIONS

Jean-Luc Marion (French)

OG   *Sur l'ontologie grise de Descartes*. Paris: Vrin, 1975; 2nd ed. 1981; 3rd ed. 1993; 4th ed. 2000.

TB   *Sur la théologie blanche de Descartes*. Paris: Presses Universitaires de France, 1981; 2nd ed. 1991.

PM   *Sur le prisme métaphysique de Descartes*. Paris: Presses Universitaires de France, 1986; 2nd ed. 2004.

IeD   *L'idole et la distance*. Paris: Grasset, 1977; 2nd ed. 1989; 3rd ed. 1991.

DSL   *Dieu sans l'être*. Paris: Fayard, 1982; 2nd ed. Presses Universitaires de France, "Quadrige," 1991.

PaC   *Prolégomènes à la charité*. Paris: Éd. de la Différence, 1986; 2nd ed. 1991.

RD   *Réduction et donation: Recherches sur Husserl, Heidegger et la phénoménologie*. Paris: Presses Universitaires de France, 1989; 2nd ed. 2004.

CV   *La croisée du visible*. Paris: Éd. de la Différence, 1991; 2nd ed. 1994; 3rd ed. Presses Universitaires de France, 1996.

QCI   *Questions cartésiennes: Méthode et métaphysique*. Paris: Presses Universitaires de France, 1991.

QCII   *Questions cartésiennes II: L'ego et Dieu*. Paris: Presses Universitaires de France, 1996.

ED   *Étant donné: Essai d'une phénoménologie de la donation*. Paris: Presses Universitaires de France, 1997; 2nd. ed. 1998; 3rd ed. 2006.

DS   *De surcroît: Études sur les phénomènes saturés*. Paris: Presses Universitaires de France, 2001.

PE   *Le phénomène érotique: Six méditations*. Paris: Grasset, 2003; 2nd ed. 2004.

VR   *Le visible et le révélé*. Paris: Éditions du CERF, coll. Philosophie et Théologie, 2005.

Jean-Luc Marion (English)

GWB   *God without Being.* Trans. Thomas A. Carlson. Chicago: University of Chicago Press, 1991.

RG   *Reduction and Givenness.* Trans. Thomas A. Carlson. Evanston, Ill.: Northwestern University Press, 1998.

CQ   *Cartesian Questions: Method and Metaphysics.* Chicago: University of Chicago Press, 1999.

MP   *On Descartes' Metaphysical Prism: The Constitution and the Limits of Onto-theo-logy in Cartesian Thought.* Trans. Jeffrey L. Kosky. Chicago: University of Chicago Press, 1999.

ID   *The Idol and Distance: Five Studies.* Trans. and introduced by Thomas A. Carlson. New York: Fordham University Press, 2001.

PC   *Prolegomena to Charity.* Trans. Stephen Lewis. New York: Fordham University Press, 2002.

BG   *Being Given: Toward a Phenomenology of Givenness.* Trans. Jeffrey L. Kosky. Stanford: Stanford University Press, 2002.

IE   *In Excess: Studies of Saturated Phenomena.* Trans. Robyn Horner and Vincent Berraud. New York: Fordham University Press, 2002.

CoV   *The Crossing of the Visible.* Trans. James K. A. Smith. Stanford: Stanford University Press, 2004.

EP   *The Erotic Phenomenon.* Trans. Stephen E. Lewis. Chicago: University of Chicago Press, 2007.

Other

AGD   Specker, Tobias. *Einen Anderen Gott Denken? Zum Verständnis der Alterität Gottes bei Jean-Luc Marion.* Frankfurt am Main: Verlag Josef Knecht, 2002.

AT   Adam, Charles, and Paul Tannery, eds. *Oeuvres de Descartes.* Paris: Vrin, 1887–1913. 12 vols. Reprint, 1964–76.

CE   Hart, Kevin, ed. *Counter-Experiences: Reading Jean-Luc Marion.* Notre Dame, Ind.: University of Notre Dame Press, 2007.

CSM/CSMK   Descartes, René. *The Philosophical Writings of Descartes.* Trans. John Cottingham, Robert Stoothoff, and Donald Murdoch (and Anthony Kenny for volume 3). 3 vols. Cambridge: Cambridge University Press, 1984–1991.

GD   Welten, Ruud, ed. *God en het Denken: Over de filosofie van Jean-Luc Marion.* Nijmegen: Uitgeverij Valkhof Pers, 2000.

GG   Leask, Ian, and Eoin Cassidy, eds. *Givenness and God: Questions of Jean-Luc Marion.* New York: Fordham University Press, 2005.

GGP   Caputo, John D., and Michael J. Scanlon, eds. *God, the Gift, and Postmodernism.* Bloomington: Indiana University Press, 1999.

MTI   Horner, Robyn. *Jean-Luc Marion: A Theo-logical Introduction.* Burlington, Vt.: Ashgate, 2003.

RGG   Horner, Robyn. *Rethinking God as Gift: Derrida, Marion, and the Limits of Phenomenology.* New York: Fordham University Press, 2001.

TT   Janicaud, Dominique, Jean-François Courtine, Jean-Louis Chrétien, Michel Henry, Jean-Luc Marion, and Paul Ricœur. *Phenomenology and the "Theological Turn": The French Debate.* New York: Fordham University Press, 2000.

PART ONE

The Constraints of Metaphysics

INTRODUCTION

"This Theological Veering
Which Is Too Obvious"

Although "overcoming metaphysics" is clearly a central concern of Marion's work, it is not nearly as clear what exactly this overcoming means and entails. *God without Being,* the book that introduced Marion to an English-speaking audience, was an attempt to think God without or beyond the language of being or ontology. Bruce Benson describes the reception of this work: "When Jean-Luc Marion's *God without Being* first appeared in translation in 1991, it was immediately clear to many that here was a new and prophetic voice in theology and philosophy of religion."[1] Marion's basic argument in this work is that the traditional metaphysical language that has often been employed to speak of God is inadequate to such a task. Metaphysics here seems to refer primarily to an ontological language that identifies God as the "highest" or "supreme being." Marion contends in this book that to designate God philosophically as the *causa sui* or as pure act or even as the ultimate grounding of morality are not only inappropriate ways of speaking about the divine, but might even be considered idolatrous. Marion tries to get beyond such metaphysically confining language and to think seriously through the implications of the "death of God," in order to move beyond both. Ultimately he seeks a kind of non-metaphysical language for theology, a speech that would be "iconic" instead of idolatrous. This desire to move beyond metaphysics was heavily criticized at the time, especially by theologians and philosophers of religion since the book was understood as primarily a theological work.[2] Most of the thinkers who comment on Marion from this theological perspective want to retain metaphysics as valuable for both philosophy and theology. This desire is often situated within an argument against Marion's "Heideggerianism." Marion is accused of making theology subservient to phenomenology and of inscribing it into Heideggerian frameworks. Wayne Hankey summarizes some of these criticisms in an article in which he claims that Marion's desire to overcome metaphysics with phenomenology is misguided and unnecessary.[3] Instead he seeks to show that Aquinas' Trinitarian theology is more useful theologically than a reduction of his work to Neoplatonism, as he suggests Marion has set out to do.[4] Jean-Yves Lacoste, in a review of *God without Being* and *Idol and Distance*, criticizes Marion for juxtaposing metaphysics and theology simplistically as the two only valid alternatives (and going on to reject metaphysics). He also feels uncomfortable with Marion's use of Heidegger, which he suggests ultimately makes theology subject to philosophy in a way that distorts Marion's account even of charity.[5] Kenneth Schmitz, too, disagrees with what he interprets as Marion's wholesale rejection of metaphysics and which he wants to preserve as valuable for both philosophy and theology. Although he acknowledges many helpful insights in Marion's work, he finds that finally it leads to "a needless misconstrual of the best of *fides quaerens intellectum*" especially because it assumes the Heideggerian definitions of metaphysics as definitive.[6] Most of these criticisms are uncomfortable with the very idea of "overcoming metaphysics" and are directed against Marion's use of phenomenology in general and his reliance on Heidegger specifically. Metaphysics seems to be equated with transcendence and is considered essential for any talk about the divine.

Other theologians agree with Marion regarding the need to overcome metaphysics, yet they do not find Marion's attempt to do so successful. This is true especially of John Milbank.[7] Milbank concurs with Marion's desire to overcome metaphysics, but finds his methods questionable and insufficient.[8] Not phenomenology but theology should overcome metaphysics, according to Milbank. He insists that Marion "effects the most massive correlation of this theology with contemporary philosophy, but in such a fashion that at times it appears that he usurps and radicalizes philosophy's own categories in favour of theological ones" (36). He further suggests that "Marion seeks to be both Barth and Heidegger at once" (37) by replacing the language of being with that of donation or givenness. For Milbank, as the title of his article indicates, "only theology can overcome metaphysics"; phenomenology is unable to do so.[9] Milbank therefore does admit that metaphysics is indeed something which needs to be challenged. But instead of taking on phenomenology as he sees Marion doing, he prefers to practice such overcoming strictly within a theological domain. While philosophical thought is to be engaged and taken seriously, it should never be appropriated or made part of the response. Any challenge to contemporary thought must be entirely theological. Milbank finds that Marion does not recognize the value of the theological tradition and misreads several theologians (especially Aquinas) in his great obligation to Heidegger.

Apart from rejecting Marion's attachment to phenomenology, Milbank also judges the theology he finds in Marion insufficient. There is not enough "Trinitarian form" in Marion's work, especially in respect to a lack of reciprocity in his account of the gift.[10] Milbank finds Marion's emphasis on the gift and rejection of the language of Being insufficient and sees him as still implicated "within a self-sufficient metaphysics" (47). Marion remains inscribed in late scholasticism, in a lingering Scotism, and is entrapped within "metaphysics" (48). Milbank even accuses him of Patripassianism[11] and insists throughout that the language of Being is essential to God and cannot be dismissed. Marion thus cannot be a proper theologian and commits various heresies, precisely because he is too much of a philosopher. The two are and remain irreconcilable. Milbank continues his criticism of Marion in several other articles which will later be examined in more detail, but the general tenor of his comments should be clear at this point.

Philosophers also feel uncomfortable with Marion's dismissal of metaphysics. The most vocal philosophical response to Marion came in reaction not to *God without Being* but to the publication of *Réduction et donation* in France.[12] In this heavily phenomenological work (translated as *Reduction and Givenness*), Marion engages in readings of Husserl and Heidegger and suggests a new approach to phenomenology that would move its exercise away from or beyond metaphysical constrictions. Here "metaphysics" seems less connected to purely ontological language or definitions of God, but designates a fascination with presence, objects, and the transcendental subject. Again it is Marion's desire to "overcome metaphysics" to which his critics object. This almost identical criticism comes especially from philosophers and is primarily philosophical in nature, concerned in particular with the definition and domain of phenomenology and its tasks. Emmanuel Gabellieri, for example, objects to Marion's facile dismissal of metaphysics and suggests that there is much of value in the metaphysical endeavor that ought to be retained. He also feels uncomfortable with Marion's radical phenomenology and his notion of the saturated phenomenon, wondering whether this saturated phenomenality has as its root less "a theophanic excess than a metaphysical deficiency."[13] He insists that instead of phenomenology relieving or replacing metaphysics, one should recover the possibilities of contemporary metaphysics. Phenomenology and metaphysics should work together in a complementary fashion.[14] In a review of *Being Given* Vincent Holzer similarly chides Marion for vacillating between "explicit transcendentality" and "metaphysical causality" in what he calls a kind of "post-Kantian christology."[15] He finds Marion's absolute immanence too radical and the "opposition between metaphysics and phenomenology" too stark. Marion is not doing "pure phenomenology" but rather appealing to and introducing transcendence in an illegitimate fashion.[16] Ricard echoes this criticism by insisting that Marion's "first philosophy" is utterly metaphysical and that givenness does not "mark an advance of phenomenology" but rather constitutes a return to a (theological) metaphysics.[17]

The late Dominique Janicaud is probably the most well-known and most strictly philosophical critic of this aspect of Marion's work.[18] Ironically in a fashion very similar to the theologians, he also finds Marion's desire to overcome metaphysics with phenomenology particularly objectionable. According to Janicaud, phenomenology has no business overcoming metaphysics, nor would it be desirable to do so. Janicaud, however, criticizes the "theological turn" with which Marion has overtaken contemporary French phenomenology, in conjunction with the work of Michel Henry and Emmanuel Lévinas. He sees the origin of this theological turn in Lévinas, whom he compares to Maurice Merleau-Ponty:

> Merleau-Ponty's way presupposes nothing other than an untiring desire for elucidation of that which most hides itself away in experience. Phenomenological, it remains so passionately, in that it seeks to think phenomenality intimately, the better to inhabit it. Intertwining excludes nothing, but opens our regard to the depth of the world. On the contrary, the directly dispossessing aplomb of alterity supposes a nonphenomenological, metaphysical desire; it comes from "a land not of our birth." (TT, 27)

Janicaud clearly prefers the "intertwining," which he associates with Merleau-Ponty because it is careful and attentive to the concrete phenomena of immanent human experience, to the "aplomb" he finds in Lévinas, which overwhelms and undoes human experience with a transcendence that is utterly "other" and thus must be (apparently) metaphysical. He suggests that all such theological interpretations or "highjackings" of phenomenology are deeply un-phenomenological and un-Husserlian.[19]

Janicaud picks on Marion as the one especially engaged in subverting phenomenology and getting away from its intrinsically immanent and scientific concerns by turning it into a field of religion and transcendence (TT, 32). In often very polemical language, he expresses what he finds problematic about Marion's project, which intends "to drive toward the 'nonknowledge' of the mystical Night in using the conceptual or terminological instruments of good old academic philosophy" (TT, 34). Not only does Marion distort phenomenology, but he is in a sense also too phenomenological, places too much value on it. It is precisely this overemphasis on phenomenology that leads Marion to a theological interpretation of it. Janicaud insists that

> phenomenology is not all of philosophy. It has nothing to win in either a parade of its merits, or by an overestimation of its possibilities — unless it is a temporary imperialism in the academic, francophone canton, or the dubious status of a disguised apologetic, of a spiritualist last stand. But is it not

a noble and vast enough task for phenomenology to seek the dimension of
invisibility that all describable idealities imply? (TT, 34)

Instead, Janicaud wants phenomenology to remain faithful to Husserl by seeking the essence of intentionality in phenomenal immanence (TT, 35).

At the same time, however, he also finds that Marion unwittingly rein-
troduces heavily metaphysical claims into his work (and in this case Janicaud seems to object to their metaphysical nature). After a more detailed
analysis of Lévinas, Janicaud takes up Marion's *Reduction and Givenness* in a
chapter entitled "Veerings."[20] He finds questionable both Marion's desire to
overcome metaphysics and the implication of an opening onto theology in
his work. In Janicaud's view, phenomenology has not replaced or overcome
metaphysics, nor is its task to do so. He goes on to criticize Marion's schema
of the three reductions and especially his notion of a pure givenness, which
he finds most troubling. He claims that Marion misreads Heidegger in attributing to him an existential reduction, when reduction and phenomenology play little or no role in the later Heidegger. Thus not only does Marion
carry further Heidegger's suggestions of transcendence and theology, but he
does so in a phenomenological guise, pretending to be a faithful Husserlian.
Janicaud calls Marion's a "pseudoreduction" which cannot be recognized
because "the path that was supposed to lead to it proves to have been too ar-
tificially flattened" (TT, 61). Janicaud criticizes Marion's notion of the call
because it is pure, absolute, and unconditioned. He demands: "Is not this
experience, slimmed down to its a priori sheathe, too pure to dare to pass
itself off as phenomenological? . . . farewell is thus bid not only to common
sense, but to the stuff of phenomena" (TT, 63). Phenomenology is always
concerned with the actual phenomena of the world and can thus never be
"pure" or "absolute."

Janicaud concludes that Marion's phenomenology is a religious endeavor,
a negative phenomenology to supplement his negative theology. Referring to
Marion's claim about the incompletion of his work at this point, Janicaud fears
"the happy, humming days to come of a phenomenology more and more negative [which] will draw out the contours of, alas, a 'more difficult' work." Marion
therefore is not really engaged in phenomenology at all.[21] His misuse of phenomenological terms indicates that he has nothing philosophically significant
to say but only wishes to explicate his theology under a slightly phenomenologically colored garb. For Marion "phenomenological neutrality has been abandoned" in this "theological veering [which] is too obvious" (TT, 68). Janicaud
continues this criticism in his more recent work *Phénoménologie éclatée* [trans-
lated as *Phenomenology Wide Open*], where he deals with Marion's book *Étant
donné* and insists that phenomenology must always remain radically atheist in
order to be authentic. He asserts, on the one hand, that Marion operates with
a confused definition of metaphysics and because of his theological concerns
remains firmly inscribed within a deeply metaphysical endeavor, and, on the

other hand, that phenomenology need not go beyond metaphysics and that it retains an important function for both Husserl and Heidegger.[22]

What really concerns Janicaud and other philosophers about Marion's project is its theological nature, and most of their criticism is leveled against Marion on that account. They fear that Marion will abandon all common phenomena, the original concern of phenomenology, and turn it into mere mysticism or "theological metaphysics." They object above all to the "theological turn" that Marion gives to phenomenology. Metaphysics is clearly central in this discussion in a twofold manner. On the one hand, Marion's desire to abandon or overcome metaphysics is found objectionable and it is insisted that metaphysics ought to be retained (though it is not always clear why). On the other hand, Marion's work itself is at times judged too metaphysical, still too much engaged in metaphysical concerns and terminology (for Janicaud especially because of its continued engagement with theology). In either case, the issue of metaphysics and the possibility of its overcoming play a central role in this debate. While we have certainly not come to a very clear and refined notion of what either metaphysics or its overcoming might mean, it does emerge that both are connected in some fashion to Heidegger's use of these terms. A fuller sense of what metaphysics means for Marion and how he wishes to overcome it will emerge only in the course of the closer examination of his work in the next few chapters. Yet two notions which he assimilates from Heidegger's philosophy ought to be briefly clarified in the beginning since Marion will use them heavily even in his study of Descartes. These are the concepts of the ontological difference and of "onto-theo-logy." As Anthony Godzieba points out,

> "ontotheology" has become somewhat like a talisman that one can whip out during philosophical debates. Its magical powers not only clinch the argument in one's favor, foreclosing any appeal, but also result in the complete annihilation of the other party . . . "Ontotheology" has developed into a code word which supposedly explains and secures a whole host of claims: the death of God, of value, and of absolute truth, along with the consequent end of Christianity as any kind of legitimate reading of reality.[23]

A basic definition of these terms is in order here, although again Marion's use of these definitions will be qualified and filled out in more detail in the subsequent chapters. At its simplest level "ontological difference" refers to the difference between individual beings (or entities) and Being as such. Heidegger argues that this difference has often been forgotten or even erased in the history of metaphysics (although it is still present even in the attempts of erasure or forgetting). This forgetting of ontological difference is a limitation of metaphysics, since it thereby becomes blind to the concealing and revealing nature of Being and understands all reality only in terms of individual entities or beings that are in no way identical to Being. As Marion points out (and I will examine in more detail later), ontological difference can also refer to the difference between the being of *Dasein* (human being) and Being as such or the difference between the being of *Dasein* and the being of other entities. Furthermore, when Heidegger first employs the term "ontological difference" in his lectures on the basic problems of phenomenology, the term also has temporal connotations.

"Ontological difference" is closely connected to what Heidegger names the "onto-theo-logical constitution" of metaphysics (both notions are elaborated in his essay *Identity and Difference* where he first speaks of this constitution). Metaphysics, according to Heidegger, is always in search of grounding and foundation. This grounding is of dual nature: ontological and theological. In the forgetting of ontological difference the two types of grounding become crossed and wrapped up in each other, when, for example, all beings become grounded in a supreme (divine) being (e.g., by being created). In this context (in which Heidegger is actually commenting on Hegel), he designates the notion of the *causa sui* as the most appropriate metaphysical name of this divine being which grounds the being of all other beings, including its own being. Marion employs Heidegger's thinking and especially these two central notions as a sort of hermeneutic framework for approaching the work of Descartes and other thinkers.

While all of Marion's critics, whether theologians or philosophers, consider and criticize Marion's attempts to overcome metaphysics in his theology and phenomenology or even his alignment with Heidegger's reading of metaphysics, few if any consider the definitions and explications of metaphysics set out in Marion's work on Descartes. Yet — so I would like to suggest — these are absolutely fundamental not only for understanding Marion's definition of metaphysics, but also for appreciating what he sees as its limitations and how one ought to conceive "overcoming" it or getting beyond its restraints. While, as I have already indicated, Heidegger is very important in both defining metaphysics and envisioning its overcoming, Descartes and Pascal are at least as (if not more) significant for Marion's project of exceeding metaphysics, in terms of both definition and procedure. Descartes provides both an example of Heidegger's evaluation of metaphysics and a much more refined definition of it for Marion while Pascal functions as an example of how this definition can be exceeded and put in its appropriate place. Much of the criticism of Marion's project fails to take these refined definitions into account.

one
Descartes and Metaphysics
"Metaphysics Opens upon Its Modernity"

Determining the nature of Descartes' metaphysics is a focal concern of Marion's study of this thinker. His first published monograph, *Ontologie grise*, deals with the question of the status of ontology in Descartes by examining Descartes' *Regulae ad directionem ingenii*[1] and the relationship of this work to that of Aristotle. Several subsequent works, such as *On Descartes' Metaphysical Prism* and *Cartesian Questions I* (as well as other articles), carry the study of the nature and status of metaphysics in Descartes further. Such an examination is usually set within the late medieval and Scholastic context in which Descartes found himself. Marion distinguishes Descartes' concept of metaphysics from that of his contemporaries, arguing that he develops a new and different definition. He also outlines Descartes' influence on following thinkers, showing that part of Descartes' approach becomes definitive for most subsequent philosophy. Marion is not merely interested in a purely historical investigation of Descartes, however. As Brandon Look points out in a review of the English translation of *Cartesian Questions*: "Marion is not principally concerned with Descartes the father of mechanical philosophy; that Descartes is chiefly a figure for historians. Rather, Marion is concerned with Descartes the metaphysician, the philosopher who continues to quarrel with the likes of Kant, Hegel, Nietzsche, Husserl, and Heidegger."[2] In this evaluation of Descartes as a metaphysician, Marion is particularly guided by Heidegger's description of metaphysics as onto-theo-logically constituted (as briefly outlined in the introduction to this part of the book). He examines whether such a foundation exists in Descartes and whether Heidegger's charge holds for Descartes' metaphysics specifically or even for metaphysics in general. In investigating these aspects of Marion's work, I will show that he develops a definition and understanding of metaphysics in the studies of Descartes and his time that becomes crucial for his later work in theology and phenomenology. Marion's definition of metaphysics, his judgment of its limitations which make incumbent the need to overcome it, and an outline of what form such overcoming may take, are all developed first in Marion's study of Descartes, the late medieval context in which Descartes writes, and his use of Pascal as a theological appropriation of and challenge to Descartes. Not only does he examine carefully whether Descartes' system may even be defined as a metaphysics (since Descartes himself does not refer to it as such), but he also interprets Descartes' search for a method and grounding for epistemology and ontology as defining subsequent metaphysics in a significant fashion. Descartes, according to Marion, is the first one to come to a clear and fixed articulation of metaphysics. Descartes delineates the boundary and limits of metaphysics in his project, but by doing so, he already indicates the manner in which these limits may be transgressed. In the end, Marion concludes that Descartes' own attempts to overcome the metaphysical system he has created and outlined remain unsuccessful. As will become obvious, however, this failure itself is significant, and even fruitful, in Marion's view.

There are two important ways in which Marion defines metaphysics in his work on Descartes. First, he outlines medieval and modern definitions of metaphysics and shows how Descartes transforms the one into the other. Descartes is therefore, to Marion, an important turning point in the very meaning of the term metaphysics. Heidegger constitutes a further such turning point for Marion. As I have already suggested in the introduction and as will soon emerge in more detail, he relies heavily on Heidegger's definition of metaphysics as onto-theo-logy. But what is particularly enlightening here is not just that Marion uses this definition in his phenomenological work, but rather that he employs it in his study of Descartes, both to illustrate and to validate what Heidegger meant by onto-theo-logy. Marion's definition of metaphysics (and what its "overcoming" might mean) is therefore much more firmly grounded and explicated than many of his readers admit (or are even aware of). Furthermore, even Marion's suggestions about how to overcome metaphysics do not begin with *God without Being*. Rather, both the meaning and the mode of such overcoming are prepared and grounded in his work on Descartes. Descartes, so Marion argues, already attempts to overcome the metaphysics he has outlined and both his partial success and his abysmal failure indicate important guidelines regarding how one might overcome metaphysics today. Even more significantly, Marion sees an example of a successful overcoming of metaphysics (especially the one he has outlined in Descartes) in the Cartesian thinker Blaise Pascal, who occupies an important — albeit not always explicit — place in Marion's work. References to both Descartes and Pascal abound (at least in the footnotes) in Marion's later works in theology and phenomenology. I will therefore begin by spelling out carefully first what metaphysics meant at the time of Descartes, how Descartes reformulates this notion of metaphysics, and what it therefore constitutes for him. We will see how Marion uses Heidegger's definition in order to "test" it on Descartes, outlining two competing metaphysical systems in Descartes' work. I will show Descartes' and Pascal's attempts to overcome this version of onto-theo-logical metaphysics and go on to explicate how Marion applies these insights gained from his study of Descartes and the Cartesian interlocutors in his later theological and phenomenological work. I will conclude by returning to the aforementioned criticisms made of Marion and see how they are illuminated by this careful attention to Marion's early work. The study of Marion's writings on Descartes' metaphysics will therefore help to clarify why Marion's work overall is so intent on "overcoming" metaphysics. More exactly it will show why he attempts to free God from the language of being or ontology (especially in *God without Being*) and why he desires to liberate phenomenology in general and the gift specifically from similar restrictions (especially in *Being Given* and parts of *In Excess*). It will also give a first indication of why such overcoming is attempted in the mode of love or charity (especially in *Prolegomena to Charity* and Marion's recent book *The Erotic Phenomenon*).

The Late Medieval Context

Marion claims that there is a definite concept of metaphysics before Descartes and an equally definite one after him, yet that the two are quite different. Somehow the very definition of metaphysics changes with Descartes. What he does to the medieval definition becomes determinative for the later tradition. While for Aquinas and others, as we will see momentarily, metaphysics refers primarily to ontology, to beings and their way of Being, for Kant and other moderns metaphysics deals "with the first principles of human knowledge" (MP, 2; PM, 2). This change is brought about by Descartes, for whom it becomes the primary way of defining the metaphysical endeavor by distinguishing himself from the late medieval tradition and its emphasis on ontology. Marion argues that Descartes' definition "clearly and consciously marks a reversal in the essence of metaphysics" (MP, 3; PM, 3). Since Descartes here serves as the determining influence on the later tradition, in which of course we still find ourselves to a large extent, the definition of metaphysics that Marion uncovers in Descartes will consequently remain definitive for him both in understanding what metaphysics is and what its death or the need for its overcoming might mean. Whether one agrees with Marion or not that we must indeed dispense with metaphysical thinking, any criticism of that suggestion must first understand what is at stake in metaphysics for Descartes and therefore for all moderns.

According to Marion, metaphysics is an absolutely essential topic for late medieval Scholasticism. He outlines various definitions of metaphysics in the late medieval literature, stemming from St. Thomas Aquinas and articulated succinctly by Suarez. For Aquinas, metaphysics is a science that has three different names: it refers, first, to "rational theology," namely to the investigation of "separated substances" such as mathematical essences, God, and other "intelligences." It refers, second, to "metaphysics" in the sense of the very meaning of that word, namely to everything going "beyond" physics. Finally, it is also synonymous with the term *sapientia*/wisdom or "first philosophy," which investigates first causes and principles (QCII, 370–71).[3] Suarez, who was very influential on Descartes' thought, gives an even firmer and clearer definition of metaphysics than Aquinas. He speaks of two sciences linked to each other: Metaphysics refers first to an analysis of being as being. It is therefore an ontology that examines being as such. This is usually entitled *metaphysica generalis* or general metaphysics. Second, metaphysics also designates the science considering God and immaterial spirits or focusing on what is called the "three most noble entities": God, soul, and world. This is usually named *metaphysica specialis*, special or specific metaphysics. In all thinkers of this time period these two definitions are assumed.[4] Marion also often compares Descartes to Marin de Mersenne, Descartes' older contemporary and mentor.[5] For Mersenne, similarly to Suarez, metaphysics can be divided into two aspects: what becomes ontology (namely, first principles and the investigation of being as such) and what might be called theology (namely certain privileged beings: God, angels, separated substances). Yet, so Marion shows, Mersenne clearly privileges the second of these and dismisses ontology as impossible (because it assumes an inadequate measure of univocity between God and creatures—being can only be attributed to God truly). As it will soon after Mersenne in Descartes, metaphysics becomes a science of first and supreme causes, yet for Mersenne it always results in theology. He identifies natural theology with metaphysics and endows it with a distinctly theological character. Furthermore, so Marion points out, for Mersenne metaphysics also has a decidedly mathematical flavor because mathematics is the only mode of certainty for Mersenne. Marion suggests that Descartes will not only adopt Mersenne's emphasis on mathematics or certainty, but more importantly will radicalize the theological primacy in Mersenne by turning it into an epistemological primacy.[6]

Descartes, in opposition to both Suarez and Mersenne, defines his work not as metaphysics but as "first philosophy."[7] He means by first philosophy something that discovers the order of how first things can be known. Although that certainly includes aspects of "special metaphysics," such as God and the soul, Descartes conceives of it as much wider in application and he thus breaks with traditional definitions. In particular, as we will see in more detail later, he distances himself from the ontological emphasis of medieval definitions of metaphysics by dividing things not in terms of what they are, but in terms of how we know them. He gives privilege not to being, but to the mind, which orders all things by the clarity of their perception. The central argument of Marion's *Ontologie grise*, especially in light of his later work on Descartes' metaphysics, is that "beyond Descartes' symptomatic refusal of the title *Meditationes metaphysicae*, his rejection of metaphysics depends upon a fierce destruction of the Aristotelian priority of being as being. Descartes avoided metaphysics because he undid the very possibility of ontology — except for a gray one."[8] As Daniel Garber has suggested, "gray" might here be better translated as "hidden" or "dissimulated."[9] It is not an explicit ontology but one obscured by the primary epistemological concern.

This move toward epistemology has several aspects which Marion outlines the most thoroughly in *Ontologie grise,* but which also concern him repeatedly in his other works on Descartes. At the same time he traces a chronological development from the *Regulae* to the *Meditations,* as Descartes' formulation of metaphysics becomes increasingly complex and more fully developed. These definitions and reformulations of metaphysics are extremely significant for Marion's own work. When he speaks in his theology and phenomenology of "overcoming" or "exceeding" metaphysics, it is always the Cartesian metaphysical system (or one defined by Cartesian parameters) to which he refers. It is therefore essential to see exactly what "metaphysics" meant for Descartes. The first stage, which one might call a preparation of metaphysics, is that of the *Regulae.* While I cannot summarize Marion's entire analysis of this work, several aspects highlight the move toward an epistemological formulation of metaphysics particularly well.[10] These include the notions of the *habitus,* of the *intuitus,* of the *mathesis universalis,* of order and the series [*ordo et mesura*], of the *figura* and the code, and of the simple natures. I will briefly explain how each of these plays a role in Marion's outline of Descartes' "gray" or "hidden" ontology.

The Move to Epistemology

Habitus

Marion shows how Descartes rewrites Aristotle by his subversion of the Aristotelian notion of the *habitus.* Most fundamentally, Descartes inverts the relationship between the act of knowing, the object which is known, and the one who undertakes this activity, the knower. The notion of the *habitus* designates the habituation of the knower to the particular object which determines how it can be known. The *habitus,* for Aristotle, is thus different for each kind of object which implies the multiplicity of the sciences. For Aristotle or St. Thomas there cannot be a reciprocal relationship between object and knowing subject,

15

but rather the "center of gravity" is always in the thing to be known. Only the divine knows things without *habitus* because "the essence of each thing appears to him immediately" (OG, 28). Marion shows that Descartes reverses this relationship in his search for a single science and thus locates the emphasis not in the activity of knowing or the thing which is known, but rather in the one who does the knowing.[11] The knowledge of the mind therefore "constitutes objects in one unique intelligibility." For Aristotle, the sciences are grounded in their genus, while Descartes grounds all multiplicity in the one human intellect. Human wisdom becomes the universal science which is general and final. Marion suggests that the entire treatise of the *Regulae* serves to establish that thesis. This implies also an ontological move. For Aristotle, the science of being and the manner of beings is grounded in their essence, all refer back to their *ousia*. For Descartes, this science will refer instead to the universal human wisdom and thus be grounded in the ego as its ultimate term. Human wisdom becomes primary and universal. For Aristotle and St. Thomas the distinction between the various separate sciences is mediated by the principle of prudence, while for Descartes all of human wisdom must be unified in a general and universal method.

Intuitus

This unification of all knowledge is achieved through the centrality of certainty. Science, for Descartes, becomes defined by certainty as the only criterion of knowing.[12] All objects that are not certain are therefore excluded from the discourse of knowledge and knowing becomes a clear distinction between certainty and uncertainty (instead of admitting a range of probabilities). Where Aristotle refers to different sciences with different degrees of probability and even at times dismisses mathematics because of its artificial character, for Descartes only matters of complete certainty count as sciences.[13] Consequently, contingency is excluded and math reigns supreme by imposing itself on all other forms of knowing. This is therefore a second step in the replacement of ontology by epistemology. Mathematical experience is indubitable because its objects are "pure and simple" and thus offer no obstacles to knowledge. Mathematical "experience" becomes determinative of all experience. The certain is perceived as such (because it is clear and distinct) by our *intuitus*, which, Marion suggests, is Descartes' term to replace the Aristotelian *nous*. The *intuitus* thus is part of experience — in fact, is its "highest achievement" (OG, 46), the locus of certain experience. *Like* the *nous*, the *intuitus* attains to its objects, it permits an anterior consciousness, and it has as its object the first principles. Yet *unlike* the *nous*, which only finds the knowledge that is already present in things, the *intuitus* comes first and makes knowledge possible. For Descartes, the object becomes an object of consciousness which is grounded upon the self. The mathematical objects of geometry are the preferred objects for the *intuitus*, which operates on the model of abstraction. The *intuitus* establishes another world which assures abstraction and universality and functions by the methods of induction and deduction of concepts.

Mathesis universalis

Unlike Aristotle, for whom the method is dictated by the thing examined, for Descartes the method must be discovered in the very act of knowing the world and is therefore imposed upon it. The method gives certainty before the object even appears. Although the method will employ mathematics and extend it to every other field of knowledge, Marion insists upon the importance of Descartes' claim that math is first in the service of certainty before it becomes applied to anything else. Descartes does not "mathematize" all knowledge, but rather organizes all sciences in terms of certainty, which is therefore the larger and more important field and principle (OG, 61). One could thus call this a "science of universal certainty," which is precisely what Descartes means by *mathesis universalis*. Derek Morrow points out the importance of the universality of this "science": "Of cardinal importance here is the unrestricted scope of *mathesis universalis*, for it is this unqualified universality that signals the distinctively metaphysical pretensions of such a *mathesis* to stand alongside of, and on a par with, Aristotle's first philosophy of *ens inquantum ens*" (GG, 19). The abstraction of math that Aristotle had already criticized is abolished for Descartes in its subordination to "order and measure" [*ordo et mesura*], which unifies all knowledge in the general method of one universal science [*mathesis universalis*]. While this claim may seem similar to Aristotle's "science of proportions," which also emphasizes measurement, such a science never has universal validity or abstract theoretical status for him. Marion argues that Descartes uses the Aristotelian vocabulary here, but only in order to institute what Aristotle rejected, namely a universal science that can guide all others in terms of order and measurement.[14] This science becomes absolutely primary for Descartes and thus replaces the science of being as being as a new "first philosophy." Descartes revises the question of the Being of being as the order and measure of beings which allows them to be known to consciousness. Order and measure replace ontology. A third step toward an epistemological interpretation of ontological concerns is made.

Order and Series

Marion argues that Descartes does not pursue the issue of measure in the *Regulae* (it will become important in later treatments) but instead carries the idea of order further in this treatise with the notion of the series and the development of the code. The question of order is absolutely central to the *Regulae* and he insists that it replaces the Aristotelian categories of being.[15] Things are ordered by the method. The mind, which must acquire a disposition suitable to it, only comprehends them because of this order which unifies all things into a totality of knowing. Since the order is not already present, only waiting to be discovered, it must be put into a certain "disposition" (OG, 73). All thoughts then follow this order. It is an order imposed by thought upon the world and thus different from it. Order is established by thought, even instituted or invented, especially because often it observes only disorder in nature. This is thus not a "natural order" and one can distinguish between the order of nature (that is often characterized by disorder) and the order of the method that attempts to make sense of the first by imposing order upon it. This is done through measurement, which forces the disordered data of nature into order. There is thus a split for Descartes between the order of thought (or the "order of reason") and the order of the world (the "order of matter"). This split will become very significant for Marion in his later expositions.

The "series" then orders things further into "categories." Marion argues that these passages refer directly to Aristotle's division of categories, but that Descartes uses them in order to replace the idea of essence with that of knowledge: "Essence (as *ousia*) hence loses the rank of an essential term, in the movement itself, where the relation to the *mathesis* comprises the absolute as relative to it, thus as respective" (OG, 81). What is absolute in Aristotle (namely essence) becomes relative, and what was relative becomes absolute (namely "pure and simple nature" as the result of the inspecting mind). The human gaze (ultimately the *intuitus*) determines for Descartes what is absolute and what relative, depending on its evidence for the mind. The world and its things are excluded together with their essences. While Aristotle makes a distinction between how we speak of things and how they are in themselves, for Descartes this distinction is collapsed and things are only as they appear to the mind. The absolute nature of something for Descartes is not grounded in its *ousia*, but rather in consciousness, and thus the conditions of the mind (cause, sameness) become the only "absolutes" "admissible for the institution of thought" (OG, 90). The method is much more important for a discovery of truth than the things themselves; truth, in fact, is not in things, but in the method of consciousness. The ego thus constitutes the world along the lines of the *mathesis universalis* and becomes its "unique founding reference" (OG, 92). "Nature" no longer refers to the being of the thing, but rather to its nature as perceived, organized, and constituted by the mind. It is understood not on the basis of matter, but on the basis of evidence.

Figura and Code

Marion interprets Rule 12 as particularly important for illustrating how consciousness is no longer inscribed in the world but the world becomes subject to consciousness.[16] This rule takes up the topics of Descartes' treatise on the soul by speaking of sensation. Marion suggests that Descartes uses the notion of *figura* to express what Aristotle means by *idea* or *eidos*. *Figura* refers to the extension of sensation as *figuration* (OG, 118). It allows both abstraction from the matter which is sensed and transcription into a kind of code which puts sensation into a comprehensible order. The primacy of the figure depends on this second element, which allows it to be measured and understood. This code becomes "a system of signs which refigures the world in the absence of its referent" (OG, 119). The substitution of *figura* for *eidos* is significant because it again moves a language of being into an epistemological register. Descartes replaces Aristotle's proportion between beings with the "figure" that can be measured in increments. Things are put into figures as into a code.[17] Sensation becomes only a variation of the coding. *Figura* makes it impossible to attain to any new beings, but rather it orders all sensation into the code. Other faculties of the soul, such as the *sensus communis* or imagination, also become subject to this notion of the code. Marion argues that Descartes consistently divests the faculties of their function and turns them into a kind of spatialization which only organizes the figures it receives from sensation. The faculties become merely epistemologically useful structures that function as certain "regions of consciousness."

Simple Natures

The concept of the "simple natures" illustrates this move particularly well. Marion not only speaks of them in *Ontologie Grise* but also devotes an entire article to them in a later study.[18] The "simple natures," as Marion points out, are neither "simple" nor are they really "natures." *Natura* refers here not to physical objects, but rather to logical elements that can be recomposed by the mind. The natures are constructed by the ego. They are "simple" only in that they are the end result of a process of simplification. Neither "nature" nor "simple" has anything to do with the object itself; rather the "simple natures" refer to the simplicity of recognizing objects. Simplicity is achieved by a division into constituent parts in terms of an analysis of figure and corporeality. Simplification and division no longer stop at the individual uniqueness or singularity of the *eidos* (its coincidence with its being), as they do for Aristotle, but end only when consciousness has achieved evidence (and when further division would imply less evidence). The process of simplification leads to the maximum amount of evidence. The simple natures, then, are not elements of the world, but rather refer to the simplest terms of understanding it. They are thus definitely established and do not have any essence.

The simple natures can be divided into four groups: spiritual (consciousness, doubt, ignorance, etc.), purely material (figure, movement, extension, instant, duration, etc.), and common things which can be sub-divided into two: certain ambivalent notions (existence, unity, duration, nothing) and common notions (quantity and relation, thus order and measure). One might suggest that there is a first preparation here of a distinction that will become extremely significant in Marion's phenomenology. Marion distinguishes between simple natures of various kinds in Descartes: mathematical, common objects, and separated substances (such as God and angels). These correspond almost perfectly to the different kinds of phenomena he will later investigate: "poor" phenomena (such as mathematical terms and equations), "common" phenomena such as technical objects, and "saturated" phenomena (of which the supreme kind is the phenomenon of revelation). Maybe Marion's choice to extend noematic distinctions in Husserl instead of noetic ones is grounded more significantly in his study of Descartes than he indicates? This suggestion will have to be pursued in more detail later. In either case, the simple natures support the move from knowledge of the object to an actual constitution of objects (and a world) by the *intuitus*. They serve as an epistemological reservoir for the primordial apprehension of the ego. Error is therefore impossible in the apprehension of the simple natures. "Error supposes a composition of the known and the unknown; but the simple nature excludes all composition, thus the simple attainment of apprehending it is true because entire" (OG, 140). Descartes puts the *eidos* and the thing in brackets and reduces them to apprehension. We thus never have knowledge of a thing "but always only of the object that is a substitute constructed by the simple natures" (OG, 141). The simple natures, then, are the only objects of consciousness. Totality and causality as measure and order guide their composition and allow them to split the thing from the object known to the mind. Heuristic principles are more important than the things themselves because they guide how things will appear in the epistemological field as objects composed of simple natures. Morrow also points out the significance of the simple natures: "Clearly, the revolutionary doctrine of the simple natures owes its central importance in the *Regulae* to that which it makes possible: Cartesian schizocosmenia understood as the mind's active construction of a world of objects reduced to evidence for the intuitive gaze — that is, the construction of (mental) constructs that can be perfectly known, because perfectly (in both senses) constructed" (GG, 27).

After this close examination of the *Regulae* and their revision of Aristotle, Marion concludes that the *Regulae* indeed form a work of metaphysics but only in substituting epistemological concerns for a "true metaphysics": "The break of the *Regulae* with Aristotelian thought thus has less to do with a 'critique' of metaphysical themes, than with their doubling and effacement through a construction of epistemological models" (OG, 181). Although the *Regulae* refuse all metaphysical discourse, they do formulate an ontology, namely that of the object. It is a kind of negative ontology by negating Aristotelian theses about being. Marion summarizes the ways in which Descartes' ontological denegation does take up ontological places and therefore makes veiled ontological assertions: a) by reading the entire world in terms of order and measure, b) by moving the grounding from *ousia* to human wisdom, c) by transposing the reversibility of relation between Being and being into the *mathesis*, which is both universal and primary, d) by negation of the categories in favor of the availability of the object. Descartes' writing therefore constitutes "a grayed ontology which does not declare itself openly, but dissimulates itself in an epistemological discourse" (OG, 186). The metaphysical nature of this "gray ontology" will consistently inform Marion's presuppositions about the nature of metaphysics in his own work. Metaphysics grounds all of reality in the ego (or a similar absolute principle) and attempts to organize all knowing into a general and universal method. This method is imposed by the mind upon things which become constituted as objects, and it is characterized by a search for certainty that is often framed in mathematical terms.

Even in this early and close textual analysis of Descartes' work, Marion is already implicitly guided by Husserlian and Heideggerian concerns. Wolfgang Röd suggests that Marion's explanation that for Descartes the being of the object is founded in the cognizing ego "sounds more like Husserl than like Descartes."[19] Marion himself talks about Descartes' "phenomenological description" and claims that the "rules of phenomenology" stem from Descartes.[20] Indeed, he uses much phenomenological terminology to analyze the shift to epistemology in Descartes which becomes a quasi-phenomenological one. Descartes re-focuses reality as grounded in consciousness and practices a version of the reduction. Things become objects of consciousness which are constituted by the Cartesian mind. Their evidence is ascertained by organizing them as they appear to consciousness. The "simple natures" especially function as the data of consciousness instead of as "objects" in the world. Furthermore, Marion's entire treatment, in a sense, has served to show that Descartes "forgets" the thought of being in favor of epistemological concerns and that he fails to formulate clearly any notion of ontological difference. Descartes not only makes no distinction between beings and Being, but he fails to examine the Being of beings entirely. This, of course, is a central claim in Heidegger's definition of metaphysics. Already in his analysis of Descartes' treatment of Aristotle's notion of *ousia*, Marion employs Heideggerian terminology by pointing out that this subversion "constitutes less the installation of a new horizon for the Being of beings, than rather the terminal catastrophe where the concern [*le souci*] for being abolishes itself" (OG, 93). Near the end he suggests that the role Descartes has given to the ego, namely as the ground for things to appear as objects, coincides with Heidegger's definition of subjectivity, in that beings (objects) "enter into relation with their Being" through the ego (OG, 188). By doing so, however, the ego alienates things from their essence or Being by turning them into objects of its perception. This move is carried even further in Descartes' later works.

The Metaphysical Systems of Descartes

After showing clearly how Descartes both uses and departs from medieval definitions, Marion seeks to ascertain in what way exactly Descartes' system might be called metaphysical, especially since Descartes himself often refused that term and preferred that of "first philosophy." In order to do so, Marion employs Heidegger's definition of metaphysics as "onto-theo-logy."[21] Heidegger articulates this definition the most clearly in his article "The Onto-theo-logical Constitution of Metaphysics" in his work *Identität und Differenz* where he argues that "the onto-theo-logical constitution of metaphysics stems from the prevalence of difference which keeps Being as the ground, and beings as what is grounded and what gives account, apart from and related to each other; and by this keeping, perdurance is achieved."[22] Marion explicates this quote (and the lecture as a whole) in the following manner:

> This determination thus indicates a doubled and crossed foundation. (i) Being [*L'être*], insofar as it differs decidedly from any being [*tout étant*], declares itself without being [*rien d'étant*], thus having nothing to do with a being [*rien d'un étant*] and especially not with the being [*l'étant*] called "God"; to the contrary by virtue of its denial of being [*néant d'étant*], it can ground all being and all beings [*tout étant et tous les étants*], including "God" because it makes them not only thinkable (according to being, due to a concept of being) but also possible (conceivable as not contradictory in the concept). (ii) Reciprocally, being [*l'étant*], in particular the first being [*le premier étant*] declared in each metaphysics, grounds not only the other beings by virtue of a first cause which also gives them reason but grounds the Being of being [*l'être de l'étant*] insofar as it accomplishes to perfection and precisely in its existence the formal characteristics of beingness [*d'étantité*]. These two principal foundations (the second doubling itself) remain furthermore articulated in their foundations crossed by the difference, which distinguishes them as Being [*être*] and being [*étant*], and for that reason (re)conciles them. (DSL, 283–84)

Marion sees ontological grounding and sufficient causality as particularly important in this context. First, metaphysics is always grounded in some fashion, either ontologically or causally. These two versions of grounding are linked in a reciprocal fashion. This doubled founding results in a third one, namely that of the Being of beings by the Being of the supreme being (DSL, 284). Marion concludes that "one cannot speak of an onto-theo-logy without seeing a triple foundation at play: the conceptual foundation of beings by Being (*Gründung*), the foundation of beings by a supreme being by efficient causality (*Begründung*), finally the conceptual foundation by efficiency" (DSL, 285). Marion also points to a second implication which he sees Heidegger making more explicitly, namely that the supreme being does not merely ground other beings but must also exercise a similar causality for its own Being, which leads to the requirements of a *causa sui* [self-caused cause] for any properly articulated metaphysical system (DSL, 286). Marion maintains that such a *causa sui* need not (in fact, cannot) refer to the Christian God, but merely designates the necessary metaphysical concept. Marion therefore sees Heidegger as attributing (at least) three aspects to any metaphysical system: First, God must be inscribed within the metaphysical system as the supreme being. Second, this system attempts to ground all other beings in the supreme being. Finally, metaphysics employs some notion of *causa sui* to accomplish this grounding.[23]

In an article that compares Marion's and Eberhard Jüngel's interpretations of the Cartesian concept of God, Paul DeHart summarizes this ambiguity well:

Thus, Descartes seeks to have it both ways. God hovers uneasily at the limit of reason, secure neither in his transcendence of it nor in his immanence to it. Indeed, Descartes must have it both ways. It is crucial to his entire scheme that God be an object of human knowledge. The human subject must know with utter certainty that God is, even if the essence of God remains incomprehensible. But then Descartes is, in effect, conceding some kind of subordination of God as object to the epistemological demands of the self-grounding knower. God grounds this knower by creation even as this knower grounds God, so to speak, by "cogitation."[24]

Thinking [-logy] and causality are then particularly important in this definition of metaphysics, as is the language of being. While Marion takes great care in explicating Heidegger, it is also clear that his definition focuses much more on the role of God in metaphysics than Heidegger's does. Marion uses Heidegger both as a measuring stick for evaluating the metaphysical status of Descartes' project and, in a reverse movement, in order to confirm Heidegger's definition of metaphysics, maybe even to deepen it. He aims to show that such a tension between an onto-logical and a theo-logical foundation, which Heidegger considers characteristic of metaphysics, is clearly to be found in Descartes. His argument will be that both the ego and God serve as measures of founding for Descartes, precisely in the way in which Heidegger envisions it, but by producing a particularly unique redoubled figure of onto-theo-logy. Marion employs this definition consistently in order to ascertain the metaphysical status of a certain thinker. In a different text he says, "the reciprocal foundation of onto-theo-logy offers a working hypothesis — in my eyes the most powerful — for the historian of philosophy."[25] But Marion does not appropriate Heidegger unthinkingly (if somewhat anachronistically). He does so because he has shown this definition to be extremely useful in his explication and evaluation of Descartes' metaphysical system, as we will see momentarily. This also implies for Marion, however, that if somebody's thinking does not comprise these particular aspects, such thinking cannot be metaphysical. (In fact, this is what he primarily intends to show for the case of Aquinas in the article used above.) Finally, these are the notions which must be overcome in our contemporary attempt to get beyond the constraints of metaphysics. But before I outline and evaluate these attempts, let me first clarify what onto-theo-logical metaphysics means for Descartes.

According to Marion, the first figure of "onto-theo-logical grounding" in Descartes is that of the ego. Of course, Marion has highlighted the importance of the knowing subject even in his examination of the *Regulae*, as we have seen above. Although the ego is not explicitly formulated in this particular treatise, Marion argues that it is prepared in Descartes' rewriting of the *habitus*, in his notion of the *intuitus*, in the focus on the employment of the method, in short in the overall emphasis on epistemology. Yet as the one who grounds this method and performs its exercise, it must remain outside of the treatment on method and must wait for a further exposition. This further exposition, he argues, is provided in Descartes' mature work, where the ego becomes the ground for a first metaphysical system. Marion elaborates this in his study *Théologie Blanche*.[26] He shows how the ego develops the notion of the code through the process of figuration (already indicated in the *Regulae*). Through these concepts of the code, the ego is able to determine the simple natures and thus attains to universal knowledge. The Cartesian mind makes possible this code, thereby confirming and grounding its own existence alongside that of its objects. By organizing the world around its perceptions, the ego attains the ontic and theoretical status of ground for everything else. The ego serves as the "being par excellence" of the first version of metaphysics in Descartes, in that it grounds the Being of all other beings which "are" as objects of its own consciousness. Yet the ego does not merely ground all other beings as *cogitatum*, but proceeds to ground even its own being in a version of the *causa sui*, what Heidegger called "*cogito me cogitare*." It thereby fulfills the Heideggerian requirements for the onto-theo-logical constitution of metaphysics. Marion summarizes this argument in his *Metaphysical Prism*:

> We have established that beings are as objects; the object thus becomes *ens* only as *cogitatum*, and with the *cogitatum*, a way of Being is at issue. Likewise, the *cogitatum* in turn implies the ego [*cogitans*]. Therefore, the ego shows up in the meaning of Being that allows the *cogitatum* to be as being in its Being. . . . A declaration about the way of Being of beings (onto-logy) and a proposition concerning the singular existence of a being par excellence (theo-logy) thus maintain a reciprocal relation of grounding. The existence of the ego accounts for (*begründet*) the way of Being of the *cogitata*; the way of Being that is manifest in the *cogitata*, by revealing them as beings, grounds (*gründet*) the ego in its privileged existence. Such grounding, double and crossed, satisfies to the letter the characteristics of what Heidegger unveiled with the name "onto-theo-logical constitution of metaphysics." (MP, 94–95; PM, 102–103)

Yet throughout his treatment Marion points to the problematic and ambivalent nature of this onto-theo-logy of the ego. Several questions are raised: If the ego really grounds and constructs the code, does this construction actually correspond to nature? If it does, is it then not merely a "discovery" of the code already in nature? Is the code "natural" or could nature have been otherwise? Furthermore, can the ego truly ground itself? If the ego is the one constructing the code, how can it also be part of it? Can the code explain the Being of the *ego sum*? It seems that this Being is forgotten (thus ontological difference is ignored). Can the code ultimately remain founded upon the ego? Marion suggests that these are the questions that lead Descartes to continue his search for a grounding and to formulate a second metaphysics of causality, in which God replaces the ego as the supreme being grounding all other beings (including the ego).

The transition from the first metaphysics to the second becomes particularly clear in a chapter of *Cartesian Questions*, where Marion examines the metaphysical situation of the *Discourse on the Method* by investigating the relationship between the method and Descartes' formulation and definition of metaphysics. According to Marion the *Discourse* works well for such an examination because it functions as a kind of transition between *Regulae* and *Meditations*. Through this examination Marion establishes that there is a clear chronological development in Descartes' work, where his metaphysics becomes worked out in an increasingly more complex form. The article received its impetus by the assertion of Ferdinand Alquié, Marion's teacher and guide on this matter, that the metaphysics of the *Discourse* is not entirely consistent. Due to the lack of a precise formulation of the *ego cogito* and its doubt, the origins of metaphysics seem lacking in this work, yet in other ways (especially theological) metaphysical assumptions are already made. Marion will end up arguing that the opposite is true, namely that the *cogito* is fully elaborated, but that the proofs for God's existence remain incomplete. The *Discourse* thus serves to distinguish the metaphysics of the ego from that of God, because only one of the two metaphysics is clearly formulated. I will leave aside for the moment Marion's claims about the insufficient role of the proofs for God's existence, since these presume arguments elaborated in a later chapter.

Against Alquié, Marion claims that there is indeed already a perfect proof of the existence of the ego in the *Discourse*, although the hyperbolic doubt is still missing. The ego is already stated, although not yet thought on the basis of thought itself.[27] Ontology is grounded in the thought of the *ego cogito*. Because the ego thinks itself, it attempts to ground its own being and that of external reality. Epistemology again assumes an ontological function. The ego serves as the ground for all beings and for its own Being. This already fulfills the Heideggerian requirement of onto-theo-logical constitution for the Cartesian metaphysics. Descartes therefore does indeed "elaborate and construct a genuine metaphysics" (CQ, 37; QCI, 65). The *Discourse on the Method* functions as a kind of transition between earlier and later stages in Descartes' work, by outlining the onto-theo-logy of the ego (namely that of thought), but not that of God (namely that of causality). The *Discourse* thus provides a bridge between the two systems of onto-theo-logy or metaphysics (CQ, 42; QCI, 73). It is only the *Meditations*, according to Marion, that clearly articulate the second version of Descartes' metaphysics, namely an onto-theo-logy grounded in God and concerned primarily with causality. Why exactly does Descartes require a second metaphysical formulation?

The code, as we have seen, is a construct of the human mind which provides order and measure for cognition in a way that establishes their certainty. Yet if the code becomes a model for the rationality of nature, then a tighter relationship between the two must be assumed, namely that the code is part of nature and not "figured" or constituted by human beings, but rather "de-figured" or discovered. In that case the code would have to be grounded in something or someone else and it would be incumbent upon humans to "de-code" it. Marion suggests that one could therefore imagine that the code would be arbitrarily imposed by God (that is, this particular appearance of the code would not be necessary and could have been otherwise). One could therefore imagine the possibility of a hyper- or super-code, a kind of over-encoding, namely that there is an order or rationale beyond the universe, which transcends humans and could not be discovered by them. Marion claims that this helps elucidate the famous passage of the evil genius and the obscure Cartesian assertion that God might be "deceiving" me. Descartes does not assume that God is actually deceptive — such an idea is ludicrous to Marion — but rather Descartes envisions the possibility that there could be a higher rationality beyond ours to which we do not have access (and thus we actually deceive ourselves), implying that the rationality of the universe we discover is dependent upon God and could have been otherwise (I will pursue the implications of this argument for Descartes' thinking about God later). Codification thus remains hypothetical insofar as it remains human. Of course, Marion is quick to point out, Descartes does not actually think that the world is arbitrary in the sense that God would manipulate it constantly in irrational ways. Rather by God's institution (that could have been otherwise) the world becomes "natural": we now discover the code that God chose to use in the specific creation of this particular world.

This institution of the code leads us to the second important issue here, that of causality. This second metaphysics that grounds all beings in the supreme divine being does so through God's efficient causality. Descartes rewrites Aristotle's notion of the four causes by combining them all in one supreme cause: *"causa totalis et efficiens"* ["a total and efficient cause"] (TB, 293). As we will see in chapter 4, this logic reaches its height in defining God as self-causing cause, as *causa sui*, a notion that was rejected by all medieval thinkers as incoherent. Marion sees the second version of metaphysics lacking in the *Discourse on Method* precisely because it lacks the idea of *causa sui*.[28] Causality is absolutely essential for Marion's definition of metaphysics. He concludes that in the *Discourse*, Descartes has not elaborated a full metaphysics because he neglects causality and cannot prove God's existence "as cause for the idea of the infinite, as cause for the ego, and as cause for Himself," as he will do in the *Meditations* (CQ, 31; QCI, 56).

Descartes therefore increasingly realizes that the ego does not suffice as grounding, but is in need of a prior causality. Causality is raised "to the rank of onto-logical reason and principle" (MP, 104; PM, 111) and becomes, in fact, more significant than perception. The "Being" of things is established even more by their being caused than by their being perceived. God thus becomes defined, for Descartes, as the total and efficient cause of the ego and as its own *causa sui*. Marion actually traces a shift in Descartes' thought here from an emphasis on the *cogitatio* as grounding to the priority of causality, which then allows him to ground even the ego. This leads to the aforementioned double figure of grounding. Descartes gives two positions to the ego — one as constituting and one as dependent — and also to God, who is thought as both inside metaphysics as the supreme being and the ground of all other beings and as outside of metaphysics as infinite and incomprehensible. Marion shows how there are two parallel and reciprocal accounts of grounding here. In one case, the ego grounds all being epistemologically through its thoughts. In the other, God grounds all beings and their way of Being in the efficient causality of the divine creation.[29] The ego cannot function as its own cause or as the cause of the infinite, and thus God must serve as both constituting ground for the ego and as *causa sui* for God's own existence. Marion concludes his study of Descartes' "metaphysical prism":

> Thus is completed Descartes' second pronouncement about the most fundamental trait of being: being is as such inasmuch as caused; this way of Being grounds beings by deploying them as *causata* and, inseparably, is itself grounded in a being par excellence, which is marked as *causa sui*. The onto-theo-logical constitution deploys the Being of beings in terms of *causa*, and thus identifies the properly and definitively metaphysical dignity of Cartesian thought." (MP, 118; PM, 125–26)

There are thus two ways of defining metaphysics, two metaphysical groundings in Descartes' thought. One is based on the language of being (subverted into epistemology through the method) and goes back to the ego and its thoughts (the *cogitatio*). The other is based on causality and refers to God as supreme cause. Metaphysics, in its Cartesian garb, is both a methodical grounding of all being on the ego who thinks and determines beings and a causal grounding that refers back to (a) God. Marion interprets this dual grounding as a more complicated version of Heidegger's own simpler analyses of Leibniz and Hegel. In fact, so he suggests, each of the two thinkers employs one of Descartes' figures of foundation, Hegel the onto-logy of thought and Leibniz the theo-logy of causality. Heidegger's definition has therefore been both confirmed and deepened in this analysis of Descartes. It has been established that there are two metaphysics in Descartes, which operate on two levels and remain unreconciled in Descartes' text. But it has also been shown that Heidegger's definition must become somewhat more complicated and thus emerges as even more useful in its new form. Marion concludes his specific analysis of Descartes' metaphysics by insisting, "Descartes' metaphysical greatness is no doubt to be found in his having distinguished them [the two onto-theo-logies], but above all in his having refused to confuse them too easily. The precisely metaphysical dignity of Cartesian thought [is] from now on something firmly established" (MP, 127; PM, 136).

These two ways of defining metaphysics will significantly determine how Marion attempts to "overcome metaphysics" in his later projects, whether treating the subject of God or that of the gift. Not only does he always assume the Heideggerian definition of metaphysics as onto-theo-logy in general; much more specifically, he interprets any metaphysics as always a project of grounding, defined by its language of being and causality. Metaphysics inscribes a supreme being (whether the ego or God or some other candidate) within an ontology. This has several consequences: The divine being becomes limited due to its reciprocal connection with all other beings whose way of Being is defined in a similar fashion to that of the supreme being. This implies an essential disregard for the unique way of Being of the supreme being (later Marion will call this idolatry, and this is the concern that occupies him the most strongly in his theological work). The supreme being also becomes determined by causality in its need to ground itself as *causa sui*, the supremely metaphysical name for the divine. Both these notions of being and of causality are deeply problematic for Marion, especially in respect to talk about God. But this metaphysical project is equally problematic when the ego occupies the position of supreme being and attempts to ground all other reality. It is this first version of Cartesian metaphysics that will become particularly influential in Marion's phenomenological work and explains why *Being Given* concludes with an extensive reconsideration and displacement of the Cartesian subject that is carried out to an even more rigorous extent in *The Erotic Phenomenon*. Marion's phenomenology of givenness is precisely an attempt to escape the constraining aspects of metaphysics, which attempts to ground all beings in a supreme being, regardless of whether this is a human or a divine being.

Furthermore, Marion's analysis of Descartes also helps us see why the project of grounding itself is problematic. Grounding is never really possible, but must redouble itself in a reciprocal crossing that becomes finally incoherent: The ego cannot ground itself if it serves as grounding for the code which it imposes on the world in order to understand all being and thus must refer back to a prior grounding in the divine causality. But such grounding would require of God to remain both outside the method as infinite and incomprehensible and to enter within it by a self-grounding in the *causa sui*. In either case, the ways of Being of beings or of the supreme being are not merely forgotten, as Heidegger insists, but cannot possibly be coherently articulated because they are incompatible. To some extent, of course, Marion does assume that the need for an overcoming of metaphysics is clearly established by Heidegger (and Nietzsche) and he therefore does not explicate this need as much as one might wish. He says, for example, that "the 'end of metaphysics' is thus in no way an optional opinion; it is a fact of reason. Whether we accept it or not, it inevitably holds sway over us as an event that has arisen."[30] Yet, despite this assumption, his project has served to highlight the various constraints of metaphysics more clearly and has confirmed the Heideggerian analysis (if not always phrased in the same fashion as Heidegger's). It is clear that the ego's attempt to gather all things into its own *intuitus* and constitute them as objects of its consciousness in its aim at complete clarity, coherence, and certainty is a project condemned to failure. Such a metaphysical project in which the ego grounds all reality cannot and should not work, as not only Marion but most contemporary philosophers maintain (Lévinas, Derrida, and Lyotard among them). Nor, as we will see even more clearly in the next chapter, is it any more satisfying to posit God as the center and originator of such a metaphysical system. Metaphysics has failed and should fail, because a project that attempts to ground all reality cannot ground its own source (an argument that Kierkegaard already made against Hegel) and the aim for complete certainty and absolute coherence turns the knower into a solipsistic and dangerous power.

This explains also to some extent why Marion's attempts to "escape" metaphysics play with the language of incomprehensibility, darkness, excess, blinding light, and saturation. The desire for full comprehension is a metaphysical one, in the final analysis a metaphysical illusion. But an overcoming of metaphysics is not easy or simple. We are inscribed in its project, often constrained by its parameters, limited by its history. Any attempt at escape merely seems to produce a new figure of metaphysics, a more complicated one perhaps, but therefore also a more elusive one. Any attempt to unsettle a previous project can easily become a new such project in need of unsettling. It is perhaps to Marion's credit that he highlights repeatedly the great difficulty of overcoming metaphysical constraints. Is any step beyond metaphysics even thinkable? Marion articulates such overcoming first in respect to two (ultimately unsuccessful) attempts in Descartes' own work and second in respect to Pascal's response to Descartes' metaphysics which he interprets as a more successful overcoming. I will summarize these versions of "overcoming" only briefly here, since they will have to be considered again in later chapters.

Overcoming Metaphysics

After having delineated the exact nature and definition of Cartesian metaphysics, Marion goes on to point out how this very definition opens the path to overcome its own metaphysical restrictions.[31] Again, Marion uses Heidegger as a guide for his critique of metaphysics and confirms Heidegger's claims regarding the insufficiency of metaphysics by his examination of Descartes. Marion thus performs carefully on Descartes what will become a more common procedure for him later on in his theological and phenomenological exercises, where he seeks to overcome the restrictions of Husserl, Heidegger, Lévinas, and even Derrida. These later "overcomings" are performed with much greater ease (and maybe less care) because Marion has laid a very thorough groundwork and explication of this same process in his studies on Descartes. "Overcoming" comes to mean defining clearly, pushing this definition to its limits, playing with it and widening it, and thus finally getting beyond its boundary. It never suggests that one ignore the thought that has gone before or the particular expression metaphysics may have found in a given thinker (be it Husserl, Heidegger, Lévinas, or Derrida). Rather, it always takes that thinker's work very seriously and works within the parameters provided in order to get beyond those very restrictions and overcome their limitations. Metaphysics is not overcome by ignoring its discourse or simplistically contradicting it. Rather, overcoming always means understanding and taking seriously the limits of a particular thought. Only by playing with those limits and by finding exceptions to them can one overcome their restrictions and discover a way beyond them. This is not a destruction of metaphysics but a transgression, an insistence that will inform much of Marion's theological and phenomenological writings.

Marion interprets Descartes as suggesting two such "possibilities of overcoming" the fixed and delimited constitution of metaphysics. He investigates this in terms of two "exceptions" to Descartes' system, two aspects that escape his order and logic (or at least attempt to do so): on the one hand, the infinity of God, and, on the other hand, the possibility of freedom for the ego. Both are impossible within Descartes' system and yet both are essential to the very make-up of God and the ego (and thus cannot be dismissed). Just as the ego and God play a pre-eminent role in the constitution of Cartesian metaphysics, they also provide the first suggestion on how one might get beyond this system. It is not incidental, then, that the primary pathway to exceed metaphysics in Marion's theology and phenomenology is a more liberating thought regarding God and regarding the human self. The topics of primary interest for Marion are then deeply grounded in his articulation of the parameters of and exceptions to metaphysics in Descartes. First, Marion shows how Descartes has difficulty articulating any notion of freedom for the ego because it is so firmly grounded in present permanence that it is unable to envision any open future. While Descartes attempts to recover a notion of the past through the concept of memory, the future remains essentially unarticulated in his system.[32] While I will examine this "temporal liberation" of the ego more closely in chapter 7, it is important to note the ego's attachment to presence and permanence. Metaphysics, for Marion, is "metaphysics of presence," in both Heidegger's and Derrida's sense of that term.[33] Charles Matthew Stapleton defines this term and its significance for Marion in the context of the Marion-Derrida debate surrounding the discussion of the gift (pointing out that the term is used very loosely):

> More or less, the metaphysics of presence is the ideology that the world can be rigidly divided into subject/object relations, and that the world is constituted of stable objects of which attributes are predicated. Said differently, because time serves as the horizon by which being is defined, and in turn beings, the prioritization of the present within the history of metaphysics has led to erroneous understandings of the phenomenon of experience.[34]

I will return to the importance of this term for Marion in more detail later, but it is significant to note the emphasis on presence already in his work on Descartes.

Second, Marion insists that the definition of God as infinite which Descartes employs in the *Meditations* points to an essential incomprehensibility of the divine that escapes the metaphysical system Descartes has outlined.[35] He suggests that infinite provides a non-metaphysical — because incomprehensible and unlimited — name for the divine. This name will remain the primary designation for the divine for Marion throughout most of his work, as we will see especially in part 2. Descartes therefore provides not only clear definitions for metaphysics but also circumscribes its limits in a fashion that makes possible their overcoming.

Marion admits that both of these are only (ultimately unsuccessful) attempts at pushing the limits and boundary lines of metaphysics. He thus employs the figure of Pascal to examine a "truer" overcoming of Descartes' metaphysics through the thought of charity.[36] Pascal will become an extremely important figure for Marion and that not merely in his evaluation of Descartes. In fact, while Marion's primary work is in the Cartesian text and context, I would suggest that the figure and spirit of Pascal guide Marion even more profoundly and inform his theology and phenomenology in a significant fashion.[37] Marion's use of Pascal allows him to formulate several fundamental contentions that will guide much of his later work. First, as already indicated, Pascal serves as model for what it might mean to "overcome" or "exceed" or "get beyond" metaphysics. Second, Pascal speaks of God and the human self in more convincing (that is, less metaphysical) fashion. Third, Pascal is able to envision a kind of rationality (of the "heart") that competes with and succeeds beyond the Cartesian metaphysical rationality (of the "mind"). Fourth, charity or love is absolutely central to Pascal's thought. In all these — obviously related — respects, Pascal hovers on the borderline between philosophy and theology. And all of these aspects will inform Marion's own articulation of these topics.

Marion begins his analysis by establishing a close link between Pascal and Descartes and by showing how Pascal is both faithfully Cartesian and intensely critical of Descartes' work. He assures us that the two thinkers met and that Pascal read and criticized Descartes as a Cartesian. Pascal both distances himself from Descartes and uses him, such as by referring to true method and using its requirements of definition. He makes very precise allusions to Descartes' texts and examples, even when ridiculing them. He can thus be said to be Cartesian also in that Descartes provides him with the supreme example of what philosophy means. Marion points out that, for example, Pascal never puts in question Descartes' distinction between thought and extension in the second Meditation and that he maintains a Cartesian doctrine of perception. Like Descartes, he defines the self primarily by thought and thus even remains faithful to "Cartesian egology." Marion finds these parallels and especially Pascal's dependence upon Descartes extremely significant as they serve to highlight the Pascalian departure from and critique of Cartesian philosophy even more clearly.[38] Pascal's criticism includes precisely an argument against Cartesian metaphysics and some of its particular features. Pascal judges Descartes' thought "useless and uncertain" and articulates a higher order of thinking that transgresses and goes beyond the Cartesian mode of knowing in terms of metaphysical certainty. For Marion, Pascal patterns the challenge to metaphysics, because he contests its very legitimacy as a coherent project. Pascal relegates the Cartesian metaphysical system to a limited place with a certain kind of knowing which is transcended and invalidated by a different kind of knowing, that of charity: "Pascal does not refute Descartes' redoubled onto-theo-logy; he simply *sees* it. But he *sees* it from the point of view of a more powerful order, judges it and leaves it destitute. Metaphysics undergoes neither refutation nor recuperation, nor even delimitation: it appears as such — vain in the gaze of charity. The metaphysics left destitute still remains, but in its order and its place, which from now on has lost its primacy" (MP, 351; PM, 377). What is this "order" of "charity" and what does it mean to leave metaphysics "destitute"? Marion examines two important aspects of Pascal's work to answer this question: on the one hand, Pascal's subversion of the Cartesian "rule of truth"; on the other hand, Pascal's distinction between the three orders.

Marion's examination of Pascal's "rule of truth" is particularly enlightening in this context.[39] In this article Marion explicates how Pascal almost consistently inverts Descartes and invalidates Cartesian theses. For Descartes, the "general rule of truth" refers to the claim that things must appear clearly and distinctly in order to be true and in order for science to be evident and firmly established. Evidence is understood as the quality of perception for an ego and truth is therefore established subjectively.[40] While the truth is that of an object, it is known "on the conditions of consciousness." Pascal at first seems to follow Descartes in these assertions, especially when he is engaged in scientific practice. Yet Marion shows that his faithfulness to this Cartesian thesis is radically replaced by a "profound modification" and "new definition of the essence of truth" that we can observe in later fragments and shorter treatises, such as the fragment on geometry, *The Art of Persuasion*, and several letters.

Already in a fragment on the "spirit of geometry" Pascal, while fundamentally adhering to the Cartesian requirements of evidence and certainty, points out that one arrives at certain primary terms that can no longer be defined or explained and must be assumed as axiomatic. Marion finds that these "extreme borders of truth" are therefore "haunted" by "indefinable evidence" (QCII, 344). Definitions are simply established in order to name things that cannot be further explained or for which no evidence can be shown. Similarly, infinite objects also cannot be demonstrated.[41] Evidence and truth thus do not coincide, but in some cases (such as first principles) there might even be a bit too much evidence.[42] Marion suggests that Pascal overcomes and transgresses these boundaries by referring truth to the heart instead of the mind. Marion asserts that one cannot simply reinscribe Pascal into a classical metaphysical position "where the gap between evidence and truth reflects simply the distinction between the discursive and the immediate faculties of consciousness" (QCII, 350). Pascal therefore recognizes the limits of phenomenality and suggests that phenomena at these limits might have to be received in a different fashion. Such a suggestion is, of course, not unfamiliar to readers of Marion's phenomenological work.

In *The Art of Persuasion*, Pascal posits several guiding rules for definitions, axioms, and demonstrations. He follows Descartes exactly, except that he excludes all rules having to do with the excess of evidence, because they are too difficult to demonstrate or even impossible to follow at times. Marion suggests therefore that Pascal does not merely relegate these difficult cases to another faculty of the mind, but rather institutes two "regimes of rationality" (QCII, 352). It is the goal of this particular treatise to distinguish these two realms of rationality. Pascal makes a fundamental distinction, namely that "the soul receives its opinions through two different powers: understanding and will: one demonstrates by proof, one makes believe through pleasing" (QCII, 352–53). Desires (such as the desire for happiness) are elevated to the rank of principles because they are as universal and general as geometrical principles.[43] The two parts of the soul thus operate in a very different fashion and assume fundamentally different principles. One refers to practical matters and the will, the other to theoretical ones and the understanding. The two might possibly even be opposed. Evidence thus no longer coincides with truth (but the mind is concerned with evidence while the will pursues truth). The second kind of evidence, that of the will, can "humiliate" and invalidate that of reason (QCII, 354). While Descartes excludes the role of the will or desire for evidence and emphasizes only that of reason, Pascal recognizes both and posits an important distinction between them.[44] Pascal sees the two particularly linked in theology, where one must love in order to know truly, but for the will this is possible even in a purely natural context. In this particular treatise Pascal outlines two methods corresponding to the two principles: one of convincing [convaincre] and one of pleasing [agréer].[45] While the first corresponds to that of Descartes, the second deals with things the other method is not able to demonstrate. This second method, however, is impossible to illuminate because the principles of pleasure are not precise or predictable.[46] Marion suggests therefore that Pascal is on the way here to formulate something radically new, but that he is not yet fully able to do so.

In a later letter Pascal begins to articulate this art of pleasing that is a sort of love and "persuades without convincing" (QCII, 360). He speaks here of a way in which one may discover God in nature through a kind of obscure evidence. Nature "hides" God and only a few are able to recognize the divine there. This hidden presence of God in nature cannot be proven by rational proof, but faith and grace must work together in order to "dispose the will to 'agree' to the evidence of God" (QCII, 363). With the will's concession faith and grace can attain to an epistemological function, but without such a disposition of the will God will remain hidden. One can thus engage two parallel hermeneutics of nature: one that is scientific and proceeds by proofs and one that is called "natural theology" and persuades by pleasures which give a different and obscure evidence for the understanding but one which is clear for the will of faith.[47] Marion assures us that this is definitely a kind of truth, although it is presented differently than by rational evidence. It is a kind of "hermeneutic conversion" into a different order (QCII, 364). This need for a different hermeneutics is due to God's desire to be loved, and love requires a decision of the will, not of reason.[48] Unfortunately, to Marion, Pascal only outlines this idea that truth can come from the will (instead of reason), but does not explicate it fully. Marion himself seeks to appropriate it later in an article on a recovery of apologetics.[49]

Pascal, then, criticizes Descartes by challenging his project as a whole. He does not merely want to modify certain metaphysical strictures, but rather suggests that there is a whole way of knowing and thinking philosophically beyond the Cartesian one, although it may include it to some extent. This procedure that Marion discovers in Pascal is precisely the one he himself follows in his own work and, it seems to me, also is the best definition of what "overcoming metaphysics" might mean for Marion himself. While he includes the insights of Husserl, Heidegger, Lévinas, and at times even Derrida, he situates them as limited within a larger project which goes beyond them and shows their shortcomings precisely in this transgression. As Pascal (at least on Marion's reading) is particularly interested in the limit-experiences and in the moments of excess, Marion revels in the language of limit, boundary, and excess. Pascal's distinction between will and reason inform Marion throughout, especially when he attempts to formulate the relation between theology and philosophy. Marion has uncovered in Pascal something that defines almost all of his own work, namely the claim that certain experiences or objects require a different kind of knowing, that they are not perceived or judged correctly by "normal" philosophy (often that means metaphysics). One must emphasize that charity, according to Marion, does not imply an abandonment of reasoning or thinking altogether. Rather, it refers to a different kind of thinking or knowing.[50]

This consideration of Pascal's notions of truth, then, has established love or the heart as another kind of truth, one as valid as the methods or versions of truth in philosophy. It therefore shows that truth must not be limited to metaphysics and that thinking is possible outside its constraints. The reasoning of the will or heart enables us to exceed metaphysics. Pascal's notion of the three orders carries this argument further by arguing that love or charity constitutes another kind of knowledge, one that is more appropriate to God and therefore frees the divine from metaphysical shackles.[51] The distinction between orders establishes the same kind of distinction between different ways of knowing, as between the two kinds of "truth" just examined. Pascal distinguishes between three different orders: those of the flesh or body, of the mind, and of charity. The second of Pascal's orders corresponds perfectly to Descartes' order of reasons. This order is transgressed, however, through the order of charity that undoes reason or the order of the second dimension and locates it within a higher way of thinking that is not accessible to someone in the second order. Pascal therefore rejects Descartes' attempts to deal in philosophy with what belongs to a different order, with what can be seen only by the order of charity. Marion describes the distinction between the three orders in different ways. First, one could argue that the three orders refer to the three objects of "special metaphysics": "body" refers to the world, "mind" to the soul, "charity" to God. Second, the three orders are ordered according to the traditional medieval divisions of major temptations: those of the flesh (concupiscence), of the mind (curiosity), and of the will (pride). Pascal transforms these not merely into temptations but into ways of seeing the world through the eyes of the body, the gaze of the mind, and the vision of charity (which replaces that of pride). Or, put in another fashion:

> In the first order, the universe is moved according to the body (extension). In the second, the *ego* thinks [itself] according to thought (Descartes). In the third, God is given to be loved according to charity. Cartesian metaphysics occupies the center of the structure of the orders — this is why it cannot constitute what the third order means by "center." Intrinsically linked to the *ego cogito*, Cartesian metaphysics shares in its subversion by charity. (MP, 322; PM, 342)

Marion shows how Descartes is employed by Pascal as the paradigm for the second order. Descartes' philosophy even serves to illustrate the transition between orders for Pascal. The superiority of Cartesian philosophy over a "natural" way of thinking shows the distinction between first and second order. A rejection of the *ego cogito* illustrates the movement from second to third order. Pascal goes from speaking of "thought" (the primary activity of the ego) to employing the language of "impulse" for the order of charity. All knowing (as certainty) belongs firmly to the second order. The three orders, then, do not refer merely to different types of "objects" but to different ways of thinking or experiencing. They designate different phenomenological realms and incompatible hermeneutic paradigms. (In fact, one might wonder whether Marion patterns his later outline of different reductions more on these orders in Pascal than on anything in Husserl's phenomenology.)

Marion makes it clear that for Pascal there is no connection or easy transition between these different topics. World, soul, and God are juxtaposed to destroy any attempt at system or common parameter between them. No single logic can apply to all three terms. Pascal thus clearly distinguishes himself from Descartes, who conflates the three terms into one system of onto-theo-logy. Marion employs the terminology of distance to describe Pascal's stance: "It is certainly the case that the elements of special metaphysics are revived and taken into account, but it falls to 'infinite distance' to mediate them. Infinite here stands for incommensurability. The 'infinite distance,' which is then 'infinitely infinite,' abolishes from the outset every commensurable relation, indeed all organization, among the three terms" (MP, 308; PM, 327). The gaps between these three orders are incommensurable and can only be "transgressed." No smooth transition between them is possible. Metaphysics is already defined by a transgression of the first order of nature. Pascal repeats this metaphysical transgression (from natural/material to immaterial/insensible) by a second transgression which "raises the first incommensurability to the next level" (MP, 309; PM, 328). For Pascal heart and mind have different orders of knowledge. The order of the heart which he at times identifies with the order of Christ has nothing to do with evidence. It is an order of reason that transgresses Cartesian evidence. Marion claims that, according to Descartes, faith and revelation only have to do with the will and are not at all connected with reason. Pascal disputes this and attributes a kind of knowledge or reason even to the third order: "Pascal, in contrast, defines a new order, which, while also privileging 'the will' (§933/460), exerts its sway and makes a criticism over and against the evidence that it drives mad, the truth whose idolatry it can stigmatize, the very science that it condemns to vanity . . ." (MP, 311; PM, 331). For Pascal, therefore, the third order has its own knowledge and reason; it constitutes its own regime of rationality. The will functions as an organ of understanding, although it is one very different from that of the mind, which is concerned merely with philosophical certainty. The third order does know, but it does so in a way that is incommensurable with the merely philosophical knowledge of the second order. It sets aside the metaphysical reasons of the second order and invalidates them from its own perspective. This is the perspective of love. Marion distinguishes Pascal and Descartes in terms of primacy of heart over mind or "love" over "knowledge." In this way, the relationship between knowing and loving God are directly reversed in Descartes and Pascal.[52]

Since the three orders are separated by an "infinite distance," they are in no way commensurable with each other. Consequently, the differences between the three orders are always bridged by a kind of transgression (instead of a neat progression). Pascal does not remain confined to metaphysics by merely doubling it, like Descartes did, but he transgresses it and gets beyond its limits. By privileging the will over reason, the heart over the mind, Pascal overcomes Descartes and institutes a new order that remains invisible and incomprehensible from the second perspective. Based on these distinctions and the distance between the three orders (especially between the second and third), Marion claims that Pascal already escapes metaphysics and contests its concepts and makes them destitute. Marion further contends that this "destitution" of metaphysics practiced by Pascal is non-violent, unlike the different "versions" of overcoming metaphysics of Nietzsche, Heidegger, and Derrida. He asserts that all three are violent overcomings because they substitute themselves for what went before (we will see this argument regarding Derrida again in considering Marion's *Idol and Distance*). Pascal, on the contrary, introduces a new and non-violent way of overcoming that passes to the limit of metaphysics and surpasses it by opening it onto "another instance besides metaphysics" (MP, 351; PM, 377). This is precisely the kind of overcoming that Marion himself will attempt to articulate, both theologically and phenomenologically. His "dislocation" of Husserl and Heidegger will become a "re-situating," a seeing differently because gazing from a different place. Pascal is so significant for Marion's project because he anticipates the "end of metaphysics": "By contesting certain Cartesian theses, Pascal accuses not only the entire metaphysics of Descartes, but also all thought, Cartesian or not, that would like to be constituted as metaphysics. In a word, Pascal would anticipate what we have learned to call the end of metaphysics" (MP, 334; PM, 357).

Marion's work on Descartes therefore contains not only an explication of the definition and nature of metaphysics but, more significantly, also an indication already of how metaphysics is to be overcome. Charity is able to exceed metaphysics and to replace the language of being and causality. Pascal hence serves as an important pointer for what Marion himself will attempt to accomplish. Pascal "sets aside" and "exceeds" metaphysics with a different kind of knowing (an affirmation of the will and heart instead of the mere certainty of the mind) and with the order of charity. This previews precisely what Marion will seek to accomplish in his own project, whether that be a theology of charity or a phenomenology of givenness culminating in an erotic reduction. The notion of the three orders also points to something else significant (but often neglected): Although the third order is superior to the second and displaces it in some fashion, when one remains within the second order its insights are quite valid. Metaphysics is thus rejected and overcome as invalid *for this third realm,* but not necessarily on its own terms where it might continue to be valid and useful.

Marion's reading of Pascal therefore serves as a useful guide in interpreting his sometimes rather strong condemnations of metaphysics in his phenomenological and theological work. Pascal does not simply ignore or simplistically reject Cartesian metaphysics. Rather, he takes it extremely seriously and perceives it as quite valid for certain limited projects (e.g., geometrical or scientific ones). Yet, he also recognizes that there are valid realms of knowing and investigating inaccessible to metaphysical method (such as the topics of love or the divine). Since Marion attempts to open access to precisely these realms in his theological and phenomenological work, one often has the impression that he simply ignores or simplistically rejects metaphysics altogether. He does not. To "exceed" metaphysics or leave it "destitute" means to show it as insufficient and invalid for these realms, to enable a different kind of thinking or knowing that is not limited to purely metaphysical certainty. Ignoring Marion's work on the metaphysics of Descartes and his explication of Pascal makes it extremely easy to misinterpret him on this point.

Based on his examination of Descartes and especially his exegesis of Pascal, Marion presupposes in all his later work that overcoming metaphysics is an essential task. Unresolved tensions (especially in terms of ultimate grounding) already exist in Descartes between the ego and God. Furthermore, post-Cartesian philosophy reduces God to an idol by insisting on the eternity, necessity, and priority of mathematical truths and by primarily speaking of God in terms of the *causa sui.* Both the self-sufficient subject inscribed in persistent permanence and this limited concept of God must be overcome by a radically different thought. Pascal serves as the paradigmatic account of such overcoming through the order of charity. Theology, specifically in its thought of God as self-giving charity, overcomes philosophy by situating it in a radically other difference. The subject, which is the center of philosophy, becomes decentered in theological discourse, and love (rather than certainty) becomes paramount.

The gap between these two orders is characterized by an essential incompatibility. For Pascal (and maybe also for Marion), theology is higher and can be neither approached nor comprehended by philosophy; it always remains invisible to it. The gap or breach between the two orders, however, can be approached from two sides. On the one hand, philosophy can attempt to push to its limits, to its extremes, have an inkling of a possibility of something other than itself, although this distance remains always in the end invisible and incomprehensible to it. This is the accomplishment of Descartes in the "exceptions" of God as infinite and the freedom of the ego. Theology, on the other hand, can look "back" with a larger perspective and reduce the differences that philosophy introduces by its own larger and more fundamental difference. This is Pascal's accomplishment with the order of charity. And similarly to Pascal, Marion attempts first a *theological* proposal for combating the restraints of metaphysics. Let me turn, then, to his theological writings on the issue of metaphysics.

two
Theology and Metaphysics
"With Respect to Being Does God Have to Behave like Hamlet?"

Of the two onto-theo-logies which Marion has outlined in Descartes, the one which posits God as ground is obviously the more significant for his theology. The terms "metaphysics" and "onto-theo-logy" are used almost interchangeably in his theological texts. He justifies this equation again in both *Idol and Distance* and *God without Being*, although it is developed the most clearly in his Cartesian texts. Marion shows how metaphysics is both misguided and limiting to the theological task, which he defines as talk (*-logos*) about and to God (*-theos*).[1] (Marion examines the nature of theology in the most detail in the introduction and the final chapters of *God without Being*, which will be explicated in more detail in the opening of part 2.) God is central to this discussion, however, not only because Marion sees theology as primarily talk about (to/from) God (not about "religion" or "faith") but because "God" as supreme being is such an important feature of the onto-theo-logical structure of metaphysics. Certainly it is true that Marion sees onto-theo-logy (and thereby metaphysics) as idolatrous in its very essence, namely because it circumscribes the divine by a concept. Because such a concept is by its very nature limiting, it does not and cannot describe the divine appropriately (any limit placed on

God becomes of necessity idolatrous). And it is equally true that this attempt to guard the divine from such blasphemy and idolatry is a fundamental concern of Marion's theological writings. Yet, to focus solely on this concern is to miss the significance of this alliance between an idolatrous concept of God and metaphysics. Both fail, precisely because they are linked in such a significant fashion. The present chapter will focus especially on the implications of Marion's theological work for metaphysics and its displacement. Chapter 5 will return in more detail to the charge of idolatry in respect to its implications for the divine.

As we have seen, metaphysics, in its onto-theo-logical structure, always assumes a supreme being which grounds all other beings reciprocally while forgetting to examine the Being of this highest being and the way of Being of all other beings. (Onto-theo-logy and a forgetting of ontological difference as the distinction between Being and beings are usually implicated with each other.) This supreme being is defined and circumscribed by the reciprocal grounding. If the divine takes the place of supreme being, which is often the case (Heidegger seems to think that this is the case in any metaphysical system, although of course Marion has attempted to qualify this by showing that the Cartesian ego can function as such a "supreme being"), "God" becomes defined and limited in a significant fashion. A metaphysical concept of the "supreme being" therefore always assumes only a *concept* of "God." And any concept that supposes that it can define and limit God is by definition idolatrous, since only idols can be defined (the truly divine as absolutely transcendent always escapes definition). Thus, it is certainly correct that any metaphysics assumes a measure of transcendence, a supreme being that grounds all other existence. Yet what is much more important to Marion, and it is this that some of his critics ignore, is that such a supreme being must always remain a concept and therefore an idol, that it cannot ever be the divine as such that is implicated in metaphysics in this fashion. Therefore while many philosophers are convinced that any system that speaks of God is of necessity metaphysical, Marion wants to insist that any true speaking of God *cannot* be metaphysical (because any metaphysical speaking of "God" would be talking about an idol and not about God). And while most theologians are certain that one must retain metaphysics because one would otherwise dispense with God, Marion wants to affirm that once one enters into metaphysics one has *already* dispensed with God and replaced the divine with a mere (idolatrous) concept. He explains:

> Now, only metaphysics is willing and able to name the *Ens causa sui* by the name of God, because to begin with only metaphysics thinks and names the *causa sui*. On the contrary, "the religions," or, to remain precise, the Christian religion, does not think God starting from the *causa sui*, because it does not think God starting from the cause, or within the theoretical space defined by metaphysics, or even starting from the concept, but indeed starting from God alone, grasped to the extent that he inaugurates by

himself the knowledge in which he yields himself—reveals himself. (GWB, 36; DSL, 57)

Therefore (and we will see this later) more appropriate talking about God might actually get us beyond metaphysics for Marion because it would transcend the false concept of God that any metaphysical system assumes and needs:

> To reach a nonidolatrous thought of God, which alone releases "God" from his quotation marks by disengaging his apprehension from the conditions posed by onto-theo-logy, one would have to manage to think God outside of metaphysics insofar as metaphysics infallibly leads, by way of blasphemy (proof), to the twilight of the idols (conceptual atheism). Here again, but in the name of something like God and no longer something like Being, the step back out of metaphysics seems an urgent task. (GWB, 37; DSL, 57–58)

Both *Idol and Distance* and *God without Being* are concerned to disconnect the link between metaphysics and the divine, and thus to disintegrate any type of "onto-theo-logical" constitution.

Marion makes one further important point in this discussion. While a concept of the supreme being certainly does not equal "God," by defining the divine in such a precise fashion, metaphysics opens the pathway to its own overcoming. Due to its precise definition and limitation, this concept can be rejected or refuted. This is why Marion can speak of the "death of the 'death of God.'" In defining the "God" who dies in this death, one can dispense with this concept and move on: "And therefore the 'death of God' expresses, beyond the death of 'God,' the death of that which announces it: the death of the 'death of God' itself" (ID, 1; IeD, 15). Marion outlines this passing through metaphysics and beyond it in the most detail in *Idol and Distance*, but it also informs *God without Being* in a significant fashion. Marion criticizes four different concepts or delimitations of God in these works. Each achieves the disposal and overcoming of the previous one (though it does so only by taking it seriously), but falters in the reintroduction of a new false concept or limitation, thus a new idolatry, a new and refined version of metaphysics. He begins with the "moral God" in Plato and Kant, whom Nietzsche displaces with the "death of God." In this death, however, new idols arise. These new idols are displaced or overcome in Heidegger with the notion of ontological difference. Yet, so Marion asserts, Heidegger himself institutes a new and more difficult idolatry. The need thus arises to displace even the ontological difference and the supreme concern with Being as such. While Marion cites both Lévinas and Derrida as two thinkers who seek to go beyond Heidegger on this point, he does not find their proposals entirely successful. I will outline each of these four "residual metaphysical idolatries" and show especially how Descartes' notion of metaphysics continues to operate in Marion's analysis. First, however, the equivalence between metaphysics and idolatry has to be established more firmly.

41

The Idolatry of Metaphysics

Idol and Distance seeks to outline and make possible a thought of distance, where the meaning of distance emerges only slowly through the study itself. The attempt to overcome metaphysics is central to this work. (In a review of this work after it was first published in France, Jean-Yves Lacoste calls metaphysics the "original sin" of Western philosophy.) From the very beginning of *Idol and Distance* metaphysics is consistently identified with idolatry, especially with that of onto-theo-logy: "The production of a concept that makes a claim to equivalence with God indeed pertains to metaphysics" (ID, 13; IeD, 28). This is the case because metaphysics thinks Being onto-theo-logically; that is, it forgets ontological difference by privileging beings in their presence and by grounding them in a supreme being which assumes the highest figure of presence. Marion here reiterates for the idol aspects he has shown to be true of Descartes' metaphysical system: the use of "God" (or something like it) as a supreme being grounding the being of all other beings, the emphasis on presence, the forgetting of ontological difference, the reciprocal relationships between these various aspects. He says of the idol:

> The supreme being in this sense, exemplarily, grounds each being in its Being, since Being plays fully in it as presence. But conversely, that supreme being itself finds its ground only in the present beingness in which Being is bound up and expressed. If Being did not announce itself in presence, the supreme being would exercise no foundational decision concerning other beings. This reciprocal play between the Being of beings in general (ontology, general metaphysics) and the supreme being (special metaphysics, theology) does not define the onto-theological constitution of metaphysics but results from it and, in a sense, marks its profound conciliation. (ID, 14; IeD, 29)

Marion reminds us in this context also that metaphysics always requires a concept of a supreme being, regardless of whether such a being is identified with a particular figure of the divine.[2] He emphasizes that this equivalence between a concept of the supreme being and the structure of metaphysics is "absolutely decisive" for his argument and that any such supreme being functions as an idol, regardless of the manner in which it serves as ground or foundation for a metaphysical system.[3] Both onto-theo-logy and atheism "force-feed us with ever more supreme beings." The God of onto-theo-logy is "rigorously equivalent to an idol," namely that of "the Being of beings thought metaphysically" (ID, 18; IeD, 33). Marion's primary concern here, then, is not merely any kind of idolatry, but the specific idolatry of metaphysics that equates the divine to the being grounding the metaphysical system. To think God as the supreme being, the being par excellence, is always to become deeply inscribed in a profoundly metaphysical system, characterized by the reciprocal (and fundamentally unthought) grounding of Being and by a focus on pure presence. John

Martis, in an article considering the theological implications of Derrida's and Marion's explication of the gift, summarizes well the Heideggerian "challenge to the whole western philosophical tradition" which Marion adopts:

> From Plato onwards, western philosophy had concerned itself with theories of existence, of what it means for something to be. These theories proposed "presence" as something real, in which beings "participated": "to be" was "to have presence." Presence itself was real only by dint of its participation in "pure presence," that which by definition could exist on its own account. Presence was described in various ways, and consequently so also was pure presence. Common to all such descriptions was the presentation of pure presence — or pure Being, Being itself — as in some way the "ground" or explanation of particular beings. In this picture, only "Being itself" required no explanation: it constituted its own explanation, its own ground.[4]

These links between Being, grounding, and presence are constant themes in Marion's analysis.

In *God without Being*, Marion pushes his definition of idolatry further by explicating a distinction between idol and icon. He begins by describing different idolatries, moving from visual to conceptual, from simple to more complex. The idol is defined by him as that which saturates our vision, provides a stopping point for our gaze which has passed over all other things in disinterest.[5] Merold Westphal explains that something "becomes an idol when the gaze that intends it is satisfied or comes to rest at its visible object" and points out that "Marion seems to have in mind Husserl's account of adequation as fulfilled intention, the situation where what is given in experience corresponds exactly to what would otherwise have been an empty intention."[6] The idol is therefore essentially metaphysical by inscribing God within human vision and making the divine subject to human concepts. Yet a God we can grasp — who fits our grasp — is too small and ultimately superfluous. Marion explains how the idol delivers the divine fully and thereby makes it available to human vision or comprehension. Yet by dazzling the gaze and allowing it to rest in it, the idol returns the gaze to itself by providing an invisible mirror to it. The gaze is dazzled by the idol because it can hold its attention fully and fill it to completion. It thus provides the exact measurement of what the gaze is capable of holding; it "fits" perfectly. Marion describes it as "the gaze gazing at itself gazing, at the risk of seeing no more than its own face, without perceiving in it the gaze that gazes" (GWB, 26; DSL, 40). The idol is grasped by the gaze without remainder, is fully exhausted by the gaze and the gaze by it. The idol therefore is the exemplary figure of pure presence, in which nothing is hidden from view. It does indeed provide a vision of the divine, but a precise vision that is fulfilled in the gaze and thus controlled by it. The observer of the idol grasps hold of the divine.

Such "idolatry" and lack of distance or transcendence is not merely found in visual gazes directed at images or statues, but concepts can also function idolatrously in a parallel fashion. An idolatrous concept of God dazzles and fills the gaze of the mind, serving as the invisible mirror of its return to itself. Marion investigates several such idolatrous concepts, beginning with Nietzsche but focusing in this work especially on Heidegger. Although he continues to rely on Heidegger's critique of metaphysics as explicated in his own work on Descartes, he also criticizes Heidegger for not carrying this critique far enough. Heidegger's emphasis on Being becomes a new idolatry that remains metaphysical in some respects. Throughout the analysis, the metaphysical nature of the idol is highlighted. Marion argues, for example, that idolatry is "a universal characteristic of metaphysical thought as such" and identifies it with the problematic of ontological difference (GWB, 33; DSL, 52).[7] In this work he focuses especially on the idolatry of "being" or ontology (thus the title *God without Being*) and throughout assumes his (and of course Heidegger's) analysis of the onto-theo-logical constitution of metaphysics, especially the insights gained in his study of Descartes. The "idolatry of being" which Marion detects in Heidegger is a kind of "conceptual idolatry" that in some ways remains profoundly metaphysical (GWB, 36; DSL, 56). Thus unlike *Idol and Distance*, which seems to be concerned with rejecting the metaphysical notion of limiting the divine by a concept in general, *God without Being* is more occupied with examining and rejecting the particular concept of "being" for God. While *Idol and Distance* seeks to get beyond metaphysics as such, one might say, *God without Being* seeks to escape one or two such versions of metaphysics, though they are particularly characteristic and dangerous ones.

As both Tobias Specker and Derek Morrow have pointed out, the concept of idolatry in Marion is not strictly limited to his thought about the divine. Morrow shows how Marion's depiction of Descartes' "gray ontology" in the *Regulae* already interprets the *ego cogito* in terms of an idolatrous gaze that turns "Being" into an "idol" by making the ego the idolatrous center of all knowledge (and precisely establishes the *Regulae* as a *metaphysical* project). Morrow juxtaposes passages from Marion's analysis of Nietzsche, which we will discuss momentarily, with insights from Marion's analysis of Descartes to show the parallels and profound connections. He concludes that

> Descartes' gray ontology transfers the site of supreme intelligibility from the divine *ousia* to the (in the *Regulae*, as yet unacknowledged) *ousia* of the *mens humana*. This substitution of the human for the divine, while literally constituting an idolatry, nonetheless serves only to institute a more fundamental and far-reaching idolatrous intention: to master the world of *ousia* by representing its being as so many *objecta* to be brought under the human gaze. . . . The Cartesian subject, it seems, does not want to *be* God so much as it wants to know what God knows. (GG, 31)

Specker, who is primarily interested in the import of Marion's thought for theology, interprets the terminology of idol and icon as the most significant aspect of Marion's thinking and sees them as determining all of his writings in an important fashion. He outlines what he calls "a phenomenology of the idol" and "a phenomenology of the icon," showing how they serve as two different structures of seeing and analyzing phenomena.[8] Specker also points to the more broadly aesthetic dimensions of the concept of the idol. Specker explicates how the idol functions for Marion as a particular way of "seeing" the divine which reduces the divine to the static gaze of the human observer. Specker also highlights the connection between the idol and the onto-theological structure of metaphysics:

> Thus we can point in conclusion to an exact analogy between the phenomenology of the idolatrous gaze and idolatrous thinking. This analogy comprises four elements: The ontotheological constitution and the concept of God, as much as the structure of the idolatrous gaze and the (material) idol. The four elements are related as follows: As that material idol is related to the gaze, so the concept of God is related to the ontotheological constitution of metaphysics. In the material idol the idolatrous structure is crystallized. In an analogous fashion the concept of God gives content to the idolatrous structure of ontotheological thinking. One can summarize as follows: Thinking is idolatrous, insofar as it posits the desire to grasp God in a concept which arises from human measure. Conversely, the concept of God can only become an idol, insofar as it is assured by the ontotheological constitution. Consequently, one can justifiably speak with Marion of an idolatry of the ontotheologically constituted metaphysics. In order to make clear the idolatrous structure of this grasp of God, Marion speaks with Heidegger finally of a "theology" and marks the God who is grasped in this "theiology" with quotation marks. Marion designates the reflective grasp of this "God" as theo-*logical*. The cursive of this part of the word places the emphasis on the logos and shows, that "God" enters the gaze only from a preconceived logos. (AGD, 103–104)

Idolatry, then, can stand in some way more generally for the limitations of metaphysics. Of course, one must keep in mind always that metaphysics here means exactly and specifically what Marion has outlined in his work on Descartes, and one may not assume some other notion of metaphysics.

Marion then has two concerns when he speaks of "overcoming" metaphysics: on the one hand, he wants to show that the "death of God" is not final, but opens opportunities for thought that go beyond this closure; on the other hand, he suggests that even the various thinkers who "destruct metaphysics" and apparently "liberate" thought remain themselves metaphysical in their thinking to some extent. One must go even further. The thinkers he discusses — Nietzsche, Hölderlin, Heidegger, Lévinas, Derrida — hence guide Marion in his analysis but simultaneously become the very figures he criticizes. This is particularly true of Marion's use and critique of Heidegger.[9] Like Pascal in respect to Descartes, Marion is deeply informed by Heidegger (and the other figures mentioned) and goes beyond them only by passing through their thought and acknowledging its importance. Throughout I will emphasize how Marion on the one hand uses a particular figure to criticize the previous version of metaphysics this thinker "overcomes" and on the other hand goes on to criticize the more complicated shape the idolatry of metaphysics takes in this figure.

The "Death of God": Nietzsche

The first idol with which Marion deals explicitly in *Idol and Distance* is the traditional metaphysical concept of God, a concept whose existence many have attempted to demonstrate. Marion sees all such attempts to prove God's existence as utterly futile because they can only prove a concept of God, and the correspondence of this concept to who God really is always remains lacking and cannot be demonstrated.[10] He argues that an unobserved slippage occurs at the end of these demonstrations: "the question of the existence of God is posed less before the proof than at its end, when it is no longer a question simply of establishing that some concept can be called *God*, nor even that a certain being puts that name into operation, but more radically that that concept or that being coincides with God himself" (ID, 10; IeD, 25). Marion shows how this is true even of Aquinas' five ways which prove certain things about efficiency and causality (a prime mover, a first cause, etc.), but all end by insisting: "and this is what everyone calls God" (ID, 10; IeD, 25). Marion questions the easy equivalence of the proven concept with the divine and therefore puts this concept of "God" in quotation marks in order to distinguish it from God as such.[11] Descartes' proofs for God's existence (but especially his formulation of God as *causa sui*) fall firmly into this category. But most often Marion uses the concept of the "moral God" and associates it especially with Kant. It is this concept, so he argues, that Nietzsche challenges in his parable of the madman who runs into the marketplace proclaiming the "death of God."[12] He often cites the phrase from Nietzsche "at bottom, it is only the moral God that has been overcome" as support for this.[13] The "death of God," then, is not a fatal occurrence for Marion. Godzieba summarizes well what many have concluded from Nietzsche's and even Heidegger's analyses:

> Heidegger's critique of ontotheology successfully articulates Nietzsche's suspicious analysis of truths and values, an analysis which supposedly undermines every claim to a transtemporal world, every assumption of metaphysical realities with which God has been identified in the Western tradition and which the Christian God represents as the highest instance. Because the Christian God has been so closely identified with being, the end of metaphysics and ontotheology equals the end of God, with no hope of redemption or replacement — because there is no other possible way to affirm God.[14]

Marion shows that this "close identification" was always a problematic one which limited God to a mere concept and that the end of this identification is therefore a cause for celebration, not for despair.

When Nietzsche announces the death of God, it is the death of this specific concept of God with which he is concerned: the "God" that is the ultimate idea or form of Christianized Platonism, the concept of the divine in which even the masses no longer believe, the supreme power that is posited as the ground of all moral values. The divine itself, according to Marion, obviously cannot die, since any notion of God would defy the very idea of death: "For a 'God' who can die harbors already, even when he is not yet dying, such a weakness that from the outset he falls short of the idea that we cannot not form of a 'God.' And is it not the least of courtesies that he should satisfy a propaedeutic concept, even if it is only our own . . . 'the death of God' sets forth a contradiction: that which dies does not have any right to claim, even when it is alive, to be 'God'" (ID, 1; IeD, 16). Marion credits Nietzsche with the recognition of this idolatry and with a rigorous attempt to annihilate such false concepts of the divine. He claims that Nietzsche and others, among whom he groups Hegel, Hölderlin, and Heidegger, recognized in the "death of God" a "paradoxical but radical manifestation of the divine" (ID, 4; IeD, 19). Nietzsche was able to come to this insight by highlighting the human tendencies to make gods and by criticizing the notion of *ressentiment,* which posits a moral "God" to justify human suffering and guilt.[15] By outlining the origin of this moral concept of God (genealogically), Nietzsche is able to eliminate it as an idol overcome by nihilism and the search of the madman. Marion again emphasizes how this concept of God is an essentially metaphysical idol because it fulfills perfectly the definition of metaphysics which he presupposes based on his analysis of Descartes (guided by Heideggerian parameters):

> Over the "God" who is an idolatrous mirror of morality is superimposed
> the idolatrous function that metaphysics imposed, or wanted to impose on
> the Christian God — after having managed to do so for the other gods . . .
> "God" is here summoned — and not only invoked — as the supreme being
> who, within the field of a discourse on the Being of beings (*ontologia, meta-
> physica generalis*), fulfills the function of concentrating its exemplary per-
> fection (*ens realissimum, causa sui, ipsum esse,* etc.) and of causally ensur-
> ing the coherence of a world. Caught within such a *metaphysica specialis*
> (*theologia,* if one will), the "God" simply answers to the name that one gives
> him. (ID, 35; IeD, 53)

He suggests that the Nietzschean concept of the "death of God" therefore helps us to envision the end of this metaphysics. In this sense, Nietzsche is an eminently positive figure who helps attack and overcome the idolatry of an ingrained and prevalent metaphysical system. Yet, Marion maintains, Nietzsche does not simply overcome this metaphysical idolatry through a simplistic atheism, but instead opens the pathway for the arrival of new gods.

For Marion, these new idols, new gods, and new concepts for the divine, which Nietzsche introduces, remain metaphysical.[16] They are metaphysical because they again become the ground for the Being of beings. The issues of "grounding" and "presence," shown to be so fundamental in Descartes, significantly inform Marion's judgment of Nietzsche as still metaphysical. Having applied Heidegger's suggestions about the onto-theo-logical structure of metaphysics to Descartes, he now extrapolates that analysis to other thinkers (ultimately even to Heidegger himself). According to Marion, the "will to power" defines all Being for Nietzsche as a grounding principle of valuation, while the "eternal return" focuses all affirmation on the present/presence.[17] Marion shows that despite the centrality of the Christ figure in Nietzsche's late writings, this "god" is still an idolatrous concept. Nietzsche rejects a "God of love" (as explicated later, the only remotely adequate talk about God according to Marion) and grounds even the figure of Christ in the will to power. He thus replicates the Cartesian metaphysics, in which the supreme being — in this case the will to power — grounds all other beings, including the divine being. The divine becomes limited to the world in Nietzsche, and Marion concludes that he is thus still limited by metaphysics' onto-theo-logical structure. Marion's definition of this new version of metaphysics deserves to be cited more fully:

> The world arouses, as a state that the will to power organizes, a god as the center from which an affirmation can come to it. The god returns to the world the will to power that gave rise to it. To the will to power that valuates each being and assigns to it its place, the god returns the global justification of the whole of beings as a world — and hence as divine. The will to power delivers to each being that which for it is Being-value, reproducing thus the investigation and the difference of the ὄν ᾖ ὄν. The god, affirming as a world the divine that gives rise to it, and therefore pronouncing in it the Eternal Return, there becomes a theological point of view: through it, the world becomes to itself its own supreme being. The god, thought as will to power, uncovers a world as the sole supreme being in affirming beings in their Being (value) . . . The god clearly finds its place, therefore, in the onto-theological structure of a metaphysics still at work. (ID, 72–73; IeD, 92)

In assigning places to being, in giving rise to the world, and especially in "affirming beings in their Being," the will to power therefore duplicates a quasi-Cartesian metaphysical and ontological grounding. Morrow points out the intense parallels between the Nietzschean will to power and the Cartesian ego, insofar as "the representative gaze of the *intuitus mentis* is joined to the valuating gaze of the *Wille zur Macht* as two sides of the same idolatrous coin; for both *ens* is represented — and representable — by 'the gaze [which] alone characterizes the idol' . . . only so that it can be manipulated by the will of the one who gazes" (GG, 32). In the figures of the will to power, the dawn of new idols, and the eternal return, Nietzsche has again outlined a world dependent upon a divine source which is limited by Being and a kind of causality.[18] Although the world itself becomes divinized in Nietzsche, it does so through the will to power which "gives rise to it" and assigns it its Being. Nietzsche repeats, even if within a different shape, the Cartesian figures of a doubled metaphysics which Marion has uncovered. Therefore, although the play of metaphysics in Nietzsche first opens toward the distance of God, that distance is eliminated in the return of new idols. Against Nietzsche's immanent gods, Marion insists that we must experience the radical foreignness of God. Only in conceiving God as radically distant does a non-idolatrous thought of God become possible. Nietzsche ultimately obliterates this distance and thus becomes the last metaphysician: "Nietzschean distance maintains, to be sure, a relation with the divine, but within onto-theology, on the basis of equivalence. Thus it reinforces the metaphysical idolatry where 'God' is defined as a state of the will to power. Within that grade-related function, the 'feeling of distance,' far from taking its distance from the metaphysical face of the divine elaborated (and presupposed) by the will to power, radically ignores the distance of God" (ID, 77; IeD, 97). Marion employs Hölderlin (in *Idol and Distance*) and Heidegger (in *God without Being*) to get beyond this particular Nietzschean idolatry. For the sake of space and clarity, I will focus on his use of Heidegger in this context.

Ontological Difference: Heidegger

According to Marion, Heidegger displaces Nietzsche's idols by envisioning a new beginning beyond nihilism. He begins by drawing a radical divide between theology and phenomenology. Marion relies here especially on Heidegger's early lecture "Phänomenologie und Theologie" [*Phenomenology and Theology*], where Heidegger posits an absolute distinction between philosophy and theology. He argues that, unlike philosophy, theology is a "positive science" concerned with a particular realm of ontic being, namely that of "Christianness" [*Christlichkeit*].[19] Furthermore, as Heidegger insisted, God is outside of *Dasein*'s search for its own Being. If Heidegger were to write a theology, as he has often been quoted as saying, the term "Being" presumably would not appear in it.[20] Thus theology is excluded from ontological concerns in a twofold manner: first, because Heidegger separates the two disciplines and insists that theology has no concern with the ontological, which is properly philosophical (or more strictly speaking phenomenological); second, because he denies rigorously any connection between Being and God.

Yet although Marion's work is deeply informed by Heidegger and he employs Heidegger to criticize Nietzsche, he goes on to point out what he perceives as insufficiencies in Heidegger's thought. (Tobias Specker says, "Marion treats Heidegger as Heidegger does Nietzsche" [AGD, 162].) Marion shows that "God" becomes a concept which is radically (and inappropriately) limited by Heidegger. On the one hand, God is confined to the limited ontic domain in which *Dasein* reflects on its own expression of faith and God appears as part of the vocabulary of that expression. Theology, for Heidegger, can only be concerned with the possible faith of an individual *Dasein* (with *Christlichkeit*/"Christianness"), and this "God" affirmed by faith would still have to be inscribed within the language of beings. God would be ontically determined and would actually not even reach ontology. God is not *Being* or ultimate ground for Heidegger, but rather dependent upon individual *beings*. (It seems that the presuppositions about ontological language which Marion has worked out in Descartes are again operative here. God appears to depend on the faith of *Dasein* here in a fashion similar to the way in which the divine becomes a *cogitatio* of the ego in Descartes.)

On the other hand, for Heidegger the divine is included in the four-fold, in which Being reigns over all beings, including that of the divine. Marion maintains that this "new beginning" "breaks with unthought ontological difference, hence with the *causa sui* of onto-theo-logy, undertakes to conceive the 'divine god,' or at least does not close itself to this possibility or, better, opens it" (GWB, 39; DSL, 61). Heidegger names the arrival of these new gods *Geviert*, the Fourfold. This multiplicity of gods remains dependent upon Being, which alone makes a question of God possible.[21] Marion insists that this is an essentially idolatrous dependence which conceives of the divine as merely ontic and regional by excluding it from the true ontological question of Being. God or gods "are" in the same manner in which other beings are and the divine comes into presence as a being among others.[22] Marion challenges this equivalence between God and a being, this assumption that God always "must be," because he interprets it as an ontic limitation. He clarifies this even further in his introduction to the English translation of the book:

> When God offers himself to be contemplated and gives himself to be prayed to, is he concerned primarily with Being? When he appears as and in Jesus Christ, who dies and rises from the dead, is he concerned primarily with Being? No doubt, God can and must in the end also be; but does his relation to Being determine him as radically as the relation to his Being defines all other beings? To be or not to be — that is indeed the first and indispensable question for everything and everyone, and for man in particular. But with respect to Being does God have to behave like Hamlet? Under the title of *God without Being*, I am attempting to bring out the absolute freedom of God with regard to all determinations, including first of all, the basic condition that renders all other conditions possible and even necessary — for us, humans — the fact of Being. . . . for God, if at least we resist the temptation to reduce him immediately to our own measure, does the same still apply? (GWB, xx)

Ontological difference expresses this problematic: while the divine has a certain kind of regional being, it never attains to Being. Marion finds this extremely unsatisfying.

Therefore, while Heidegger does indeed get rid of the metaphysical idol of God as *causa sui* and regards it as insufficient, any other appearance of God becomes limited by the overall question of Being. As Jeffrey Bloechl puts it:

> Marion takes this last point, the claim that thought and appearing always presuppose being, as an assertion that being is thus the screen on which beings must appear in order to have meaning. And whereas he agrees that

this does pass without notice when it is a question only of things found in the world, he interjects that it is profoundly unsuited to what arrives from wholly outside. Contrary to Heidegger's original concern to describe the transcendence of being over its disclosure to us as beings, Marion thus considers being as the original projection of a subject which assumes itself to be the proper locus of all meaning. Regarding the self-revelation of God, the screen of being would therefore also be a filter (*l'écran*) which Heidegger has imposed on the effort to think about religious experience.[23]

In order to escape onto-theo-logy, in order to think profitably about God, we must get outside of metaphysics and that means, for Marion, not just outside defining God in terms of grounding causality but also beyond making the divine dependent upon both Being and being. In order to rid ourselves of the difficult Heideggerian idolatry that turns the divine into a being and makes God subject to Being, we must escape not merely metaphysics but, more specifically, ontological difference: "Or again, does not the search for the 'more divine god' oblige one, more than to go beyond onto-theo-logy, to go beyond ontological difference as well, in short no longer to attempt to think God in view of a being, because one will have renounced to begin with, thinking him on the basis of Being? To think God without any conditions, not even that of Being, hence to think God without pretending to inscribe him or to describe him as a being" (GWB, 44–45; DSL, 70). We must be able to hear from or see a site beyond the site of Being as such, a more radical difference that dislocates ontological difference. Being and ontological difference thus become a higher and more complicated idolatry, a further and more refined version of metaphysics.[24] As Specker says: "The constitution of metaphysics, its critical overcoming, and the question of God in its metaphysical and non-metaphysical version are tied to the question of Being. The question of Being is therefore the point of departure from which Heidegger's perspective arises and thinks toward God" (AGD, 176).[25] Or, as Felix Ó Murchadha puts it:

> The glory of God is precisely that to which no correspondence is possible, that for a fundamental reason: because God reveals Himself in the world as beyond the world. . . . to put the question in relation to Marion and Heidegger, can there be an exception to the ontological difference? If there can be, then the sameness of thought and being is superseded, thinking is liberated from being, and a place for faith is philosophically underscored by reference to phenomena that point beyond any account in terms of nature, understood in the widest sense.[26]

For Marion, to get "beyond" ontological difference means to highlight that there is a more fundamental difference that goes beyond and situates ontological difference.

Marion's reading of this has not gone unchallenged. Béatrice Han thinks that Marion's "reading of Heidegger is at best incomplete and often faulty" because he oversimplifies "considerably the relationships between transcendence, disclosure, and intelligibility."[27] According to her, Marion makes "three fundamental mistakes in his exegesis" by reading Heidegger through Husserl (i.e., failing to appreciate Heidegger's advance beyond Husserl), by interpreting Being solely through the *Dasein* analysis (and thus disregarding Heidegger's later work), and by ignoring the hermeneutic circle (in her view a result of the strong emphasis on Husserl). She claims that Marion reads *Dasein* solely in terms of intentionality and ignores the facticity of *Dasein*, its pre-given structure of pre-understanding. Overall, she finds Marion's account "interesting" but "unacceptable."[28] One should point out, however, that she limits her remarks to Marion's analysis of Heidegger in *God without Being* and does not consider his later treatments (for instance, in *Reduction and Givenness*), where Marion marks the delineations between Husserl and Heidegger much more carefully and clearly considers Heidegger's later work. Michel Henry, in contrast to Han, praises Marion's reading of Heidegger (in *Reduction et donation*) as "incontestably powerful."[29]

Tobias Specker points out how in Marion's interpretation of Heidegger, ontological difference itself is wrapped up in the metaphysical project because the forgetting of the question of Being seems to be reinforced by the withdrawal of Being, which thus is implicated in producing the onto-theo-logical constitution of metaphysics (AGD, 174). Furthermore, by making itself the supreme question and the only difference worth considering, the question of Being and ontological difference imposes semi-metaphysical constraints upon the thought of God and therefore remains idolatrous. Specker emphasizes that for Marion, Heidegger envisions the question of Being as a precondition for any thought about God (AGD, 175). Yet, for Marion, God must be thought radically without conditions, even without the conditions of Being and representation. Marion thus goes even a step further in this work. Although Heidegger's recognition of the ontological difference has highlighted something important about metaphysics and even overcome it in a certain sense, it still remains on its borderlines. Marion points out, however, how ontological difference in its peculiar idolatry, in its hovering on the borderlines of metaphysics, proves eminently helpful at the same time. By revealing the limits clearly, by posing conditions rigorously, it marks the path of the cleft which one must traverse: "Ontological difference, *almost* indispensable to all thought, presents itself thus as a *negative* propaedeutic of the unthinkable thought of God. It is the ultimate idol, the most dangerous but also the most educational and, in its own way, profitable, since it offers itself as an obstacle that, beaten down and trampled, becomes an ultimate scaffolding—*scabellum pedibus tuis*—without entering into the unthinkable, the indispensable unthinkable" (GWB, 45–46; DSL, 71–72).

Ontological difference, which in *God without Being* appears to designate primarily philosophy's focus on the question of Being in light of which all beings are considered, is a thought that closely approaches the gap and the excess that Marion seeks to think. It has passed to the ultimate edge of metaphysics and can thus serve as a springboard to an approach different from and other than it. In this way it outlines the boundaries and marks the path to exceptions to metaphysics (maybe similarly to the way in which the figures of the infinite and of freedom function in Descartes: exceptions to a metaphysical system that remain on its boundaries). Heideggerian thought in general and ontological difference specifically become useful for Marion because of the manner in which they point to the ways in which *not* to speak of God nonmetaphysically. They show that a destruction of metaphysics which dispels the traditional forms of onto-theo-logy (the thought of God as *causa sui*) is not enough, but that in doing so God can again become subject to an even more regional thinking (personal faith or *Christlichkeit* in Heidegger) and the horizon of Being can become a quasi-metaphysical totality. To liberate God from philosophy does not immediately imply that God is named adequately. Yet, it can forge the path toward a more appropriate naming.

An Older Difference: Lévinas and Derrida

Most of *God without Being* is devoted to overcoming this more difficult Heideggerian idolatry, which Marion attempts with the use of certain passages of Scripture and the proposal of a thought of charity (both of which will be examined in more detail later). Yet, in *Idol and Distance*, Marion actually employs Lévinas' and Derrida's projects in order to "overcome" even Heidegger, although he sees them as ultimately unsuccessful ways of getting beyond Heidegger's ontological difference. He criticizes Lévinas for merely inverting the ontological difference by giving priority to the other human being instead of Being as such (which is what Heidegger does).[30] Lévinas therefore replaces one kind of being for another. Instead of challenging Heidegger's ontology in general, he simply criticizes Heidegger's emphasis on the Being of *Dasein* and replaces it with a concern for the Being of the other. This mere reversal remains inscribed in ontological difference.

Yet Lévinas does present a very fruitful aporia for Marion which spells out even more precisely the direction in which we must (not) look in order to speak adequately of God and to overcome ontological difference. A reading of Lévinas tells us that "beings do not depend uniformly on Being, since the Other and its ethical justice transgress the ontological Neuter," while also showing us that a mere inversion of ontological difference does not suffice. We must therefore find "a distance that passes beyond ontological difference, all the while remaining homogenous with it." Instead of solely inverting the terms of difference, one must get beyond both the terms and the "field" of ontological difference by opening a different terrain or game altogether. Lévinas' notion of exteriority is not sufficient but instead we need a notion of exteriority that "would not mobilize, following its example, Being and beings, but would reinscribe them in a place of exteriority, in a grid of separations, a combination of differences that, together, would situate and relativize them. The ontological difference would remain, but as transgressed" (ID, 220; IeD, 269–70). Lévinas, although unsuccessful in his own attempt to overcome ontological difference, points to the ways in which such overcoming would become possible, even more so than had Heidegger. For Marion, Lévinas' infinite seeks to escape Heidegger's difference and yet remains inscribed in it in some way. Lévinas, in a sense, stays too close to Heidegger and thus is unable to go beyond him. What Marion claims to learn from Lévinas' aporia parallels what he has said about the relationship between Descartes and Pascal. The point is not to destroy or ignore or invert the thought which one seeks to overcome. Rather, one leaves it standing but empties it of its significant thrust by viewing it from a stance outside it, by finding another terrain that will situate it as merely partial, as neither absolute nor ultimate. Is that not, however, precisely Derrida's project? Marion thinks not.

According to Marion, Derrida attempts to resurrect another and older difference that defers the ontological one. *Différance* is not a particular difference but the very structure of difference.[31] *Différance* dispels the ontological difference by situating it as a particular case of differences in general. None of these differences can be preferred over any other. Each is its own center and no difference or center has any priority over any other. Stapleton points out how Derrida's "trace" of writing that does not become an object within language is in fact very similar to the "God" of the "Abrahamic traditions": "To think *différance* or God within the present, thus subordinating them within being, is to attempt to think otherness while also trying to include them in the category of the same, which is exactly what cannot be done. The mysterious God hidden in the burning bush, speaking silently in the wind, whose ways are unknowable cannot be encountered as, noting that everything turns on the 'as,' knowable and un-mysterious." There is also no possibility for this God/trace to become present, no secret code that allows access to it. Both God and *différance* "provide for something like the possibility in which beings can appear, or present themselves" but are different than they are and do not appear in presence.[32]

Yet Marion finds that *différance* only transgresses ontological difference by reproducing its fold on a higher level and does not actually get beyond it. In an interview Marion explains that the notion of *différance* lacks the anonymity that Derrida claims for it:

> For Derrida there is a neutral difference (*différance*), which at first has nothing to do with time. In my opinion, however, this difference does not mean anything except "belatedness." Yet this belatedness does not remain nameless or anonymous. There is no namelessness of the difference [*der Differenz*] in the strict sense of the anonymous. The difference is rather belatedness in respect to the appeal, and there is no belatedness without appeal. Whether this belatedness comes from the Other or not, is secondary for me. But a belatedness in the neutral sense of Derrida seems to me phenomenologically impossible.[33]

Différance, then, only leads to a new region of interpretation, an older kind of difference, but not truly to a transgression or an escape. For Derrida, God still remains inscribed in Being; thus his thought is also idolatrous (ID, 231; IeD, 280). Derrida rejects any possibility of non-onto-theo-logical theology, which is precisely the only kind of theology possible for Marion. By traveling through ontological difference and only pushing at its edges, one does not overcome it. Neither Lévinas nor Derrida succeeds in doing so. Victor Kal summarizes Marion's use of Lévinas and Derrida in a useful fashion:

> Marion adopts Derrida's insight radically. For, according to him, it becomes clear in Derrida that the theology being sought can only be found *on the far side of ontological difference.* This theology situates its subject on the far side of the sense of destination and the play that takes place in difference, experienced indifferently or not. It does not help to think of this difference as pure attention (Heidegger), as radical substitution (Lévinas), or even as complete indifference (Derrida), for each puts God in the context of human hearing. It is true that a person can only hear within and in the context of this Being, this creation or, even, this indifference, but, says Marion, this exactly indicates that God Himself is distant. Nothing is learned of Him. He is *still further* away.[34]

Marion thinks that we can only truly succeed in overcoming metaphysics by playing with, expanding, and invalidating the boundaries of its philosophical project. In *Idol and Distance* he employs somewhat militaristic language in talking about the advances [*marches*] which defend this metaphysical territory and which one does not get beyond by ignoring them, but only by attacking them. He accomplishes this especially with the notion of distance, which I will examine in more detail later. In *God without Being,* he employs the language of "play"—one plays with the boundaries, suspends, and opens them. He does this with several biblical texts that employ the philosophical terminology of *on/onta/ousia* and displace its meaning and significance. Marion first cites a verse from Romans 4:17 where God gives life to the dead by calling "nonbeings as beings." God gives being to nonbeings, regards them "as if" they had being. The philosophical categories of ontology are used in kerygmatic fashion and therefore introduce another kind of difference. This difference of faith does not destroy ontological difference but is "indifferent" to it by setting it out of play: "That ontic difference should thus be struck with indifference, as when a luminous contrast hitherto quite visible is effaced in a general bedazzlement, refers back to another difference, still anonymous, but already at work" (GWB, 88; DSL, 131). The biblical text serves to indicate a difference that is clearly distinguished from philosophical difference and yet can invalidate it by that very distinction. Marion substantiates this with a second text from 1 Corinthians, in which Paul assures his audience that although they are nothing in the eyes of the world, literally have no "being," God grants them being by seeing them differently than the world does, which, in fact, is nothing in God's eyes.

God reverses the ontological categories in which the world measures and invalidates them through love or charity.

This becomes even more obvious in his analysis of the parable of the prodigal son, the only passage in Scripture in which the word *ousia* (or "essence") occurs. It refers here to the *ousia* or "essence" (literally: inheritance or goods) of the father: the younger son asks for his share of the father's *ousia*. Marion finds that this resonates legitimately with the idea of *ousia* in philosophy. He interprets the parable as a misunderstanding on the part of both sons that *ousia* is something that can be possessed or grasped, instead of a generous gift to be enjoyed. The younger son not only asks for the "ousia" of the father, but then squanders it and thus loses his filiation. Even the older son considers the father's ousia only in terms of possession. Yet the father's love returns the filiation of the prodigal through his generous pardon. For the father "ousia" defines the gift of forgiveness and charity: "The father is not fixed on the ousia because with his gaze he transpierces all that is not inscribed in the rigor of a gift: giving, received, given." The father therefore invalidates the importance of ousia and inscribes it in a higher game, that of charity or love: "Ousia is inscribed in the play of donation, abandon, and pardon that make of it the currency of an entirely other exchange than of beings" (GWB, 100; DSL, 146). It becomes a game of the gift, indifferent to ontological difference, transgressing it, opening horizons unknown to it. Charity, Marion concludes on the basis of these biblical passages, overcomes being. Or, as Thomas Guarino puts it, for Marion, "the inadequacy of the language of Being forces a cathartic turn to the more poetic forms of agapic love. Such a shift successfully subverts the enclosing dimensions of ontology. Rather than freezing the idolic gaze, the agapic turn yields to an iconic attitude, recognizing the Gxd who is both ungraspable and unknowable."[35] Marion therefore suggests that the Scriptural language has led us beyond the philosophical dilemma and has succeeded in overcoming and invalidating its categories:

> It is important here to point out this unique attainment: biblical revelation offers, in some rare texts, the emergence of a certain indifference of being to Being; being thus makes sport of Being only by outwitting ontological difference; it outwits it only inasmuch as it is first distorted by another instance, the gift. The gift crosses Being/being: it meets it, strikes it out with a mark, finally opens it, as a window casement opens, on an instance that remains unspeakable according to the language of Being — supposing that another language might be conceived. (GWB, 101; DSL, 147)

Both gift and charity are here interpreted as strictly theological.[36] We will see that in Marion's more recent work, however, they will become philosophical categories.

Marion therefore employs Scriptural texts in order to challenge philosophical categories. Theological concepts, such as gift and charity, are able to move us beyond metaphysical constrictions by dislocating any notion of grounding or even of ontological difference: "The Pauline text outwits Being by setting being in motion as if it were not bent to the fold of Being" (GWB, 91; DSL, 135). The two texts — biblical and philosophical — operate on different planes, use the ontic terminology in incommensurable fashion. The theological is able to

> *distort* the play of being by withdrawing it from Being, by *undoing* being from the rule of Being. This crossing traces a cross over ontological difference, a cross that *abolishes* it, *annuls* it without annihilating it, *distorts* it without contesting its right. In the same way that a window opens the view to an immense space that it nevertheless measures by a crossbar, this crossing opens ontological difference to a differing that renders it indifferent only by excess and that places it in reserve only in that it preserves it from an entirely different dilemma. (GWB, 95; DSL, 139–40; emphasis mine)

Although Marion assures us that this neither "contests the right" of philosophy nor "annihilates" it, his language of distortion and abolishment is rather strong. By invalidating and undoing philosophical categories and by opening onto another plane, the insight of revelation is able to lead beyond the confining philosophical categories and free the divine from its restrictive definitions. Scripture, although on a different level than philosophy — apparently on a decidedly superior one — can thoroughly unsettle the philosophical discourse. Theology, he seems to assume here, is superior to philosophy and can invalidate and displace it. The "attainment" of revelation is an invalidation of philosophy, a superior solution that solves the problematic idolatry of philosophy. It introduces a plane that philosophy cannot grasp or discover by itself, a type of third order.

In retrospect, Marion has repeatedly pointed to the theological nature of his work at this point and also has frequently highlighted the polemical atmosphere in which the work originated. In an interview he emphasized that "one must understand that a book like *God without Being,* if not provocative, was at least combative. When one simultaneously criticizes Derrida, Heidegger, and St. Thomas Aquinas in one breath, in order to conclude in some fashion that now only the New Testament or nothing counts, it is a matter of provocation."[37] Yet, the arguments of *God without Being* and *Idol and Distance* cannot be dismissed as mere provocation. Apart from the obvious parallels to Marion's phenomenological work, to which I will turn in the next chapter, they also develop an important paradigm that remains consistent throughout Marion's work: namely a conception of a superior or different language of charity that challenges and dislocates purely rational thought. Marion adopts precisely what he has outlined as Pascal's challenge to Descartes: a third order of charity which views and unsettles the second order from a place outside and beyond it. Jeffrey Kosky suggests in a footnote to an article outlining the progression from *God without Being* to *Being Given* that "a fruitful comparison could be made between Marion's position as regards theology and metaphysical thought of God in *God without Being,* and the position he reads in Pascal confronting Descartes in the final chapter of *On Descartes' Metaphysical Prism* . . . In brief, in *God without Being* Marion adopts the position that he attributes to Pascal in *On Descartes' Metaphysical Prism.*"[38] Kosky is certainly right in this suggestion, although I would maintain that the parallel is much more extensive, applying not only to *God without Being* but to most of Marion's writings, both theological and phenomenological in nature. We might compare Marion's theology to the Pascal of the *Pensées* and his phenomenology to the Pascal of the *Art of Persuasion:* while Pascal is informed by and criticizes Descartes, who represents the paradigm of philosophy for him, Marion is informed by and criticizes Heidegger (and Husserl, Lévinas, and Derrida), who represent(s) the paradigm of philosophy for him. And the challenge is dual for both: while at times the philosophical paradigm is challenged from something outside it, namely theology, at other times it is displaced by something at its own boundary, namely a different way of thinking philosophically. Of course at this point this must remain a mere assertion. The next chapters will confirm this suggestion more fully. Let me turn, therefore, to Marion's more strictly philosophical work.

three
Phenomenology
and Metaphysics
"Unfolding the Fold of the Given"

Marion's phenomenology has in some ways gained even more attention in the contemporary debate than his theology. It also constitutes his most recent work, yet it is still significantly marked by a desire to overcome metaphysics. I will outline first how he proposes such overcoming in his trilogy outlining a radical phenomenology of givenness, paying particular attention to the continuity between his early work on Descartes and this more recent phenomenological project. Three aspects central to this work deal directly with metaphysics and the need for its overcoming. First, Marion's general proposal of a phenomenology of donation or givenness (which he outlines in *Reduction and Givenness*) is supposed to go beyond the continuing metaphysical restrictions of Husserl's and Heidegger's projects, while explicating their potential for this transgression. Second, in *Being Given* Marion not only continues this argument but deals also with the notion of the gift and shows how it helps us escape metaphysical restrictions. Third, he develops (in both *Being Given* and *In Excess*) the notion of saturated phenomena, as the aspect of phenomenology that can move us beyond metaphysics. I will conclude this section with a brief look at Marion's most recent work on the erotic phenomenon, since the influence of Descartes on this work is even more explicit. In this book Marion very clearly juxtaposes his own "post-Cartesian" meditations with those of Descartes (and Husserl).[1]

A Third Reduction

Already *Reduction et Donation/Reduction and Givenness* announces Marion's desire to expand phenomenology beyond metaphysical restrictions with the notion of donation or givenness.[2] He spends most of this preparatory work in outlining what he sees as the unfulfilled potential of Husserl's and Heidegger's phenomenological projects. He finds that both thinkers place metaphysical restrictions on the appearing of phenomena: Husserl seems too preoccupied with the constitution of objects, while Heidegger is too obsessed with the language of Being. The grounding of these two issues in Marion's exploration of Descartes is immediately obvious, if rather general at this point. Marion shows how these projects of the constitution of phenomena and of investigating the meaning of Being both end up limiting the self-showing of phenomena, because they must appear either as objects or within the horizon of Being. He suggests that one ought to push Husserl's project further by employing the phenomenological reduction more radically. By making reduction an absolute principle, something he contends Husserl's own definitions of the basic principles of phenomenology justify, we can move beyond these metaphysical restrictions to a point where phenomena can give themselves purely and unconditionally. Pure givenness liberates phenomenology and allows philosophy a non-metaphysical outlet. While *Reduction and Givenness* is occupied primarily with a critique of Husserl and Heidegger in light of these contentions, *Being Given* constitutes a comprehensive attempt to outline such a new phenomenology of givenness. Let me briefly summarize Marion's analysis in order to see how he proposes metaphysics ought to be overcome. I will be less concerned here with determining whether his readings and criticisms of Husserl and Heidegger are correct and adequate than with showing how his analysis is significantly indebted to and prepared by his work on Descartes.

The preparation for an overcoming of metaphysics and an opening of phenomenology to its ultimate conclusion (or limit or excess) happens in *Reduction and Givenness*. Already here Marion defines his project as an attempt to complete or end metaphysics: "In undertaking to free presence from any condition or precondition for receiving what gives itself as it gives itself, phenomenology therefore attempts to complete metaphysics, and, indissolubly, to bring it to an end. Phenomenology therefore remains exactly on the line — the watershed: by soliciting the liberation of presence, it fulfills the expectations of metaphysics, but in thus stealing from it the object of its quarrel, it abolishes it" (RG, 1; RD, 8). The project intends to think phenomenology to its end, to go farther than did Heidegger with his thought of Being, which in Marion's view remained ultimately unsuccessful. Phenomenology must give a new beginning to philosophy by pushing the notion of possibility to its limits.[3] Marion thus employs certain aspects that he sees as essential to phenomenology (for example, its emphasis on possibility or the notion of the reduction) in order to overcome other (more detrimental and less essential) aspects of this project (for example, its actualization in Husserl or Heidegger and especially Husserl's search for constitution or evidence). This preparatory work is supposed to make thinkable the third reduction, which Marion seeks to perform in *Being Given*. *Reduction and Givenness* is a detailed examination of Husserl and Heidegger and the possibilities and figures of phenomenology. Phenomenology must be freed even from itself, from the thoughts which have already attempted to think it but insufficiently so. In his phenomenological project, then, Marion seeks to enlarge the domain of philosophy, to push its limits, to delineate its boundaries and outline a possibility of its overcoming.

Marion begins his project by examining carefully the "breakthrough" that Husserl assumes to have accomplished in the *Logical Investigations* and the readings and critiques of this breakthrough by Derrida[4] and Heidegger.[5] Marion suggests that Husserl does not think donation or givenness radically enough and that Heidegger seeks to overcome these limitations, to push phenomenology further by making it into a method for ontology:

> It seems permissible to suppose that Husserl, submerged by the simultaneously threatening and jubilatory imperative to manage the superabundance of data in presence, does not at any moment (at least in the *Logical Investigations*) ask himself about the status, the scope, or even the identity of that givenness. This silence amounts to an admission (following Jacques Derrida's thesis) that Husserl, leaving unquestioned the givenness whose broadening he nevertheless accomplished, does not free it from the prison of presence, and thus keeps it in metaphysical detention. Heidegger, on the contrary, seeing immediately and with an extraordinary lucidity that the breakthrough of 1900–1901 consists entirely in the broadening of givenness beyond sensible intuition, assumes precisely the Husserlian heritage by making the entire question bear on what such a givenness means — and therefore in being careful not to reduce it too quickly to presence, even under the figure of categorial intuition. (RG, 39; RD, 62)

Marion seeks to push this "broadening of givenness" beyond a reduction to "presence" even further. The thought of Being/being will again become a major issue in *Reduction and Givenness*. Not only is it significant for a treatment of Heidegger, but it will occupy much of the space in which the argument between Husserl and Heidegger is conducted for Marion. This is not only because Heidegger emphasizes the question of Being, but precisely because since Descartes this issue determines for Marion the metaphysical status of a thinker. To delineate carefully what Husserl or Heidegger have to say about ontology, grounding, and presence is to make a judgment about the metaphysical quality of their thought.

Marion does not agree with Heidegger's claim that Husserl does not think ontology. Rather, both Husserl and Heidegger deal with ontology, but think it differently. For Husserl the mode of Being of phenomena depends on their constitution in appearing to the presence of consciousness. They are the lived experience of consciousness and are reduced to their appearing in presence. All of Husserl's phenomena thus remain flat and uninteresting in Marion's view because they all become objects to be constituted by consciousness. To some extent this judgment corresponds to what Marion has said about presence in his study of Descartes' objects. Just as the Cartesian method of the code arranged all objects by their perfect presence to consciousness, Marion chides Husserl for a similar obsession with objects, evidence, and presence. He finds that Husserl's notion of *Gegenständlichkeit* (which he translates as *objectité* ["objectity" or "objectness"] in order to distinguish it from *Objektivität/objectivité* ["objectivity"]) reduces phenomena to objects which are not only perfectly present to consciousness but actually completely controlled by its constitution of them in signification.[6] Signification (or intention)[7] for Marion therefore seems to correspond to the Cartesian notion of the code and its method of figuration. As signification anticipates the constitution of the phenomenon and supplies what is missing from intuition for its apprehension, the code through figuration constitutes objects for consciousness in perfect clarity. In another context, Marion explicitly associates Husserl's attempt to "raise formal logic to the rank of ontology" with the Cartesian *mathesis universalis* and points out that Husserl himself uses the phrase (RG, 148–53; RD, 220–28). As Marion's Descartes looks rather Husserlian in some ways, Marion's Husserl is also rather Cartesian in some respects.

According to Marion Heidegger takes issue, however, not only with Husserl's account of appearing phenomena and their Being but also with the phenomenological reduction. He wishes to pass beyond the Husserlian reduction "toward the meaning of the Being of beings" (RG, 66; RD, 103). This doubled (or second) reduction is executed through the analytic of *Dasein* and ontological difference. For Heidegger, "the privilege of *Dasein* comes to it only from its disposition to undergo a redoubled phenomenological reduction; the latter passes from being to the 'meaning of Being' only by working that being which is determined above all by the Being of beings" (RG, 70; RD, 110). Martin Gagnon chides Marion for forgetting the level of interrogation and careful investigation that is necessary for reduction even to become possible. It has an "interrogative implication" which Marion ignores.[8] Marion does employ the terminology of "reduction" rather freely to refer to the "bracketing" or "setting" aside of certain assumptions, questions, or frameworks. He does not make a distinction between several levels of (phenomenological, eidetic, etc.) reduction as Husserl does. Heidegger's quest for the truth of Being, whether in terms of the *Dasein*-analytic or in terms of the generous givenness [*es gibt*] of *Sein*, is an example of "reduction" for Marion because both moves interpret the appearance of beings in light of the horizon of Being. Marion interprets Heidegger as moving beyond Husserl's desire to return to the things themselves in a second breakthrough that attempts to reach the Being of beings, as defined by the problematic of ontological difference:

> Phenomenology is accomplished by accomplishing, with the *Logical Investigations*, a first breakthrough: that of the intuition at play with intention in order to reach the things themselves. But phenomenology accomplishes a second breakthrough when Heidegger calls intentionality to return, as concerns things, not only to beings, but to the very Being of beings. Superimposed on, if not added to, the distinction between intuition and intention is the difference between Being and beings. The ontological difference wholly defines the breakthrough carried out (if not completed) by Heidegger. It does so, first, because it displaces phenomenology from the knowledge of beings to the thought of Being, first according to fundamental ontology and then according to the *Ereignis*. It does so, secondly, because the ontological difference alone allows one to make the distinction between metaphysics — attached to Being only as the Being of beings and with a view to beings — and the thought of Being as such; that is, it alone allows one to practice a "destruction of the history of ontology" that, in fact, allows and requires one to rewrite the history of metaphysics as the history of the forgetting of Being, as an unthought history of Being. In short, the ontological difference decides on both the phenomenological thought proper to Heidegger and the site of all preceding metaphysics. (RG, 108; RD, 163)

We see here again the importance for Marion of the notion of ontological difference that we have already observed him utilize in his evaluation of Descartes' metaphysical system. Marion will now employ this in order to judge the metaphysical quality of Husserl's thought. With Husserl, phenomenology is still enslaved by metaphysics because it is beholden to the constitution of objects through intention and because he fails to realize the ontological difference. With Heidegger, it begins to free itself from metaphysical shackles (although, as we have seen, not entirely successfully). The ontological difference helps to clarify this relationship to metaphysics.

Again, Marion engages in a careful delineation of the ontological difference, which in fact he discovers to have several different definitions in Heidegger.[9] Not only does it designate the difference between "beings" [*Seiendes*] and "Being" [*Sein*], but it refers also to a further difference between the "Being of *Dasein*" and "Being as such." Through a comparison of Descartes' ego with *Dasein* and more generally Heidegger's relationship with Descartes,[10] Marion asserts that Heidegger cannot really delineate ontological difference in *Sein und Zeit* because the analytic of *Dasein* hinders him from thinking it fully. The *Kehre* thus becomes necessary even to remain faithful to his project of thinking Being as such. Furthermore, it is not true that Husserl does not have an ontology; rather the problem is that Husserl confines ontology to the horizon of objectness, the object-character of things viewed by intentionality.[11] Marion suggests that Husserl even conceived of an "I" prior to and outside of ontology, a self beyond being. Yet he never thematized such a "horizon outside of Being" because of "his intoxication with the constitution of objects according to the innumerable regional ontologies, and then his inability to recognize the ontological difference and therefore to see clearly what it is a question of transgressing" (RG, 162; RD, 241). Rejecting this "intoxication" with objects, Marion instead intends to expand the horizon beyond the issue of Being. He sees this as being faithful to the main impetus of phenomenology, if not always to Husserl's particular instantiation of it (RG, 162; RD, 241). Husserl, in Marion's view, had an inkling of the path out of metaphysics and toward a pure phenomenology. In a sense, he already opened a way even beyond Heidegger. Yet, according to Marion, Husserl was too timid to pursue this path, too focused on poor phenomena when he could (and should) have been dazzled by the abundance which he glimpsed. Marion here clearly seems to align Husserl with Descartes, in the sense that both are able to show the limits of metaphysics and yet remain unable to get beyond them. In fact, Marion likens Husserl's confusion of ontology to the "gray ontology" he has discovered in Descartes (RG, 160; RD, 239). Even the experience of bedazzlement that Husserl is unable to overcome or utilize parallels Descartes' awe before the infinite whom he is incompetent to describe adequately, but whom he instead confines to *causa sui*.

In *Being Given* Marion deepens this critique of both Husserl and Heidegger. Again, he criticizes Husserl's sense of objectness [*Gegenständlichkeit*] as the originary horizon of the phenomenon and finds that it threatens pure givenness.[12] Husserl jeopardizes his own project by giving universality to objectness, which is only one mode of givenness. Heidegger also does not think Husserl's project radically enough by shrinking back "before the originarity of givenness" (ED, 51; BG, 33). Heidegger thinks the withdrawal of Being and ontological difference together in a way that limits givenness and makes it subject to the *Ereignis*. James Dodd summarizes Marion's criticism of Husserl and Heidegger helpfully as follows:

> Marion often characterizes manifestation as something restricted, or regulated either by an intuitivity (which in his reading of Husserl always seems to take the form of an intentionally fulfilled, and in turn discursive intuition), or the meaning of Being thought as disclosure (truth). Why restricted? First, because intuitivity marks out a space for phenomenality by regulating structures of the visible, thereby binding the scope of the given to what can be experienced in the mode of the understood, the assimilated, the set and fixed as something *seen*. Second, because Being, thanks to its departure in the enactment of givenness, thereby relegates this enactment itself to a derivative moment of its principal movement of concealment. The Being in being-given in this way circumscribes givenness, turning thought away from the gift (*Gabe*) to its own becoming, thereby ensuring that Being remains the essential theme. Each move in turn embeds the phenomenality of the phenomenon into a web of principles or ties (18), and each fails to "admit

... the phenomenality proper to the phenomenon — its right and its power to show itself on its own terms" (19).[13]

Marion wants to maintain against both Husserl and Heidegger that the "it" which gives must always remain radically anonymous. Heidegger, however, subsumes the origin of givenness in the advent of the *Ereignis* and thus limits it to this advent of Being.[14] Instead, the horizons of objectness (Husserl) and beingness [*étanité*] (Heidegger) must be eliminated, the phenomenon freed from both the language of objectness and that of being.[15]

Marion's readings of Husserl and Heidegger on this point have been criticized repeatedly. Bruce Benson wonders, for example, about Marion's phenomenology whether "there is something inherently problematic with the project itself," namely whether "Marion's reduction to pure givenness obliterate[s] the very conditions that make it possible to understand and appreciate that which is given?"[16] Gerhard Höhn in a German newspaper reviews recent developments in France, particularly in light of Janicaud's claim about the supposed theological turn. He summarizes Marion's work (up to *Reduction and Givenness*) and sees it culminating in the definition of God as love. He also wonders whether it is really possible to have a phenomenology of the "invisible originary" or whether that is not a contradiction in terms (although he does not agree with Janicaud that Marion's work can be dismissed simply as a "theological turn").[17]

Natalie Depraz provides a more extensive critique, although she does not always explicitly apply it to Marion. She is rather unhappy with what she judges a subversion of Husserl's project.[18] In a thorough investigation into Marion's phenomenology, she asserts that it radically changes the very nature of phenomenality. On the one hand, Depraz objects to the translation of *Gegebenheit* with givenness/donation: "*Gegebenheit* ist nicht *Gebung*" (117). It does not equate to the given.[19] She thinks that it is a non-negotiable aspect of phenomenology to examine the mode of appearing. By identifying givenness and intuition with each other, phenomenology would be limited to a "static dimension" (119). She claims that a reflection on the infinite would be able to question this connection between givenness and observation (*Anschauung*). The givenness of a normal object is already infinite, since many experiences of it are necessary to grasp it in its fullness (even to see all sides, for example). Unlike that of Descartes, Husserl's concept of the infinite therefore is a negative infinite that implies the imperfection and definitive negativity of knowledge (125). On the other hand, she criticizes Marion for changing the reduction into a method with a far more universal application than seemed necessary for Husserl. To turn reduction into an obligatory procedure is to step outside primary phenomenology.[20] She asserts that by making the reduction a founding phenomenon Marion is led back into the scholastic sterility that Heidegger condemned under the name "ontotheology."[21] The charge of "onto-theo-logy" is clearly false. Most of Marion's work is precisely an attempt to combat onto-theo-logy. Nor can one describe the function of reduction in Marion as found-ing, in the way in which he has shown Descartes to be grounding all reality in the ego or in God. As pointed out above, Marion does seem to employ the term of reduction quite liberally. He sees Descartes to have practiced such reduc-tion by setting aside beliefs and challenging convictions through radical doubt. Heidegger performs an "existential" reduction or a reduction to being, while Marion himself puts everything in parenthesis for the sake of givenness (or later for eros). This is not a metaphysical grounding, however, because what made Descartes metaphysical was not his doubt but his constitution of objects. Reduction similarly does not ground everything, but instead opens a space that allows things to appear of themselves. It neither causes them nor organizes them along a *mathesis universalis*.[22]

In a review of *Reduction and Givenness*, Claude Piché explains Mari-on's distinction between a phenomenological/transcendental reduction and an existential reduction or reduction to the appeal by focusing especially on the chapter about ontological difference. He summarizes how according to Marion, *Sein und Zeit* distinguishes (ontological difference) not only between Being and beings, but also between genres of being. He concludes that Mar-ion was able (in the book) to root his phenomenology historically while also "adopting new accents."[23] Rolf Kühn also reviews Marion's phenomenology favorably. He refers to Marion's "fourth" definition of the principle of phenom-enology as the one which "encompasses the entire phenomenological devel-opment of method and functions as its hidden presupposition," although he does insist that Marion's reduction is still to appearance and manifestation.[24] He affirms as enriching Marion's translation of *Gegebenheit* as donation or givenness and praises him for giving reduction a positive meaning, in that re-duction "opens" and "gives" instead of limits and reduces. Overall he approves of Marion's critique of Heidegger and finds that Marion's fourth principle is useful because it opens phenomenology in the direction of Henry's "material phenomenology" and makes it possible.[25]

Similarly, Jeffrey A. Bell in a review of the English translation of *Reduc-tion and Givenness* finds that "Marion presents a finely nuanced, sophisticated case for interpreting the work of Heidegger and Husserl in light of Husserl's call to return to the things themselves."[26] He suggests that "a defender of Hei-degger might respond by arguing that this apparent circularity is what one nec-essarily encounters when one attempts to return to the things themselves; that is, in carrying forward Husserl's phenomenological reduction one inevitably encounters what Heidegger called the hermeneutic circle," but he finds "con-vincing" Marion's claim that Heidegger is not radical enough in his return to the things themselves. Bell does criticize Marion for not paying more attention to Heidegger's late works, which he suggests would have made Marion realize that his "discussion of the 'unconditional call' simply echoes Heidegger's later theories on the 'presencing of presence' and the 'House of Being.'"[27] Marion should have engaged in a critique of these later works. Considering how much time Marion does spend on Heidegger's later works (especially in terms of his reading of Heidegger's *Ereignis*), this critique seems somewhat unjustified.

Regardless of how faithful Marion is to Husserl or Heidegger (or how much he reads one through the other), it is clear that his interpretation of phenomenology is deeply grounded in his earlier insights. The rejection of ontological and "object" language corresponds perfectly to what Marion has determined as deeply problematic metaphysical groundings in the Cartesian project. Marion seems to interpret Husserl's project as a renewed version of the first metaphysics he has uncovered in Descartes. Like Descartes, Husserl allows consciousness to arrange all phenomena as so many objects of consciousness. And in some way like Descartes, Heidegger allows Being to become the sole framework for the appearance of all other beings (although of course Heidegger's Being is not divine). In order to overcome metaphysics, in Marion's view, phenomenology must move beyond its obsession with the constitution of objects as well as beyond its infatuation with *Dasein* and the language of Being. Husserl, on Marion's reading, opened this possibility but did not pursue it.[28]

Givenness

Marion thinks that he can free philosophy from metaphysics by pursuing more radically this phenomenological project beyond being. In order to do so, he must perform a third and more rigorous phenomenological reduction exceeding those of Husserl and Heidegger. In *Reduction and Givenness*, he describes this as a third reduction which will free phenomenology from the restrictions of both object(iv)ity and the question of Being by opening itself to an appeal that comes from a further and anonymous distance. This is not the claim of Being [*Anspruch des Seins*] or even that of God, but a pure and unadulterated claim, the appeal as such.[29] Both Husserl's and Heidegger's phenomenology can be led back to this originary form of the call, to a third and prior reduction. The call of the other, the appeal as such, goes beyond the Heideggerian call of Being and thus liberates itself from these semi-metaphysical constrictions.

This new, third reduction Marion attempts to think more fully in *Being Given*, where he identifies it as a reduction to pure donation or givenness. He interprets the principle "as much reduction, so much givenness" as the primary principle of phenomenology.[30] Phenomenology must allow what shows itself to be seen without imposing any kinds of limitations upon the self-showing of the given. Just as Marion attempted to think God "without" or "beyond" Being, he now intends to think all phenomena in this way. Phenomenology seeks to overcome metaphysics. Marion insists that for phenomenology the thing or object comes to me and appears to me in its "flesh" or in person and therefore overcomes the restrictions of being and constitution. The goal of phenomenology is always to uphold this privilege of pure givenness. Phenomenology must allow for the manifestation of the thing without manipulation by the viewer (ED, 15; BG, 9). This becomes possible through the method of reduction, whose goal is not the possession of certainty or the elimination of doubt or the imposition of a priori conditions of consciousness, but rather the "undoubtability" of the appearance of things. In order to protect the phenomenon, all obstacles must be removed, all violent or illegitimate theories must be excluded. The rigorous phenomenological reduction thus takes the initiative only in order to give it to that which manifests itself, so that it can finally do without it. This principle, so Marion suggests, is thus not a first principle, but a last or final one. When reduction reduces utterly, the given appears as such. Reduction leads back to the full givenness of the phenomenon. The phenomenon must be understood from givenness as such, from the self of the phenomenon (instead of from the limits of consciousness). To reduce givenness means to free it from all other limits, including those of intuition. Phenomenology, unlike metaphysics, does not oppose the object and its representation, but rather tries to think them together as two modes of the same thing and thus gives them integrity. That which Husserl thinks only implicitly and not yet rigorously, Marion seeks to think fully and explicitly.

Some readers of Marion have objected that this is no longer phenomenology, because phenomenology always requires the notion of horizon and of the constituting ego. Even Lévinas, to whom Marion is highly indebted especially for his critique of Heidegger, made this objection at some point. Marion retells the encounter: "I said to Lévinas some years ago that in fact the last step for a real phenomenology would be to give up the concept of horizon. Lévinas answered me immediately: 'Without horizon there is no phenomenology.' And I boldly assume he was wrong" (GGP, 66). What Marion wants to argue is that the idea of horizon limits the self-givenness of the phenomenon in that it appears to me only within the parameters I set for it in my act of constitution. Instead, the phenomenon ought to be allowed to show itself on its own terms. Because the self-showing is still received in some manner (the phenomenon still appears even when it is no longer constituted by a transcendental ego), this reception can still be described and examined in Marion's view, even when it ruptures or even suspends the horizons of the recipient. Marion maintains that this is therefore still phenomenology, in fact, a phenomenology more faithful to the self-giving of the phenomenon.

Against Dominique Janicaud, who argues that Marion is abandoning classical phenomenology by attempting to eliminate the phenomenological horizon (and ultimately the cognitive ego),[31] Dodd, in his review of the English translation of *Being Given*, affirms that its central concern is "to make the phenomenality of the phenomenon once again the central question of phenomenological philosophy. The attempt here," so he suggests, "is thus not to go beyond phenomenology, but to return to its original insights, its fundamental accomplishments, in order to discover again, in a new form, what had been the driving force at its inception."[32] In his view, "the contribution of Marion's work is arguably to have shown that a specific problem, that of the givenness of the given, provides, in an unexpectedly direct and complete manner, a potentially decisive mode of orientation thanks to which the ambiguities of all the basic concepts and intellectual moves that make up the phenomenological philosophy can be both exposed and addressed."[33] Marion himself vacillates in whether he wants to claim his project as profoundly faithful to "classical phenomenology" and merely working out implications already inherent in Husserl's thought, or whether he sees it as a significant overcoming of Husserl and Heidegger and an independent phenomenological project in its own right. Since I am concerned primarily with showing the overall coherence of Marion's thought and not with evaluating his faithfulness to Husserl, I will leave the question of his phenomenological "orthodoxy" open and instead turn to explicating the proposal of givenness itself.

Givenness gives itself and confirms itself not through possession and certitude but by abandoning itself, by holding nothing back (though this certainly does not mean that we are able to grasp or make present all that is so freely given). It "perfects itself by undoing itself" (ED, 89; BG, 60). Givenness designates the pure phenomenological act of self-giving. As pointed out above, Marion's interpretation of *Gegebenheit* as givenness has not remained unchallenged. Depraz criticizes his use of the term, which she judges un-Husserlian. Janicaud has similarly objected to Marion's "mis-translation." Marion justifies his employment of this translation again in *Being Given* by emphasizing that *Gegebenheit* always refers both to the process of giving and the character of the giving. Marion admits that the various terms connecting giving or gift are related ambiguously and equivocally. Yet, givenness does have necessarily an act of giving, the stake of the gift, the actor who is the giver, the mode of what is being accomplished, namely the given. This polysynomy is meaningful in Marion's view. He therefore equates the self-showing of the phenomenon with its pure givenness: "Showing oneself thus goes definitively back to giving oneself: the fold of givenness, in unfolding itself, shows the given which dispenses givenness. Showing oneself, for the phenomenon, equates to unfolding the fold of givenness where it surges up as a gift. Showing oneself and giving oneself play in the same field—the fold of givenness, which unfolds itself in giving" (ED, 102; BG, 70).

Marion outlines at this point a phenomenology of the "gift" before fully correlating it to his analysis of givenness. Since his analysis of the gift has elicited particular criticism, I will devote the next section to that subject and here finish outlining the aspects of pure givenness he elucidates somewhat later in his treatment.[34] His analysis orients itself along Lévinasian parameters. Instead of being interrupted by the face of the other that comes from otherwise, from an immeasurable distance, and surprises and affects me, Marion applies this same description to all phenomena. He depicts the givenness of phenomena with four figures: *anamorphosis, arrivage, fait accompli,* and *incident*. Throughout he insists that givenness is the very mode in which phenomenology is able to get beyond metaphysics. Givenness gives outside of Being, can even give Being; it determines the phenomenon in its giveability and acceptability and thus exceeds metaphysical restrictions. No phenomenon can appear without givenness as such, and this "as such" does not reduce phenomena to their "beingness" but to their status as given. The phenomenon always comes to us from "somewhere else," from a distance, from its "self" from which it abandons itself in its giving. Marion does not always explicitly connect this exposition of givenness to his analysis of Descartes. Yet, as I will seek to show, it is very clear that the insights gained earlier are operative here and that his outline of the ways in which givenness functions are a direct response to what he has analyzed as the shortcomings of metaphysics in Descartes.

Marion names this "coming from otherwise," first, an *"anamorphosis"* (ED, 174; BG, 123). The phenomenon takes form from itself and arises from its own ground (which is other), comes across a phenomenological distance. This appearing happens in contingency, touches me, falls upon me, affects me and pushes me: the phenomenon comes to me as an event that modifies my field (of vision, of knowledge, of life). It happens to me. I must give myself to the phenomenon, must allow it to engage me in its play. Phenomena inhabit and surround me. *Anamorphosis* touches me in some way, traverses a distance which leads (*ana-*) to its taking form (*-morphosis*). It determines the direction of its own arrival. I would suggest therefore that *anamorphosis* reverses the epistemological direction of the Cartesian subject. While Descartes rethinks ontology in terms of the *intuitus* which imposes its own view on all objects, the self-giving phenomenon arrives without any such prior view and takes form as a surprise. Its arrival is not determined by the human *cogito* (or by a divine grounding) but rather comes upon me suddenly and unexpectedly. Phenomena do not require the Cartesian grounding of the code and cannot be organized in an all-embracing *mathesis universalis*. Marion has therefore sought to eliminate essential features of the Cartesian metaphysics.

This unforeseen and sudden arrival of the phenomenon, second, Marion calls *arrivage* (an arrival distinguished from a simple *arrivée* that might be predicted or known beforehand).[35] This *arrivage* leaves no initiative to me except my absorbing the shock of the *anamorphosis*, receiving it in awaiting. The phenomenon constitutes me as the recipient, makes itself to be accepted (Marion calls this a "counter-experience" that reverses the direction of Husserlian constitution). The contingency of the phenomenon thus becomes a necessity for me, although it never has necessity in itself, but always remains contingent upon its arrival as a given. *Arrivage* thus, in Marion's view, assures the individuation, unpredictability, and temporality of the phenomenon.[36] With this, *arrivage* seems to rethink the Cartesian insistence on self-presence and permanence in the present. It is neither determined or predictable along the parameters of the code. It underlies neither figuration or abstraction, because it escapes all such control of the *ego cogito*. The fact that figuration, abstraction, and *mathesis universalis* are impossible destabilizes and indeed invalidates the Cartesian *intuitus*. Knowledge is not grounded upon the self which perceives and organizes it, but comes as a surprising event. Again, Cartesian assumptions about metaphysics are being invalidated and displaced.

Third, according to Marion, this arrival is always an accomplished fact. The phenomenon as purely given arrives in the mode of facticity, as a *fait accompli*. This facticity of the arrival (which might be likened to Lévinas' notion of the *il y a* but with Heideggerian connotations of generosity which Lévinas explicitly excluded) has no prior causes, is always already there, befalls me like an accident. The given cannot be fit into a logical progression of time, since it has neither past (cause) nor future (permanence). Although this certainly recalls Heidegger's terms of facticity and the thrownness of *Dasein*, Marion wants to emphasize even more radically the role of the phenomenon in this instead of its effect on the mode of *Dasein*. Far more phenomena, for Marion, have the character of revelation in some fashion: they have always already taken place. They are absolutely first and originary. They are in each instant completely irrevocable. The facticity of the phenomenon does not reduce me to factuality but comes to me as a fact. This fact erases itself in order to accomplish itself. I am constituted by this phenomenon, not it by me. Marion speaks of this as a reversal of intentionality, in which I become the objective of the object.[37] The given phenomenon is a *fait accompli* in that we find ourselves always already within it, are preceded and constituted by it. This not only carries further the refusal of permanence and presence which dislocates metaphysics, but it also displaces the causality of the metaphysical system in which everything must be grounded in a prior rationality. Not only is the causality of order and series set aside by this *fait accompli*, but we can also not refer back to a divine (or human) *causa sui* in Cartesian fashion. Instead Marion likens the *fait accompli* to Descartes' insistence on the creation of the eternal truths, which I will examine in the next chapter. This important Cartesian thesis (of the creation of eternal truths) serves as an illustration of the *fait accompli*, which gives facticity as an act of prior establishment.

This "falling upon us" of the fact finally happens as an *incident*. Its first and last moment always coincide. Its "incidental" and free appearance comes as surprise and cannot be predicted. It does not define itself as an essence, does not show itself within the horizon of being. The incident always dispenses with all profundity, all background. It comes as a kind of explosion without antecedent or essence. The phenomenon in Marion's view invalidates the ontological categories of metaphysics. It does not allow itself to be described in terms of "objectness" or "beingness" but instead transcends all such horizons. It undoes the metaphysical categories of being and causality by withdrawing from them both and making any constitution, prediction, or control of the subject (or even of a divine *causa sui*) impossible. The phenomenon which gives itself does not do so within metaphysical parameters. Marion therefore concludes that his radical phenomenology of givenness has indeed accomplished the step outside metaphysics by invalidating all the categories of a metaphysical system

71

which he had outlined in his reading of Descartes (informed by Heidegger). And it is specifically these categories that Marion has sought to invalidate. He is not really concerned to eliminate all references to transcendence or religious experience, since metaphysics is not primarily defined by such notions or concerns. Rather, grounding, need for certainty, ontology, causality, and perfect presence circumscribe the metaphysical project. These are the notions that must be replaced if one wants to get beyond metaphysical restrictions. We are able to see this even more clearly in Marion's writing about the gift.

The Gift

In order to determine the modes of givenness, its possibility, and the equivalence between self-giving and self-showing, and to avoid a metaphysically causal determination of the given, Marion engages in a close analysis of the gift, starting from the aporiae outlined by Derrida.[38] Marion suggests that Derrida's aporia of the impossibility of the appearing of the gift only posits the problem, but does little to resolve it. He proceeds to show how the gift can indeed become possible by getting outside the economy of exchange and the metaphysics of presence, to which Derrida maintains it remains always resigned (by showing its impossibility to appear otherwise). If a gift is to appear it needs different conditions of possibility than this impossibility. The economic horizon of exchange must be renounced in order to interpret the gift from the horizon of givenness itself. Marion shows how the gift can become possible when one of the terms of exchange is bracketed (or placed under phenomenological reduction) and thus eliminated — i.e., when the gift is thought without donor or without recipient or without a gift-object. Each time one of the terms is "put into parentheses," the gift can appear in some way "as such." First, we can (and must) eliminate the recipient as the benefactor who renders a debt of thanks or gratitude. I must give as if the recipient did not return the gift, as if no recipient existed. Marion suggests the examples of love of one's enemies or the case of an ungrateful person who recognizes no gift as given. He also analyzes the parable of the sheep and the goats in which Christ claims reception of a gift of which the givers had no idea that he was to be the recipient (Matthew 25:31–46). A gift can thus be given without any respecting of persons and in complete ignorance of any eventual reciprocity, that is to say, without a recipient. Secondly, one must put the giver into parentheses, which Marion illustrates with the examples of an inheritance or the joy caused by an athlete or artist where the giver has no sense or experience of the response of the recipient. To give truly, one must be ignorant of one's gift and of its effect upon the other, although the recipient must at the same time recognize his or her indebtedness to this unknown giver.[39] Finally, one must think an elimination of the gift-object itself where it loses its status of being or object. Marion examines the symbolism of the transferal of power or the promise of love through insigniae or signs (e.g., a ring) and insists that the highest kind of gift is precisely one that has least real "being," is least of a concrete object. The more considerable a gift is, the less it becomes a transfer of property. The gift is reduced to the point where there is no object, no property, no possession or economy of exchange. This gift is accomplished perfectly when it is received and accepted. After performing such a bracketing for each of the terms, Marion insists that he has been able to distance himself from Derrida, has been able to eliminate reciprocity and the metaphysics of causality.[40] Both givenness and the gift are radically immanent and do not, for example, refer back to a transcendent giver. He ends his analysis of the gift by connecting it explicitly to his phenomenology of givenness, suggesting that the givenness of the phenomenon is indeed to be read as a generous gift in this sense.

Some readers of Marion have taken issue with his insistence on the indebtedness of the self to an unseen giver. They find such an account of prior debt confining and inhibiting. Robyn Horner, for example, objects to Marion's insistence upon debt for theological reasons. She finds his discussion problematic because "the notion of indebtedness seems to fly in the face of the very possibility of the gift" (RGG, 183). According to her, such a reading would be Pelagian.[41] She argues that the gift, if it is to be read as a symbol for God or for God's self-giving in grace, must be debt-free. We do not owe anything to God. To suppose otherwise would be "too much to bear" (RGG, 247). John Caputo objects to Marion's notion of indebtedness on more philosophical grounds.[42] He distinguishes Marion's and Derrida's accounts of the gift in terms of their willingness to grapple with darkness or lack of light. He finds Marion too reluctant to deal with such darkness and thus able to deal with only "partial blackouts" in his account of the gift. From a Derridian point of view, therefore, Marion is unable to escape the economy of the gift because he still reduces it to debt even as he escapes a certain causality. He emphasizes visibility or invisibility of the gift, while Derrida focuses on its identification and is thus more comprehensive. For Marion, a gift escapes economy (or, as Caputo claims, is situated in a higher economy) as long as it is not implicated in any kind of causality and has no causal agents or results. Yet Marion does not mind that debt is still present; rather he emphasizes such debt because in his view it dislocates the self-sufficiency of the subject. For Derrida, any kind of debt is poison to the gift and annuls it, while for Marion lack of indebtedness re-institutes the autarchy of the subject. While Marion worries about causality, Derrida is concerned with credit. Both wish to dispel the narcissism of the subject, but Marion seeks to escape it by reminding the subject of its prior debt requiring humility and gratitude, while Derrida attempts to speak of a responsibility without duty or debt. Caputo summarizes what he surmises as Derrida's response to Marion: "It is trouble enough to owe an identifiable debt to an identifiable creditor, but to situate the whole of life within an horizon of insoluble debt to an anonymous donor seems even worse. The gift ought to lift us up, not flatten and depress us. The debt mourns, but the gift pipes" (GGP, 214).

John Milbank's criticism of Marion is almost diametrically opposed. He finds Marion's account of God as self-giving love deeply dissatisfying. He contends that Marion's gift is still Cartesian because he continues to separate subject and object and does not intermingle them.[43] Marion's distance remains an abyss that cannot be crossed. Instead, in Milbank's view, a gift must be given in some sense in order to become real and specific. He condemns especially the language of purity in Marion and asserts that "just as Marion's divine gift is in this aspect a hypostasization of a modern, free, post-Cartesian, capitalist and 'pure' gift, and thereby 'indifferent to content', so it is also (as a concomitant) relatively indifferent to a counter-gift, or to relation and reciprocity."[44] Even in respect to God, Milbank contends, some interaction has to be possible and the gift has to be returned in some fashion. Milbank is troubled by Marion's attempt to liberate God or the gift from metaphysical dependence on being and causality which he finds misdirected.[45] The gift must be received and used, gratitude must be rendered for it and a return gift can and must be given. He repeats this criticism in a later text in even stronger terms: "For this reduced gift which is no identifiable object, derives from no known source, and passes to no known willing recipient, can only be 'recognized' in a fashion that can make no conceivable difference to actual ethical life . . . both Derrida and Marion remain trapped within Cartesian myths of prior subjectivity."[46] Overall Milbank seeks to conceive of a theological conception of the gift that would do justice to the Christian message of creation and redemption and for which ontological categories in his view are indispensable. He censures Marion for abandoning faith in favor of a philosophical exercise that ultimately remains irrelevant to theology. Of course, the primary concern of his criticism is theological. He is less concerned to evaluate Marion's reading of Derrida or to safeguard a philosophical consideration of the gift and its phenomenological implications.

It is true that Derrida's aporia is clearly not eliminated by thinking the gift without one of the terms. The point is not to suspend one term, but to realize that one would have to get rid of all of them simultaneously in order to be able to speak of the exchange of a "gift." Also, for Derrida, the major point seems to be debt and not causality. Marion, on the other hand, clearly thinks that causality and reduction to presence are the main issues. By suspending one of the terms of the relation, he can show how the gift can escape the cycle of exchange, which is tied within the causal relationship of Aristotle's four causes. He has few qualms about re-introducing debt into his analysis of the gift. In fact, the indebtedness to an unknown giver serves an important function for Marion. Merely to criticize this move is to disregard what is at stake for him. He seeks to escape metaphysics, to push phenomenology beyond its metaphysical prison. Metaphysics, however, as we have seen in Marion's analysis of Descartes, is concerned with causality and the language of ontology. As we have observed above, Marion uses the term "metaphysics of presence" in a sense congruent with this conception of metaphysics. To be able to speak of the gift without causality and while suspending in turn the "being" of each term of the relation (thus showing that "being" is not most essential to it, that it can be struck with "vanity") is precisely to describe the gift successfully beyond its metaphysical fetters. In fact, to make it dependent upon something else (a "debt" that is not a "cause" because unknown and unidentifiable) is to show clearly its non-metaphysical character, since metaphysics is all about self-sufficiency and self-presence without any dependence upon another. Marion's analysis of the gift is entirely consistent with his given parameters (the doubled definition of metaphysics), starting point (Cartesian metaphysics), and desired goal of pushing the boundaries and limits of phenomenology beyond metaphysics.

Furthermore, Marion's suggestion of a certain indebtedness, although admittedly problematic, is also meant to overcome the Cartesian self-sufficiency and autarchy of the transcendental subject, which I will examine in much more detail in chapter 7. To erase his suggestion of debt would be to return to a subject that can "make it on its own" and has no need of any other. Marion insists on prior indebtedness, therefore, in order to challenge the autarchy of the transcendental subject. The self is always already obligated, responsible, given over to something prior to itself. This is not to deny that it might have been more helpful had Marion used the language of responsibility, as does Lévinas, instead of speaking of a prior debt, especially in light of Derrida's account of the gift in terms of economy. While Marion's explication of the gift is sufficient for his own project and does indeed overcome the requirements of metaphysics as he writes them, it is true that his analysis of the gift does not constitute an adequate response to Derrida and in fact seems to disregard aspects of Derrida's argument. While Marion's "putting in parentheses" of one or several of the players in the gift-exchange does indeed help him get beyond the causal relationship which he wants to avoid, it does not enable him to get beyond the depiction of gift-exchange in terms of economy, which is precisely what Derrida criticizes in the first place. Yet while Marion's depiction of the self as indebted might pose a theological problem, it does not seem to me to jeopardize thereby his account of subjectivity. If the goal is to describe a self that is no longer subject and center of the world, then a notion of indebtedness certainly contributes to accomplishing that goal. One should also note that Marion seems to have modified his position in his most recent book on the erotic phenomenon, where he repeatedly contrasts the erotic relation with that of economics or commerce. While economy depends on reciprocity, pure gift-giving can never be mere exchange and defies reciprocity. It does not expect anything back and is not indebted. Marion seems to attempt to get beyond the issue of debt in this case and to articulate mutual dependence without economy.[47]

In order to identify his analysis of the gift with that of the given as such, Marion returns to thinking phenomena as purely given by outlining (as I summarized above) the terms that would have to describe such a pure given as *anamorphosis, arrivage, fait accompli,* and *incident.* By correlating these various figures and terms directly to his analysis of the gift, Marion concludes that the "being given" can indeed be paralleled by the gift, can be described like it, gives itself as a gift.[48] The determination of the phenomenon as *anamorphosis* corresponds to the experience of the recipient when the giver is eliminated. The determination of the phenomenon as event corresponds to the experience of the giver when the recipient is bracketed. The determination of the phenomenon as *arrivage* corresponds to the reduction of the gift-object itself. The characteristics of incident and *fait accompli* confirm this reading. One can thus safely conclude, according to Marion, that the self-showing of phenomena is a self-giving that parallels the phenomenology of the gift. In both Marion's analysis of the gift and his depiction of a pure phenomenology, the determinations and definitions of metaphysics are therefore reversed and rejected. Phenomenology precisely suspends the metaphysical language of being and causality. In its purity, it speaks of phenomena beyond being and beyond the normal relation of cause and effect. Givenness trumps being; effect overwhelms cause. Marion's phenomenology overcomes precisely the metaphysics he has outlined in Descartes. This analysis is clearly guided by his explication of Descartes. Metaphysics does not primarily mean transcendence, but rather ontology and causality, a project of grounding and certainty. The limit of metaphysics which was so clearly demarcated by Descartes (and even more so by Husserl and Heidegger) is crossed when phenomena appear in their purity. These phenomena, however, precisely because they escape or go beyond the normal metaphysical conditions of ontology and causality, must appear to us in a radically different mode, must somehow subvert these very same metaphysical conditions in their appearing.

Saturation and Excess

Marion therefore confirms his analysis (and also shows that it is valid for all phenomenology and not just for a region) by investigating the possibility of a phenomenality of givenness to pass outside or beyond impossibility in defiance of metaphysical limits. He takes as his guiding thread the possibility of impossibility of phenomenality in metaphysics, especially in its Kantian determinations of the formal conditions of experience. For Kant the conditions of possibility for any phenomenon depend upon our power of knowing and agree with the sufficient reasons for any appearing (which, as we have seen, they of course also do for Descartes). A phenomenon can only appear if it justifies itself according to these parameters. Reason alone gives it its sole effectivity or actuality. Any possibility for objects of experience, including the appearing of phenomena, is ruled by the principle of sufficient reason. Phenomena are only given to a consciousness and always directly linked to consciousness. Marion shows how Husserl at first apparently departs from Kant by positing a pure apparition and the self-justification of intuition. Yet Husserl unfortunately goes on to limit phenomena by imposing the conditions of the horizon and the transcendental I which must combine the flow of lived experiences and assemble them in order to give them meaning through constitution. Marion thinks of these as constricting and limiting the self-showing of the phenomena. Phenomena should be permitted to shift and even explode our horizons, to transgress what we can grasp or bear. Under the figures of the horizon and the transcendental I Husserl compresses and homogenizes all experience, in Marion's view, and is unable to receive any radically new or surprising event. Marion therefore insists that givenness must free itself from the justification and limit of the horizon of phenomenality and from any pretension of the I to pose itself as subject and condition of experience in either synthesis or judgment. The I cannot decide the phenomenon but must receive it. We must make an attempt to define the I without any recourse to transcendentality. Only in this way can givenness be thought unconditionally and irreducibly.

On Marion's reading, furthermore, for Husserl as for Descartes, intuition has a kind of penury; it lacks in respect to intention and never gives itself fully. Marion interprets Husserl's emphasis on the role of intention and signification as a serious shortcoming because it limits intuition (ED, 268; BG, 191). Husserl believes that the field of signification is much larger than that of intuition. Signification always surpasses intuition and fulfillment. The adequation between intention and intuition becomes a simple limit, an ideal that is always missed. Evidence only realizes itself for very poor phenomena, while full phenomena can never be seen adequately and are always given only imperfectly. Marion suggests that such is the case only because Husserl focuses his analysis on poor phenomena, in which the concept is indeed fuller than the intuition. Instead he calls us to examine an excess of intuition, where intuition gives more than intention can hold or conceive.[49] This kind of intuition does not expose itself in a concept, but instead saturates it and shows it to be super-exposed. The hypothesis of a phenomenon saturated with intuition "imposes itself on our attention because it designates the possibility of a phenomenon in general" (ED, 280; BG, 199). Bruce Benson, in a review of *Being Given*, paraphrases this: "In other words, there's so much there that we can never get our puny little minds around it."[50] Instead of being its cause, the I then becomes a mere witness to this self-giving of the phenomenon: the given comes as a kind of revelation.

Ruud Welten explains helpfully that there is indeed "a certain surplus of intention" in Husserl's phenomenology.[51] He shows how Marion regards all this as a deficiency or failure in Husserl's work, because the latter is intent upon reaching full evidence. Yet according to Welten, "saturation is not possible without this aiming at fulfillment (without intentionality). It is difficult to understand how fulfillment of any kind works without any intentionality of consciousness because it makes no sense to understand the saturated phenomenon outside consciousness, outside experience, or outside affection."[52] Welten insists that a kind of disappointment is essential to Husserlian phenomenology: "In the saturated phenomenon, intuition is not fulfilled to a point of adequation but exceeded, resulting in an inadequate surplus." For Husserl this disappointment "is inherent to the basic intentional structure of consciousness."[53] Welten does not think that Marion takes sufficient account of this aspect of disappointment and concludes that "in fact, disappointment is the state of consciousness in which man experiences the finitude of his consciousness. As a positive mental process, disappointment reveals the borders of finite consciousness. In disappointment, my intention strikes against the border of the possibilities of consciousness. Intention is pushed back and left behind without intuition. Therefore, disappointment is the experience of the impossibility to phenomenalize fully what is intended" (94). Marion does actually speak of the absolute importance of disappointment in a recent interview with Richard Kearney: "The very experience of the excess of intuition over signification makes clear that the excess may be felt and expressed as disappointment. The experience of disappointment means that I make an experience which I cannot understand, because I have no concept for it. So the excess and the disappointment can come together." He applies this explicitly to the saturated phenomenon: "The saturated phenomenon doesn't mean that we never have the experience of being in the desert. The reverse is the case: the desertification is an excess, in some way. The experience of something that is unconditional is, for me, something occasioned by the fact that I am disappointed, that I am in the situation of encountering something without having the possibility to understand it. This is not nothing. This is a very important figure of phenomenality."[54]

Depraz takes issue both with Marion's definition of Husserl's phenomena as "flat" and with his introduction of saturated phenomena, which for her are indistinguishable from the former type. There can be little or no distinction between "poverty" and "richness" in phenomenality. The very terminology is "non-sense."[55] Ricard also objects to what he regards as an "abusive" reading of Husserl which places phenomena into a "universe neighboring on magic."[56] John Caputo is somewhat less critical of Marion's designation of flat phenomena and instead shows how this extension of intuition is grounded in a particular reading of Husserl (which he contrasts to an extension of signification in Derrida's reading of Husserl) (CE, 67–93).

Why does Marion focus so much on the "range" of phenomena and on the noematic aspect of their appearing? Marion is dependent here again, it seems to me, on his prior analysis of Descartes. The distinction between different levels of phenomena seems to arise from the Cartesian terminology of the simple natures. The three kinds of simple natures between which Descartes distinguishes correspond almost exactly to the three categories of phenomena which Marion posits in his phenomenology. Descartes' "mathematical" simple natures seem to preview the "poor" phenomena Marion discovers in Husserl, Descartes' common objects the "technical objects" of Husserl, and his separated substances (such as God and angels) the "saturated phenomena" which

Marion seeks to introduce. In some sense, of course, Marion already reads the simple natures in Descartes as phenomena of a sort. Simple natures are constituted by consciousness and come in different kinds of increasing complexity. Furthermore, Marion chides Descartes already for focusing on the "flat" and mathematical ones in particular. While this organization of phenomena along a spectrum of increasing saturation may then be somewhat questionable as a straightforward reading of Husserl, it certainly is consistent with Marion's overall framework. Marion is obviously concerned with reversing the Cartesian emphasis on the ego, which he has outlined earlier, as determining all knowledge. In this new phenomenological proposal there is no *intuitus* that would organize and control all incoming phenomena. Quite the opposite: it is the phenomenon that imposes itself onto consciousness, which becomes a mere passive recipient. Marion goes on to examine four (or five) kinds of saturated phenomena by showing how they invert Kant's categories, which limit intuition by the concept.[57] He employs the categories of quantity, quality, relation, and modality.[58]

Quantity

The first saturated phenomenon is saturated according to *quantity*. Thus it destabilizes and undoes Kant's definition of quantity as the sum or combination of all parts in a homogeneity given to intuition as an aggregate. For Kant each phenomenon has a clear quantity which is its extensive size. The totality of phenomena equals and results from the sum of its parts. This quantity is always finite, can be perfectly predicted and previewed. It is enclosed by its quantity and measurement. The saturated phenomenon according to quantity thus is *incommensurable*, goes beyond measure in an enormity of quantity without limit. This phenomenon cannot be previewed or predicted; it surprises in its suddenness. Marion identifies this phenomenon as the historical (or cultural) *event*.[59] Events are distinguished from other phenomena (objects) because they are not produced, and are therefore unforeseeable and unrepeatable. Yet they do manifest themselves and can thus be analyzed. The event is always already there even before we can describe it; its past is uncontrolled. It provides a scene for a very particular event in the present, and the occurrences of that moment are unplanned, unforeseeable, and unrepeatable. What appears in this particular moment escapes any and all constitution. The hermeneutic of the event must by definition always remain infinite.[60] We thus have only indirect access to the event as self-given. Instead of us awaiting, reproducing, or describing the event, it affects us, modifies us, and maybe even constitutes us.

Although Marion does not make this explicit, the event seems to dislocate and undo the Cartesian obsession with order and measure. By being immeasurable and defying all comprehension that might establish certainty or prediction, it is in clear opposition to the Cartesian need for "clear and distinct" notions of truth. The event does not fit into a code and it defies any desire for *ordo et mesura*. It cannot be contained in a *mathesis universalis* since its quantity cannot be established and its hermeneutic remains limitless. Figuration becomes impossible for an event that can be neither foreseen nor repeated. Not only does this analysis provide a phenomenological description for the experience of an historical event, but it also defies all Cartesian parameters for containing such an event.

Quality

The second phenomenon is saturated in terms of *quality*. It overturns the Kantian category by its *intensity*, which cannot be supported by the gaze but bedazzles it and blinds it. It can thus be identified as the "fullness of the visible" or the *idol*. The gaze accomplishes itself fully in the idol; it saturates this first visible that it can neither transpierce nor abandon and it thus becomes the center of all admiration. The idol gives truth to my ipseity, it defines the maximum of intuitive intensity that I can endure while keeping my gaze on a distinct and visible spectacle; thus it defines what I can support of phenomenality. In the case of the idol the gaze is finally incapable of seeing (sensible intuition) or perceiving (intelligible intuition) because it is saturated by a bedazzlement that is too brilliant.[61] While Marion here refrains from any theological inferences, his terminology of course connects clearly with the notion of the idol which he has explicated in his theology, although it disconnects the idol from metaphysics and now interprets it as going beyond metaphysics and escaping its restrictions. Marion expands the somewhat narrower definition of "idol" as the painting or statue of an experience of the divine (which stopped the gaze in admiration and bedazzlement and filled its entire visibility) to extend to all such dazzling experiences (especially paintings but also works of art in general). The idol therefore appears to set itself in explicit opposition to the Cartesian *intuitus* (as we have seen already to be true more generally for a phenomenology of givenness). The experience of art is so overwhelming and bedazzling that it cannot possibly be controlled by the gaze of the *intuitus*. The ego is unable to ground this experience or to impose its own measure upon it. The experience of the idol is so intense that it defies the control of the gaze and shatters its attempt to assign it a place in a range of experiences.

Relation

The saturated phenomenon according to *relation* is the *flesh*. This phenomenon, in order to invert Kant's category of relation, must appear as *absolute* and as making impossible any analogy with experience. It is unforeseeable, non-comprehensible, non-reproducible, absolutely unique. An absolute phenomenon has no analogy to experience. Thus, according to Marion, any horizon that would forbid such absolute manifestation must be eliminated. This does not mean that it dispenses with all horizons but that it must be read according to several horizons which overlap and must all be considered simultaneously. The flesh establishes my ipseity, my uniqueness.[62] I cannot ever take distance from my flesh. I don't *have* flesh but I *am* flesh, which becomes very visible in the experiences of suffering, pleasure, and aging.[63] The taking on of the flesh accomplishes facticity much more radically even than does the existence of *Dasein*. Marion insists that I am completely tied to my flesh. I do not give myself to my flesh but it is my flesh that gives me to myself and which therefore defines me phenomenologically the most clearly. According to Marion, the flesh actually eliminates the distinction between appearance and appearing, between intuition and signification, *noesis* and *noema*. Signification cannot contain intuition in this case, because intuition precedes and makes possible all intentionality and thus also signification. The flesh is the very place where the fold of donation unfolds most directly. There is no distinction or separate relation between me and my flesh but I am utterly tied to it. Marion suggests that the flesh is the only saturated phenomenon which allows the ego to find itself in some fashion. Yet it does so not by giving me anything outside myself, but by opening me to all other given phenomena. It thus sets in motion a new kind of subjectivity and destroys the metaphysical subject.[64] Marion will use this category of the flesh even much more thoroughly when exploring the erotic phenomenon.

The phenomenon of the flesh therefore makes impossible the Cartesian project of figuration. While figuration allowed for the possibility of abstraction from sensation and placed all sensible experience into a comprehensible order, the experience of the flesh is one of utter immediacy that does not allow for such abstraction and coherence. We can no longer think of subject and object as utterly separate, nor can we envision an ego that calmly contemplates and rearranges all things as objects of consciousness. The sensing of the flesh cannot be placed into a series or a code. The flesh denies any notion of causality but denotes a radical passivity. Although Marion appropriates most of what he says about the notion of the flesh from Maurice Merleau-Ponty and especially from Michel Henry (to whom he usually gives credit for his analysis), he describes it in a fashion that responds to the two systems of metaphysics that he has outlined in Descartes.[65] The experience of the flesh makes impossible the ego's constitution of all things by a thought separate from them and turning them into objects. It also defies the kind of efficient causality that Marion outlined as a second metaphysical system in Descartes by refusing to ground the ego externally in a prior grounding or creation.

Modality

The fourth phenomenon, which saturates and inverts the category of *modality*, is *invisible* to the I and destroys the correspondence of object to thought that Kant presupposes in this category. This phenomenon does not accommodate itself to the strict conditions of experience of the transcendental I and its power of knowing but instead has phenomenal autonomy and appears in and by itself. It is a phenomenon that cannot be turned into an object, cannot be constituted as an object. It gives itself to be seen [*vu*] but not to be looked at [*regardé*]; it is not under the control of the gaze and cannot be reproduced by it.[66] The saturated phenomenon thus no longer appears under the conditions of possibility, but instead is an experience of the impossible that makes any reification impossible. Marion outlines how the I is submerged by the phenomenon, is constituted by it, follows it as its witness. No longer do I give meaning to the lived experience and the intuition; they give their meaning to me. This saturated phenomenon can come to me as the *icon* which Marion identifies as the face of the other.[67] If there is any intentionality here, it is that of the other acting upon me. Intuition does not proceed from me but comes toward me and envisages me. *Noesis* does not prepare any *noema*, but rather unleashes a *noetic* uncontrollable and hopeless superabundance. The *noema* appears as infinite and overflows all *noesis*. The saturated phenomenon in this case does not appear as visible but as excess. I must submit myself to the view of the face, to its *anamorphosis* par excellence. The face raises up an endless diversity of always possible, provisional, insufficient significations. The face comes as an event without cause, as a *fait accompli*. The expression of the face has an infinity of significations. In fact, even what the face says is only an approximation to what it really meant to express. The face, according to Marion, thus opens the phenomenon of the other.

This experience of the other is Marion's attempt at describing a genuine experience of other human beings that he interprets Descartes as incapable of providing (as we will see in more detail later). Everything he says about this experience of modality defies the Cartesian desire for control and certainty. This is an experience that is impossible to reduce to an object, which is of course what Marion contends both Descartes and Husserl do to all phenomena of consciousness. One cannot serve as the ground for an experience of the other, but it is always an event that breaks in, surprises and overwhelms me. In signifying infinitely, no certain knowledge, no comprehension of this experience can ever be established. Constitution becomes impossible. Marion's outline of saturated phenomenality thus clearly inverts the Cartesian constitution of objects and desire for certainty (and the Husserlian constitution and desire for evidence).

Revelation

After examining the four cases of saturated phenomena, Marion suggests that these degrees of phenomenality allow us to investigate whether there is an absolute maximum of saturation, a phenomenon that gives itself with a maximum degree of phenomenality. He therefore examines the possibility of a fifth phenomenon that is saturated in all four respects, inverts all four categories. He calls this the "paradox of paradoxa" or the phenomenon of revelation. Of this phenomenon, he insists, we can only speak in terms of possibility, not actuality. Phenomenology can say absolutely nothing about whether or not revelation has actually taken place, but it can suggest that if such a thing were possible, its phenomenality should be described in a certain fashion. Marion claims that this project has been an enlargement of phenomenology and that it has absolutely nothing to do with justifying the fact of Revelation. (He marks the distinction between the possibility of a phenomenon of revelation which phenomenology can explore, and the theological "fact" of Revelation, by employing lower-case in the first and upper-case in the second instance.) He asserts that it is not even the primary goal of his project to show the possibility of revelation, but rather to push the limits, definitions, and resources of phenomenology as far as they will go.[68] Phenomenology is now able to describe an experience that is so excessive and overwhelming that it appears at the very limits of phenomenality.

To have pushed phenomenology to its most pure form, then, is fruitful for Marion in two complementary ways. On the one hand, it makes possible a thought of the possibility of revelation. On the other hand, it successfully overcomes metaphysics and denies any constitution of onto-theo-logy. Although Marion has not always made the relationship of his phenomenological enterprise to Descartes explicit, he does so to some extent in his conclusion:

> Phenomenology does not break decisively with metaphysics until the moment when and exactly to the degree to which — a degree that most often remains in flux — it names and thinks the phenomenon (a) neither as an object, that is to say, not within the horizon of objectness such as, starting with Descartes, it defines the epistemological project of constituting the world and excludes from phenomenality, and therefore from the truth, all that, whether by lack (the pure sensible) or by excess (the divine and the insensible), does not fall under the order and measure of the *Mathesis Universalis*; (b) nor as a being, that is to say, within the horizon of Being, whether we understand this in the sense of the metaphysical *ontologia* or claim to "destroy" it in the name of the Dasein analytic or protect it under the cover of *Ereignis*—for a number of phenomena simply are not, or just don't appear inasmuch as they are. (BG, 320; ED, 439)

In this quote from the final pages of *Being Given*, Marion again clearly relates an overcoming of metaphysics to the parameters of metaphysics worked out in his analysis of Descartes. Metaphysics is defined by its constitution of objects in perfect presence and its exclusion of everything that does not submit to the universal method that gives structure and order to all experience. Furthermore it grounds all beings within the horizons of Being and causality. To allow phenomena to appear means not to impose any semblance of a horizon on them, since this will always exclude some of them. The apparition of phenomena must be unconditioned; they must be permitted to give themselves as pure givens. These phenomena are thus no longer metaphysical, no longer subject to the language of Being or causality or the *mathesis universalis*.

The Erotic Reduction

In Marion's most recent phenomenological work, an analysis of love, the influence of Descartes is even more explicit. While I will leave a thorough consideration of this work to the final part, even a brief perusal makes it abundantly clear that Marion's phenomenology of eros is posited as an explicit rebuttal of Descartes' metaphysics of the ego. He subtitles the work "Six Meditations" and explains in the introduction that this reference to Descartes (and to Husserl) is intentional, as he wants to "substitute erotic meditations for the metaphysical meditations" (PE, 19; EP, 8). The first meditation especially is an explicit rebuttal of Descartes. Marion contends that Descartes' obsession with knowledge and certainty is misdirected. We desire not knowledge but assurance. We do not want to know who or what *exists,* but rather whether we are *loved.* Love therefore overcomes and goes beyond being and plays outside of ontological categories. While metaphysics is obsessed with certainty and with proving the existence of the ego, this obsession completely misses the point of the human condition: "The products of technology and the objects of science, the propositions of logic and the truths of philosophy can well deploy the whole certainty of the world, what does that have to do with me — I, who am not a product of technology, not an object of science, not a proposition of logic, not a truth of philosophy?" (PE, 33; EP, 16). While all these provide knowledge and results of facts, they do not provide wisdom nor can they make me certain of myself. Although metaphysics gives the same certainty to the ego with which it endows objects, this certainty is not worth a whole lot because it cannot give meaning to my life. Furthermore, Cartesian certainty is circular: either I assure myself of my own certainty while still doubting whether I am (the first Cartesian version of metaphysics) or I am utterly contingent on some prior instance and thus can no longer be sure that I will continue in existence on my own (the second Cartesian version of metaphysics). The metaphysical demonstration of the existence of the ego thus leads us to a realization of our radical uncertainty and lack of direction ("the attack of vanity"). In Marion's view Cartesian certainty leads only to autism, solipsism, and narcissism. The Cartesian project must therefore be rejected in favor of an exploration into the experience of eros.

Marion goes on to rethink essential terms of metaphysics in light of this erotic reduction, namely those of the world, of space, of time, and of ipseity. To emerge as "loved" or at least as "loveable" opens an entirely different terrain than the traditional question of being and replaces it as insufficient and misguided: "The erotic reduction does not modify the figure of the ego in order to attain the same goal by other means — to certify one's being. It renders destitute the question 'to be or not to be?'; it deposes the question of being from its imperial rule and exposes it to the question 'what's the use?'; it considers it seriously from the point of view of vanity" (PE, 50; EP, 28). This is a completely new reduction that displaces the traditional priority of ontology and metaphysics, and it requires a completely different attitude (which Marion distinguishes from the traditional "natural" attitude).

The question of vanity attacks, first, the homogeneity of space. No longer can space be thought metaphysically as a distinction between "here" and "there" oriented by change of place and the constant possibility of occupying a different place. In the erotic reduction, I am concerned with another place, the one where my prospective (or actual) lover dwells. "Here" and "there" are not interchangeable in the erotic reduction, which is particularly evident when I am far away from home. Space thus becomes heterogeneous and non-substitutable (PE, 55; EP, 31–32). Similarly, the erotic reduction destroys the succession of time. In a natural or metaphysical attitude time moves successively from the past via the present to the future. Instants follow each other, constantly moving from "before" to "after." Metaphysical time, Marion suggests, has no center because every present moment becomes immediately part of the past and is succeeded by a new moment that suffers the same fate. The erotic reduction, however, turns time into an event. As we have seen in the analysis of the event, it cannot be predicted, produced, or re-produced. I cannot simply decide to find an answer to the question of whether I am loved, but must await it. While I wait, Marion points out, time does not really pass because nothing happens.[69] Of course lots of things happen during this time, but for the erotic reduction they are irrelevant and do not count. "Time is thus no longer defined as an extension of the mind, but as the extension of the event" (PE, 59; EP, 34). Although I await the event, it always comes as a surprise and it accomplishes itself not as an "enduring permanence" but as "given present" (PE, 59; EP, 35). The arrival of the other gives me my "present," although it itself always remains awaited and never present. Its absence is more important to me than any thing actually present. The temporality of this awaiting thus also makes possible my individuality, in that it is the only thing that makes any difference to me. To speak of the past in the context of the erotic reduction does not refer to memory, as it did for Descartes, but to the burial of one's hope to be loved, to death. The past refers to complete absence but it remains always suspended by the hope of the awaiting, thus by the future. Time in the erotic reduction bears all the characteristics of the event: *arrivage, anamorphosis,* and radical contingency.

In this first meditation, Marion clearly resumes his concern with Cartesian metaphysics and even more obviously attempts to transgress it. In fact, this is probably his most systematic proposal of a different way of philosophizing, a path that is not beholden to metaphysics and yet addresses the human condition most fundamentally. Yet Marion relies heavily here on his earlier analysis. This work certainly does not arise out of a vacuum. Not only has he spoken of the experience of vanity in both his theological and his phenomenological work, but he also employs several of the saturated phenomena he has analyzed earlier, most prominently the event and the flesh. His previous metaphysical and phenomenological analyses aid him in reconceiving what has been his concern from the beginning: overcoming metaphysics with a thought of charity or love.

And, as I have tried to show, Marion's analysis of Descartes informs him throughout his phenomenological project, even when he does not make this influence explicit. All the terms of Descartes' "grayed" ontological epistemology are displaced in Marion's phenomenology. Causality and even being as ground are attacked. Neither the ego nor God is in control in Marion's phenomenology. Phenomena are not objects; rather they come as experiences of saturation that overwhelm consciousness and have none of the Cartesian connotations of certainty and clarity. This, in my view, is why Marion opts for the terminology of saturation and bedazzlement. Metaphysics, in its Cartesian and therefore its modern form, is poor because mathematical and fully controlled by the human gaze. To exceed metaphysics must mean to expand and enrich our experience, to give it more to see. While Descartes thinks that we can obtain the clearest vision of a piece of wax by abstracting from it and eliminating all information given by the senses, Marion suggests that we open ourselves to the plentitude of this phenomenon and not allow our preconceptions and desire for certainty to limit its appearing. And this is particularly important to do when we face not a piece of wax, but deal with the complexity of a historical event, admire the beauty of a great work of art, encounter another person, or have a religious experience. To interpret such encounters in terms of presence in being or their having been constituted in some fashion is simply inadequate for Marion. They cannot be grounded either by the ego or by God.[70] And it is this final contention — the refusal of (doubled) grounding — that makes it so imperative for Marion to examine the status of God and the self in a thought that would attempt to exceed metaphysics. As has been implied throughout this analysis such overcoming has implications for how we speak about God, how we conceive the self, and how we approach the other. I will therefore now go on to explore in more detail how God, self, and other are radically displaced and re-thought in this project at and beyond the boundary of metaphysics.

PART TWO
A God of Excess

PART TWO

A God of Excess

INTRODUCTION
"To Pass Over to God's Point of View"

Marion's talk about God is probably the aspect of his work that has received the widest attention. *God without Being* has been discussed for years as an independent work, since for a long time it was the only book translated into English. From the responses to this work and to Marion's proposal of the saturated phenomenon (especially in the wake of his presentation at the first Villanova Religion and Postmodernism conference, "God, the Gift, and Postmodernism"), all the way to very recent treatments of his work (e.g., Hart's 2007 *Counter-Experiences*), two fundamental tenors can be distinguished. On the one hand, Marion's work is judged as too determined and as radically compromised by its particular references, either to Christianity in general or specifically because of its Roman Catholic character. On the other hand, his talk about God is seen as too undetermined, too transcendent, lacking any clear hermeneutic connection to concrete religious experience. Furthermore, as pointed out already earlier, it is far from clear (in Marion or in his commentators) whether Marion's talk about God qualifies as *theology* or as *philosophy*. And even if some of his writings are described as theological — as I have already done especially for *God without Being* and *Idol and Distance* throughout the first part — this might be the place to investigate more carefully what "theology" would indicate for Marion, before I begin analyzing his talk about God. I will therefore first examine briefly what Marion means by theology when he employs the term and then go on to see whether he actually exercises such theology himself or whether it is a term used only to designate an endeavor in which he does not himself engage. Both of these will help us in outlining what one may want to say about theology in general and his theology specifically in this context.

Marion makes one very broad distinction between two different kinds of theology: natural or rational theology and revealed theology. *Natural theology* refers to rational discourse about God, especially to the exercise of arguing from the immanent to the transcendent, such as happens, for example, in most proofs for God's existence. He usually dismisses any such attempt because of its metaphysical nature. It is subject to exclusion by phenomenological method because of its appeal to transcendence and has been thoroughly refuted by Kant and Hume. In a final section, "Concerning the Use of Givenness in Theology," of the first chapter of *In Excess*, for example, he distinguishes between these two kinds and argues in respect to what he here calls "theology of philosophy" or "metaphysical theology": "Concerning the theology of philosophy, that is to say, 'first philosophy,' comprising onto-theo-logy, no ambiguity remains: since it is based on real transcendence, causality, substantiality, and actuality, it cannot resist a phenomenological reduction. Phenomenology would not be able, in any manner, to admit speculative arguments that go beyond the given, ignoring the constraints of givenness and asserting a non-immanent foundation" (IE, 28; DS, 33). All the terms Marion employs here ("reality," "causality," "substantiality") clearly refer back to what he has outlined as essential characteristics of metaphysics and onto-theo-logy. The God of *causa sui* is the pre-eminent subject of such a theology. Marion speaks of this way of doing theology only to reject it and assures his critics repeatedly that he is not involved in any such metaphysical endeavor.

Revealed theology, however, Marion affirms and defends. Revealed theology, in contrast to the above, is not confined to metaphysical restrictions. It does not speculate about existence but instead reports experience. In this emphasis on immanent experience, it hence also escapes reduction by phenomenological method. For example, in a footnote Marion identifies the "God" of whom Husserl speaks as a "transcendent being." Since Husserl limits God to this particular metaphysical definition, so Marion suggests, other manners of speaking of God are not thereby excluded:

> Again it must be noted that here the bracketed "God" is defined only as the ground (*Grund*) of the facticity of the world, therefore according to its metaphysical sense as a transcendent being outside the world. This narrow sense would therefore leave intact *any definition of God not based on a transcendence of this (metaphysical) type*. Now, it is precisely the case for revealed theology that it approaches God by immanence as well as transcendence . . . Would this immanence more radical than the region of consciousness

also fall beneath the blow of the reduction? (BG, 343, note 4; ED, 106, note
1; emphasis mine)

Obviously for Marion the answer to this question is "no"; the experience of an
"immanent" or "revealed" God is not excluded by phenomenological method.
Within the text he clarifies by distinguishing between theology as revealed,
which he calls *sacra doctrina,* and "*theologia rationalis,* which belongs to *metaphysica specialis* and arises solely from metaphysics" (BG, 72; ED, 105). The
distinctions in this passage rely at least provisionally on the medieval definitions of metaphysics which I have examined earlier. By defining God as one
object or being among others (even if the highest and most powerful), one
reduces God to metaphysics.

As Tobias Specker develops in detail, Marion does also make a distinction
between *theo*-logy and theo-*logy.* In fact, Specker sees three different discourses
at work in Marion. *Theo*-logy refers to a discourse in which God's appearing
determines the shape of the logos. Theo-*logy,* on Specker's reading, can refer
either to a discourse in which rationality determines and covers over the divine
or to a more critical (also philosophical) discourse which uncovers this discrep-
ancy and domination. Specker views Marion as condemning the first type of
theo-*logy* but affirming (and even practicing) the second, which does not itself
engage in *theo*-logy but prepares a space for it. Marion's phenomenology of
givenness constitutes one such attempt at more appropriate theo-*logy.*[1] While
Specker's distinctions are helpful and not incorrect, I find them somewhat
cumbersome in practice (especially since Marion himself does not make such
a three-fold distinction). The distinctions between natural theology and revealed theology or between theology and philosophy are much more frequent
in his writings.

Marion never fully defines the term "revealed theology," yet he does circumscribe the activity of theologizing repeatedly. I will therefore rely on these
statements about the activity of theology to guide us at least in the direction of
a definition. We will see that revealed "*theo*-logy" is quite literally a *logos* about
the revealed *theos.* It attempts to explicate and testify to the ways in which God
has become known. Its core and content is revelation. It thus originates from
God and only then passes to human speaking. Marion defines the theological
task in the most detail in *God without Being* where he emphasizes strongly its
source in God rather than in human logic (here he does italicize "*theo*-" and
not "-logical").[2] Since this is also one of his most controversial statements, I
will look at it in a bit more detail. Already in the introduction to *God without
Being,* Marion speaks of the pleasure of doing theology that is greater than any
other, because it passes from mere words to the divine Word whom it addresses
and allows to become present within one's speaking or writing. True theology
does not originate from ourselves: "Theology always writes starting from an
other than itself. It diverts the author from himself (thus one can indeed speak
of a diversion from philosophy with all good theology); it causes him to write

outside of himself, even against himself, since he must write not of what he is, on what he knows, in view of what he wants, but in, for, and by that which he receives and in no case masters" (GWB, 1; DSL, 9–10). While Marion does not explicitly claim to be doing theology here himself, this strong introduction speaking of the pleasure of doing theology, of its direction toward God, and of the need to "obtain forgiveness for every essay in theology" (GWB, 2; DSL, 10) seems to suggest that at least at this time Marion still saw himself as engaged in a theological task. The book begins with this reflection on theological writing and ends with an essay on the task of theology that grounds it in the Eucharist.[3] The actual argument of the book is therefore enfolded in a dual reflection on the nature of theological thinking. Although Marion is clearly not defining only what he is doing but rather making statements about what theology usually does or should do, it is implied that he sees himself as involved in and contributing to that endeavor at least to some extent.[4]

Apart from the implication that this is indeed an essay in theology, Marion also repeatedly emphasizes the divine origin of theology. It is talk that ultimately proceeds from God. The reflection on the task of doing theology which concludes the text proper and is entitled "Of the Eucharistic Site of Theology" emphasizes this abundantly and has therefore elicited sharp criticism. I will first examine what Marion says about the task of theology and then briefly look at some of these critiques. Marion insists that theology can speak of God only "in such a way that this 'of' is understood as much as the origin of the discourse as its objective . . . following the axiom that only 'God can speak well of God' . . . Theology should expose its logic to the repercussions, within it, of the *theos*" (GWB, 139; DSL, 197). It is theology insofar as it speaks of Christ who erases gap between sign, speaker, and referent. The Word of God speaks the only authentic word of God. If we started from a merely human point of view and remained entangled in our own speech and its concerns, it would be impossible for us to reach the divine. Rather, we must allow the Word to speak through us perichoretically in the way in which the Trinitarian relationships inhere in each other, speak each other, and pass through each other in loving relationship. Theology must be decidedly Christian and that means that it not be guided by the fad of current epistemology or linguistics, but instead must control and guide it: "To justify its Christianity, a theology must be conceived as a logos of the Logos, a word of the Word, a said of the Said — where, to be sure, every doctrine of language, every theory of discourse, every scientific epistemology, must let itself be regulated by the event of its redoubling in a capital, intimate, and anterior instance" (GWB, 143; DSL, 201). The direction of the hermeneutic endeavor is thus reversed. We do not speak the word, the Word speaks us. Marion does not shrink back from asserting the divine nature of the theological task. God, "in his Word, will speak our language and teach us in the end to speak it as he speaks it — divinely, which means to say in all abandon" (GWB, 144; DSL, 203). He suggests as the first principle for any true theologian — i.e., one who speaks of God and does not merely utter words — to aim through the text toward God. As the Eastern Fathers emphasized, theology must become a kind of prayer. Although the theologian's main task is to comprehend the text and to present it, this means that this interpreter must first be in communion with the divine in a way that makes God the starting point of the exposition.[5] Theology is not merely an exercise of interpretation of a text or even a history, but it implies a direct connection to and responsibility before God. Theology must be directed toward God and ultimately finds its origin in God, in order to be justified and authentic.[6] Marion anticipates here some of the criticism he indeed received, namely that this puts the theologian apparently in the place of God and presumes a kind of divine authority for one's theology: "But, one will object, does this principle not lead at all to a delirious presumption, strictly to a delirium of interpretation, which asks a man to take the place and position of the Word himself?" (GWB, 149; DSL, 210).

In order to guard against such hubris, Marion uses the event of the disciples on the road to Emmaus to establish a Eucharistic hermeneutics that is grounded in the practice of the fellowship of all believers. The Emmaus disciples are confused and unable to interpret the event they have witnessed, namely Christ's death and the first hints of his resurrection. Even when Christ himself comes to walk with them, they do not recognize him. Although they obviously "see," they do not understand, but require an interpretation.[7] Christ himself tells them how the Scriptures speak of him, yet even then they do not understand fully. Only in the breaking of the bread do they finally both recognize Christ and comprehend the interpretation given them. He concludes from this that "the Eucharist alone completes the hermeneutic; the hermeneutic culminates in the Eucharist; the one assures the other its condition of possibility: the intervention in person of the referent of the text as center of its meaning, of the Word, outside the words, to reappropriate them to himself . . . If the Word intervenes in person only at the eucharistic moment, *the hermeneutic (hence fundamental theology) will take place, will have its place, only in the Eucharist*" (GWB, 151; DSL, 212; emphasis his). Theology is thus always exercised within community and for the community, centered around the event of revelation, rather than merely the pure word of the theologian. Marion stresses the important role of the Christian community for the task of theology, but employs this at the same time in order to highlight the role of the bishop:

> The community therefore interprets the text in view of its referent only to the strict degree that it lets itself be called together and assimilated, hence converted and interpreted by the Word, sacramentally and therefore actually acting in the community. Hermeneutic of the text by the community, to be sure, thanks to the service of the theologian, but on condition that the community itself be interpreted by the Word and assimilated to the place where theological interpretation can be exercised, thanks to the liturgical service of the theologian par excellence, the bishop. (GWB, 152; DSL, 214)

This insistence that "one must conclude that *only the bishop merits, in the full sense, the title of theologian*" and that "*only the saintly person knows whereof he speaks in theology, only he that a bishop delegates knows wherefrom he speaks*" (GWB, 153, 155; DSL, 215, 218; emphases his), coupled with his refusal of any "progress" in theology except for a repeated interpretation of revelation, are the claims which have been taken as most offensive by many readers. I will briefly outline these critiques in order to set the stage for my analysis of God-talk in Marion's project(s).

Many critics have objected to the supposedly "dogmatic" character of Marion's work. Graham Ward, for example, in attempting to situate and outline Marion's "theological project," which he sees located within clearly identifiable postmodern parameters, argues that it "forecloses the postmodern questioning with an uncritical dogmatism" (229).[8] He sees a turn in Marion's philosophical stance (evident, for example, in *Idol and Distance*) to a "Marion-as-Conservative-Catholic who places upon that site the transubstantiated host elevated by an ecclesiastical authority," which is centered precisely in the chapter ("Of the Eucharistic Site of Theology") I have just examined.[9] He accuses Marion of engaging in natural theology (later in a "negative natural theology") because his notion of revelation is so closely tied to visibility, and comments in the same sarcastic tone we will encounter in other critics: "But we move into much clearer water in his later work. Untroubled by the will-to-power and Being's all too visible idolatry, his French prose is washed in a more rarefied, mystical light" (232). What is problematic about *God without Being*, in Ward's view, is the "metaphorical slippage" that takes place as Marion applies the terminology of idol and icon to conceptual and not merely representational models. His hermeneutics therefore becomes circular and "time and sign collapse into participation in a current liturgical event." In consequence, "theology as a textual practice, as writing, is subsumed beneath theology as liturgical praxis, as transubstantiation" (233). Throughout Ward accuses Marion of Platonism, since his use of metaphor supposedly emphasizes and elevates the spiritual over the physical. Furthermore, his negligent use of metaphor dissolves the achievements some of his early philosophical analysis provided: "The analysis of the idol and the icon, then, is always slipping into metaphoricity and the metaphors are saturated with an eternal light to the point where they are purely translucent. The dialectical tension between them, instituted on the basis of human intentionality, its limitations and its narcissism, is continually being dissolved" (234). Ward insists that this ultimately evades hermeneutics or interpretation and becomes self-affirming: "Marion's a priori faith in the testimony of revelation itself confirms (proves?) a God beyond Being [which] reinforces Marion's faith in his own interpretation of this testimony. Any boundary between, any attempt to distinguish, exegesis and eisegesis is obviated. There is no room for self-critique" (235). He thinks that Marion's move from phenomenology to dogmatism requires at the very least "a doctrine of scriptural inspiration which might legitimize such reading" (235). Marion's reference to the role of the bishop cited above Ward finds particularly objectionable and claims that it invalidates "any ontological or phenomenological or hermeneutical investigation" (236). Both Marion's "slippage of metaphor" and his "evasion of hermeneutics" therefore lead directly to a "Gnosticism" that refuses the physical and speaks of a pure gift (which Ward judges an impossible task). Marion therefore does not get beyond post-modernity but rather returns to pre-modernity: "He turns the icon, the face, of Christ towards post-modernity, offering it a return to a pre- and post-secular cosmology: the world as sacrament of love mediated by and on the authority of the community called the Church" (237).

Peter-Ben Smit similarly criticizes Marion's Eucharistic hermeneutic by focusing especially on the controversial claims surrounding the bishop as theologian.[10] In response to Marion's reference to Veronica's veil, he finds that "this observation has one important implication: it is impossible to say that text and event are the same. Rather, they belong to each other as sign (text) and referent (event)" (30). Smit is bothered by the maleness of the bishop, by his solipsism (apparently he can do theology without the community), and by his close identification with Christ. He asks: "But is it really only the bishop who occupies the hermeneutic site of the Eucharist? This would sound suspiciously like claiming that the bishop is celebrating the Eucharist for the community, without the community taking part in it" (35). He wants to insist instead "that it is not only the bishop who occupies the Eucharistic and theological site. As the Eucharist is a celebration of the whole community, to which the bishop also belongs in his/her own person, the only true theologian is Christ, present (as the above citation from Gregory of Nazianze already points out) in his representative the bishop. Therefore all who are present in their own person can only follow St. Gregory, and imitate, as human theologians, that theologian who is superior to us: Christ" (35). Overall he thinks that his reflection leaves everything in Marion intact: "all that changes is the identity of the 'hermeneut,' the interpreter" (36).

John Caputo's criticism of *God without Being* in general and the passages we have examined above in particular echoes that of Ward.[11] He argues that "writing from God's point of view" implies a kind of privileged access to the divine that becomes quickly militant and exclusive and cites Marion's Roman Catholic allegiances as confirming this analysis. He finds that Marion is in need of a hermeneutic "chain" that would tie his talk about God to actual experience of some kind (even as the "chain" of signifiers must always be "destroyed" in order to speak adequately of God). Although "what is called for is an expenditure without reserve in which one tears up the balance sheet of divine names," "it is important first . . . to insert the assertion into the chain for it to work, important first to weave the concatenation that is going to be ripped up, to create the tension that is going to be burst, to set up the measure and the horizontality that is going to be exceeded, to establish the cool and sober ratio that will be interrupted by an instant of divine madness" (190). Thus, "God

is wholly other — almost. As long as you hold on to the chain" (191). Because
it lacks such a hermeneutic chain and proposes to begin directly with God,
Caputo judges Marion's talk about God as beyond Being in his theological
work to be incoherent. Indeed, he finds it very "risky to begin with the Wholly
Other, to insist throughout on utter alterity," because this "thing" that cannot
be defined will take over and swallow both "God" and us. He continues, "then
things will begin to slip a little and we will begin to lose our grip. We will not
know what is wholly other, whether it is God or something else, or whether it
even has a *what*. We will not know whether *wholly other* is a predicate of some
being, however exalted, or itself a subject, or a quasi-subject, some kind of
dark halo of indeterminacy and anonymity that surrounds and eventually seeps
into — and saturates — our lives" (191). God would become only one possible
(and already idolatrous) name for this utterly undetermined "wholly other."
Marion is held to provide an example of such indeterminate speaking about
God and God's otherness and serves to point both to the dangers and possibilities of doing so in particular ways.

Caputo's language of "slippage" and of lack of hermeneutics mirrors that
of Ward. It is Caputo's overall argument in this article that Marion approaches
God's alterity in two distinct ways, one that is beyond phenomenality altogether
and has no textual chain [to erase/*rature*] and one that remains within the phenomenological field by filling and overloading it with excess [to saturate/*sa-
ture*]. In the second case, which refers to Marion's writings on the saturated
phenomenon, a textual chain is maintained. Since I have not yet explicated
Marion's later phenomenology of revelation very carefully, I will focus here
only on the first part of Caputo's article, which rejects this first mode of naming God that appears in the passages of *God without Being* examined above.
According to Caputo, Marion advocates an unconditioned relation with God
which approaches the divine on its own terms.[12] He rejects this version because
"Marion asks for something unthinkable, and flatly impossible — as opposed to
the more textured, textual impossibility" (194). He finds that Marion's account
is "wedded to a fatal strategy" because it requires that humans abandon their
finitude. Furthermore, Marion is inconsistent in his account by becoming very
theological and conditioned through his use of Scripture and historical faith
in Christ and by defining God in terms of love.[13] Finally, Caputo condemns
Marion's strategy as "a terroristic hermeneutics" by his Scriptural literalism
and extreme obedience to the authority of the Church's magisterium.[14] He
concludes:

> *God without Being* confirms Derrida's suspicion that it is just when some-
> one purports to speak or to teach without mediation that we are visited by
> the most massive mediations. It is precisely when someone claims to have
> reached, or been granted, God's point of view that things start getting very
> ungodly. It is just when someone thinks to have laid hold of the Wholly
> Other that we are visited by the human, all-too-human. Marion's love of
> episcopal authority is something of a giveaway, a telling tip-off to the vio-

lence of the unconditioned. The unconditional corrupts; the absolutely unconditioned corrupts absolutely. (195)

Both Caputo and Ward, therefore, object intensely to what they see as a clearly theological project in Marion, advocating a rather conservative Roman Catholic position that threatens to invalidate his more philosophical insights. This is similar to the position James K. A. Smith espouses in his article "Liberating Religion from Theology," where he criticizes especially Marion's claim regarding the impossibility of a phenomenology of religion by comparing Marion's work to that of Heidegger, finding the latter much more useful for the construction of a phenomenology of religion that is distinct from theology.[15] He criticizes Marion's theology as "colonizing," as reducing all religion to the Christian (more specifically Roman-Catholic) interpretation of God. He argues that

> Marion's "religious phenomenon" is in the end collapsed into a very particular theological phenomenon; correlatively, his (albeit im/possible) "phenomenology of religion" slides toward a very possible, and very particular, theology. The result of this rather insidious movement is twofold: first, this conception of a phenomenology of religion reduces religion to theology; that is, it effects a certain levelling of the plurivocity of (global) religious experience and forces it into a rather theistic, or at least theophanic, mold. Religion, for Marion, turns out to be very narrowly defined and, in a sense, reduced to its theological sedimentation. Second, and as a result of this, Marion particularizes religion and the religious phenomenon as quite Christian — at best, monotheistic, and at worst, down right Catholic. . . . This particularization is yet another kind of reduction: a reduction which reduces the size of the kingdom, which keeps the walls close to Rome and makes it impossible for any who are different to enter.[16]

Smith seems to have few problems with Marion's phenomenological outline as such, but objects only to the examples Marion uses, to what he sees as Marion's theological (rather than religious) determination of phenomenology. Marion's project fails not because it is phenomenologically incoherent or misinterprets Husserl or Heidegger, but because it is too Roman Catholic and is reluctant to use wider religious examples. Smith distinguishes carefully between religion (which for him is inclusive and plural) and theology (which is particular and concrete, thus apparently by nature colonizing). He suggests that "Marion's piety leaves no room for difference and will not permit any other gods to appear, indeed, one may be concerned that this pious phenomenology of religion is not beyond crusading to eliminate such paganism."[17]

While Caputo, Ward, and Smith judge Marion too determined, Richard Kearney instead suggests that Marion is lacking in determination. He finds both Derrida's and Marion's accounts too empty, too indeterminate, too atheistic as thought about God.[18] In his recent work *The God Who May Be* he seeks to articulate a God of possibility and eschatological promise. He endorses an

eschatological rather than an onto-theo-logical or purely negative interpretation of the divine. Kearney seeks to inhabit a middle space between what he
considers "two polar opposites in contemporary thinking about God."[19] These
constitute: "(a) the hyper-ascendant deity of mystical or negative theology; and
(b) the consigning of the sacred to the domain of abyssal abjection." He criticizes the first group (Lévinas, Marion, Derrida) for aiming at a language that is
"high" or too transcendent, because it speaks of "a divinity so far beyond-being
that no hermeneutics of interpreting, imagining, symbolizing, or narrativizing
is really acceptable." Rather, "God's alterity appears so utterly unnameable and
apophatic that any attempt to throw hermeneutic drawbridges between it and
our finite means of language is deemed a form of idolatry." The second group
he sees as going to the opposite extreme: "the divine slips *beneath* the grid of
symbolic and imaginary expression, back into some primordial zero-point of
unnamebility which is variously called 'monstrous' (Campbell, Zizek), 'sublime' (Lyotard), 'abject' (Kristeva), or 'an-khorite' (Caputo)." What he finds
lacking in both positions is any attempt at mediation or narrative imagination. For both groups, he suggests, "the divine remains utterly unthinkable,
unnameable, unrepresentable — that is, unmediatable" (7).

Instead, Kearney insists upon the need for narrative hermeneutics,[20] according to which he understands "religious language as an endeavor to say
something (however hesitant and provisional) about the unsayable" (7). Kearney suggests that negative theology (including that of both Derrida and Marion) pushes God too far away and allows for no hermeneutic exegesis. A God
who is that distant is finally religiously useless. Religion is precisely defined as
passionate response to the divine. In an analysis of Moses' experience at Mount
Horeb, while rejecting certain traditional onto-theo-logical interpretations, he
insists that "the most appropriate mode of human response to this Exodic revelation is precisely that: *commitment to a response . . .* we may say, consequently,
that the Exodic act of disclosure signals an inextricable communion between
God and humans, a radically new sense . . . of fraternity, responsibility, and
commitment to a shared history of 'becoming' . . . God may henceforth be
recognized as someone who *becomes with us*" (29).[21] God does not remain
utterly undetermined but is indeed disclosed by the hermeneutic reading of
certain texts and as a wager of their confluence. He insists that these texts and
the religious experiences which they portray call us to a response of commitment: "Faced with the burning bush, one doesn't merely speculate; one runs,
or if one holds one's ground, one praises, dances, acts" (30). In Marion, on
the other hand, transcendence becomes "too transcendent." He suggests that
Marion merely wants us to accept his account of God without being open
to debate or a variety of hermeneutic interpretations. Referring to Marion's
explication of Dionysius, Kearney criticizes its absence and indetermination.
He calls this complete lack of determination "a serious hermeneutic muddle":
"If the saturating phenomenon is really as bedazzling as Marion suggests, how
can we tell the difference between the divine and its opposite? How are we to

distinguish between enabling and disabling revelations?" (33). Throughout his work Kearney insists that, however hesitantly, we must say something about the divine, we must be able to recognize or identify at least to some extent, primarily in order to make distinctions of justice and ethics that would otherwise remain impossible. Some guidelines, preferably hermeneutic ones, are necessary in order to distinguish between the divine and the monstrous. In Kearney's view, Marion does not provide such hermeneutic guidelines for the necessary distinctions and recognition.

Marion's talk about God, then, has elicited a variety of responses, of which some seem diametrically opposed. While most of this second part of the book will be a kind of response to these critics (and I will return to them explicitly later), two preliminary remarks are in order at this point. First, one should point out that Marion has recently modified or at least clarified some of his strong statements about the bishop as theologian in an interview with Richard Kearney, where he points out that he meant to emphasize primarily the necessary connection between the rigorously intellectual exercise of theology and the living faith and practice of the church. Let me quote his comment in full:

> I would like to say this. When I said that "only the bishop merits the title of the theologian" I was not, of course, taking sides in the present-day differences between, say, bishops and theologians, I was referring back to the tradition where most of our great theologians were, at the same time, bishops in their communities. I am thinking here of examples such as the two Gregorys, Basil the Great, or John the Chrysostom. For a long time in the common tradition of the Church, the *place* to teach theology was the pulpit from which the bishop, during the liturgy, had to explain the Gospel. All our great Patristic books were, in fact, connected to these homiletic practices.

In response to Kearney's objection that some theologians have also been condemned as heretics, Marion judges this a subversion and admits that "it is difficult for us to think today about how theology was originally not supposed to be the outcome of intellectual curiosity, logical dexterity, or academic career." He insists:

> Theology grew out of the task of commenting on the Scriptures. Not because you chose to be a professional exegete of the Scriptures but because that was an essential part of the liturgy, of the Eucharistic gathering of the faithful. In this sense, theology was a communal event. It was the theology of a community and not the solitary research task of a theologian. The great theologians of the tradition were not writing books because they wished to get published but because they needed to address specific questions that were of importance in their communities.[22]

This statement is significant not only because it clarifies Marion's earlier claims and interprets them as referring to a historical situation that is no longer our present one, and maybe therefore mitigates or even eliminates the demand for ecclesiastical hierarchy to sanction theological endeavor. Rather it is important because it emphasizes much more strongly something evident already in the original statements, namely the intimate connection between the task of theology and the liturgical practice of the church.[23] Of course, Caputo and Ward object not only to Marion's reference to hierarchy, but precisely also to this emphasis on liturgical connection. They seem, however, somewhat inconsistent in their criticism on this point. On the one hand, they condemn Marion's "Platonism" and "Gnostic" emphasis on the spiritual, his lack of connection to the physical and to the world. Yet on the other hand, they criticize precisely this connection to the physical ecclesial community of believers and the actual physical practice of participation in the Eucharist. Ward criticizes Marion both for his "translucent Platonism" and for his interpretation of "the world as sacrament of love mediated by and on the authority of the community called the Church." Similarly, Caputo condemns in almost the same breath Marion's supposedly unconditioned relation with God that lacks any connecting chain and his conditioned use of the Scriptures and ties to the Catholic community and its hierarchy. Surely an emphasis on the community and its actual practices provides precisely some connection to the world that guards theology from disappearing into flights of mysticism or intellectualizing to such a degree that theology degenerates into a playing with words that no longer has meaning for the community whose practices and Scriptures it is meant to illuminate.

This also leads us to a further important point. Marion's admittedly somewhat unguarded statements of writing from God's point of view or letting the Word speak through our words do not imply in my view that the theologian has a privileged access to the divine that is severed from any meaningful hermeneutic connection. Rather, a theology of revelation speaks of the ways in which God has been acknowledged by various sources as having been revealed, the Scriptures and the experience of the church primary among them. It assumes these experiences and attempts to illuminate them as having their source in a God who has chosen to speak through them. When Marion makes any statements about God or about revelation, they are always deeply grounded in the Scriptures and often supplemented by references to the Fathers or the past experience of the Christian community. They do not constitute mystical assertions of Marion's own invention. There is therefore a clear hermeneutic connection here (a point I will take up in more detail near the end of this part). The supposed "hubris" in Marion's writings is balanced by a good dose of humility precisely in the way in which he employs the sources he regards as constitutive for theology and sees them as grounded in the community whom this theology is meant to serve. Theology, then, for Marion does require a kind of commitment that philosophy eschews. A comment Marion made in the above-mentioned interview is particularly illuminating in this context. Marion tries to explain what it might mean that "blessed are those who believe without seeing." He comments:

It may be to some extent the distinction between philosophy and theology, simply that. Because in philosophy we have to "see" to believe. What does that mean, to believe? For us, because we start from a philosophical point of view, we spontaneously think that to believe is to take for true, to assume something as if it were true, without any proof. This is our interpretation of belief. In that case, it is either belief or seeing. But is this the real meaning of belief? In fact, belief is also to commit yourself, and in that case, it is also, perhaps, a theoretical attitude. Because, by committing yourself to somebody else, you open a field of experience. And so it's not only a substitute for not knowing, it is an act which makes a new kind of experience possible. It is because I believe that I will see, and not as a compensation. *It's the very fact that you believe which makes you see new things*, which would not be seen if you did not believe.[24]

Commitment to a community and to the God whom it worships does not then only lead to blind submission to hierarchy. Instead it actually opens one's eyes in a new way for things one would not have seen or understood otherwise. A theology of revelation is able to experience and speak of things to which it would not have access without any commitment, with a purely philosophic and critical stance. We will have occasion to return to this point.

Finally, both Marion's statements about the character of theology and the criticism of his theological statements require familiarity with his work on Descartes' theology. Not only will Marion's claims become much clearer when seen in the context of his investigation into Descartes' theology, but much of the criticism needs to be mitigated by this earlier preparation and its implications for Marion's more recent work. To proceed from God to humans instead of the other way around does not mean a complete lack of hermeneutics and a solitary divinized mysticism. Rather, as Marion will develop in relation to Descartes and Descartes' late medieval context, it points to the traditional doctrines of analogy in which any term finds its fullness and grounding only in God (who is beyond even such terminology) while the same term can be applied to humans only by deficiency. It is an acknowledgment of human finitude rather than a hubristic stance of privileged knowledge. Theology of revelation is one that does not fall into univocal language between God and humans as natural theology is wont to do, but rather maintains a distance between the human and the divine which may be expressed most appropriately through the methods of analogy or the traditional ways of naming God characteristic of "negative" or "mystical" theology. The task of theology is to bear witness to experiences of revelation without falling into the blasphemy of metaphysics. This becomes possible (or at least easier) when theology makes use of the methods that have been employed successfully in the past in order to articulate such experiences and especially to talk about the source of revelation and the central subject of theology: God.

As I have pointed out already in the introduction, the parallels between Marion's theological talk about God and his phenomenological talk about the phenomenon of revelation have often been noted and criticized. Thomas Carlson, for example, suggests that Marion's theological text "maintains a strikingly deep resonance" with his phenomenology.[25] It has the same "core concern," namely that of liberating various phenomena from conditions and limits.[26] Both Marion's theology and his philosophy are concerned with overcoming metaphysics and thereby liberating God and the subject respectively. Carlson objects that there is no clear distinction between philosophy and theology in Marion's discourse.[27] Instead Marion presupposes his theology and specifically his talk about God in his philosophy.[28] His phenomenological goals are parallel to his theological ones and constitute a "generalization" of his theological concerns. Both projects engage in a parallel elimination of boundaries: "Just as Marion's theology would pass beyond metaphysics by freeing God's self-revelation in distance from every limiting concept that would seek to render that God present under the idolatrous conditions of thought, so his phenomenology would pass beyond metaphysics by freeing the phenomenon's self-showing from any a priori conditions, whether those of the thinking subject or those of a metaphysical God" (ID, xix). A similar parallelism is true for Marion's analysis of the gift.[29] What is more, not only conditions and particular objects are parallel or find a similar explication in Marion's two fields; the two even share the same hermeneutic paradigms. Again and again Carlson points out the "striking isomorphism" of Marion's language.[30] Carlson finds that "the logic of a faith that sees only to the degree that it receives the necessary will to see is a logic equally decisive to Marion's phenomenology and theology — even if the latter has an actual content while the former articulates only possibility" (ID, xxx). He therefore apparently concurs with Marion's own distinction between his two projects in terms of actuality and possibility, and merely objects that Marion has not recognized how intensely parallel they are.

He interprets these parallels as an opening toward more fruitful thought but also comments on their problematic character: "Such an isomorphism would not mean, as many argue or assume, that Marion's phenomenology is 'really' or 'only' an indirect means to advance his theology. It could mean, however, that Marion's theology and phenomenology inform one another in more subtle and complex ways than Marion himself sometimes wants to allow . . . it could well be the case that one's conception of the possible is substantially and inevitably shaped by what one already takes to be actual — just as one's understanding of the actual would always already be framed by what one imagines to be possible" (ID, xxxi). Yet, while many critics observe such close connections between Marion's theological thinking about God and his phenomenological analyses of phenomena of revelation, few have seen any need to go beyond that. It is this topic especially, however, that is the most firmly grounded in Marion's early work in Descartes, as he himself often indicates.[31] In one of Marion's more recent papers this is particularly obvious. In a paper written originally for the fourth Villanova Religion and Postmodernism conference ("Transcendence — And Beyond"), Marion develops the notion of God as the "Impossible."[32] He grounds his analysis not only on several Scriptural texts (such as Christ's healing of the paralytic and the story of the annunciation, which both refer to God's ability to do what is impossible for humans). Rather, these Scriptural analyses come only after a long detour through the history of philosophy and its statements about transcendence, focusing especially on the late medieval discussion that is exemplified in St. Thomas, Duns Scotus, Suarez, and finally Descartes. Marion clearly sees this medieval context as significant for his phenomenological and theological reflections. A closer analysis of his writings on Descartes' theology will make clear why this is the case.

four
Descartes and God
"A Solitary . . . Abandoned on a Field in Ruins"

Marion is especially interested in Descartes' "theology" and in his relationship to the particular theological questions and systems of the time. He refers to Descartes' theology as *blanche* ["white" or "blank"] because it is precisely a refusal to engage in theology and to reduce God to philosophical or metaphysical language. Marion emphasizes three aspects of Descartes' refusal to subject God to idolatrous definitions. First, Descartes sets himself in explicit opposition to the trend of speaking of God univocally, of assuming that God is subject to the same rational thought processes as humans are, or even of applying the terminology of being to God and created existences univocally. Descartes finds abhorrent the idea of mathematical truths as equivalent or even superior to God and instead insists on the creation of "eternal truths" and their dependence upon God. Furthermore, in formulating his proofs for God's existence, Descartes can be put into explicit conversation with the medieval doctrines of analogy and ways of naming God that he both invalidates and complicates. Finally, even in rendering the traditional ways of approaching God impossible for subsequent philosophy by his confusing of the traditional paths of naming God, Descartes ultimately recognizes the infinity and incomprehensibility of

God. With the exception of Pascal (whom Marion sees primarily as a theological writer), he is the last (philosophical) thinker to do so. One can say, then, as DeHart rightly does: "What makes Descartes the great thinker he is for Marion is that he acknowledges the failure of rational comprehension of the divine even as he refuses simply to abandon the drive to comprehend."[1]

This engagement with Descartes' "blank theology" therefore serves as a further preparation for Marion's subsequent work and provides important insight into fundamental presuppositions of his later claims. For example, Marion's strong insistence on the ineffability and incomprehensibility of God and his repeated concern to protect God from definitions of "being" or other restrictive concepts arise out of his reading of Descartes and the Cartesian theological context. Marion's desire to safeguard God's name, his selection of tools for accomplishing such protection, and his choice to speak of God in terms of excess are grounded firmly in these earlier insights. I will examine three significant aspects of Marion's treatment of Descartes' theology. First, I will look at his summary of Descartes' stance against any kind of univocity between the created and the uncreated. Second, I will explicate what Marion says about the breakdown of the doctrines of analogy before Descartes and the influence of this disintegration on Descartes' project and subsequent philosophical thinking about God. In *Théologie blanche*, where Marion outlines most of this argument, he moves back and forth between the assertions of univocity and the breakdown of analogy, as they are indeed closely linked. In this treatment, however, I will separate the two and outline the move toward univocity first. That will make it clearer why the theories of analogy are so important in this context and why their breakdown is detrimental for Descartes' project. Third, I will investigate Marion's argument about the three proofs for God's existence in Descartes that he connects with the three medieval and patristic ways of naming God and that are also linked to the methods of analogy. Finally, I will consider the implications of these analyses, in particular their strong emphasis on apophaticism and the essential incomprehensibility of God.

The Language of Univocity

The defining text for Marion's interpretation of Descartes' theology is a quotation from Descartes' letter to Mersenne which insists that "the mathematical truths that you [Mersenne and others like him] call eternal were established by God and depend entirely upon Him. To say that these truths are independent of God is in effect to speak of Him as a Jupiter or a Saturn, and to subjugate Him to Styx and the fates."[2] Marion examines both parts of this text (first, the philosophical statement about the mathematical truths; second, the poetic reference to fate) in several contexts and sees them as key for Descartes' stance toward talk about God.[3] According to Marion, Descartes firmly rejects a movement toward univocity and a subjection of God to mathematical or other rational truths.[4] "Univocity" refers to speaking of God in the same manner and with the same terms as of creatures. (For example, both God and humans could be described as beings and the term "being" would be applied to both God and creatures in the same fashion.) At the same time certain truths, such as those of math and logic, were beginning to be interpreted as "eternal" and unchanging. They were necessary for all thought and especially for the construction of the world. It was therefore implied both that God must have made use of math and logic to create the world and that God understands these truths in the same fashion as humans do (since they could not be otherwise). Marion judges both of these (related) claims as idolatrous and blasphemous. He attempts to show that Descartes insists against such assertions that God is always far superior to human thinking, that no terminology can be applied univocally to God and creatures, and that all truths — albeit eternal or rational ones — are dependent upon and created by God. In this stance, Descartes is fundamentally opposed to most of the theological, philosophical, and scientific thought of the time.

Furthermore, far from seeing the reference to Saturn, Jupiter, and the fates as a mere poetic allusion, as most other interpreters have done, Marion emphasizes its significance and claims that it actually makes a precise argument further supporting the first assertion (namely, that the eternal truths depend upon God and are created). In an article devoted entirely to this part of the quote, Marion illustrates with several passages from Homer, Herodotus, Hesiod, Horace, Virgil, Plato, Cicero, and Seneca how the pagan gods were indeed often subject to fate and destiny.[5] Descartes, so Marion argues, rejects this pagan submission of the gods and finds it menacing to God's transcendence and incomprehensibility. Descartes thus opposes himself to the entire philosophical discussion of his time and consistently distances the Christian God from fate, destiny, or pagan divinities. This particular sentence in a letter to Mersenne, then, clearly summarizes what Marion wants to highlight as Descartes' most fundamental claim: that God is utterly different and distant from any human attempt to assimilate or comprehend the divine, whether it be pagan, poetic, philosophical, or scientific in nature and intent. According to Marion, Descartes is radically opposed to the philosophical and theological thrust of his time in this emphasis. In honoring and highlighting Descartes' emphasis on divine distance and ineffability, Marion is simultaneously expressing his own concern.

Marion outlines how — in contrast to Descartes — late medieval thought moves to increasingly univocal ways of speaking about God and creatures. Univocity, in this context, assumes that very similar or even identical language can be used to speak about God and about humans or the world and that no fundamental difference distinguishes them. Marion claims that such univocal language leads to a subordination of the divine to the human and the hubristic assumption that God can be understood and maybe even controlled by human beings. Both the intent and the procedure of this thinking limits or even eliminates God's transcendence. This movement has several representatives and different aspects. Marion distinguishes between ontological univocity (such as in Suarez and Vasquez), spiritual univocity (as articulated by Bérulle), and epistemological univocity (seen in Mersenne, Kepler, Galileo, and to some extent even in Descartes himself). Marion spells this argument out in great detail in the first section of *Théologie blanche*. I will outline two of these moves toward univocity that illustrate Marion's argument and its implications the most clearly, namely those connected to the language of being (ontological) and to the language of mathematics (epistemological).[6]

Ontological Univocity

Marion begins his treatment with Suarez, who first posits an ontological univocity between God and humans by diffusing the traditional analogies between beings and making the divine being comprehensible.[7] "Being" becomes a unified concept that to some extent can be applied univocally to both divine and human beings. For Suarez, "being applies in the same sense (logically or intrinsically) to both creatures and God: the ontological gap between the finite and the infinite distinguishes God from his creatures less than the conceptual representation of them as beings joins them" ("Idea of God," 267; QCII, 225). Not only is God conceived from this univocal concept of being, however, but understanding between humans and God is due to the same concept. Univocity of essence and univocity of thought become closely linked. Marion insists that for Suarez, "The *ratio* of essence, as logical truth, becomes a univocal and universal logic of a neutral truth. The univocity of logic follows the univocity of essence. Univocity thus dominates the attribution of logical identity of an absolutely sufficient *ratio*, even for God" (TB, 49). This logical truth leads not only to an objective concept of being in the later philosophical tradition but also to the possibility of dispensing with God entirely. It hence becomes even more evident why Marion will later be so eager to reject this language and will interpret it as an idolatrous way of speaking about God. Ontological univocity quickly brings about epistemic univocity, and both are equally problematic: "The univocity of the concept of being thus gives rise to a kind of epistemological univocity; representation governs the knowledge God has with respect to possibilities (creatures), as much as it does the knowledge which finite understandings claim with respect to the infinite. To this extent, at least, God's knowledge is like ours" ("Idea of God," 268; QCII, 227). How could this move happen? How can Suarez claim that God understands in the same way we do, when much of scholastic theology would never have admitted such a suggestion?

Marion claims that univocity is closely linked to a separation of God and truth which ultimately posits truths as prior to and possibly even superior to God. Suarez sees truth as prior to God's knowledge of it; truth is thus founded on an exterior reason (TB, 29). The truths themselves assure the place of reason, even for God. It is this claim to which Descartes (and Marion with him) is most fundamentally opposed, because such truth or reason then becomes superior to God, determines the divine, and ultimately eliminates it as unnecessary. For Descartes nothing is or can be prior to God, neither truths nor reason (which is itself a prior truth). Reason must be grounded in the divine causality and be dependent upon it (TB, 31). We can see here why Marion sees Descartes' insistence on the creation of the eternal truths as deeply linked to a rejection of univocity. For Suarez truths have become separated, so that God can have a relation with them (as different from Godself) and they are founded separately. Concepts apply in equal measure to God and to other beings and are thus imposed upon God. Marion claims that this later leads to the principle of sufficient reason in Leibniz (TB, 48). Logical truth gives birth to independent reason and dispenses with God (TB, 49). Real essence becomes something independent from God, who only perceives its eternal possibility and is bound to its rules (TB, 53).[8]

For Descartes, there is a clear distinction between divine and human knowing. They are as separate as the finite is from the infinite. As much as the finite expands, it can never reach the infinite; there is no simple progression from one to the other. The two are incommensurable and the finite can never attain to the infinite (TB, 71). Nothing can be said in the same way of us as it can be said of God. God creates truths, and divine truths infinitely surpass our truths. Descartes always denies any notion of univocity between God and humans. God is the author of the essence and existence of creatures and they are never independent of him (TB, 73).[9] Marion claims that because many of the arguments regarding univocity are made by theologians and because Descartes no longer has the theories of analogy available to him, he cannot make a theological argument here and is reduced to a simple rejection of univocity and an affirmation of complete equivocity. There is no way for Descartes to bridge the gap that separates divine from human.

This is of course precisely what Marion intends to do in his later work: bridge the gap between the divine and the human in a way that preserves the distance between them, does not erase their differences, and does not speak of them univocally. Suarez' use of the concept of being as the highest definition of God and at the same time as a term that can define both God and humans equally clearly shows why Marion later wishes to "free" God from this language of being, why he refuses ontological univocity between the divine and human. As I have tried to show in the last part and will continue to explore in the present one, metaphysics for Marion invariably moves toward univocity, by tying God and humans together into a system in which the relations between the two can be clearly delineated and thus finally erased.

Epistemological Univocity

The strongest move toward univocity, however, becomes connected to the desire to interpret the physical world in terms of mathematical language. Johannes Kepler and Galileo Galilei, for example, assert that God understands math in exactly the same way that we do. Marion finds that "Kepler goes so far as to identify mathematical rationality with God" ("Idea of God," 268; QCII, 228). Again, this has epistemological implications: "This epistemological univocity in fact implies that we understand God's divinity to the same extent that we understand mathematical possibilities" ("Idea of God," 269; QCII, 230). Kepler was of great importance to Mersenne, who then strongly influenced Descartes. Kepler's ideas thus become transmitted to Descartes through Mersenne.[10] For Kepler, eternal truths are equal to God and the very reasons for creation are mathematical.[11] God is glorified through the study of mathematics and geometry. A devotion to mathematics leads to a devotion to God. By considering mathematical truths, the astronomer can attain to the divine ideas or even to God directly. The mathematical ideas are as intelligible to God as they are to us and are understood by both in the same fashion. Doctrines of analogy are therefore not necessary.[12] Marion shows how for Kepler, astronomers can fulfill a much better theological function than priests, because they can actually ensure a certain knowledge of God by their exegesis of the book of nature which describes perfectly the order of the world and of God. Geometrical and quantitative ideas are thus identified with God.[13] Math is God's gift to humankind and its exercise brings humans closer to God. The mathematical truths, in consequence, are co-eternal with God, are identified with the divine, preside over all creation, and give privileged access to God. Humans share the same intellect with God and their knowledge works univocally. For Kepler, we know and perceive in the same manner as God does. Human understanding thus must even define the divine nature. Marion insists that this is completely and utterly contrary to Descartes' claims in every respect.

According to Marion, Kepler speaks about God with almost "barbaric simplicity," without any sensitivity at all to the possibility that the nature of that discourse might be inappropriate for the divine subject. For Kepler, God can be measured by our comprehension; his language thus is idolatrous. It is still an authentic experience of the divine, but an idolatrous one because it reduces God to what can be grasped by the human mind. Marion accuses Kepler of "measuring God by the cubit of our comprehension, by the span of our hand, by the measure of our finitude, in short by substituting an idol for him. The idol, without doubt, consigns an authentic experience of the divine, and hence it is not appropriate to underestimate it or to deny the religious elan of the pastor turned astronomer. But, the idol, just as much, does not attain to the divine which it desires to comprehend, and thus reduces it at the price of its comprehension" (TB, 186). Marion's use of the terminology of idol and icon is clearly being prepared here. Kepler's language is idolatrous because it measures the divine in human terms and regards it as a reflection of human vision and achievement. It lacks the iconic vision (in this case of Descartes) that realizes that the infinite is far beyond the human grasp who is always dependent upon it. In any case, for Marion the move to univocity is completed in Kepler. Truth is as transparent to the human mind as to the divine; it does not matter who understands or interprets it. Mathematical knowing becomes the model of all rationality, and univocity becomes inevitable. Any insistence on God's infinity or distance is abolished. God is not free to create, but is submitted to the logical laws of geometry, which preside at creation and provide the norm for divine action. God makes an ideal archetype for the world according to the mathematical truths imposed upon creation (and on God). God becomes effectively reduced to a governor of the machine of nature who only realizes its inherent potential. Humans can describe this rationality of the world perfectly; they can "think God's thoughts after him" (TB, 192). For Kepler, even the Trinity can be understood according to geometrical models.[14] Although Descartes follows Kepler in his optics and is strongly influenced by him, Marion maintains that he rigorously rejects Kepler's other claims. The *Regulae*, for example, on Marion's reading establish the finitude of human knowing in a manner radically contesting Kepler's contentions. Descartes insists that mathematical truths do not give us access to a knowledge of God, but only to knowledge of the physical world.

Although Galileo does not emphasize mathematics quite as much as Kepler does and does not explicitly identify God with math, he does also describe God as master-mathematician and divine architect who organizes the universe according to a coherent geometrical plan. For Galileo, too, mathematics is the highest version of truth, and its evidence and certainty assure exactitude. He argues, in fact, that geometry and the study of nature give more exact and definite access to God than the Scriptures do, since the latter are subject to human interpretation.[15] Scripture, for Galileo, becomes a mere supplement for the truths already given clearly by mathematical investigation. Ultimately, math shows the design and the revelation of the Creator better than Scripture because math is responsible for the creation of the world while Scripture speaks primarily of its redemption.[16] All rationality is thus understood for Galileo by mathematical truth, including the God who exercises it. Marion concludes that for Galileo, human and divine knowing become univocal and equivalent, because both depend upon the exactitude of truth.[17] Galileo even at points chides God for not organizing the heavens even more mathematically.[18]

Marion concludes his section with a brief comparison of Galileo's *Dialogo* with Descartes' *Regulae*. He argues that the method plays the role in Descartes' epistemology that math plays in Galileo's. Yet while Galileo extends that epistemology to God and assumes univocity between divine and human knowing, Descartes establishes differences of knowing only between humans and refuses to extend such distinctions or relations to God at all. Rationality is not independent for Descartes, as it is for Galileo and Kepler, but rather it is radically dependent upon God, who is prior and superior to it.[19] For Descartes, distinctions between knowing operate only on the level of human understanding, while for Galileo these are parallels between finite and infinite understanding.[20] Descartes, in fact, explicitly condemns Galileo on this point and accuses him of confusing the infinite and the indefinite. He claims that Kepler, Galileo, and Mersenne treat the infinite as if they were above it, while

he himself has always submitted himself to the infinite when writing about it.[21]
Marion often refers to this particular passage to point out Descartes' reverence
for God's incomprehensibility.

Mersenne is a further figure in this context and a particularly significant
one, due to his close association with Descartes. And like Kepler and Galileo,
Mersenne "continually invoked the identity of mathematics and the divine
understanding . . . mathematics constitutes the language and activity of God
Himself" ("Idea of God," 269; QCII, 231). As we have seen in the opening to
this section, it is to Mersenne that Descartes addresses his letter, condemning
the stance of making mathematical truths equal to God. In his various letters to
Mersenne, Descartes consistently refuses to address theological questions, yet
he sees the issue of the creation of eternal and mathematical truths as a philosophical one and therefore engages in it.[22] In his responses, Descartes insists
that the mathematical truths, although eternal, are created by God, depend
upon God as much as other creatures do; that they could have been otherwise
than what they are presently, that they do not emanate from God, and that they
are not produced in the same sense in which the divine Word (Christ) comes
from the Father. "In short, the mathematical truths which are perfectly comprehensible, do not at the same time make God comprehensible, but presuppose instead an 'infinite and incomprehensible being' with 'incomprehensible
power'" (TB, 166).

For Mersenne, in contrast to Descartes, God's actions are submitted to
geometry. The eternal truths of mathematics have a divine dignity because
God proceeds geometrically. Furthermore, because God has made everything
mathematically, we can know God through geometry. God imitates mathematical truths and the divine essence can be described through mathematical
idealities. Thus knowing a science is not only knowing *like* God but knowing
God. In Mersenne, as a theologian, this identification of God with math is
particularly problematic and Marion sees it as having serious implications:
"Thus Mersenne transforms the traditional theological thesis that the divine
ideas in the end vanish into the divine essence (as in Augustine, Bonaventure
and Thomas) by identifying God's omnipotence with respect to creation with
the requirements of mathematical rationality; mathematical rationality is held
to be the *only* possible and thinkable kind of rationality. In this way divine omnipotence is subordinated to mathematics" (IG, 270; QCII, 232). Marion consistently condemns this—with Descartes—as leading to anthropomorphism
and idolatry.

In a review of several of Marion's writings on Descartes, David Marshall
claims that Marion neglects to deal with Descartes' insistence that God is incapable of destroying even the smallest part of matter. Overall, he finds problematic that Marion apparently neglects Descartes' writings on physics almost entirely and ignores the importance of the *res extensa* (thereby giving insufficient
weight to Descartes' dualism).[23] In fact, so Marshall contends, the *res extensa*
actually functions as a kind of analogy in Descartes (135). Marion overempha-

sizes ontological concerns in his interpretations of Descartes and therefore disregards (illegitimately) Descartes' physics. Marion transposes Descartes' dualism between physical and mental into a dualism between divine and human. Descartes is not concerned with God but with physics (138–39). While Marshall is certainly correct that Marion is not particularly interested in Descartes as a physicist, it does not seem right to say that Descartes is not "interested in God." Marion's careful analysis of Descartes' repeated insistence on God's alterity and infinity especially in light of the general move to univocity serves precisely to highlight that less-well-known side of Descartes. While it might be a selective reading, that does not seem to disqualify Marion's conclusions about this aspect of Descartes, as Marshall himself admits by calling Marion's writing about late Scholasticism "great" [großartig] (132).

The Demise of the Doctrine of Analogy

As we have seen, according to Marion, Descartes fundamentally opposes the reduction of God to human knowing and especially to mathematics. Although Descartes agrees with much of Kepler's and Galileo's optimism about human knowledge and insists upon clarity, method, and certainty, Descartes always locates God *outside* of the realms of human knowledge and judges a comparison of divine and human ways of thinking impossible. Yet Descartes' position is primarily one of rejection, not of affirmation. Although, according to Marion, Descartes clearly recognizes the blasphemy and idolatry in the assumptions and claims of his contemporaries, he is unable to formulate a clear positive position against them that would speak of God more adequately and coherently. Marion claims that this is due to the demise of the traditional theological ways of talking about God available in medieval times, in particular the doctrine of analogy. Marion examines how this doctrine functioned in Aquinas and outlines its demise in the subsequent commentators, a process that reaches its height of distortion in the thinkers most influential for Descartes on this particular issue: Cajetan and Suarez. A doctrine of analogy that would escape univocity in speaking of God's relation to creatures is thus no longer available to Descartes.[24] Descartes is not only largely alone in his refusal to submit God to clear definition, but he must also articulate this refusal without having the appropriate language for doing so. Descartes thus can only escape idolatry and blasphemy by refusing to articulate a theology. His "theology" remains white, blank, erased.[25]

The theological doctrine of analogy derives from the theory of the divine names (which I will treat in the next section). It was falling into disuse at the time of Descartes and, according to Marion, he is the last one to attempt to use it.[26] Analogy is a way of using terminology of both God and creatures without assuming that the same term is employed in the same fashion of both. It maintains a relationship between the two without implying either complete identification (univocity) nor complete difference (equivocity). Furthermore,

Marion insists that analogy always assumed a move from God to creation, not the other way around. The traditional position of this relationship is that of St. Thomas Aquinas.[27] According to Aquinas no clear proportion can be calculated between divine and human, but they are related to each other as cause and effect. The transcendental causality of the Creator, however, has only a "relation of reference" to the finite, not one of "measurable relation." According to Marion, it always remains epistemologically indeterminate.[28] This epistemological indetermination makes analogy possible and confirms incommensurability between the divine and the human. Thus, perfections (such as goodness, beauty, etc.) are not really attributed to God but rather proceed from God and have an infinite status in the divine.[29] Even the most intrinsic perfection of the creature is dependent upon God and proceeds from this infinitely other. Names can hence be predicated of God and of creatures by an analogy of proportion (reference). Although they refer to the same term, this does not make them univocal. Not the same thing is predicated of both, but they refer to it in a similar way. No outside term is thus imposed upon God, but creation always refers back to God. The reference of God to the finite remains both real and incommensurable.[30]

Cajetan and Suarez

Cajetan provides the standard [though false] interpretation of Aquinas on this point. He outlines three types of analogy: one of inegality, one of reference, and one of proportionality. According to Marion, he invents the first one. The last two are indeed Thomistic, but Cajetan reverses them.[31] For St. Thomas, perfection is in God first and creatures participate in it really but secondarily and deficiently. Marion thinks that Cajetan misses this fundamental point in St. Thomas and makes perfection constitutive of creatures.[32] For Cajetan this way of analogy only applies to two precise cases: the good and being. Both constitute creatures first of all (formally). He does not realize that the same being and goodness could simultaneously define both God and creatures without assuming univocity between them by being constituted by God and possessed by creatures in only a derivative fashion.[33] For Cajetan (and later for Suarez) perfection defines both God and creatures intrinsically and reciprocally. Not only is this a profound rupture with Aquinas and a complete misunderstanding of what he actually says, but Marion suggests that it confuses the thesis of analogy so profoundly that it becomes useless. He therefore insists that Suarez receives from Cajetan a misinterpretation of analogy that refuses Descartes any access to it.

Suarez summarizes the tradition of talking about divine names in Aquinas and Dionysius in terms of univocity, equivocity, and analogy, which help to distinguish between the finite and the infinite.[34] Univocity sees God and humans as the same; equivocity claims that there is no relation between them.[35] Suarez sees equivocity as a cause/effect argument: God is the cause; creatures are the effect. Aquinas, however (as we saw above), had used this argument to deny univocity in favor of analogy, not of equivocity.[36] Furthermore, Suarez takes the concept of univocity from Duns Scotus and defines it (falsely, in Marion's view) as an identity of the principle of being in God and creatures. The name "being," therefore, becomes attributed equally to God and to humans. This makes a doctrine of analogy impossible because it erases meaningful distinction between the divine and the human. According to Marion, Suarez rejects analogy of being in favor of a direct relationship between beings and Being. Suarez' doctrine of analogy, then, leads directly to a univocal concept of being.[37] And in his critique of Cajetan's confusing doctrine of analogy, Suarez actually ends up claiming more or less the opposite of Aquinas, in Marion's view. For Thomas, terminology is always applied first to God and then to creatures, while Suarez reverses this movement.[38] Furthermore, he eliminates Thomas' emphasis on creation and the causality of creatures (something else that Descartes will attempt to recover). In desiring to make the concept of being univocal, Suarez finally denies the doctrine of analogy altogether.[39]

What is essential to Marion in the doctrines of analogy, then, is a way of describing the relationship between the divine and the human, the uncreated and the created, that would neither collapse the distinction between them nor eliminate any relationship at all. It is, one might say, a way of describing a "distance" between creation and God that separates them and yet could be traversed through the theology of the divine names. Furthermore, Marion points out repeatedly that it proceeds from God to creatures, not from humans to God. While humans indeed approach God as humans, they quickly realize that their conceptions and language of the divine are inadequate. In order to preserve the divine incomprehensibility, analogous naming must proceed from God and refer to creatures only derivatively. This does not mean that the theologian has some mysterious privileged access to God that lacks any hermeneutic intermediary, but rather it means that beauty, love, goodness, and other such attributes are found first in God and grounded in the divine. Humans participate in them only derivatively and by analogy. Descartes seeks to articulate this kind of continuity between divine and human knowing that preserves distance without having available to him the traditional theological language just explicated. Marion argues that the creation of eternal truths which Descartes maintains in order to combat the move toward univocity constitutes a (failed) attempt to speak of God in terms of the doctrines of analogy and that this idea, in fact, governs all of Descartes' thought. The entire second part of *Théologie blanche* is devoted to supporting this argument. The creation of the eternal truths constitutes a kind of search for a foundation or grounding of science and knowledge, which Descartes achieves through the *mathesis universalis*, the code that governs all understanding. Since I have already summarized that argument in the last part, I will only point out the implications Marion derives from it for the topic of God.

The Code and Causality

Through the notion of the code, Descartes had maintained a relationship between human construction of knowledge and the discovery of an order already inherent in nature. Descartes argues that such encoding of nature, which refers to the pattern employed by God in the creation of the world, transcends human knowledge, is grounded in God as its cause, and therefore could have been otherwise. There is thus a kind of analogy between the code constructed by human rationality and the superior and original encoding dependent upon God. Both requirements of analogy are fulfilled: the code establishes a relation without being identical for God and creation, and it proceeds from God to creation and not the other way around. The creation of the eternal truths establishes the arbitrariness of the code, because it shows that the geometry of nature is not necessarily "natural" (i.e., "necessary"). The process of defiguration (or decoding) produces the rational model of a new world that is based upon certain laws established by God. Since these laws are established definitively by God they constitute the rationality of any possible world. The truths are present before the world and the mathematicians found their own rationality on it (but do not impose it on the world). According to Marion, for Descartes there is definite equivocity, an unbridgeable gap, between creatures and Creator. The eternal truths are not in the least semi-divine nor do they have aseity [self-subsistence], which belongs to God alone, but they are creatures like everyone and everything else. This immense gap between God and creation is a "radical abyss," and yet there can be an approach across this space precisely through an understanding of science because it examines the principles which God has instituted for the world: "The human spirit, who rearranges the definition of science starting from the norms of knowing in order to produce the evident certainty of a science; God, who arranges the conditions of all rationality which is itself without any prior condition, disposes originally the eternal truths, in order to render thus all evidences and certainties possible" (TB, 273). Discovering God as founder of the code thus enables knowledge of God while this remains a relative knowledge, a knowledge of incomprehension.

Furthermore, Descartes establishes a second relationship between humans and God, based on humans being created "in God's image." Descartes locates this analogy or similarity in the human will, which is infinite as God is infinite. Yet this similarity between God and humans, Marion points out, actually serves to separate rather than unite them because human independence and autarchy posits humans against God and often leads to separation. The "univocity" of independence (God and humans both have independent will) therefore results in an ontic equivocity (humans go their own way). Marion claims that this is a precise formulation of analogy because human independence is only a tangential univocity (i.e., freedom means the same thing in God as in humans but does not function in the same manner). While it establishes a relation between God and humans (even a certain likeness), it does not define the essence and dignity of God because infinity always implies a measure of incomprehensibility. In Marion's view, Descartes does not attempt to define the nature of God until he devises the divine name of *causa sui*. With this name God does indeed imitate human self-sufficiency [*contentment de soi*] to some extent. Marion maintains that the notion of the *causa sui* (despite its insufficiency and even logical incoherence) does constitute a further attempt at analogy. Descartes actually explicitly refers to it as "*per analogiam*" (of the cause to efficiency), namely establishing an analogy between God's grounding of beings and human grounding of knowledge. Analogy then is only used explicitly in Descartes "in order to reduce the essence of God to the general rule that governs all finite beings — causality. That is the case, because far from reducing the tendency to univocity, this *analogia* increases it" (TB, 428). This "analogy," then, does not fulfill the requirements of analogy because it moves from humans to God and ultimately collapses meaningful distinctions between them. It applies the language of causality and self-sufficiency to humans and God in univocal fashion and patterns God in the image of humans. Descartes' only explicit attempt at the use of analogy therefore fails miserably.

Aza Gourdriaan examines the doctrine of analogy in Descartes in light of Marion's exegesis. He gives a thorough summary of Marion's treatment of univocity, analogy, and *causa sui* in Descartes, but suggests that Descartes is far from as reluctant to enclose God within a univocal naming as Marion claims (GD, 104–108). Although he complicates Marion's argument by pointing out other places in which God seems subject to the system instead of different from it, Marion would agree that the divine does finally become subject to the Cartesian metaphysics. And, as we will see in the next section of this chapter, Marion does recognize the tension between these various Cartesian definitions of God.

By outlining this search for foundation and grounding (that culminates in the *causa sui*) Marion has shown us Descartes' attempt to come to terms with the questions of analogy which he never resolves satisfactorily. The grounding remains analogous in its radical fragility:

> Here appears Descartes' highest singularity: in the same moment in which he opens metaphysics to its modernity in covering up definitively the question of analogy (and thus of the divine names), and in instituting the univocity of the *causa sive ratio* to the point of forging the God of *causa sui*, he opens, in quite another sense, metaphysics: he inscribes the incomprehensible idea of the infinite (and of infinite power) into an ontic transcendence that no formal univocity can ever finalize. (TB, 443)

Descartes, so Marion concludes at the end of his study of the relationship between univocity and analogy, is the only exception to the evolution toward mathematical and ontological univocity. He holds in tension univocity and radical equivocity because he lacks a doctrine of analogy and thus remains in "a provisional and untenable equilibrium" (TB, 453). After Descartes, the doctrines of analogy disappear from the theological vocabulary and are displaced (at least in philosophy) by the question of the ground/foundation. Marion concludes his comparison of Descartes and Suarez in *Théologie blanche* with the following words that summarize well Marion's estimation of Descartes' stance toward thought about God in general: "But, now, far from advancing as an iconoclast, does not Descartes rather discover himself as a solitary, without weapon or army, abandoned on a field in ruins, for an immense task: to become the first Christian thinker who must think the created and the uncreated, the infinite with the finite devoid of the theology of the divine Names and thus of the doctrine of analogy" (TB, 139).

The Proofs for God's Existence and
the Language of Divine Names

So far Descartes' talk about God seems to consist almost entirely of refusal. Much of Marion's argument has served to display the erasure and even explicit lack of any theology in Descartes. Yet Descartes does speak of God in his philosophy. The most prominent locus of this philosophical talk about God is, of course, in the proofs for God's existence. We have seen already that Descartes' metaphysics portrays God in a very ambivalent fashion: on the one hand, as a simple *cogitatum* of the ego; on the other hand, as the being par excellence which grounds the ego. This equivocal status corresponds to the divergent proofs for God's existence in Descartes' work that Marion will end up showing to be incompatible with each other.[40] He argues that we need to understand Descartes in the context of the discussion of the divine names which is, in fact, closely linked to the doctrines of analogy. Names, such as goodness, wisdom, or being, are applied to God "analogically"; they are both like and unlike human goodness, wisdom, or being. In the traditional theology of naming, which derives its origin from the work of fifth-century theologian St. Dionysius the Areopagite, several moves are outlined. Names can be applied to God affirmatively (through *kataphasis*): God is indeed good, wise, loving. Yet it is immediately realized that these names do not describe God fully or adequately and they are therefore denied in a second move of *apophasis*: God is not good or wise or powerful, in the way in which humans are or understand those terms. Finally, according to Marion, both of these descriptive moves are transcended by what he calls a "way of eminence": one of prayer, in which description culminates and is suspended in praise. Marion interprets Descartes' project as an attempt to "give metaphysically rigorous names to God and to the God of Christian revelation" (MP, 209; PM, 220). Descartes is involved in a philosophical explication of the theological exercise of naming God appropriately. Marion therefore proposes "reading the Cartesian discussion of the attributes of God as a metaphysical repetition of the theological treatise on the divine names. Only on this condition will it become possible to answer the crucial question: how and within what limits does God enter, with Descartes' redoubled onto-theology, into metaphysics?" (MP, 210; PM, 221).[41] Marion outlines these three proofs in the *Metaphysical Prism* and correlates them to the traditional ways of "naming" God through the three Dionysian ways: that of affirmation (*kataphasis*), of negation (*apophasis*), and of praise (*eminentia* or *aitia*).[42] By thinking of Descartes in conversation with other (theological) writers, Marion is able to show the incompatibility of the various assertions which Descartes makes about God. Descartes uses these three ways, but makes them equivalent and subverts them in a way that makes them lose their theological coherence and order. He simply juxtaposes the different proofs, without making a clear decision between them, thereby revealing their inherent contradictions and incompatibilities while refusing to resolve them. In consequence, the traditional ways of naming God are excluded from the subsequent philosophical discussion.

Infinity and Perfection

Descartes' description of God begins with "indetermination and dissimulation" (MP, 214; PM, 226), because almost the first mention of God in the *Meditations* suggests a possible confusion of God with the evil genius. It is only later that he moves to more affirmative and more definite statements about God. Marion consequently argues that from the very beginning Descartes deliberately reverses the order of the traditional affirmative and negative ways of speaking about God. Usually, theologians started with definitions of and affirmations about God, which they then went on to deny. Yet, instead of denying something that can be said affirmatively about God, Descartes begins with unknowing and dissimulation which leads him to a later definite determination. In contrast to this first indetermination, Descartes goes on to identify God, second, in terms of substance and causality. Substance, as applied to God, means perseity: "self-subsistence referred to itself" (MP, 223; PM, 235).[43] Descartes' definition of substantiality thus becomes confused: he applies the term to both God and many other things, yet he denies any univocity between substance as applied to God and applied to creatures or things. This equivocity of the term "substance" leads to Descartes' first significant definition of God, namely, as an infinite substance, which Marion suggests becomes, at least at first, Descartes' most important name for God. Certainly this will always remain the most significant name in Marion's own work, because this definition of God in terms of infinity implies for him an insistence on incomprehensibility and immeasurability. God is beyond the order of the method (so significant for Descartes), and so cannot be defined by it. Marion explains, "if the infinity of God in principle passes beyond (creation of eternal truths) the strictly objectifying method, incomprehensibility will not betray an imperfection, a deficiency, or an irrationality in the definition of God; on the contrary, it will attest to its perfection, as the sign of another rationality. God the infinite is not known despite his incomprehensibility, but through it" (MP, 231; PM, 243). Wolfgang Röd summarizes: "Because God due to his immeasurability cannot

be subjected to any measure, then he can also not become object of a methodical cognition."[44] This first definition is open-ended and seems to be the
most significant and primary one for Descartes. It recalls, in a sense, the path
of eminence of negative theology, because "the infinite does not give itself to
thinking except in refusing comprehension, does not reveal itself except in dis-
simulating the bedazzlement of its brilliance without equal" (TB, 456). The
infinite imposes itself on the human mind from the outside. It is a thought that
humans cannot invent.

Descartes goes on to propose a second definition of God in terms of
"power, perfection, and omnipotence" (MP, 235; PM, 247). Marion asserts
that omnipotence actually becomes a significant name for God that almost replaces that of infinity in importance, recurring especially strongly in Descartes'
later writings. He sees it as a supreme attribute that speaks of permanence and
immutability and which is incompatible with other attributes such as supreme
intelligence.[45] The notion of omnipotence becomes linked with the idea of
God as Creator. Omnipotence thus acquires a notion of efficient causality (a
point that will become important for Marion). This omnipotent Creator God
is finally defined further as the most perfect being, *ens summe perfectum.*[46]
Marion concludes about this second name for God in Descartes that it designates not merely a certain accumulation of perfections, but rather the move to
a superlative infinite power.[47]

God is therefore named first as infinite substance (a move that denies any
clear descriptions of the divine) and then later as perfection and omnipotence
(a move that assumes an apparently clear definition of the divine). Marion
points out the inherent contradiction and tension of this juxtaposition:

> This carries a twofold consequence. First of all, eminence no longer con-
> stitutes a third moment, autonomous if not equivalent to the first; rather, it
> simply crowns the other two ways, without really surmounting them. Next,
> since they do not open onto any third term, the negations (positive) and the
> affirmations (superlative) run the risk of being juxtaposed, indeed of con-
> tradicting each other, without there being any possibility of a final arbiter or
> a court of appeals. This gives rise to an incurable tension in the Cartesian
> doctrine of the divine attributes and names. (MP, 235; PM, 247)

The idea of God's perfection or omnipotence can be reached by the
human mind through successive additions and reconciliations of human
thought about God. It is therefore clearly contradictory to the idea of God's
infinity and superiority to any human attempt of comprehension. Kenneth
Winkler in his article "Descartes and the Names of God" argues that the Cartesian names for God are not incompatible, as Marion claims.[48] He finds that
especially the first two names of infinity and perfection are dependent upon
each other (453). He analyzes the use of "summus" in Descartes and decides
that "the evidence I have assembled — the order of words in (1), details of the
relationship between (1) and (2), Descartes's descriptions of the Third Medita-

tion proof, and the apparent equivalence of *supreme* and *supremely perfect*—strongly suggests (though it by no means proves) that the name of God that dominates the Fifth Meditation—*ens summe perfectum*—also dominates the definitions of God in the Third" (458). He concludes by suggesting "that as the *Meditations* progresses, the notion of God as infinite is reduced to (or unpacked in terms of) the notion of God as supremely perfect. Hence a positive (though inevitably inadequate) conception of God is achieved in the *Meditations* only when we have a clear and distinct idea of God as supremely perfect" (462). The two names are therefore neither divergent or incompatible and "Descartes's leading notion of God, in the Third Meditation as well as in the Fifth, is that of supremely perfect being" (463–64). Winkler does not refer to Marion's assertions about the third name, *causa sui*. In showing how the name "most perfect" comes to dominate the name "infinite," Winkler is not in as serious a disagreement with Marion as he seems to think, since Marion argues something very similar (e.g., MP, 238; PM, 251). Philip Clayton similarly argues that Marion is wrong to distinguish between the two names of "infinity" and "perfection" and that his analysis of infinity is limited if not mistaken. He finds that it commits an "egregious error" because "if infinity is, as he thinks, the 'most divine' of the names of God, this must be because it is the most appropriate, the best, in short—the most perfect. Thus one would place infinity over perfection for the paradoxical reason that infinity is the more perfect of the two. But if one's criterion is to find the most perfect ultimate name for God, then surely perfection itself, not infinity, is the best candidate."[49] Clayton does not recognize, however, that Marion is not searching for the "most perfect ultimate name" but that what he finds attractive about the "name" of "infinity" is precisely the fact that it escapes all "perfect" or "ultimate" namings. Furthermore, it is not "perfection" but "omnipotence" that weighs the most strongly for Marion in the second Cartesian name. Géry Prouvost, on the other hand, does recognize the importance of the divine name of infinity for Marion, but wonders about its unique status. He finds that Marion's reading is too much influenced by Lévinas here.[50] While Marion's analysis certainly is inspired to some extent by Lévinas, it is not entirely clear why that would be so detrimental. As Wolfgang Röd points out, the major difference or even incompatibility between the two names is that omnipotence/perfection is an intelligible idea that can be clearly grasped, while God as infinite can only be recognized but never comprehended.[51] It is this distinction that is the most significant for Marion and guides his analysis.

Causa Sui

Finally, the thought of God's omnipotence for Marion becomes grounded in causality such that a third definition of God as *causa sui* emerges.[52] This name of God is unique to Descartes and refers to God's grounding of the foundation of all thought of the ego and God's own self-causing. Marion compares the *causa sui* to a third manner of naming God, that of affirmation.[53] Descartes is the first to use this term for God, because the very notion of *causa sui* was considered incoherent by the medieval thinkers. Jean-Marc Narbonne claims in an article responding to Marion's work that Descartes was not the inventor of the notion of *causa sui* but that it can be found in Plotinus and many medieval thinkers. The notions of *causa sui* and aseity are not alternatives, as Marion seems to indicate, but one contradictory concept. He admits, however, that this issue is "marginal to the work of J.-L. Marion," which he finds "admirable in more than one respect."[54] Marion responds to this criticism in *Questions cartésiennes II*, maintaining in greater detail his original position that Descartes is indeed the originator of this concept, since it connotes an impossible contradiction in all medieval thinkers and is not employed as a coherent concept by Plotinus.[55] He goes on to show that Aquinas had outlined two inconsistencies in the notion: (a) A cause must precede its effect while *causa sui* would imply that an effect can precedes its own cause (or is at least simultaneous with it); (b) God is not caused at all but causes all other things.[56] Efficient causality especially is specifically rejected by Aquinas, while that is the very notion that Descartes emphasizes in the *causa sui*.[57] Marion contends that even thinkers who usually have absolutely nothing to do with each other agree in finding the notion of a self-caused cause contradictory: Anselm, Aquinas, Duns Scotus, Ockham, Suarez, Schopenhauer, and Nietzsche.[58]

Marion cites the three responses that deal with this notion and claims that the clearest and maybe even the only way that God can be proven by the natural light of reason is as an efficient cause.[59] Descartes establishes causality as a kind of principle of existence that applies to everything including God. This idea of causality therefore makes possible both an ontology and a theology, therefore results in an onto-theo-logy.[60] Marion even claims that Descartes specifically chose to contradict the entire medieval tradition with this notion in order to establish such an onto-theo-logy. Tradition before and contemporaneous with Descartes insists strongly upon the impossibility of proving God a priori, because God admits of no cause.[61] Causality and a priori proof of God are therefore linked, even for Spinoza who affirms both notions. Marion concludes from this that Descartes introduces the notion of *causa sui* not because he has resolved its internal difficulties — that is far from the case — but rather because he must do so in order to give a proof for God from a priori knowledge, and *causa sui* is the only way to accomplish that.[62] In order to deal with the apparent incoherence of the term, Descartes introduces a notion of analogy between *causa sui* and efficient causality. As indicated above, in Marion's view this notion of analogy does not really work, and it certainly does not recover the theological notion of analogy but rather reverses it: *causa sui* in God is understood by analogy to efficient causality in humans; the finite therefore explains the infinite.[63] Three things result from this: causality becomes not just a divine attribute but defines the divine essence, it remains in tension with Descartes' insistence on divine incomprehensibility, and the logical objections are never answered. This makes an entry of God into metaphysics possible and allows for an onto-theo-logy. It is in this context that Marion makes the rather startling claim that God did not really enter into metaphysics before Descartes. Since the medieval thinkers reject the notion of *causa sui* for God and do not construct an onto-theo-logical system, the supposedly metaphysical status of their thought and especially the role the divine might play in it must be reexamined much more carefully before they can be judged guilty of subjecting God to metaphysics.[64]

Théologie blanche argues that the *causa sui* actually re-establishes analogy between God and humans in a way that leads Descartes also to univocity. Causality and self-sufficiency are attributed to God in the way they function for humans.[65] Efficient causality is not thought starting from God, but is imposed upon God (thus reversing the move of analogy as we have seen above). As do all other beings, God submits to causality and also achieves existence in the same fashion since it is defined by causality.[66] Descartes here consciously rejects St. Thomas' argument that an effect cannot be its own cause and needs to be distinguished from it (and that therefore a notion of *causa sui* is incoherent) by combining and rethinking the idea of efficient causality and divine aseity.[67] He introduces an idea of analogy between divine and human efficiency, which modifies both the idea of efficiency and that of the essence of God. Anything that happens (even when nothing does) must be maintained by divine causality and that includes God: God must thus cause the divine essence which is defined by that very causality. The divine essence itself becomes an efficient causality. The notion of *causa sui* thus establishes epistemological univocity in Descartes, although it does so only tangentially, because God's essence, even interpreted as efficient causality, remains finally "immense and incomprehensible" (TB, 438). Thus "the existence of God does not become causally intelligible except on the condition that its essence appears intrinsically incomprehensible" (TB, 438). Descartes thus asserts both univocity and equivocity at the same time.

Confusion and Incoherence

The combination of these three proofs for God's existence within Descartes' text constitutes an amalgamation of incompatible ways of naming God. According to Marion, Descartes not only confuses the traditional Dionysian ways and their inherent order, but also juxtaposes several traditions of affirming God's existence that are incompatible with each other. Furthermore he adds a third notion, that of the *causa sui*, that is in conflict with the others and illogical within itself. Having outlined these three names in Descartes' argument, Marion wonders whether this juxtaposition does not make the proofs for God's existence incoherent. If they are no longer organized in a clear hierarchy and become disconnected from their theological contexts, they must end up contradicting each other.[68] As we have seen, Marion suggests that each of the three different definitions of (or names for) God is privileged in one of the Cartesian proofs for God's existence (idea of an infinite substance, divine essence that is sum of perfections, ultimate causality). At the same time, as we have seen, each of these names goes back to one of the Dionysian ways or paths toward God (affirmative, negative, eminence), and finally each takes up one figure of evidence for God from medieval thought (infinity from Duns Scotus, perfection from Ockham, *causa sui* invented by Descartes). Descartes thus provides a kind of summary of all the available options of the tradition. Yet, in thus taking up different and even contradictory positions on divine determinations, Descartes exposes a tension that is an essential incompatibility: "Descartes at once and successively holds two determinations of God . . . which, historically, were posited as adversaries, and irreconcilable ones at that" (MP, 256; PM, 269–70). Corresponding to the three proofs, Descartes has three metaphysical names for God: (1) the idea of an infinite substance (that causes the idea of God in me) and is characterized especially by infinity and incomprehensibility; (2) the idea of a divine essence that encompasses all perfections and according to which God is the supremely perfect being (ontological argument); (3) the idea of *causa sui* (which later becomes the principle of sufficient reason). According to the second definition, God perfects properties in us, but this contradicts the first idea of transcendence and incomprehensibility. While the first way of infinity is an apophatic name, the second is more akin to a version of the *via affirmativa*.[69] The first definition of infinity is contradicted by the second definition, which refers to God as an accumulation of finite perfections. In the first proof, God is assumed to be outside the method (incomprehensible), while he is enclosed within it in the second determination (perfect but not incomprehensible). This tension is exacerbated by the introduction of defining God as *causa sui*, which might be interpreted to refer to the way of eminence. By submitting God to a principle depending upon the light of reason (namely that of "sufficient reason"), this proof contradicts the insistence on incomprehensibility of the first one. Furthermore, in speaking of God as "overabundant power," the proof of causality is in accord with the first definition (infinity) but in opposition to the second. Marion draws out the incompatibility of these various proofs and definitions and concludes, "Descartes employs several determinations that can no longer be used interchangeably as soon as their origins all refer to theological debates in which these determinations earned an irreducible singularity" (MP, 270; PM, 285). Instead, he insists that Descartes' thought about God becomes so tenuous that it becomes "a complex web of contradictions" (MP, 271; PM, 286).

That these three ideas or proofs are contradictory is not a failure, in Marion's view:

> Rather, it attests to the fact that God cannot adequately be conceived within the limited discourse of metaphysics. Descartes here boldly and explicitly confronts the tension between the demand for a conception of God that is intelligible to humans and respect for His transcendence. The fact that Descartes's metaphysical theology remains indeterminate and breaks down into several theses (just as light breaks down when it passes through a prism)

makes it, somewhat paradoxically, *the* radical position on the question of God at the beginning of modern thought. ("Idea of God," 278; QCII, 249; emphasis his)

Descartes' followers will carry his thought further and highlight its essential incompatibility by emphasizing only one of these proofs and focusing on only one definition of or name for God. In fact, according to Marion, the metaphysical systems that emerge after Descartes will all take up one of his definitions of God and allow their metaphysics to be determined by it.[70] Since Descartes has destroyed the precarious balance between the three ways of naming God in a specific hierarchy, he has also condemned all subsequent philosophical thought to metaphysics and idolatry.

This concern with the divine names and the hierarchy that organizes them can be traced through all of Marion's work. He will engage in a detailed analysis of Dionysius in his theological work (specifically in *Idol and Distance*), a similar analysis (as a response to Derrida) will crown his phenomenological work (in the last chapter of *De Surcroît/In Excess*), and in his recent book *The Erotic Phenomenon* he makes the startling claim that an erotic experience must necessarily be expressed in the language of the divine names. It is thus significant that Descartes' metaphysics emerges as a deliberate confusion of the theology of the divine names. Only an appropriate use of this theology, especially a recovery of the Dionysian way of eminence, according to Marion, can make possible an adequate naming of God.

Pascal and Divine Incomprehensibility

After considering Descartes' metaphysical system and especially its culmination in the proofs for God's existence, Marion goes on to employ Pascal as a critique of Descartes on this point. This challenge in respect to Cartesian metaphysics has already been outlined earlier. According to Marion, Pascal is even more strongly opposed to Descartes' proofs for God's existence, which he rejects as "useless, uncertain, and prideful" (MP, 289; PM, 307). Metaphysics cannot know about God. The questions of Being and existence are struck with idolatry for Pascal, as they will become idolatrous for Marion. While Pascal follows Descartes on many philosophical points, he consistently disagrees with him on all theological issues, especially regarding the definition of God. Like Descartes, Pascal emphasizes God's infinity and incomprehensibility, but he does so far more strongly and usually in opposition to Descartes. And, as Wolfgang Röd recognizes, in the final count Marion is closer to Pascal than to Descartes.[71] I will outline briefly what Marion highlights about Pascal's response to Descartes to show how Marion's use of this thinker previews and reflects his own concerns that become more explicit in the theological and phenomenological work.

Marion shows how Pascal dissolves any neat division between notions of the infinite and the indefinite (which Descartes thought necessary, especially to distinguish between the three "objects" of special metaphysics: God, soul, and world) and refuses any articulation of these beings in a system of special metaphysics. Marion claims that Pascal trivializes Descartes' infinite to the point where it becomes a meaningless notion: "God is said by the infinite, for Pascal as for Descartes; but for Pascal, infinite no longer says anything, while for Descartes it utters a privileged concept. From now on, as the infinite is dissolved, God, drawing back in the same degree, fades away. His nameless silence abandons the discourse — grown idle, gregarious, and vain — of the sciences, and first of all of metaphysics" (MP, 293; PM, 310). For Pascal, God becomes a *deus absconditus* of whom no proofs are possible. He consistently refuses to "prove" God and rejects all metaphysical discourse about God. "Metaphysics," for Pascal, becomes a synonym for "proofs for God's existence," both of which are judged pointless endeavors. Pascal thinks that any proofs for God are futile and useless. They induce pride. They are uncertain and thus to be rejected. Marion interprets the argument of the wager as taking up Descartes' metaphysical argument especially, because it implies a necessary move of faith. Marion emphasizes Pascal's complete rejection of any relation between philosophical knowledge and an experience of God and insists that for Pascal knowledge of God is possible only in a loving relationship: "The goal and the stakes of a discourse on God are not summed up in the knowledge of God; knowing God even exposes one to a fearful danger: pride. It is not a matter of either first or only knowing God, but of loving him. . . . The pride of knowing God (deism) does not draw any closer to God than does ignorance of him (atheism), for the knowledge of God is made worthy only by loving him" (MP, 296; PM, 314). One does not approach God through metaphysical language but only in complete submission of faith. Pascal here employs less philosophical and more traditionally theological language. He has moved from a justification of belief in God or a presumption to have knowledge of the divine to the desire for complete devotion and a decision of submission that is outside any interest in divine existence or "being." Marion summarizes the import of this on the relation between God and metaphysics:

> The ultimate question is no longer pursued in view of grasping the relation between God, the being par excellence, and existence in general, but in view of the relation between man and his own pride (or sin), thus between man and charity (Jesus Christ). The irruption of the parameter instituted by charity or pride disqualifies the pretense that metaphysical discourse has to posing the highest question about God. With respect to God, it is not a matter of knowing if he exists or not, as if *to be/to exist* would benefit, vis-à-vis God, from an unconditioned and unquestionable precedence and similar excellence. In contrast, faced with God, *to be/to exist* are seen as one idol among others, though no doubt the most radical, since it permits the metaphysician to dodge, by dissimulating, the reversal of interrogation. (MP, 297; PM, 315)

The language of existence that is applied to God in the metaphysical proofs and that is seen as such a primary question instead emerges as idolatrous. As Marion will show in *God without Being*, the language of charity or faith is more pertinent to God than that of being or existence. To inquire only into God's existence is to turn the divine into an object and is therefore an idolatrous — if not a blasphemous — project. Marion points out the implications of this recognition: "With Pascal, this interrogation, far from setting out from the metaphysician and heading toward God . . . is now deployed from God to man, who has been despoiled of the ontological idol and charged with the task of deciding if he loves God — or not. God no longer has to prove his existence before the metaphysician so much as the latter, unveiled in his humanity, has to decide if he can say 'Lord, I give you all'" (MP, 297; PM, 315). Unlike for Descartes, for Pascal we move from the divine to the human, not the reverse. This, of course, corresponds exactly to the requirements for the doctrine of analogy that Marion has outlined. Instead of emphasizing the human control of the divine, who has to submit to having the divine existence proven, humans ought to open themselves in receptivity to God.[72] The fundamental direction of this divine-human relation must be reversed. Although Marion does not spell this out for Pascal (and in fact sometimes distances himself from Pascal's "fideism"), he does seem to indicate that Pascal is proceeding in the right direction and is correcting what is problematic in Descartes.

Pascal suggests that Descartes makes mere utilitarian use of God, but has nothing to say that would encourage and support faith.[73] For Pascal, the very issue of existence is missing the point of God (an obvious parallel to Marion's argument in *God without Being*). According to Pascal "Descartes misses the question of God, not just because his metaphysical proofs remain uncertain, but above all because they remain useless for salvation — in short, because they simply do not see that with God, it is less an issue of his existence than of our decision concerning him" (MP, 298; PM, 316). Marion goes on to analyze §556 in Pascal's *Pensées*, where he explicitly opposes himself to Descartes' project of establishing existence of God and immortality of soul. Pascal thinks that it is blasphemy "to claim to deal in a strictly philosophical rigor with what belongs first of all to charity, thus to theology" (MP, 300; PM, 317). Pascal cites Descartes' most original and most powerful thesis, the doctrine of creation of eternal truths, and condemns it as the "pagan blasphemy par excellence." Any proof of God then is condemned by Pascal as a heretical or blasphemous endeavor. He maintains adamantly that God can only be known in Christ. Although the notion of the creation of the eternal truth seems to escape metaphysics and Descartes insists on this thesis in order to guard God's infinity, Pascal criticizes precisely this argument the most sharply. Metaphysics can never accede to real knowledge of God because it begins with a false starting point that obscures the question from the very outset. A desire to know God in a purely intellectual fashion shows an idolatrous stance, before any inquiry has even taken place. God cannot be known by human intellectual knowledge.

Pascal makes the shortcomings of metaphysics in respect to God abundantly clear: in its obsession with certainty and clarity, evidence and method, metaphysics misses the divine completely, because God is always beyond anything that can be grasped by the human mind and could be submitted to methodical investigation. This is not merely a recognition that our human knowledge is too limited to reach the divine and that God is a little bit beyond our capacity to understand. Rather it constitutes the rejection of *any* philosophical attempt to reach God. Pascal therefore serves as the figure of a *theological* overcoming of metaphysical thought, as a language of charity and not being. As pointed out already at the end of chapter 1, Marion maintains that Pascal is thoroughly and faithfully Cartesian in his philosophy and yet completely "overcomes" it with his theological thought. He does so not by showing it to be wrong but by rendering it irrelevant in light of a higher thought. Theological talk, for both Pascal and Marion, transgresses and renders metaphysics "destitute." The step outside of metaphysics in Pascal is accomplished by a decentering of the Cartesian ego and its metaphysical concepts through the divine gaze and the mystery of Christ. This higher thought is an explication of the God of Scripture (as opposed to the God of the philosophers), the God of Christ, the God of abundant and self-sacrificing charity.[74] Much of Marion's own work attempts to carry further such a theological overcoming of metaphysics, especially in *God without Being* and *Idol and Distance.*

We can also already see how Marion's theological work is profoundly grounded in his analysis of the late medieval context. First, it shows why Marion insists on an "infinite distance" between God and creatures: it is precisely such distance, which collapses into neither univocity (as it does for most of the thinkers) nor into complete equivocity (as it does for Descartes), that he wants to articulate in his work and that he thinks is the only appropriate fashion of approaching God. Second, it also illuminates what Marion means by starting from "God's point of view," an expression and move for which he has been sharply criticized, as we saw in the introduction to this part. It does not mean that he claims to have some privileged access to the divine and can talk of God without context. Quite to the contrary, Marion is always extremely aware of the context of any argument, as this analysis of Descartes' theology surely has shown. Rather, it means that he wants to preserve the kind of analogy between God and humans that Aquinas and Dionysius express (as opposed to Suarez or Cajetan), one that moves terminology from uncreated to created, from infinite to finite, not the other way around. Finally, it illustrates the profound importance of the language of the divine names for expressing an appropriate doctrine of analogy and the dire results of a breakdown and confusion of this language. All of these concerns and presuppositions will inform Marion's theological and his phenomenological work significantly.

I would contend that Marion's work in theology especially, but possibly even his phenomenology, constitute attempts to recover a language for the divine that would escape univocity, namely an attempt to recover a new version of analogy employing a modified version of the language of the divine names. And it seems to me that it is precisely for that reason that Marion makes the two assertions for which his God-talk has been most often criticized: on the one hand, that one must speak "from God's point of view," and on the other hand, that one must employ a language of excess, brilliance, and saturation when speaking of the divine or of a possible phenomenon of revelation. Yet the foregoing analysis of Marion's writing on Descartes and the Cartesian context are helpful not only to clarify some of these (for many critics) troubling remarks, but also help us understand better what is going on in Marion's theology and even in his phenomenology. What I want to argue is that not only is it Marion's continued concern to guard against univocity in contemporary language for God (a fairly obvious point), but also that both his theology and his phenomenology precisely are attempts to recover a new version of a doctrine of analogy (with the notions of distance and the icon) and a quasi-Dionysian *via eminentia*. Marion *does not* speak of either his theology or his phenomenology in terms of analogy, probably partially due to his critique of the confusion about this discourse in the late medieval context.[75] Yet, as I want to show in the following chapters, his reading of what constitutes analogy in the best sense of that term — namely one that preserves proper distance and does not collapse into either univocity or equivocity, one that proceeds from God to human instead of the reverse — is a good way also for understanding Marion's primary concern regarding the divine in his theological and phenomenological writings. As in part 1, I will explore this thesis first for Marion's more theological texts and then for his more recent phenomenological work.

five
Theology and God
"The Glory of the Divine
Befalls Us Only Obliquely"

Already in his study of Descartes, Marion is deeply concerned with appropriate language about God. I have examined how Marion interprets the late medieval move toward univocity, the decline of the language of analogy, and the Dionysian ways of naming God as important contexts for ascertaining the status of Descartes' theology. We have seen how Marion views Descartes' writings as more faithful theologically than those of some of his contemporaries, precisely because of his refusal to engage in the movement toward univocity and to speak of God or define the divine explicitly. In chapter 2 I also outlined Marion's presentations of more recent versions of univocity and metaphysical idolatry, for example in Nietzsche and Heidegger. Although some of them try to escape metaphysics or reject traditional idols of God, all of them either institute new idols or do not exceed the old ones sufficiently or successfully. In Marion's more theological works he therefore attempts to outline such an overcoming himself by formulating a kind of language about God that would escape metaphysical constrictions and speak of God more adequately. He does not do so in a vacuum. The insights gained in his study of Descartes and the late medieval context will serve as important pointers for Marion's desire to free God from the past idolatries of thought, to protect God's name. He attempts to distinguish the concept "God" from non-conceptual thought about God, whom he even "crosses out" in his *God without Being,* in order to indicate the difference. God must always be thought in terms of distance. Marion defines this as a kind of crossing, in which God's coming toward us is crossed by our worship/praise/prayer toward him, although the two are never identified or confused with each other. God is never subject to our thoughts or definitions, but always escapes them. God remains at a distance: a distance that recedes with our approaching it and that can only be traversed or crossed, but never eliminated. The language of being and causality must be replaced with one of distance and charity. Philosophical definitions *of* God must be replaced by theological talk *to* God. Or, as Ruud Welten puts it: "If there is a God, it is not because I feel the urge to speak about Him, but because He speaks to me. This is the key to Marion's work as I see it. . . . Thought, according to Marion, is indeed capable of opening up to God."[1]

There are several figures to Marion's thought about God that all point to the same irreducibility and distance of the divine. They closely correspond to his Cartesian project and are firmly grounded in it. Like Descartes he refuses univocal language for God and seeks to articulate a renewed doctrine of analogy. In the legacy of Dionysius he attempts to update the language of the divine names. And like Pascal he searches for a language of charity, a place other than philosophy and beyond its logic. I will thus investigate the terms and imagery that Marion uses for God or for more appropriate language about the divine while arguing for them as representing certain fundamental theological moves already outlined: (a) a refusal of univocity, in particular with the terminology of the icon; (b) a reformulation of the doctrines of analogy, especially with the notion of distance; (c) a recovery of the language of the divine names as culminating in praise as a kind of performative language; and (d) a proposal of a theology of kenotic charity in a realm other and beyond philosophy. Of course these moves cannot be distinguished quite that neatly insofar as the importance of distance arises already in the terminology of the icon, the language of the divine names is closely linked to the notion of distance, and love or charity plays a role in all of them. Just as the refusal of univocity was linked to a demise of the language of analogy and the language of analogy employed the ways of naming God, the different aspects of Marion's theology also interweave and inform each other.

The Icon: Refusal of Univocity

Marion opposes the theological icon to the metaphysical idol. In chapter 2 I already outlined the idol's deep implication in metaphysics. More importantly in this context, however, the idol establishes univocity between the divine "object" and the human observer. While Marion himself does not put it in these terms, that Cartesian concern always stands behind his rejection of idolatry.

Marion emphasizes that although the idol presents a true vision of the divine, it is a particular and limited vision that matches exactly the human gaze that has captured it. He highlights a kind of mirroring function of the idol that displays exactly as much as the human gaze can bear and thus sends this gaze back upon itself. Hence this is a perfectly univocal gaze, where the divine mirrors the human gaze precisely. Marion is troubled not merely by the control the observer exercises on the idol, but far more by this limitation imposed by the gaze. The divine becomes confined entirely to the scope of the human gaze that sees it. As Marion puts it, "the idol consigns the divine to the measure of a human gaze . . . it presents a certain low-water mark of the divine; it resembles what the human gaze has experienced of the divine" (GWB, 14; DSL, 24). Not only are both measured with the same gaze, but it is the human gaze that determines the measure.[2] Whether visual or conceptual, such idolatry perfectly corresponds to the epistemological univocity Marion has outlined in Kepler, Galileo, and Mersenne (even though it speaks the language of art or philosophy and not of mathematics). Like the late medieval and early modern moves to make the divine subject to human measure and comprehension, idolatry delimits the divine image or concept by the measure of the human gaze and thus eliminates any true difference or distance.

The icon serves as Marion's response to this univocity. Most importantly, the icon does not serve as a "stopping point" for the gaze in the way in which that is the case for the idol, but rather it becomes a kind of window through which the gaze travels toward the "unenvisageable," that which cannot ever be contained in a human gaze.[3] The icon therefore essentially refuses univocity between divine and human by insisting on the impossibility of the gaze being filled by the divine according to its own measure or by appropriating the gaze to itself. The icon allows the divine to "saturate" the visible without being fixed by it. It makes possible a kind of separation or distance between the human and the divine. Idols abolish distance, while the icon preserves it. In *God without Being*, the icon is interpreted as the best manner of speaking about God. The icon opens onto the invisible without exhausting it or giving it to be seen. It allows the invisible to travel through it and to strike the observers, to envisage them. Marion says: "The essential in the icon — the intention that envisages — comes to it from elsewhere, or comes to it as that elsewhere whose invisible strangeness saturates the visibility of the face with meaning" (GWB, 21; DSL, 34). The icon thus preserves God's transcendence by refusing the mirroring function of the idol. While the idol assumes univocity between the viewer and the divine by circumscribing what is seen by the terms in which it can be grasped by the one observing, the icon refuses any such limitation. The gaze travels through and beyond it and indeed originates from God, not from the viewer, who finds him- or herself envisaged by the divine other. As Marion had criticized the false reversal of terminology in the late medieval writers in which purely human categories, such as being, become applied to the divine in a univocal fashion, he now reverses that movement with the terminology of the icon. Marion emphasizes especially the inability to measure or contain the divine in the icon: "The icon recognizes no other measure than its own and infinite excessiveness [*démesure*]; whereas the idol measures the divine to the scope of the gaze of he who then sculpts it, the icon accords in the visible only a face whose invisibility is given all the more to be envisaged that its revelation offers an abyss that the eyes of men never finish probing" (GWB, 21; DSL, 33). Ruud Welten summarizes:

> The icon thwarts that which applies to the idol. The icon is not apparent, not analysable, not visible, not comprehensible. Representing a non-idolatrous attitude, the icon is the counterpart of the idol. The icon overcomes the invisible mirror, the fixing, and the intentional gaze, which applies to the idol. The icon itself claims the gaze of the onlooker. The gaze no longer belongs to the onlooker but to the icon itself. . . . the icon recognizes no standards but its own infinite transgression.[4]

While univocity establishes a common measure between divine and human and allows the human to measure the divine, the icon refuses all measure and acknowledges the essential incomprehensibility of God. Marion establishes this also for "conceptual icons": "Every pretension to absolute knowledge belongs to the domain of the idol" (GWB, 23; DSL, 37).

The icon, however, does not merely speak of the difference between divine and human, but also makes possible a connection between them. Hence it does not merely preserve the divine from univocity with the human, but also opens toward analogy. Welten is right to point out in this context that Marion rejects the medieval doctrine of "analogy of being."[5] Marion does not reject, however, the concern and paradox of analogous naming, namely the need to speak of the divine neither univocally nor equivocally. It is this concern and paradox that the terminology of icon and distance seeks to recover in my view. Analogy holds in tension God's immanence and God's utter ineffability. Marion wants to recover and uphold this tension. Contemplating the icon becomes a way of opening oneself to the invisible gaze that comes from a distance and cannot be grasped. Here "union increases in the measure of distinction, and reciprocally" (GWB, 23; DSL, 36). The icon makes it possible to meet God without reduction because it opens the self to the gaze of transcendence. Marion explicates this aspect of the icon further in *The Crossing of the Visible*, where he engages in a detailed analysis of the iconography of the Eastern tradition and its theology of veneration.[6] The icon allows for a crossing of gazes in prayer where both partners are separated by an immeasurable distance even as they envisage each other in love. The icon thus recovers a first essential function of the doctrines of analogy. It reverses the movement from humans to God that characterizes the idol (and metaphysics) and instead allows the gaze to originate from God and envision the human being. Of course, Marion has pointed to this as a particularly important direction of the doctrines of analogy, namely that they begin their move of analogy with God and proceed from God to humans. Only thereby can they avoid the blasphemy of attributing merely human categories to God. Humans are consequently defined as derivative from and dependent upon God. The terminology of the icon attempts to achieve a similar movement in its reversal of gazes. This is not a mere reversal, however. Welten points out: "What is important is not just that the intentionality of the icon is orientated towards me instead of the reverse, but the consciousness experiencing this as a gift that is given. The icon is the intentional gaze of the other in me. The icon approaches me, gives itself. The point is this gift to consciousness."[7]

The terminology of idol and icon is probably the most well-known aspect of Marion's work, especially since it reoccurs in a different form in his phenomenological writings. Both Stijn van den Bossche and Tobias Specker have argued that this terminology identifies what is most unique and most important in Marion's work and that the rest of his writings must be read in light of the analyses of idol and icon. While I try to show the reverse (namely that icon and idol have to be read in light of the insights established in the engagement with Descartes), their arguments bear consideration at this point, especially considering the extensive analysis Specker provides. Specker emphasizes especially the importance of the invisible in the icon. He argues that the invisible becomes to some extent visible in the icon while remaining invisible. It becomes visible as invisible and therefore points to the difference between the icon and the one represented in it (AGD, 212). He goes on to show how the saturated phenomenon has a similar iconic structure. He summarizes his insights as follows:

> The theology of the icon confirms that on final count the icon is not realistic, without being anti-realistic or surrealistic. The theology of the icon also emphasizes that the icon does not represent [*darstellt*] anything divine, but rather destroys [*macht zunichte*] any representation. The material icon serves as pure pointer to the unrepresentable holy and divine, which in turn is highly present precisely in its effectiveness. By the divine being present and effective in the icon precisely as nonrepresentable, the theology of the icon shows a parallel to Marion's crossing of opposites. Finally, in the required reversal of the intuitive understood from its responsorial status, one also hears echoes of the theology of the icon, which proceeds from an inspired, if not glorified, painter who responds to the ethical demand. (AGD, 217)

Specker also highlights the importance of iconic language and the relation between the icon and faith. Unlike Specker, who emphasizes the continuity between Marion's theology and his phenomenology, Stijn van den Bossche makes a distinction between what he calls Marion I and Marion II.[8] The former is concerned with theology, the latter with phenomenology. Similarly to Specker, he sees the issue of idol and icon as all-pervasive and as Marion's most fundamental concepts. Bossche's argument is primarily apologetic, and he is particularly interested in the apologetic promise of Marion's work. He claims that "throughout the study this [whether God cannot be perceived as immanent in phenomenology] is the sometimes hidden theological-apologetic agenda of *Étant donné*—which does *not*, however, in itself submit the phenomenology to theology: Marion's laying down of theology means at the same time its deposition in phenomenality—as nothing more but also nothing less than a rational possibility" (329). He repeatedly insists that both Marion I and II are "apologetes" (337). He in great detail outlines Marion's suggestion of the doubly saturated phenomenon of revelation, focusing entirely on the figure of Christ (340–41). He concludes that Marion gets rid of recent philosophy's tendency to relativism and refusal of transcendence. "The particular—even revolutionary—character of Marion's phenomenology consists in this: truth in it adopts a strictly *immanent* character, and hence need no longer be founded by a transcendent God or one of His transcendental surrogates" (344). He thinks that Marion combines the God of the philosophers with the God of faith and shows that they can be flip sides of each other, and summarizes what he sees as Marion's central achievement: "Marion lets God, remaining the Invisible, appear for reason" (345). While Bossche maybe moves too quickly to an apologetic interpretation of Marion's language, he is right to point out Marion's concern both to preserve the divine ineffability and infinity and to maintain that the divine is indeed given to experience in some fashion. This concern becomes even more explicit in Marion's terminology of distance.

Distance: A Recovery of Analogy

The language of distance carries the analysis of the icon further by recovering the second aspect of the doctrines of analogy, namely their intent to keep a separation between divine and human that makes relationship possible without falling into either univocity or complete equivocity.[9] Marion argues that one can speak of God only in terms of distance. Distance guards against univocity. It introduces something irreducible between God and the world, especially between the divine and the human. Distance thus refers to the relation between God and humans, to a certain paradox of withdrawal and advent, nearness and distinction which alone makes an encounter with God possible. Horner defines well what Marion means by this term:

> Distance primarily refers to a separation or spacing that makes relationships (intra-trinitarian, divine with human, and human with human) possible. But it is also that which protects those relationships from totalisation, that is, it prevents us from reducing the other (divine or human, or even work of art) to our own dimensions. However, distance is used in its strongest sense to mean God, or grace, the self-giving of whom resists comprehension even while pointing towards the origin of such excess. (MTI, 60)

We have seen already that for Marion only God's infinity gets beyond ontology and causality, and only God's incomprehensibility escapes epistemology. Distance designates both infinity and incomprehensibility and emerges as more radical than ontological difference (Heidegger), *différance* (Derrida), and the thought of the Other (Lévinas).[10] Marion's theological category of distance, and specifically his thought of God, are asserted to be more successful than all present philosophical transgressions of metaphysical constrictions. Distance is able to get beyond metaphysical restrictions of God to a more appropriate speech. Marion, then, does not conceive of distance only negatively, in order to distinguish it from ontological difference or to guard against any too close identification with the divine. In my view, it also makes the more positive and constructive move of allowing for analogy. As analogy made it possible to speak of God, humans, and their relationship without falling into the extremes of either univocity (as in Suarez, Mersenne, and others) or complete equivocity (as in Descartes), the terminology of distance attempts to accomplish the same balance. Distance both speaks of the similarity between the divine and the human and enables relation between them while never losing sight of the immeasurable and infinite distinction between them. Coupled with the terminology of the icon, distance begins from God and is traversed from God to humans instead of the reverse, just as the doctrines of analogy emphasized. Let me establish this by examining more carefully what Marion argues in respect to distance.

First, distance guards against univocity. It goes beyond the simple distinctions between beings drawn by ontological difference. It emphasizes the divine transcendence that can never be measured by human beings and is completely beyond anything we can fathom or describe. It speaks of a God even beyond Being, a God of absence, a God who is crossed out and cannot be grasped by any definition. It makes any language of univocity impossible, because in it "intimacy with the divine strictly coincides with withdrawal" (ID, 139; IeD, 178). Distance, Marion insists, cannot be defined, because we know always only one pole in the relationship that it attempts to traverse.[11] In distinguishing it from ontological difference, Marion points out that distance always hovers on the brink of becoming a simple absence. While ontological difference is still at work even when (or especially when) it is forgotten, the forgetting of distance leads to its abolishment, resulting either in idolatry or the death of God, appropriation of God or complete atheism. Distance hence tries to maintain the fragile balance of analogy between complete univocity and utter equivocity. In the distance it establishes between divine and human it threatens to become a simple absence.

Some commentators have stopped here. In a comparison of Marion's work with that of Jean-Yves Lacoste, Jeffrey Bloechl for example fears that there is a danger in the notion of distance that God would be "not only beyond names but also without names, which comes perilously close to being simply anonymous."[12] He summarizes that "what will suffice for both Marion and Lacoste is that it proves possible, on their terms, to turn from religious experience to philosophical descriptions of events and structures which the believer then does indeed recognize" but asks in response, "Is it not the case, contrary to everything Marion and Lacoste have argued, that it is precisely the content of the object or practice where God is revealed that stimulates religious desire and shapes religious experience?"[13] He concludes that "Marion and Lacoste offer us a general theory of human existence and experience in which the religious horizon is extended beyond the reach of any particular denomination or creed—one that risks, then, becoming detached from the particularity of the experiences which those denominations and creeds profess."[14] A strictly apophatic theology threatens to collapse into utter equivocity" and no longer allows any meaningful relation between the divine and the human.

Second, therefore, distance must also guard against equivocity and be able to establish some kind of relation. If God is so immeasurably distant, how do we encounter the divine at all? In what ways is "analogy" between God and humans still possible? Despite the great emphasis placed on the divine transcendence and ineffability, Marion also repeatedly speaks of God's presence or immanence in several ways. In *Idol and Distance* he does so through the terminology of the gift (that opens a fourth dimension). He takes up this language in *God without Being*, but goes on to stress especially the movement of love or charity. Both of these will of course become important for his phenomenology also (the terminology of the gift has already been examined in chapter 3). Yet Marion engages in two more explicitly theological affirmations of God's immanence and the possibility of speaking about God. On the one hand, he takes up St. Dionysius' language of the divine names as an appropriate manner for speaking of the divine. This should not be surprising, considering what he has argued about the link between the failure of the doctrine of analogy and the confusion of the language of the divine names in Descartes. On the other hand, in the context of his analysis of charity, Marion also provides an explication of the incarnation and an articulation of a Christian theory of atonement, neither of which seem to have received much attention in the secondary literature. This may be due to the fact that it is such an explicitly Christian and theological account (in fact, a rather Eastern one). To disregard it completely, however, is to miss something important in Marion's work. I will consider both of these attempts to hold in tension God's incomprehensibility and the human need to speak of and approach the divine, beginning with Marion's use of St. Dionysius in *Idol and Distance*.

The Three Ways: Naming God in Praise

Marion continues his recovery of analogy in terms of distance by speaking of the kind of language that might be appropriate to traverse such distance: "distance must, in order that we might inhabit it, be identified. It will be identifiable only if we can say it and speak of it. We will be able to speak of it only if we come from it and remain in it. To speak of distance: concerning it, and also starting from it. But what language can be suitable to distance?" (ID, 139; IeD,

178). In response Marion returns, not unsurprisingly, to Dionysius for inspiration. This return is significant, not only because it is directly grounded in the medieval appropriation of this thinker and Descartes' deliberate confusion of these ways of naming God, but also because Dionysius will continue to guide Marion even in his phenomenological writings, in particular in his criticism of Derrida. It is not at all difficult to perceive the continuity in this case. Although we cannot determine God or name God appropriately, Dionysius provides a way to speak of this distance, or at least to indicate it. We have seen in our discussion of Descartes how the medievals marked this distance by the language of analogy. Marion suggests that a recovery of the language of divine naming becomes possible through the discourse of praise.[15] He insists that this particular language escapes the idolatry of marking God as an object by speaking of God "divinely," a contention that will also inform his more phenomenological writings on this topic.

Marion outlines Dionysian theology by distinguishing between three ways or paths toward God. The first way is the *kataphatic* or affirmative way: we use many terms of God (often derived from Scripture) that at first seem quite appropriate, such as those of being, goodness, power, wisdom, etc. We affirm that God is good, has power and wisdom. We realize, however, that these terms do not describe God fully or might in some sense even be false. In a second move, the *apophatic* one, we therefore deny this human terminology of goodness, power, or wisdom of God and judge it inappropriate to describe the divine.[16] In Dionysius, affirmation and negation thus "play with each other" and show the failure of all human approaches to transcendence. Marion interprets Dionysius to continue beyond these two ways that predicate (or deny) certain things of God to a third way which no longer predicates anything at all, neither positively nor negatively. He calls this the "way of eminence," a final movement of praise or adoration that is no longer concerned with either affirmation or denial.[17] Marion therefore does not merely summarize the traditional Dionysian pathways, but seeks to recover them as appropriate ways of speaking of the divine today by constantly pointing to the implications of this language for metaphysical idolatry and linguistic reference.

The theology of St. Dionysius has two important implications for Marion. On the one hand, it protects and dissimulates the name of God, making it impossible to locate the name in a clear concept or an object humans might control. On the other hand, Marion highlights the pragmatic function of this discourse which turns its referent into an actor who affects and transforms the speaker. First, Marion insists that through this theology the divine Name remains unnameable and obscure. The Name withdraws even as it gives itself.[18] Predication becomes impossible. To some extent, apophasis — the negative movement — already accomplishes this: "apophasis no longer only frees discourse from the obvious improprieties; it also eliminates the highest conceptions as impertinent. Struck in their assurance, they are inverted and abolish their illusory primacy" (ID, 146; IeD, 185). Yet simple negation is not enough, but the third movement is indeed necessary in order to overcome even the "categorical pretension" and idolatry of apophasis (ID, 147; IeD, 186). The combination of both movements (kataphasis and apophasis) while balancing each other "indexes the failure of our linguistic approach" (ID, 149; IeD, 187). The third movement, that of eminence, which goes beyond both, does not reestablish predication. Rather it insists even more strongly on the impossibility of all definition for or predication of the divine by moving to a discourse of praise or prayer. According to Marion, the only way to speak of God appropriately is to praise or to bless instead of to name or predicate. This is a new kind of discourse, one of silence that keeps distance and is finally unable to speak.[19]

This silence of praise results in a union with God that becomes much more performative than descriptive. Instead of "saying something," it acts. We do not define God but render ourselves and receive even this rendering as a gift: "we discover ourselves, in distance, delivered to ourselves, given, not abandoned, to ourselves" (ID, 153; IeD, 192). Victor Kal summarizes this performative use of language: "Being unable to speak is only a pause, a temporary period. Ultimately, it is quite possible to say something relating to God, even to utter a word we find 'fitting for God.' Something true can be said when it is 'made true,' namely, in performative speaking. But the 'performance,' the action that makes the speaking true, is not the speaker's accomplishment; it is a *gift* from the other side. Truth, concerning God, *resounds* in me."[20] We can only receive distance as gift, not appropriate it. We cannot speak of God but are changed by God's address, receive our identity from this distant appeal. Marion concludes that this notion of distance does not separate us from God, but rather allows us to establish a relationship in which we actually discover ourselves in a new fashion.[21] In attempting to speak of the divine distance, then, we are ultimately given not God but ourselves. Instead of determining God's name, we ourselves are given a name by God. God remains always unthinkable, always escapes us. We cannot comprehend the unthinkable but must receive it in love.

Thomas Guarino embraces most of Marion's account, although he reads it as too critical of the tradition. He interprets as Marion's project "to establish the limits of the being question, discarding, in the process, the classical and transcendental metaphysical baggage that has led to a distorted image of divine life. . . . what Marion ultimately offers is a kind of deconstruction of attempts to name God, a project undertaken precisely in service to God's Otherness."[22] Of Marion's account of Dionysian language he says specifically,

> To claim that predication must yield to praise appears to limit theological language to its doxological and anagogical dimensions, thereby enervating its cognitive spine. Of course, if one's understanding of revelation is epiphanic, then the status of theological language will be largely symbolic, in the sense of allegorical and suggestive rather than analogical, in the sense of predicable and referential. Such an approach allows a much wider berth

for constructive theology than has been the case classically, but it moves in a very different direction than the tradition on the issue of the intelligible yield of theological statements.[23]

Although he lauds Marion for his effort to preserve the divine otherness, he also sees problems in Marion's account: "Marion underestimates, in a significant way, the extent to which the tradition was on guard about excessive presence. All are aware of theology's long history of attempts (not always successful) to avoid monism, univocity, and conceptual idolatry, to shun reference without difference when speaking of God. One may clearly identify a palpable 'idoloclastic' fervor in the tradition that Marion does not acknowledge."[24] In light of Marion's careful work on Descartes and the late medieval tradition, and his frequent references to the early Eastern Fathers, this argument does not hold water. It is simply not correct to say that Marion does not recognize attempts in the tradition to preserve the divine difference and ineffability.

Yet, for Marion, the loving reception of the gift does, in fact, make participation in God possible. It is precisely such participation that guards against a complete equivocity between divine and human: "Participation therefore never jumps over distance in claiming to abolish it, but traverses it as the sole field for union. Participation grows by participating in the imparticipable as such, and it increases the imparticipability of the imparticipable all the more insofar as it more intimately participates therein" (ID, 156; IeD, 196–97). Marion explains that to participate in the unthinkable is to acknowledge it as unthinkable. It never eliminates distance but always invites one to further participation. This opens to the Eastern thought of *theosis* (deification, participation in God): "God is not jealous of his divinity — but man lacks ambition. He does not grasp that nothing less than the distance of Goodness offers itself to be traversed through an imparticipable participation" (ID, 160; IeD, 198). In his appropriation of the Eastern theological tradition, Marion does articulate clear accounts of incarnation and atonement, despite Guarino's (and also John Milbank's) assertions to the contrary. Through the language of praise, then, Marion has moved through several and increasingly more complicated versions of distance. From simple distance that acknowledges only that God cannot be identified as an object that might be possessed, to a realization of finding ourselves given by God as a gift, we have been set on a path that actually allows for participation in God's divine life, even as it preserves the immeasurable distance between God and humans. Marion carries this theological explication even further in his occasional interpretations of the incarnation.

The Wounds of Christ: Encounter with Charity

Both *God without Being* and *Idol and Distance* had emphasized Christ as the icon of God and as the one who practices distance the most faithfully. In *Idol and Distance*, employing the language of the early Patristic Trinitarian controversies, Marion suggests that the poet—who in some sense represents Christ—is "the one who receives in his humanity the divine overabundance and who, so to speak, absorbs its shock in his flesh, to the point that the human and the divine are translated one into the other with neither confusion nor separation" (ID, 107; IeD, 136–37). That is a good summary of much of what Marion will say about Christ and God's visibility or self-revelation. Christ gives his body as the visible evidence of the measure of divine distance. The filial distance between Son and Father alone allows for a human vision of God. In this filial play between Son and Father we experience distance. Yet even Christ's filiation is possible only in poverty, kenosis, dispossession, and distance. Christ must utterly abandon himself to the Father, live only for and toward the Father, in continual reference to God. Only this voluntary dispossession allows for revelation of divine distance. The suffering of the Son makes manifest the glory of the Father. Marion says, "the glory of the divine befalls us only obliquely, in the naked form of the Son" (ID, 113; IeD, 141). He suggests that this is the only measure of distance that humans can bear. The distance of the human Christ to the divine Father is the only inkling we have of the Triune distance in the life of God. God becomes visible only in suffering and self-emptying, which by its very nature is a very obscure visibility—one that speaks of love and self-giving, not of glorious height or convincing logic. This theological discourse of charity, then, becomes a way of recovering Pascal's third order of charity, which is also characterized by the Christic kenosis. Charity deploys its own logic and truth that is outside that of rational philosophical discourse and cannot be comprehended by it. As Kathryn Tanner says: "Theology has in Marion's hands all the rigor of an alternative logic of love" (CE, 201). Love is the only appropriate way to speak about God, since it is a manner of speaking that does not impose limitations on God but rather allows the divine to overflow in kenotic self-giving.[25]

The final interpretation of the icon and of distance, in all of Marion's accounts of it, is the figure of charity. Already the "fourth dimension" that Marion introduces in the final chapter of *Idol and Distance* is described as a dimension of charity.[26] Marion plays on the Heideggerian connotations of generosity in Being in order to interpret this giving as a gift of love.[27] He suggests here already that the language of gift and love will help carry us beyond the limits of metaphysics. Charity constitutes a fourth dimension beyond that of ontological difference, namely one that maintains distance faithfully. Charity, for Marion, is a different point of view that arises beyond Being and ontological difference.[28] He interprets this dimension of charity here as primarily theological: it is the paternal distance of the Father to the Son, the Trinitarian difference within the divine life, or the experience of the Christian vis-à-vis the divine.

Marion carries this further in *God without Being*. While arguing that God is limited and idolized by the language of being, he suggests that the divine is more correctly named by the language of love or charity. Charity is God's preferred and most appropriate name.[29] Love is the only term that names God non-idolatrously. It goes beyond ontological difference and frees God from the language of being: "If, on the contrary, God is not because he does not have to be, but loves, then, by definition, no condition can continue to restrict his initiative, amplitude, and ecstasy. Love loves without condition, simply because it loves; he thus loves without limit or restriction. No refusal rebuffs or limits that which, in order to give itself, does not await the least welcome or require the least consideration" (GWB, 47; DSL, 74). Love overcomes being and renders it insignificant. It thus gets outside of metaphysics, distorts its boundaries, becomes limitless. Love overcomes all the metaphysical idols of God and thinks of God most authentically:

> God can give himself to be thought without idolatry only starting from himself alone: to give himself to be thought as love, hence as gift; to give himself to be thought as a thought of the gift. Or better, as a gift for thought, as a gift that gives itself to be thought. But a gift, which gives itself forever, can be thought only by a thought that gives itself to the gift to be thought. Only a thought that gives itself can devote itself to a gift for thought. But, for thought, what is it to give itself, if not to love? (GWB, 49)

Marion here postulates a relationship between vanity and agape (in fact, he often makes this connection), in that although opposed to each other, both show the question of being as irrelevant: "That which is, if it does not receive love, is as if it were not, while that which is not, if love polarizes it, is as if it were" (GWB, 136; DSL, 194). In the same way, a complete commitment to love often results in everything else being rendered utterly vain and meaningless.[30] Marion explicitly grounds this relation between vanity and love in Pascal and his notion of the three orders.[31] It is Pascal who has shown that a metaphysical depiction of love is insufficient, especially when it comes in its Cartesian guise (i.e., an occupation with being and/or causality).

Kurt Wolf points out the centrality of love in Marion's thought about the divine. He summarizes Marion's central claims as on the one hand an insistence on the absolute unconditionality and sovereignty of love for discourse about God and its escape of any grasping delimitation of human thought.[32] The categories of being are absolutely insufficient for doing justice to this abundant and unconditional love. He also highlights how love is not mere irrational emotion for Marion but pursues its own logic and rationale (similarly to the way in which the third order of charity does for Pascal). Robyn Horner also explicates how love is a kind of knowing for Marion (CE, 236–38). She summarizes him in helpful fashion:

> In sum, from a theological perspective, love is knowledge first in the sense that it forms the content of what is known, albeit that this content is known as unknown, since it is "sealed," or given as "distance." In this sense it is superior knowledge, which judges all other knowledge and shows it to be

worthless. It is visible by way of the distortions it reveals in that knowledge. Further, it functions to reveal new phenomena and operates as a herme- neutic principle. But love is also knowledge in the second sense that it en- ables us to know. Love enables us to recognize love, and we only know by choosing to love. The "how" of love here overlaps with the "what" of love, since new phenomena are seen through the will to see and are interpreted in accordance with that choice. Marion's recognition of the role of herme- neutics and of the will is significant, for he has implicitly (and perhaps un- intentionally) identified the limitations of a theological understanding of the knowledge of love: we have to interpret the (sealed) content of love as love, and we do this by willing it, in love, to be love. In fact, the knowledge of love — and more specifically God as love — only comes to us by way of a theological decision, which means that theology is subject to the charge that it only overcomes metaphysics by repeating one of its central moves. While Marion never withdraws from his theological commitments, his thinking of love eventually comes to be supplemented by a phenomenological working out of love as knowledge. (CE, 239)

Some readers have questioned Marion's emphasis on love as the only appro- priate "name" for God. Provoust, for example, criticizes Marion's replacement of God's name as *causa sui* or "being" with the name of charity. He finds that the point is not that of finding a better name and insists that charity still remains idol- atrous, that it remains also in an unresolved tension as a creaturely (or human) concept. No names can be attributed to God.[33] Lacoste criticizes Marion's posi- tion in a similar manner.[34] He suggests that analogy is no longer possible after Heidegger, but that one must reconceive something like analogy in terms of both proximity and transcendence of God. No analogy between gods and humans is possible for Heidegger except within the framework of the question of being. Analogy becomes blasphemy. While Lacoste objects to Marion's complete rejec- tion of philosophical language about God in *God without Being* (of course, this is before the publication of any of Marion's phenomenological works), he also finds that Marion's elevation of love over being is arbitrary and no less philo- sophical. For Marion, according to Lacoste, there are only two alternatives: either metaphysics or traditional Christianity. In order to recognize God some kind of thought must be permitted; otherwise theological discourse remains incoherent. Lacoste does recognize that "love" also functions as a type of analogy, namely that of the good.[35] One must combine the analogy of being and that of the good:

> It is not sufficient, in order to enter rigorously into theology, to think beyond the question of being, and to dispense God from "being" because he "loves." One must still thematize the *analogia caritatis* according to which God still greater is also a God always nearer, and according to which the question on the good, on relation, on charity, and the gift, and the question on the created after having been the question on God. One cannot think (of) God without conceiving that the question of being must be posed in new terms if God is [has been] named.[36]

God is when/because God loves. As Specker rightly points out, however, Lacoste seems to disregard the fact that love has a kind of logic for Marion and thus qualifies as thinking and not merely as senseless emotion devoid of content (AGD, 224). Bradley also points out that "in anticipation of the inevitable question of why agape, alone, should be the name that remains unthinkable by ontotheology, Marion replies that it is because it is a gift of divine charitable love which hyperbolically exceeds the conditions of both giver and recipient."[37] The notions of gift and charity are open-ended and do not limit the divine.

An account of love becomes Marion's measuring stick for all appropriate talk of God, self, and other. For example, already Nietzsche is judged by Marion for his deficient account of love. Nietzsche's Christ is revealed to be idolatrous precisely because of this incapacity to love.[38] In Marion's treatment of Dionysius we learn that love is the ultimate figure of distance, for without distance love is impossible. Charity requires distance and allows it to give itself. It ultimately makes possible participation in God. As we have seen, this participation does not eliminate distance. Love alone is the ultimate traversal of distance. Love consecrates and performs distance in prayer. Christ is central here as the one who opens distance in Dionysius and serves as a paradigm for all human giving.[39] The Son receives himself from the Father and continually offers himself in utter dependence and poverty. The icon and charity both point to the loving kenosis of the Son. Yet in the same way, we must render ourselves as gift in appropriately measuring the divine distance. Charity describes a love of total abandonment and devotion:

> To receive the gift amounts to receiving the giving act, for God gives nothing except the movement of the infinite kenosis of charity, that is, everything. Receiving the gift and giving it come together in one and the same operation, redundancy. Only the gift of the gift can receive the gift, without appropriating it to oneself and destroying it in a simple possession. He who would not give would not receive anything that he does not immediately freeze in his possession. Receiving and giving are therefore achieved in the same act. (ID, 166)

Kathryn Tanner finds Marion's account too kenotic and disembodied. She opts instead for a more "enfleshed" account of the incarnation, criticizing Marion for over-emphasizing Christ's self-emptying and not giving any role to human response to God (CE, 219–28). Yet while Marion's treatment of love certainly is very kenotic in character, he requires a similar kenotic response from humans. Even his phenomenological account of eros will describe the response in a similar fashion. The lover and the beloved (whether divine or human) give and receive in abundance.

In his theological works, charity for Marion usually means gift. We cannot possess the divine but must accept its gift. The measure of this coming and self-giving, this revelation, must continually be fixed by God. God disappears as giver of the gift and cannot be identified. God's absence, in fact, only makes possible the gift of revelation which would otherwise annihilate itself. Only the withdrawal of the divine manifests God.[40] The language of gift and love thus applies supremely to God. God's Trinitarian life is characterized in itself by outgoing love and self-giving. Father and Son continually give each other their very selves in the Spirit. Anything that Christ is and does always and immediately refers back to the Father and gives glory to the Father. The divine becomes present in that God gives Godself to be broken and given to the world in the church and in the Eucharist: "The consecrated bread and wine become the ultimate aspect in which charity delivers itself body and soul" (GWB, 178; DSL, 252). Only love gives fully and the gift exemplifies love supremely. For Marion, love and gift are more or less synonymous at this point. Love is like the gift because it does not attempt to comprehend, does not gather together, grasp, or possess. Instead, love lets go, pours itself out, abandons itself, gives without limits. Love does not master or limit, but transgresses limits and goes beyond itself. Marion defines love as free gift in the absence of conditions or even a stipulation of reception or comprehension.[41] Both are utterly kenotic in their complete and limitless self-abandonment to the Other. Love reverses movements and undoes restrictions. In Marion's view, it allows a bridging of distance that becomes non-possessive and non-determining. Only love can traverse the distance between the divine and the human (or later even that between humans) in a continual movement that does not freeze it in thought or image. Love undoes the restrictions and delimitations of being and non-being.[42] Charity is the only way to live the Christian life rigorously and in abandon. This love is one of utter kenosis, complete self-emptying. Christ is the supreme example of such love that loses all attachment to Being, even to one's own identity. To abandon oneself to such love is to love with the same excess (ultimately to become a martyr).[43]

Marion carries this argument to an even greater extreme in *Prolegomena to Charity*, where he explores the "sinister logic" of evil that always seeks a culprit to alleviate the hurt I have suffered.[44] Evil [*le mal*] automatically leads to hurt or pain [*faire* or *souffre mal*] and the desire to inflict pain on others [*faire* or *rendre mal*].[45] This is the case because evil elicits almost automatic desire for retribution and thus always leads to a kind of "counter-evil."[46] Evil always calls forth another evil. Revenge seems to impose itself by necessity and thus the call for justice (for the evil that has been suffered) necessarily becomes a violent injustice (in calling for the imposing of pain on another).[47] Ultimately, so Marion asserts, the only way to stop evil is to absorb it, not to return and thus not to perpetuate it. One can only excuse oneself by passing the responsibility and the suffering on to another, thus perpetuating the chain of on-going and self-generating pain and evil. This continual and logical transmission of evil is stopped by Christ, precisely because he refuses to assert his own innocence but instead absorbs the guilt and the pain of evil.[48] Christ is just only and precisely because he becomes supremely guilty. He absorbs evil and pain by suffering it instead of handing it on. Suffering becomes the very possibility for a manifestation of God.[49] Marion shows how we accuse God with responsibility for evil and suggests that God responds by taking on the position of the culprit. By choosing not to avenge himself, Christ absorbs our evil and stops the chain of transmission of evil. God gives Godself as the culprit, as the one to absorb evil and pain. We establish our innocence by practicing our revenge on someone who does not go on to inflict revenge for the suffered pain on a further victim. The only way that God can absolve the guilt of the world is to become guilty in Christ. Marion here uses the notion of the "death of God" in a very different sense:

> Which is not possible, except at only one price: that, effectively, he be absolutely guilty, and thus, absolutely punished, and thus, absolutely dead. The "death of God" descends in this manner from the spirit of revenge, in a direct line. For the world, the only good God is a dead God. In as much as a living God appears odious to the world, so much does he, dead, become almost bearable, in order to satisfy the hate exerted by revenge. The world recognizes God only in order to be able to kill him — and God renders the world even this ultimate service. (PC, 10–11; PaC, 23)

God becomes visible to the world only as dead, as the culprit and not the judge. God, then, clearly does become immanent for Marion, but only in the utter self-emptying of the divine kenosis. God is seen and experienced only in suffering and death. In his analysis of the crisis that death constitutes, Marion plays out the following paradox: "in the crisis between men and God, man always claims the role of judge, the judgment is always the death sentence, and the condemned is always God" (PC, 117; PaC, 139). God's self-giving is a judgment only in the sense that we judge ourselves. We must make a decision; God does not judge us. God never comes as judge, but always appears only as the one condemned, the one suffering. The "death of God" proclaimed by modern and postmodern philosophy is consequently read by Marion as a further example of this divine kenosis.

In his work *The Crossing of the Visible,* Marion gives a complementary account by describing how the invisible can become visible. He makes a careful distinction between the "unseen" which the painter brings forth in the visibility of a painting and the "invisible" that is given only in the icon and is not available to sight. God, he suggests, only becomes visible in the wounds that we inflict on God, only in the divine kenosis which goes all the way to death.[50] Only a dead God is ultimately rendered visible, and that is precisely why God gives Godself up to death. God is rendered visible only in God's agony and thus recognized only in love.[51] God's suffering and self-emptying in Christ bridges the gap between immanence and transcendence for Marion. God, for Marion, is always crossed out, always only visible through the marks of the nails we drive into God's hands. God allows Godself to be "nailed down," not by the desire for knowledge expressed in definitions and philosophical logic, but only because of a love that recognizes the need for redemption from evil. Divine immanence is always deeply kenotic for Marion and retains its ambivalence. Even in this case, although utterly unlike the idol, the only God we can "see" is a dead God.

Marion recently carried this even further in the context of a (philosophical) consideration of God as the "impossible."[52] He attempts to rethink traditional accounts of omnipotence in light of certain biblical passages that speak of God's possibility to do the impossible in a very different fashion. Marion employs the account of the annunciation in which Mary responds to God with impossibility and the angel assures her that for God all things are possible. Both the angel and Mary in her response focus on God's "word" or "saying" ["*rhema*"] instead of an abstract notion of divine omnipotence.

> The point is not to acknowledge simple omnipotence (which commits to nothing and permits, on the contrary, every lie) but to have faith in God's good faith. To have recourse to God's omnipotence is useless, since it still remains immanent to our own finite point of view (like the reverse face of possibility according to represented non-contradiction). Instead, the task is to transcend our own finite point of view in order to pass over to God's point of view — or at least to aim for it, to admit it as an intention. In contrast to us, where saying commits to nothing (we lie), on God's part, saying and carrying out what is said coincide absolutely. More than the power to do anything, God has the power to say anything — not in virtue of his omnipotence but in virtue of his fidelity. God can say whatever and all that he wants because what he says, he does. (34)

God makes the impossible possible through faithfulness to the divine word which here brings about the incarnation. God's ability to accomplish the impossible has nothing to do with an arbitrary power to do ridiculous things, but rather refers to God's power to accomplish the divine will, which is always defined by love. (Marion's analysis here parallels in an interesting fashion what he has argued about Descartes' insistence that the creation of the eternal truths does not imply that they become arbitrary or capricious.) This does not limit God, but rather attempts to say something about how we experience God and the way in which we have experienced God acting: "Neither logic, nor contradiction, nor the principle of identity, nor efficacy, nor the principle of sufficient reason, retains the slightest relevancy here, namely when the task is to conceive that to which God's word commits itself and commits God" (35). The relevant question to ask is not *whether* God is, but *how* God is, not what God *can* do, but what God *will* do: "God does whatever he wants, but the main thing is that he wants only what it becomes him to want — which is to say only what comes from him and answers to his love" (35).

Marion sees the apex of this divine (im-)possibility in the radical possibility of forgiveness that transcends anything humans might accomplish. In Marion's view, the Scriptures affirm that only God can forgive sins. He employs two brief stories to illustrate this, that of the rich young ruler and that of the healing of the paralytic. The first story illustrates that true conversion can be accomplished only by God. We lack God's holiness and perfection, just as the rich young man lacks the ability to lack, to become poor by complete identification with Christ. The story of the paralytic makes this even clearer in that it emphasizes Christ's divinity precisely in his unique ability to forgive sins, which no human can do. The healing of the paralytic further substantiates Christ's ability to do the impossible (36–37). God's power thus does not refer to what seems to us the most difficult to accomplish for God (healing), but rather what God sees as the most difficult to accomplish for us, namely conversion or forgiveness.[53] In light of the greatest evil we acknowledge our impotence to forgive and revert to metaphysical definitions of moral responsibility in order to justify it. Only with love is nothing impossible.

This explication of the incarnation and especially of its intensely kenotic character connects, of course, with Marion's repeated emphasis on the Eucharist that has elicited so much criticism. If the primary (or even the only) way in which we can experience God is in the wounded and broken body of the Son, then participation in the Eucharist is the preeminent manner of experiencing God's presence now. This is precisely why Marion stresses the centrality of the Eucharist (and its hermeneutic potential) in any truly *theo*-logical talk in such passages as the following:

> The Word intervenes in person in the Eucharist (in person, because only then does he manifest and perform his filiation) to accomplish in this way the hermeneutic; the hermeneutic culminates in the Eucharist; the one assures the other its condition of possibility: the intervention in person of the referent of the text as center of its meaning, of the Word, outside of the words, to reappropriate them to himself . . . If the Word intervenes in person only at the eucharistic moment, the hermeneutic (hence fundamental theology) will take place, will have its place, only in the Eucharist. (GWB, 150–51; DSL, 212)

The celebration of the Eucharist combines many of the aspects that Marion has sought to stress throughout his more theological work. While it certainly establishes analogy with human bread and wine, it is clearly to be distinguished from simply human nourishment. The Eucharist is, at least for the Roman Catholic and Eastern Orthodox believer, truly the broken body and shed blood of Christ, and yet simultaneously it certainly is no "proof" for God's existence. Its nature is essentially iconic, serving as the entrance of the believer into the divine life. As instituted by Christ it derives from God and invites humans into its participation, thus imitating the direction of analogous language. The language of the Eucharist is not predicative but performative, in Marion's interpretation of that term. Kraftson-Hogue concludes the following about Marion's interpretation of the Eucharist:

> To talk of God is to remain after the event of Christ in the gift of memorial. Such talk, aware of the gift of the memorial and of its distance from the event (a distance that as distance simultaneously separates and unites, for it is a giving distance), ceases to predicate and turns to praise. God exceeds

predication, exceeds the bounds of language and time and being, "giving Himself to be known as He gives Himself." To talk of God, or to memorialise the event of Christ, is also to be with God. For Christ gives in and through the memorial, accompanying us in the hermeneutic adventure that is the mystery of being language-using human creatures of God.[54]

The Eucharistic liturgy gives praise to God by participating in the angelic celebration of the divine and by instantiating the kingdom of heaven.[55] The Eucharist speaks of divine immanence, even as it is always coupled with God's absence, as Marion illustrates in his interpretation of the experience of the Emmaus disciples.[56] In Kraftson-Hogue's words again:

> To return the gift is to offer up all discourse in honour and praise of the Word who [is] ultimately always and already speaking. So, the claim made in the introduction that memorials attest to events that occurred, to the absence of a presence that once was there, requires revision. Memorials attest to events and presence only insofar as the event or presence returns to the memorial. This return is the gift of charity, the mysterious and gracious distance-crossing of the Gift. Thus, in saying only words in the saying that "once things have happened only words remain," one is saying also that in all words is the presence of the Word.[57]

The traditional theological affirmations about the Eucharist then corroborate well what Marion seeks to say about the balance between God's immanence in Christ and divine transcendence.

Thus although Marion begins with Nietzsche, Hölderlin, and Heidegger, he quickly moves beyond them. His explicit talk about God is a clearly Christian theology that is heavily Catholic (with multiple Eastern Orthodox resonances). God is pictured as a God of self-giving and abundant love, a God who is Triune relationship and becomes incarnate in the person of Christ and explicated through the Eucharist. We are here, as Marion himself makes clear, in another dimension, a fourth or theological one paralleling Pascal's move to another order, a dimension that remains faithful to the Church's tradition of interpreting its message.[58] Only theology can speak from the other side of distance in this way, can claim to traverse distance and become involved in the Trinitarian play of the divine persons. This God withdraws, is present only in absence, known only in ignorance and incomprehension. We no longer speak of the God of the philosophers, but, like Pascal, of *Deus absconditus*, of the God of Abraham, Isaac, and Jacob. Yet has Marion really been able to preserve the balance between univocity and equivocity? Does his language of the divine names work, and can it become a non-predicative way of speaking about God as he claims? Is this God still too transcendent without possibility for relationship? Or is it maybe a God too immanent, too Roman Catholic, too determined already? These questions will have to be explored in more detail, but let me first turn briefly to Marion's phenomenology, which — as has often been noted — in many ways parallels the more theological explication I have just examined.

six
Phenomenology and God
"It Is Impossible for God to Be Impossible"

Despite all of Marion's protestations to the contrary, it seems rather evident that the possibility of speaking of phenomena of revelation constitutes one of the most significant goals of his phenomenological project. Marion attempts to articulate a phenomenology that allows us to speak of religious experience, or more specifically of an experience of divine revelation, within strictly phenomenological terms and categories. In some sense he clearly wants to recover an opportunity that he interprets Descartes as having closed: the possibility of considering revelatory phenomena philosophically. Just as the doctrines of analogy and the language of the divine names enabled coherent talk about God that became impossible with the degeneration of these means into univocity and epistemologically grounded metaphysical thinking, so Marion seeks to develop a new kind of language that would make possible an articulation of the thought of God and religious phenomenality within the philosophical exercise. These are not, of course, proofs for God's existence, as Marion emphasizes constantly. He fully agrees with Pascal's rejection of such proofs and with his judgment of such talk as utterly useless and even blasphemous. Philosophy has no right or capacity to speak of the actuality or efficacy of God or Revelation. It only qualifies as a language that might give a certain coherence to such thought. That is, however, a useful exercise. To show that one might describe religious experience and qualify the nature of its phenomenality, to situate its location and the parameters of its appearance in the field of consciousness, to delineate the possibility and coherence of God-talk within phenomenology, are clearly not without merit to religious believers, especially when they seek to articulate their faith intellectually. Furthermore, Marion does emphasize that this is a philosophical or "rational" discourse, although the type of rationality appropriate to it might differ from what we often understand by reason or rationality. Although he does not always make this clear, he seems to be employing the distinctions between two types of truth or reasoning he has uncovered and examined in Pascal. There is an evidence and rationality of the mind (the logic of metaphysics) and a different type of evidence or rationality, namely that of the heart or of the will. Yet, this different kind of "evidence" or rationality is now not solely theological, but rather is worked out phenomenologically. Ultimately, it will be a "logic of love" which pursues its own kind of rationality.

As has been pointed out but must be emphasized again, according to Marion phenomenology cannot explicitly think about God as an actuality; it can only examine the possibility of a phenomenon of revelation, i.e., a phenomenon that deals with the immanence of God. Such a question as the existence of a transcendent Creator cannot be explored within phenomenology. Divine transcendence is always excluded by the phenomenological reduction. Thus, even in this limited situation of mere possibility, the investigation deals not with God as such (whatever that might mean) but with God as a possible phenomenon, a given to intuition.[1] This given (if there is one) would be the most radical one, the paradox of paradoxa, a saturated phenomenon par excellence, that saturates and subverts all four of the categories simultaneously. Marion investigates the possibility of such a phenomenon while always reminding us that we are only dealing with the *experience* of revelation, not with any proof of its actual existence or occurrence. In *Being Given*, he treats the supreme Christian figure of revelation: the human Christ who claims to be an icon of God. In the final chapter of *In Excess*, he switches instead to an investigation of the divine name in an attempt to refute what he takes to be Derrida's argument against negative theology.[2] He again suggests that all phenomenology can do is to "protect" the divine name through a certain deliberate kind of silence or unsaying that follows the figure of the third way (of eminence) in Dionysian theology.[3] Finally he explores the "impossible" phenomenon of the divine further in the aforementioned paper entitled "The Impossible for Man — God." I will begin by examining Marion's arguments for God as supremely saturated phenomenon and then see how his later treatments modify and add to this proposal.

The Saturated Phenomenon Par Excellence

Marion repeatedly reminds us that phenomenology even in its mode of pure donation radically reduces. All assumptions about the existence of a transcendent God must be set aside. "God as such" cannot even constitute a thought for phenomenology. In an interview Marion deplores the fact that revelation becomes unthinkable for phenomenology as it is articulated by Husserl and even Heidegger. Marion seeks to open this possibility again by "formulating phenomenology in a way that makes Revelation possible and thinkable."[4] One may think the possibility of a phenomenon of revelation, which would be a phenomenon at the very limit of the excess already indicated. The phenomenon of revelation goes beyond even the experience of a historical event, a beautiful painting, the immediacy of my flesh or the encounter of another person. Marion calls it a "variation of second degree" over the saturated phenomena or the "paradox of paradoxa."[5] Like the other phenomena, it gives itself completely without measure yet is not measured even by them. Although Marion insists again that he is dealing here only with possibility, not with the ontic status of this paradox, he goes on to use the manifestation of Christ as the supreme example of such a possible doubly saturated phenomenon.[6] This phenomenon saturates and inverts all four categories. According to quantity, it is radically unforeseeable [*un événement parfaitement imprévisible*] and has the character of event. According to quality, it cannot be supported [*insupportable*]; it is immense and suspends all general perception. It arrives as *arrivage* and escapes from its past in the marking of a new beginning as *fait accompli*. According to relation, it is the revelation of the flesh par excellence and escapes all horizons. The agony and simultaneous exaltation of the flesh on the cross opens a plurality of worlds, an infinite number of horizons of nominations and hermeneutics. According to modality, the "I" is constituted by Christ as witness; the saturated phenomenon par excellence effects the counter-gaze of the other who makes me a witness.

Welten has pointed out the difficult nature of this example:

> The saturated phenomenon actually becomes manifest *in this revelation* [of Christ]. The saturated phenomenon is a *possibility* of phenomenology. Without this possibility, Marion's phenomenology would not be phenomenology at all but empirical science with God as its object. Without the saturated phenomenon, the phenomenological status of Marion's philosophy would wane. Therefore, Marion will not say that Christ shows himself to mankind; rather, Marion outlines a phenomenology with room for revelation. . . . As a result, Marion will not claim that Christ is the only possible saturated phenomenon: Christ is the ultimate saturated phenomenon, the possibility that is itself saturated by the possibilities of saturation. The saturated phenomenon is not to be fixed; however, its phenomenological *possibility* needs to be demonstrated. The saturated phenomenon does not represent Christ, but it shows us the structure of God's appearance.[7]

Kathryn Tanner finds that Marion cannot sustain God's unconditionality because his phenomenology of revelation imposes undue restrictions on the divine:

> This possibility — this eventuality — that Revelation would exceed the bounds of phenomenological description, however purified, is just what Marion's phenomenology ultimately disallows. If a revelation were to occur (and I agree with Marion that his phenomenology does not prejudge this question) it would have to conform to the dictates of phenomenology concerning the givenness of what appears. Givenness as a universal law of phenomenality permits no exceptions, not even for Revelation, not even for God's coming to us in Christ. (CE, 203)

In fact, so she suggests, Marion's phenomenology functions as a conceptual idol in his own sense of that term. While Marion wants to free the divine from restrictions, he actually limits and confines any notion of revelation: "Marion has so well integrated impossible phenomena such as Revelation into phenomenology by reconfiguring its terms of analysis, so well justified the appearance of saturated phenomena such as Revelation thereby, that the coming of Revelation in fact loses its capacity ever to disturb the discipline. . . . Phenomenology, just because it has become such an apt instrument for describing a God beyond measure, becomes God's measure" (CE, 205). God cannot enter phenomenology in the way in which Marion prescribes. Welten, conversely, judges Marion's attempt to be successful precisely because phenomenology has not surrendered to theology here. He emphasizes the important distinction between appearance and perception in Marion. While Marion's phenomenological structure allows the divine to appear, that does not mean God must be perceived: "Marion will not show us God; he just makes sure there is room for God to show *Himself*!"[8]

God thus can be inscribed within phenomenality if self-emptied to the point of appearing as a phenomenon. Yet the divine is not defined or limited by this appearing within phenomenality. Just as the face gives a surplus which is perceived as a lack, saturation gives too much to intuition, but gives no concrete object that can be seen or identified. The thought of a revelation occurring, or of God giving God-self to be seen as a phenomenon, is thus not incoherent but thinkable on phenomenological terms in Marion's view. Phenomenology pushed to its utmost extreme can approach this unthinkable thought. It neither directly touches nor grasps it, but approaches it from afar and can delineate some of its conditions of (im)possibility. The possibility of God or revelation can be thought as a doubled paradox, as thought strained to its very extremes.

Again it seems clear that in this proposal Marion is attempting to find a balance between univocal and equivocal attempts to speak about God. On the one hand, he affirms that the divine appears as a phenomenon, becomes utterly immanent to the human consciousness which experiences this divine in-breaking. On the other hand, the saturated and paradoxical nature of this phenomenon, its remove to a "second degree," clearly attempts to preserve the transcendence, difference, and distance of God without reducing it merely to human experience. Although Marion does not use the language of analogy in this context (as, of course, he does not do explicitly in his theology either), I would suggest that this constitutes at least the attempt of an analogous manner of speaking. By emphasizing the coming of this phenomenon from itself, its overwhelming nature that saturates the intuition and is more than anyone can bear, defying any sense of signification, Marion stresses phenomenologically what he has outlined in his work on Descartes as the fundamental origin of any notions of analogy. In fact, most of Marion's proposal regarding a pure phenomenology has insisted on this primacy of the phenomenon. Regardless of what one might think about the viability of this pure givenness of the phenomenon or of its faithfulness to Husserl, it is clear that "freeing" the phenomenon from the restrictions of consciousness, and allowing for its pure self-giving in the manner in which it chooses to do so, is one of Marion's primary concerns. One might suggest that he actually extends the notion of analogy to apply to all saturated phenomena, not merely to the phenomenon of revelation. That is to say, for saturated phenomena neither a uniformly univocal nor an entirely equivocal account is adequate. The phenomenon can neither be described adequately as merely an object of my consciousness over which I have complete control (and which is thus univocally like me to a great extent), nor can it be said to be so equivocally other that I cannot receive it at all (as we will see, the recipient must still identify the incoming and self-giving phenomenon).

Furthermore, one can also see how, just as analogy enabled the application of "divine terminology" in a lesser measure to human beings, his proposals of saturated phenomena end up informing the rest of his philosophy, such as his recovery of a non-metaphysical self as the subject and his consideration of the other as the Beloved. I will examine both of these in more detail later. Marion speaks of both human (event/painting/flesh/face) and divine (revelation) topics as phenomena, thus establishing a clear analogy between them. They appear in a very similar fashion and all saturated phenomena challenge the Kantian phenomenal categories Marion subverts in a parallel way. The phenomenon of revelation, as blinding and bedazzling as it might appear, does perform its blinding work in exactly the same manner as the other saturated phenomena, merely going a step further by combining all their characteristics. Marion is emphatic at times to insist on the importance of this theoretical framework. All phenomena of revelation, whatever or whoever they might be, *must* appear according to these conditions of experience.[9] The phenomenon of revelation, despite its extreme character, establishes a clear parallel or analogy with other experiences of intensity, saturation, or excess, other "uncontainable" experiences.

If, however, this phenomenon of revelation offers itself so fully, under such similar parameters as all other phenomena, and threatens to transform all other phenomena to quasi-revealed ones, how is one then to distinguish between phenomena of revelation and other phenomena? Is the experience of revelation merely "more excessive," subverting more categories? How are we to speak of God and to preserve the divine transcendence that Marion has been so anxious to guard throughout his work? Marion addresses this question in his contribution to the first Villanova conference, "God, the Gift, and Postmodernism," by taking up again the Dionysian language of the divine names.

The Phenomenon of the Unspeakable

In *De Surcroît/In Excess*, Marion engages in an analysis of negative theology and a strong criticism of Derrida.[10] Again, he says less about God directly than about the kind of speech that would be appropriate to employ to describe an experience of God. He outlines the three ways in Dionysius' theology and concludes with an account of prayer and praise as a language that is outside of predication. Marion begins by analyzing Derrida's criticism of negative theology and wonders whether such theology must reduce itself necessarily to a metaphysics of presence and be subject to deconstruction, as Derrida appears to claim.[11] He reminds us that there are three moments or ways in the Dionysian discourse: the kataphatic, the apophatic, and the way of eminence. This third way Derrida misses or at least does not take seriously, but instead claims that negative theology finally does arrive at predication even while it claims to deny all names of God. Marion wants to assert that the third way plays outside the duality of affirmation or negation, synthesis or separation, true or false. It transgresses the values of truth which are exercised by logic and metaphysics and thus evades saying the truth. It has no interest in affirmation. Mystical theology (a term Marion prefers to negative theology because it does not collapse the distinction between the second and the third move) attempts to surpass the duality of truth in which metaphysics plays by instituting a clear hierarchy. There can never be an adequate name for God, but only a multiplicity of names. The point is not either naming or not naming God, but un-naming or de-nominating.[12] This is an undoing of all nomination; it carries in its ambiguity the double function of saying and undoing all saying of the name. This third way or voice denies the very pertinence of all predication; it surpasses all affirmation and negation.

Prayer or praise, the language of this third way, has a strictly pragmatic function and is no longer predicative.[13] The word no longer says or denies, but rather acts in giving itself to God, whom it unsays. Dionysius does not merely oppose affirmation and negation, but transgresses both in praise. With the third way the point is no longer to say (or to deny) something of something, but to say no longer, to unsay. The point is to refer oneself to the One whom nomination no longer touches. One does not designate the referent, but the speaker is pragmatically lifted up to the inaccessible Referent. To attribute a name to

God is not to name God's essence or presence, but is rather to refer to the experience of God's absence, to anonymity and withdrawal; such naming only indicates but never manifests. Prayer always assigns a name. Yet it "does not consist in causing the invoked one to descend into the realm of our language," but rather raises us to God in a "sustained attention" (IE, 144; DS, 173–74). Mystical theology is not inscribed in a horizon of Being; nor is it subject to metaphysical causality. God cannot be named or known; to assume either (or to attempt to inscribe God in metaphysics) is idolatry and blasphemy. As Martin Laird summarizes regarding what he calls a "logophatic apophaticism" in Marion, logophatic discourse refrains from

> positing God as an object and then predicating something of this object. Logophatic discourse is not trying to reach God with speech; nor does it attempt to seek God. . . . when kataphatic discourse concerning God is abandoned in apophatic union, the Word indwells human deeds and discourse; the Word manifests itself in them. The clenched fists of predicative, attribute discourse have relaxed, and in these open palms of discourse, the Word speaks itself, "labile inhabitant of our babble." Language is no longer grasping but revealing.[14]

Marion himself insists that "incomprehensibility therefore belongs to the formal definition of God, since comprehension would put God on the same level as a finite mind (ours), would submit God to a finite conception, and would at the same time clear the way for the higher possibility of an infinite conception, beyond the comprehensible" (IE, 154; DS, 186). The Name of God does not have as its function to inscribe God within a horizon, but rather to allow us to enter within that name and to receive our name by this excess. That is why liturgy does not talk *about* God but *to* God. Mystical theology does not find a name for God but helps us to receive our own name. Marion concludes that "the theologian's job is to silence the Name and in this way let it give us one — while the metaphysician is obsessed with reducing the Name to presence, and so defeating the Name" (IE, 158; DS, 190).[15] Marion therefore suggests that the heretics, in their desire to define God's name, are the real metaphysicians.[16]

The relation between theology and phenomenology in this particular piece is much more fluid than in other of Marion's works. Yet, while Marion appears engaged in a theological task in *God without Being* and to some extent also in *Idol and Distance*, in this context he seems to describe the task of theology from a phenomenological standpoint. His analysis is mostly concerned with determining how one might speak phenomenologically of the experience reported by the theologian. A comparison with Marion's analysis of Dionysius in his more theologically oriented work makes clear how carefully he separates the two discourses. Although Marion speaks of prayer, praise, God, and even baptism in this article, his focus is much more clearly phenomenological than in his theological writings. In both cases he speaks of the necessity of withdrawal, of being named by God, of the third way that goes beyond affirmation and negation. Unlike in his discussion of Dionysius in *Idol and Distance* Marion here does not appeal to the inner workings of the Trinity, to the incarnation, or to the Eucharist. Although he cites certain Patristic writings he does so primarily to show that mystical theology defies a "metaphysics of presence" in favor of a "pragmatic theology of absence." He then considers the possibility of a doubly saturated phenomenon as distinct even from these more theological reflections. Even to consider whether the divine is ever given as such a phenomenon is to cross into theology. Phenomenology can only consider its possibility.

For Marion, two figures speak of the possibility of such a phenomenon: first, the stupor or terror in the face of the incomprehensibility and excess which forbids all approach and, second, the obsession with the constant evocation of this name, with discussing and even denying it.[17] Philosophy remains haunted by the divine name, even though it cannot pronounce it. Marion concludes that we must live in the Name not by saying it but by allowing it to say us, to name us, to call us:

> For if no one must say the Name, this is not simply because it surpasses all names, passes beyond all essence and all presence. In fact, not even not saying the Name would suffice for honoring it, since a simple denegation would still belong to predication, would again inscribe the Name within the horizon of presence — and would even do so in the mode of blasphemy since it treats it parsimoniously. The Name must not be said, not because it is not given for the sake of our saying it, even negatively, but so that we might de-nominate all names of it and dwell in it. (IE, 162; DS, 195)

Even in praise, only the response is identifiable. The Name itself remains anonymous; only its impact is retained through the one praising in response to who or what remains anonymous.

Marion's essay, originally delivered as the keynote address for the first Religion and Postmodernism conference at Villanova University, has become the center for most of the criticisms of his talk about God. John Caputo, Thomas Carlson, Robyn Horner, James K. A. Smith, and others have argued against certain aspects of it in detail or have it used it as a starting point for a wider criticism of Marion's work. Before looking briefly at some of these critiques, however, let me conclude this survey of Marion's phenomenological considerations of the divine and revelation by considering his most recent statements on this topic. In his keynote address for the fourth Villanova Religion and Postmodernism conference, he explores the notion of God as "the impossible," both synthesizing his earlier work and carrying it a step further.

The Phenomenon of the Impossible

In "The Impossible for Man — God" Marion outlines the relation of God to the notion of "impossibility."[18] He begins by summarizing the argument he has made over the years, both in his study of Descartes and in some of his earlier, more theological arguments. He then goes on to reject some of the philosophical definitions for linking God and impossibility through the notion of omnipotence. Instead he employs the Scriptures, in particular the stories of the annunciation and the healing of the paralytic, in order to speak of God's ability to do the impossible in terms of forgiveness. Similarly to earlier treatments and to the conclusion of his work on the erotic phenomenon, he ends by linking God with love or charity. I will employ this article to bring together the various things Marion has said about God and in order to set the stage for an evaluation of this project and its critics.

Marion begins by analyzing the notion of transcendence and showing how it remains linked to being in Husserl and Heidegger: "The transcendence of Being does not disclose transcendence, but instead closes and limits it" (18). Marion links this notion of transcendence, even in phenomenology, to the definitions of metaphysics in Duns Scotus, where the transcendentals are still inscribed in the realm of being to which even God's transcendence is limited. Consequently, God's essence is defined by a univocal concept of being and remains limited to its horizon.[19] We must therefore get outside of ontological language. God's existence is not the primary issue for belief and cannot serve as its primary criterion. Any proofs of God's existence presume a "perfect hegemony" between the horizon of being and the question of God which becomes operative in Suarez. Metaphysics, however, is not able to "define conditions of intelligibility and possibility for 'God' by means of a glaringly unquestioned univocity, God can only be instaurated [instituted] as God on the basis of his pre-ontological condition and pre-transcendental freedom" (20). Here Marion is clearly bringing together his concern with univocity in his work on Descartes and the late medieval context with his more recent phenomenological claims about the limitations of ontological and metaphysical language (which are, of course, also rooted in these earlier concerns). Univocal language is blatantly inappropriate for God because it applies human ontological and epistemological categories to the infinite in a fashion that limits the divine to mirror the human.

Marion goes on to question the notion of impossibility. He reviews the definition of the phenomenon, which is defined through the relationship between intuition and concept. In the case of God I have neither adequate intuition nor any concept. God does not fit into my notions of time and space but transcends them infinitely. The very notion of divinity requires this for Marion.[20] Every concept to which I could assign intuition would be invalidated in the case of God. Marion is here referring to his work on the saturated phenomenon and its incomprehensible nature. Incomprehensibility is an absolute requirement in the case of the divine.[21] Marion links to this phenomenological analysis his earlier theological explication of the idol and the icon. The concepts we impose upon God, he reminds us, say a whole lot more about us than about God: "the concepts that I assign to God, like so many invisible mirrors, send me back the images that I make up for myself of divine perfection, which are thus images of myself. My concepts of God turn out in the end to be idols — idols of myself" (22). The death of God thus gets rid of a particular concept of God and is simultaneously tied to that concept. Any atheism of a particular concept becomes ideology. Similarly, every theism that tries to define God by a concept turns into idolatry. Trying to define God's essence makes God subject to the idolatry of being. Marion brings these theological and phenomenological insights together to insist that the phenomenon of God is therefore impossible: "Speculative theology, however, which conducts its thought within faith and in view of belief, diverges radically from atheism when it comes to interpreting this phenomenal impossibility. For speculative theology, the very impossibility of a phenomenon of God belongs to a real and indubitable experience of God. Indeed if God cannot *not* be thought as beyond phenomenal conditions — unintuitable and inconceivable — this impossibility results directly from his infinity, taken as the hallmark of his incomprehensibility" (23). Impossibility is a kind of "counter-experience" of God.

As he has already suggested at the end of his article on the saturated phenomenon, the very fact that the question of God always becomes posed again seems to attest to its validity for Marion. While God's existence cannot be established, according to Marion "God's pertinence" cannot be doubted, since the divine question always arises anew in our experience. Somehow this paradox which is at the limits of our rationality must be explained. Marion therefore argues that God becomes "defined by impossibility as such" and "begins where the possible *for us* ends. . . . In God's case, and in God's case alone, impossibility does not abolish the question but actually makes it possible" (25). Marion therefore seeks to examine "how the impossible is converted into the possible when we pass from man to God" on the basis of Scriptural passages that affirm that what is impossible for humans is possible for God (27). This "definition" still says more about us than about God, because it delineates our boundaries and finitude instead of saying anything positive about God. For God nothing can ever be impossible. Nothing, therefore, can make God impossible: "It turns out, as a matter of principle, that it is impossible for God to be impossible" (28). The impossibility of God established by phenomenology only has meaning for us (who are limited in phenomenal experience), but not for God (who is not thus limited). God is always thinkable as the impossible. One must therefore rethink the ontological argument which falsely assumes that any concept could define God's essence. We must renounce all concepts and stick strictly to incomprehensibility. Impossibility becomes "the distinctive hallmark of God's difference with regard to man" (28). The argument becomes turned upside down and the impossibility of God's impossibility proves precisely divine possibility: "The necessity of God's possibility flows from the impossibility of his impossibility" (29). Marion suggests that we write this "the [im-]possible" (30).

He then analyzes the metaphysical definition of omnipotence which attempts to speak of this relationship between divine possibility and human impossibility. This omnipotence, however, is defined in terms of human boundaries of what is possible, which God is not permitted to transcend. Reason must still determine God, and based on our earlier analyses we know that this is deeply unsatisfying to Marion. In speaking of mere metaphysical impossibility, we confine God to our understanding. We thus have to allow for a radical possibility that transcends all impossibility. This means, for Marion, that God's relationship to possibility "can no longer be thought in terms of omnipotent efficiency" (33). Abstract and arbitrary omnipotence is disqualified as unsuitable. We must somehow describe God's relation to possibility without "*reducing* or *degrading* it to the level of omnipotence" (33; emphasis his). Already in Descartes Marion had rejected mere omnipotence, or even more so, efficient causality, as inappropriate names for God. He shows here even more clearly why that is the case and how a more phenomenological notion of impossibility and dynamic efficiency might be recovered to speak of the divine. Using certain biblical passages Marion suggests that divine power must be thought in terms of kenotic love expressed as forgiveness and faithfulness, not in terms of an abstract notion of omnipotence.[22] Again "being" and "power" are overcome by love in a fashion that clearly mirrors Pascal's overcoming of the Cartesian definitions of God (among which omnipotence figures prominently) with his third order of charity.

Transcendence or Immanence?

Marion's attempt to free God from the language of being and his proposal of the saturated phenomenon are probably the aspects of his work that have received the widest attention and criticism. Especially his presentation to the first Villanova conference and the subsequent article have been taken up by several commentators. I will therefore briefly consider some of these critics in a separate section and respond to them by way of concluding this consideration of Marion's work on the topic of God. I will begin with John Caputo, Thomas Carlson, and Robyn Horner and then move on to a different critique by Richard Kearney, Bruce Benson, and John Manoussakis.

John Caputo

In his response to Marion's presentation at Villanova, John Caputo finds that Marion simply repeats Derrida's intent in *Sauf le nom*, namely, to protect God's name and keep it safe from idolatries and from being brought into presence. But while for Derrida this implies a loss of the divine name which never becomes present, for Marion it results in a confession of non-knowledge, leading to a higher form of knowledge (that overflows our comprehension with its excess). Caputo asserts that Marion turns Husserl on his head by interpreting the lack of fulfillment in intuition into an overflowing or excessive intuition in the case of God. Derrida's and Marion's readings of Husserl are thus diametrically opposed.[23] For Marion, presence is associated with the concept and thus any idolatrous naming of God is inscribed in the metaphysics of presence, while any pragmatic naming of God in praise escapes presence: "we are given access to God by God's own self-giving or givenness, beyond or without a concept" (GGP, 195). Derrida, on the other hand, does not see this hyper-essentialism escaping presence, but finds that it designates precisely a "meta-metaphysical" or "meta-ontological" "meta-presence" (GGP, 195). According to Derrida and Caputo, this kind of "hyper-Husserlian" way of describing "hyper-essentialism" is still inscribed in an economy. Furthermore, mystical theology continues to affirm God, even as it does so in praise or hyper-language and terminates in "*Gelassenheit*, a deeply affirmative assent to God's advent" (GGP, 197). This affirmative assent to God's advent is apparently to be condemned (unlike Derrida's) because it is rooted in a religious tradition.[24]

In the essay examined earlier (criticizing *God without Being*), Caputo is a bit more generous toward what he calls Marion's second position (namely, the more phenomenological instead of theological one). He suggests that Marion recognizes the need for limits and conditions better in his work on the saturated phenomenon. Even in his desire to dispense with the conditions of the transcendental I and the horizon, Marion plays at the limits of phenomenality and thus allows for a path toward excess (instead of excess without path). Caputo explains that "for Marion, the saturated phenomenon is a *liminal* phenomenon, one that breaches or transgresses ordinary phenomenological limits or horizons but that nonetheless plays on these limits and thus remains dependent upon these constraints and horizons that continue to be *indispensable*."[25] Rather than being completely without limits or conditions, the saturated phenomenon is described as saturating a horizon or transgressing a limit, as possibility of the impossible.[26] This possibility is one that Caputo finds more congenial, because it remains dependent upon certain conditions even as it defies them. The impossible thus remains inscribed into a certain relation between possibility and impossibility and plays on its boundaries, instead of being entirely disconnected from all conditions or relations.[27] Caputo thus judges this account of the saturated phenomenon more successful because it remains within the orbit of Derrida's *différance* (and Heidegger's difference), which means that Marion's project as a whole ultimately precisely fails insofar as it seeks to go beyond Derrida and Heidegger.[28]

Caputo goes on to suggest that the saturated phenomenon (read as a version of Derrida's *différance*) is far too determined. He asks ironically: "Surely the saturated phenomenon is worlds removed and infinitely protected from the blur, the fog, the confusion, the disseminative morass, the sheer noise of deconstruction?"[29] Obviously he will conclude that such is not the case for Marion. He insists against him that this phenomenon might as well be interpreted as the "rustling of the anonymous" instead of as God. Instead of attributing richness to them (as Marion does), one might as well interpret these phenomena as poor and confused, even superficial. Just as for Lévinas God can possibly be confused with the *il y a*, this may also be true of the saturated phenomenon, which might as well be saturated with anonymity and abandonment.[30] In contrast to Marion's emphasis on excess, Caputo favors anonymity, abandonment, melancholy, saturation in terms of zero quantity, confusion, differences; an undecidability that is "vulnerable, ambiguous, frail."[31]

In a recent address, Caputo similarly condemns Marion's "Platonism" (again interpreting Marion's language of excess as recalling Plato's imagery of the "good beyond being"). He compares Marion's degrees of givenness to Plato's divided line and contends that saturated phenomena are phenomena of imagination, because they are not actually given and are merely phenomena of possibility. Therefore phenomena of revelation cannot be distinguished from other kinds of imaginative phenomena (such as centaurs or unicorns) and do not constitute a higher degree of phenomenality. And while great literature or poetry may actually "reveal" something about our lives, it cannot "lay down the one and only way God can reveal or give Godself." Marion has not established that the phenomenon of revelation is the only or even the best way in which God could appear. Caputo thinks that Marion's "account is open to numerous objections: that it confuses Revelation with magic or simply with imagining things; that by its literalization of Scriptural narratives it runs the risk of treating the Scriptures not as icon but as idol; and finally that it cuts off in advance other approaches to Revelation and in particular other approaches to Scriptural hermeneutics." Again Caputo worries about Marion's allegiances to a conservative Roman Catholic agenda and objects to "the particular flavor of his theology," which he contends is non-correlational. In Marion we get "an attempt to identify God's own self-donation with a very literalizing understanding of the Christian Scriptures by way of a contrived rendering of phenomenology." Marion aligns himself far too much with "the bishop," the hierarchy, and the Vatican.[32]

Others have also criticized the "unconditioned" nature of Marion's discourse or accused him of "colonialism." Eric Boynton, for example, wonders,

> can the traditional concept of revelation and the phenomenological exploration of the enigmatic site agree that the happening of the mysterious self-manifestation (which strictly does not appear) be nominated the God of a determinate tradition? Does the "appearance" of God, however mysterious or ineffable, in the enigmatic site remain a requirement held for reasons pertaining to phenomenological inquiry or for reasons of theological commitment? Can the unconditioned event of the gift, merely signaled within phenomenology, properly and surpassingly be explored through a determinate tradition without conditioning the unconditioned? Can a Christian theology, whose language requires and insists upon a referent that is neither indeterminate nor dispensable, help but identify and determine the wholly other, the utterly unnameable? Does the phenomenological discovery of the unconditioned mark God's disappearance, at least an explicitly Christian God? Asked differently, does the bringing together of the concept of

revelation and the enigmatic site make questionable the very idea of revelation expressed in the Christian tradition?[33]

In what follows, Boynton engages in a comparison of Marion's writing about the icon and Heidegger's analysis of the work of art and complains on the one hand that the icon is too transcendent and not rooted in a historical reality, and, on the other hand, that it is too determinate and carries pre-ordained theological content. He suggests that "if Marion seeks to liberate God from conditions of Being or thought (for Marion, from conditions altogether) this is only possible by a gesture that submits God to the anteriority of iconic givenness or love." Although he does not explicitly name Marion in his conclusion one must assume he means him when he condemns

> the more enthusiastic, overstated, even indefensible claims of postmodern theology — claims insisting upon a theological surpassing of critical or reductive philosophical thought, claims that inevitably misfire in a theological determination or fetishizing of a professed otherness ... The God of phenomenology in the hands of theology becomes a form of violence not only visited theologically on the forms of religion generally, but even subjects a specifically Christian expression to a kind of theological colonialism.[34]

Marlène Zarader similarly criticizes what she perceives as Marion's introduction of transcendence into phenomenology. She wonders "whether, and under what conditions, is it possible to affirm a transcendence within a strictly philosophical discourse, in particular when this discourse claims to be phenomenological."[35] In general she follows Janicaud's criticism by chiding both Marion's and Lévinas' attempts to make transcendence thinkable within phenomenology. She concludes "that philosophy has no access to transcendence, whether transcendence is understood as a being, as God, or as the Other. A fundamental closure of philosophy makes it, in principle, unable to grasp transcendence, insofar as this is understood according to the category of an excess with respect to presence."[36] She suggests that radical phenomenology attempts to escape this dedication to presence and thus allows for something like transcendence to be considered, but judges Lévinas' and Marion's attempts to do this as insufficient because they cannot read transcendence only by its evidence in experience but make dogmatic assumptions. Their phenomena are not "situated within experience." The requirements seem contradictory: transcendence both must and cannot enter into experience. She concludes: "The phantasm of a pure or absolute alterity proves to be unachievable."[37]

Thomas Carlson

Thomas Carlson in many ways agrees with Caputo's presentation, although his analysis is overall more careful and more generous. While Caputo simply rejects Marion's religious commitments and apparent determinations with their concurrent emphasis on excess rather than lack, Carlson actually articulates in what way such commitments might become problematic for Marion's phenomenological project. Carlson concludes his work *Indiscretion* with a chapter comparing Marion and Derrida on the question of the gift.[38] He detects three figures of the gift as "impossible" in contemporary theology and phenomenology: as goodness beyond being, as saturated givenness, and as death. Carlson judges the first primarily theological (Neoplatonic) and associates it with Marion's theology, the second primarily phenomenological and associated with Marion's phenomenology, the third a possibility of conversation between the two opened by Derrida. He summarizes both Marion's theology and his phenomenology in detail. Regarding Marion's analysis of the language of praise, he points out that Marion and Derrida differ on whether this language refers to a "Requisite" (i.e., a clear referent). For Derrida, the referent is empty or even dispensable, while for Marion the referent always remains required. Carlson insists that Marion is making claims not only about theology here, but indeed about the "very essence of language," and that a very similar analysis of language reappears in his phenomenological work. Carlson finds this close alignment between Marion's philosophy and his theology troubling, because it brings a theological determination into a phenomenology that is supposedly undetermined.[39]

Although Marion maintains that his phenomenology is without theological determinations, Carlson sees the two interacting far more closely. He points to profound parallels between the two projects. Language functions in Marion's phenomenology, for example, in a very similar fashion to the language in Marion's theology. In both cases, according to Carlson, language appears as a gift from a distant origin and to which the recipient must respond (205). Carlson indicates that Derrida suspects behind this anonymous call the determinate claim of the Father which therefore would inscribe Marion in an economy that annuls the gift. Although Marion's phenomenology does indeed keep the call unknown and anonymous, the structure and appearance of the one claimed or responding parallels his theological account.[40]

Carlson finds these parallels troubling because they seem to jeopardize Marion's project. In his theological work, Marion determines phenomenological descriptions through theological ones (such as using Christ as the paradigm for any icon). While he attempts to eliminate these determinations in his phenomenology, Carlson does not judge this move successful. He finds that Marion's taking up of the notion of revelation within strictly phenomenological domains "leads to a strange bind: either the phenomenology of revelation sheds no light on Revelation — which leaves one to wonder what meaning or purpose such a phenomenology might have — or else Revelation can indeed be described according to the phenomenology of the saturated phenomenon — in which case one is left to wonder how the saturated phenomenon's 'unavailability' relates to the real, historical experience that would define Revelation" (209). Unlike Caputo, who speaks of them as two distinct projects, Carlson sees a profound continuity between Marion's theology and his phenomenology. He compares Marion's analysis of revelation in phenomenology with his treatment of God in theology and decides that they are "nearly identical," in that they are both "purely self-authorizing because unconditionally self-manifesting" (211). He goes on to outline the parallels between Marion's treatment of "God" in both accounts and judges them identical or at least parallel in terms of the lack of restraint or reserve with which God is given, the lack of horizon or emphasis on invisibility in both, and the notion of abandon which functions significantly in both. Carlson wonders whether the historical determination God receives in Marion's theology does not jeopardize Marion's phenomenological account, where the phenomenon of revelation is given without community or history as a pure and unconditional gift.[41] It is not clear, in Carlson's view, that Marion's phenomenological God is distinguishable from his theological one.[42]

Carlson turns to Derrida in order to alleviate (or at least explicate) this problem in Marion's accounts. He parallels the tension between the determinacy of Marion's theology and the indeterminacy of his phenomenology to Derrida's analysis of negative theology as always undoing its own tradition, drawing particularly on Derrida's objections to Marion's analysis of praise or prayer as non-predicative. Despite all of Dionysius' negativity, the one whom he praises or to whom he prays is still the Christian God and his language can be clearly identified as Christian; thus his prayer is not pure. In fact, "the condition of possibility for such a determinate, tradition-bound prayer — namely, its iterability or citationality — might well call the possibility of pure address as such into question" (218). Derrida, in other words, is held to provide us with a balance between the possible and the impossible in theology.[43] Carlson thus desires a balance between determination and indetermination. An account that is theologically committed and rooted in a community and tradition must be balanced with and encircled by an indeterminate discourse which constantly challenges it.

Carlson further explicates these suggestions by contrasting Marion and Derrida in terms of a theological and a thanatological account of the impossible, one that parallels Caputo's distinction between excess and *khora*. While Marion circles "in endless desire" around the "inconceivable and ineffable generosity of the Good beyond Being," in Derrida death becomes the "figure of the gift in its 'impossibility'" (229). For both Heidegger and Derrida, "death marks a possibility that can never be realized in experience, the horizon of all possibility that itself *remains* at every moment possible and thus marks the impossible."[44] Carlson views this indeterminacy between the excess of the Good and the lack or absence of the gift in terms of death as indispensable. And although he sees both aspects in both figures, he suggests that "in the end, Derrida may sustain this undecidability in a way that Marion does not, since Derrida recognizes the possible indiscretion between revelation and death, whereas Marion wants finally to avoid it — but Marion's own phenomenology, despite such avoidance, could nevertheless invite a similar undecidability" (231). Marion does not free the referent in the same way that Derrida does, nor can his exclusion of indiscretion be justified on phenomenological terms. Although outlining a certain indecidability between presence and absence, Marion is "unfaithful to such indeterminacy" (232). Marion excludes the thought of death in a most ungenerous fashion by presenting it as confiscating possibility.[45] Carlson wants to see the phenomena of the saturated phenomenon and of death as indistinguishable figures of impossibility and finds that Marion draws distinctions between them that are too stark and are meant only to preserve a more determinate naming of God. He concludes that "while Marion's phenomenology points powerfully toward the undecidable, he in fact seems nevertheless to have decided" because he remains too much a prisoner of his own Neoplatonism (234).

Thus Marion ultimately resembles Aquinas rather than Dionysius because he is so convinced of the "unlimited plentitude of the saturated phenomenon" and has always already decided for it and against lack or death. Carlson wants, instead, to go with Derrida "in the other direction, in the direction where one really could not decide, or where one could really only *decide*—without knowing—whether the impossibility one faces is that of plenitude or poverty, revelation or death" (235). He therefore advocates a philosophy of religion that maintains the interplay between apophatic mysticism and phenomenology.[46] While Carlson's criticism of Marion is more balanced than that of Caputo, he too ultimately interprets Marion as limiting transcendence to notions of excess and as not being sufficiently "discreet" in his account of the divine. A similar sentiment is expressed by Robyn Horner.

Robyn Horner

In *Rethinking God as Gift*, Horner dedicates three chapters to Marion, comparing him to Derrida in a fashion very similar to that of Caputo. Like both Caputo and Carlson, she writes from a more theological or religious perspective and yet ironically examines mostly Marion's phenomenology. She gives a careful and thorough outline and summary of *Reduction and Givenness*, as well as of parts of *Being Given*. She also reviews both Janicaud's and Derrida's criticisms. In doing so, she discovers many parallels between Marion's phenomenological and theological work, defending him against some of his more violent philosophical critics. Yet Horner finds, similarly to Caputo, that God is too clearly determined in Marion's work. Speaking about Marion's theological works she claims, "there is no undecidability about this giving. 'God' may be 'crossed out,' but it is certainly God who orients the given that exceeds being. Marion tries to protect God from reductionism not only by withdrawing God from intelligibility (by using the device of crossing out), but by introducing the horizon of distance" (RGG, 112–13). She continues, "the question is whether or not distance can separate the terms sufficiently to allow for infinite interpretability. It seems to me that in making God an absolute term, Marion has potentially compromised his reading" (RGG, 113). Horner, too, then, finds Marion's decision for God or excess, rather than for emptiness or indetermination, objectionable. She also sees this decision as influencing his more phenomenological works.

For her, therefore, it becomes impossible to demarcate the border between philosophy and theology in Marion in a meaningful fashion. Marion's project fails, however, if the two discourses cannot be clearly distinguished. After examining to what extent *Reduction and Givenness* is theological, Horner decides that it is indeed a phenomenological work, but is guided by theological concerns:

> Marion is not writing an explicit work of theology: it demands no theological commitments and does not articulate theological themes. Instead, he sets out to develop a phenomenology, one that is expanded to encompass not only what is given in fullness of intuition but also that which gives itself without the completion of signification. Nevertheless, in so doing he is working at the border of phenomenology and theology because he wants to allow for the possibility that less usual "objects" (that is, we learn more fully in *Etant donné*, phenomena of revelation) might be brought within the realm of phenomenological study. (RGG, 114)

She then judges that the question of whether Marion's project "fails" or might be "relevant for a renewed consideration of the relationship between philosophy and theology" is left open in this work (RGG, 114). She goes on to explore *Being Given* in greater detail but does not find that its argument finally resolves the issue.[47] Ultimately, both theology and philosophy fall short in Marion's work. She defines the impasse under which he labors as follows: "Phenomenology cannot deliver phenomena of revelation/Revelation as such, and therefore it seems that the conversation between phenomenology and theology cannot take place, at least not without doing violence to the neutral (as distinct from the natural) attitude of phenomenology. . . . Like the gift, a God handed over into intellectual custody would be no God at all" (RGG, 158). Theology fails in Marion because it cannot give a determined God, cannot make Revelation actual in any sense. Phenomenology, on the other hand, is taken captive by Marion's Christian theology of revelation and thus cannot remain neutral. Marion's gift still "gives too much" (RGG, 180). Horner therefore aligns herself with Caputo and ultimately with Derrida in judging Marion's analysis of the gift insufficient and too determined.[48] She reiterates repeatedly Caputo's judgment that "Marion still argues for the success of phenomenology, and for excessive phenomena, whereas Derrida puts forward the failure of phenomenology and opts for aporetic experience," finding Marion convincing only insofar as "he lays his bets on the Name, [and if] 'his' Name gives — from the outside at least — no more than Derrida's," but she is not convinced that such is the case (RGG, 246). Horner, Carlson, and Caputo concur, then, that to describe God in terms of excess and saturation instead of deficiency, lack, or *khora* is too determined and so undesirable. They all seek to reach a greater indecidability or indeterminacy and find Derrida more useful in that respect.

In contrast to Kearney, whose criticism I examined in the introduction to this part and to whom I will return momentarily, Horner actually does find a hermeneutic at work in Marion. She even sees the value of Marion's work mostly in its hermeneutic promises. She sharply criticizes Marion's tendency to interpret revelatory phenomena instead of merely describing them, pushing the readers to make decisions and committing them to a particular interpretation. The interpretation of the phenomenon of excess cannot be left open for Marion because "the undecidability of the excess risks an encounter with 'the Devil,' so to speak, as much as an encounter with God" (RGG, 174). Apparently, she does not see such an encounter as particularly problematic, while this, of course, is a major problem for Kearney, who criticizes Marion precisely for leaving this excess too undecidable. She thus does observe a hermeneutic at work in Marion: "To risk God rather than the Devil involves 'seeing' the icon in a particular way. Seeing makes use of the light; phenomenology is a science of the light. Perhaps that is why Marion refers to phenomena of revelation/Revelation as blinding in their excess, overwhelming, while Derrida's undecidable gap is a black hole" (RGG, 174–75). She interprets Marion as following von Balthasar in this interpretation of light and revelation. For both theologians, the phenomenon is seen by the ones committed to a particular community of faith.[49] She recognizes also that there is not merely structure or form in Marion (as in Derrida), but also some content, in that God can be known as a phenomenon (RGG, 176). For Horner, Marion's particular determination of God jeopardizes his hermeneutic and gives God too much content.[50]

Ruud Welten

Welten investigates Marion's project from a more clearly phenomenological perspective. His central argument against Marion is that one cannot dispense with intentionality but that it plays a much more important role in a recognition or reception of the divine phenomenon than Marion admits. He approaches Marion's work within the framework of a more clearly Husserlian focus, but does concentrate his reflections on implications of this framework for the possibility of speaking of phenomena of revelation. He wonders about Marion's "faithfulness to Husserl" precisely because he is interested in the possible relationship between phenomenology and theology. He formulates the problem as follows:

> From a phenomenological starting point, the question becomes: how is God given to me? Leaving theology aside, the issue becomes a question of givenness; a phenomenological question. The point is that we can only do phenomenology if we leave all theological motivations between brackets. However, if we do so, we never can reach the point where givenness is God's givenness without adjusting our intentionality to our religious desire. We can only describe a kind of givenness in which the phenomenality of

God can be described; a phenomenology that opens up the possibility of God's pure givenness.[51]

He insists that "disappointment" is not only essential for Husserl in the appearing of the phenomenon but also an important feature of revelation. Marion, in his view, does not take sufficient account of this important aspect of the self-revealing of the phenomenon. He insists that "disappointment is not the counterpart of revelation but, rather, one of its true manifestations. Understood from its noetic side, God disappoints me. From a theological point of view, however, this might mean that disappointment belongs to the paradoxical structure of religious belief itself."[52]

Yet, in Welten's view, "disappointment does not abolish knowledge; it yields knowledge. . . . in a case of disappointment, the intuition disagrees with the intention. The object appears as 'other' than the object of the intended act. This disappointment seems to be the radical counterpart of fulfillment; it is a kind of un-fulfillment."[53] He thinks that this structure describes the saturated phenomenon well, but insists more than Marion on the lack of fulfillment in this context: "The saturated phenomenon can be described as a phenomenon that I do not expect. However, this 'not expecting' is not accidental, but fundamental. It belongs to the paradoxical structure of belief. The Messiah is 'longed for' but he comes always unexpected. He does *not* exactly *fulfill* our expectations."[54] Indeed, he thinks that this structure of disappointment is particularly characteristic of religious experience. Welten emphasizes that although this thinking is useful for describing religious phenomena, it only describes possibilities and affirms nothing about the reality of God: "The possibility of a saturated phenomenon cannot guarantee the appearance of God if my intention does not long for him."[55] He concludes that he has shown that "the saturated phenomenon cannot escape intentionality. The saturated phenomenon remains possible only because intention is already involved. . . . To read Marion through Husserlian eyes discloses this fundamental human experience: no *promises* without disappointment."[56]

Richard Kearney

Since I have already examined Richard Kearney's criticism of Marion in the introduction, I will only recapitulate it briefly here. It is important in this context, however, since it is almost diametrically opposed to that of Horner, Carlson, and Caputo (less so to Welten's). While they see Marion as determining God too much and being too committed to a particular religious tradition, Kearney sees Marion as too indeterminate. Marion's God is "too transcendent" and therefore in danger of becoming "so unknowable and invisible as to escape all identification whatsoever."[57] In Kearney's view, "Marion distills negative theology (as enunciated by Dionysius and Gregory of Nyssa) into an uncompromising 'theology of absence.' The 'saturated phenomenon' of mystical eucharistic encounter with the divine is informed by such a *hyper*-excess that it cannot be seen, known, or understood. Its very superabundance surpasses all predication and narration" (32). On the one hand, Kearney feels that this God becomes so overwhelming that there is nothing left for humans to do: "there is nothing further for us to think, say, or do to make the Word more fully alive in this world" (32). On the other hand, this God becomes so hyper-excessive and hyper-absent that no experience of the divine is possible. Kearney sees this as a very dangerous move:

> We hit here upon a serious hermeneutic muddle. If the saturating phe-
> nomenon is really as bedazzling as Marion suggests, how can we tell the
> difference between the divine and its opposites? How are we to distinguish
> between enabling and disabling revelation? Who is it that speaks when God
> speaks from the burning bush? And if it is true indeed, as Saint Paul con-
> cedes, that the Messiah comes like a thief in the night, in the very same
> passage (1 Thessalonians 5), Paul, pace Marion, calls for sober and enlight-
> ened vigilance . . . Such Pauline sobriety seems a far cry from Marion's
> celebration of blind mystical rapture (33).

Throughout, Kearney is deeply critical of any talk about God that—like Marion's—lacks hermeneutic connection and is unable to make clear distinctions
between enabling and disabling revelations, between the divine and the monstrous, since he judges this to dispense with all considerations of ethics and
justice.

In contrast to what he sees as the limitations of Marion's project, Kearney
wants to hold open God's transcendence as much as possible, while acknowledging that we must make judgments and distinctions for the sake of justice
and ethics. Such judgments, he suggests, although always made in fear and
trembling, become possible through narrative or diacritical hermeneutics.
Thus although he conceives of his own commitment to a particular religious
tradition as widely as possible, he acknowledges such commitment.[58] It matters, on Kearney's account, whether the God of whom we speak cares about
widows, orphans, and strangers or devours them. It matters whether we can
face this God with hope in the future and whether we are challenged to be
transformed into people who will help the divine to become immanent and
welcome the kingdom of justice and peace. We "help God be God" when we
"offer a cup of cold water" to a person in desperate need. In order to be committed to such a vision of God and not a monstrous or unjust one, we require
hermeneutic judgment that recovers eschatological interpretations of the stories which narrate this divinity of hope, peace, and justice. It is this emphasis
on justice and peace that Marion neglects.

John Milbank concurs with this judgment to some extent. Most of his criticism of Marion is a contention that Marion remains Cartesian because he
does not allow for content in his talk about God and the self and allows for
no genuine relationship between them.[59] He insists that the biblical account

must feature more prominently in any consideration of the possibility of God's self-giving: "The countervailing movement of a faithful, ecclesial reception of God's offer — Christ's person and finally his suffering — commences as soon as Christ commences, and accompanies him throughout his path. Otherwise there would remain no trace of him in human records at all." Instead, in his view Marion "ignores the hermeneutic priority of the necessary reception of Christ by Israel in the person of Mary. Without this reception, without this 'reciprocity,' the gift would be so thwarted that it could not even begin to be this gift — the incarnate God."[60] He therefore concludes that a phenomenology of revelation (or of the gift) requires an ontology. In a later text, where he again strongly censures Marion's account of the gift, he contends that Marion's recognition of the divine phenomenon "acknowledges only the idol of an abstract God, whose gift is as effectively abyssal and absent as that of Marion's atheistic interlocutors." He continues by speaking of this giving as "arbitrary," of its reception as a "violent rupture," and of its giver as "hostile."[61] Marion's account, then, remains insufficient, because it is not filled with Christian content and because it claims to access a pure experience beyond metaphysical parameters.

Bruce Benson

Bruce Benson's exploration of "modern idolatry" deals with the same aporia we have uncovered in Marion: "Is there a way to speak of God that both makes God present and allows God to remain other to us?"[62] How might one negotiate between absolute transcendence and complete immanence? How to speak of God without determining the divine in a fashion that becomes idolatrous? Benson responds to these questions by employing the work of Nietzsche, Derrida, and Marion. He sees Marion especially attempting to take up precisely this task of overcoming onto-theology and idolatry through negotiating the balance between saying too much of God and remaining completely silent (187). After outlining Marion's analysis of idol and icon, Benson goes on to highlight what he sees as the "fundamental problem with Marion's account," namely that it is too located in the Roman Catholic tradition and excludes other experiences of God, thus becoming idolatrous itself. In Benson's view Marion lacks a "mediating logos" (200). Marion is so focused on the divine Logos that he is unable to establish any clear hermeneutic that might transmit the divine Word in(to) human words. In a more recent review of *Being Given*, Benson expresses his worry in the following fashion:

> Put in a theological context, does the revealed Logos break through as a "pure phenomenon" without any horizon? Or does that Logos depend upon the context of, say, Old Testament prophecies for its very identity (at least for us)? Or, alternatively, when the Logos becomes present to us in the breaking of the bread, how much does its meaning (again, at least for us) depend upon the very ordinary biological reality that bread sustains life and the very particular historical occurrences of the Passover and the Last Supper?[63]

Benson summarizes Marion's account of the saturated phenomenon, focusing especially on his proposal for a language of praise that might get beyond metaphysical predication. With Derrida he censures Marion's suspension of the phenomenological horizon and like Kearney would suggest that such suspension makes it impossible either to maintain the anonymity of the call (as proceeding from any other and not merely from God) or to distinguish meaningfully between different calls. Like Kearney he concludes that "it would seem that only if God can be identified can there be theological talk" (212). While this might eliminate certain kinds of idolatry, Benson fears that it will merely institute new idols. Furthermore, God-talk becomes so "apophatic" that it can be no longer distinguished from any other indeterminate discourse: "If God's primary characteristic becomes the lack of identity, then does not all talk of things that cannot be properly identified have the potential to turn into talk about God?" (213).

Benson therefore ends up agreeing with Kearney by likening Marion to the early Christian heretic Marcion.[64] For both, God cannot truly appear and incarnation is therefore impossible:

> Although an invisible and inapproachable icon may be saved from being defiled by the flesh, such cannot be the true God-man who is seen. So Marion's God still ends up sounding a bit too close to the god of the philosophers. In the end, Marion and Marcion both shy from accepting the fundamental christological aporia, that Christ is fully God and fully man. Instead of facing the excruciating demands of an orthodox Christology that attempts to navigate between the Scylla of transcendence and the Charybdis of immanence, Marion denies the true iconic nature of Christ and so succumbs to the idolatry of transcendence. (223)[65]

For both Kearney and Benson, then, Marion's talk about God is ultimately too transcendent, too un-identifiable, too abstract. It lacks hermeneutic grounding and theological determination, because it does not become "incarnate" (or at least does not acknowledge an incarnate God).

John Manoussakis

John Panteleimon Manoussakis uses Marion in his own attempt to elucidate a phenomenology of God (or in describing the possibility of God being given to consciousness as a phenomenon). He defends Marion against his critics who think him too theological: "For today's Anytoses and Meletoses, the fact that for Marion 'God' is the 'God of Abraham, Isaac and Jacob,' the God who Jesus dared to call 'Abba,' that is to say, the God of the tradition in which Marion grew up, lives and writes (as if it could have been otherwise), that fact amounts to a betrayal of rigorous science. For such thinkers, it seems, phenomenology ought to have been, to borrow Thomas Nagel's expression, the view from nowhere!"[66] He implies that Marion's phenomenon is too limited in failing to envision the possibility that God might appear as a phenomenon in more than one fashion. No such phenomenon could ever give a complete experience of the divine. He also emphasizes the pole of the recipient as essential. He therefore stresses, like Kearney and Benson, the need for an *incarnation* of the phenomenon:

> It seems then that God can choose from a whole repertoire of epiphanies, from an idol to an icon, and from a trace to a saturated phenomenon. None of these, however, will ever give us the entire God-phenomenon as such, in that all of the theophanies to be found in Greek, Judaic or Christian sources, no matter how opaque or elusive, are made possible by means of an *if* or an *as*—that is, they are made possible by means of hypothesis, imagination, representation, signification—all of which are modalities operated by the I. Revelations and apparitions of God, saturated or otherwise, still have to be perceived somehow and by someone. They have to be seen and felt somatically (to return to the Husserlian principle), they have to become *incarnated* in certain figures, schemes, colors, sounds and smells if they want to be epiphanies at all (*epi-phany* is what appears (*phainesthai*) to or upon someone and thus, is still a phenomenon). Prophets and mystics speak of their apocalyptic visions in metaphors, in similes and in narrations, that is, they process them through language in order to be experienced by them and communicated to others. All of these, though, constitute horizons, conditions as they are, that exclude the possibility of any 'pure,' unconditional giving of God.[67]

He claims that Marion tries to go beyond this and attempts to think a phenomenon that is not conditioned or in some way constituted by consciousness. He concludes that such a phenomenon would be blinding in an intense degree: "Thus, if God is ever to appear, He has only two options: either to be reduced to the modalities of the *as* and the *if*, conditioned by the subject's imagination and experience, or to appear unconditionally in all His excessive glory but at the subject's own risk." Instead of these rather extreme alternatives, he favors a third option, "where the I does *not* look and does *not* see but experiences the Other's look."[68] Overall Manoussakis emphasizes the need for relationship that he finds missing in Marion. God should neither be turned into an object nor become so unknowable that no relation is possible at all. He summarizes his central concern as follows:

> We have seen that every effort to seek God's givenness among various intuitions or by means of an intuition that will correspond or even exceed my intention amounts to seek God ontically, as a thing among things; it also amounts to an attempt to turn God into an object that the I will eventually *know* or *possess*. However, the only way to "know" God *and* the only way for God to know me is not as a being (ontically), but as a person (ontologically)—a person with whom I have (and He has) a relationship. On the other hand, we have also seen that it is possible for God to "appear" in the experience of His look in me. In this way, I have an experience of God as the invisible gaze that sees but is not seen. Strictly speaking, then, God "appears" while He remains invisible; He appears, nevertheless, in me and

only in me, a fact that indicates that, insofar as I am the Other for God, an Other that He can look at and be in relationship with, God is in *need* of me as the horizon that possibilizes His (otherwise impossible) appearance. The human person, and therefore every human person, is understood as the sacred place of God's epiphany.[69]

Manoussakis, then, does not criticize Marion as harshly as some of the other thinkers but rather employs him as an opening for his own thinking about the possibility of God's appearing. Yet, in emphasizing the need for relation and for a multiplicity of ways of divine appearing, he does imply that Marion's account is both too transcendent and too limited.[70]

Is Marion's talk about God, then, too transcendent, as Kearney, Benson, and to some extent even Manoussakis claim? Or is it too immanent, as Caputo, Carlson, Horner, and Welten seem to suggest? Does Marion connect the saturated phenomenon too much to his particular ecclesial tradition or does he sever all ties to an authentic Christian sense of the incarnation by disappearing into flights of disembodied mysticism? Or is he maybe committing both errors at once, one in his theological, the other in his phenomenological work? I would suggest that the thorough preparation and deep roots of Marion's later work in his earlier treatments of Descartes guide us further here also. It seems to me that the manner in which Marion situates the Cartesian attempts to talk about God, especially the proofs of God's existence (regardless of their obvious failure), serves to indicate the fashion in which his own work is grounded. Marion argues that Descartes is interacting with the traditional medieval ways of naming God, although he does not clearly articulate such interaction in his explication of the proofs. Similarly, I would say, Marion is articulating his own talk about God clearly within the context of a tradition, even when he does not always highlight all of the ways in which his work is indebted to that tradition. In closing this chapter I would like to go back to a possibility I suggested earlier, namely that Marion's theological and phenomenological talk about God can be read as a recovery on the one hand of medieval notions of analogy (appropriately understood) and on the other hand of the Pascalian distinctions between different types of truth or evidence (or "orders"). Both of these I think will serve to highlight how Marion does maintain a clear balance between transcendence and immanence, between phenomenological freedom and hermeneutic contextuality.

First, as I pointed out in the introduction to this part, it seems somewhat incongruent to condemn Marion's work both for its indeterminacy and for its determinacy. His language of excess and saturation is interpreted *both* as lacking hermeneutic connection and making it impossible to identify or experience God *and* as limiting the divine to the good instead of leaving open the indeterminacy of *khora*. On the one hand, Marion is criticized for his emphasis on transcendence, on purity, on anonymity, on separation of God from particular historical idols. On the other hand, he is also censured for his emphasis on immanence, for his use of biblical examples and the incarnation, for his faithfulness to the Roman Catholic tradition, sacraments, and hierarchy, and for theological resonances in his phenomenological analysis of God, self, and other. Yet it is precisely the latter that guards against excess in the former. Clearly interpreters and critics work with preconceptions about how much transcendence is acceptable and how much immanence is required in order to speak adequately of the divine. And one's judgment about the appropriate balance to a great extent shapes how one interprets or judges Marion's work on this issue.

In contrast maybe to a purely philosophical endeavor, theology — it seems to me — requires commitment and not merely empty desire. It requires commitment to a community, in order to guard against individualistic fideism and disembodied mysticism. Talk about God that is not connected to a community and a tradition quickly degenerates into individualistic speculation that lacks responsibility. Similarly connection to community and tradition preserve God-talk from becoming so abstract that it is no longer concerned with bodies, with suffering and redeemed flesh. It seems to me that it is precisely Marion's commitment to his particular ecclesial tradition that preserves his theology from becoming too transcendent and his focus on the Eucharist that reminds him of the embodied flesh of the incarnation and guards against a disembodied "god of the philosophers" only. It is clear, furthermore, that Marion does get the inspiration for his analysis of the divine phenomenon from the sources of Scripture and the Christian tradition. At times he is even rather insistent upon the need to rely upon a community of faith or even an ecclesial hierarchy or an apostolic tradition in one's talk about God. Although such statements are set within the context of his theological writings, obviously his phenomenological description of revelation is also informed by such sources. In some sense, in fact, his discourse about God is accomplished as a hermeneutic move. The liturgical acts of the sacraments and of one's participation in the liturgy serve as the hermeneutic framework for interpreting an experience of God. The fact that this is not always an interpretation of strictly biblical texts, but very often one of liturgical actions and experience, does not seem to detract from its essentially hermeneutic character. Marion's work, it seems to me, is hermeneutically grounded in the tradition of the church (including an interesting balance of Western and Eastern theological aspects) and specifically in its liturgical experience, especially in its apex, the experience of the Eucharist. It is no surprise, then, that even Marion himself speaks of "Eucharistic hermeneutics." That hermeneutic grounding of Marion's work, it seems to me, has only been condemned as limiting but too little acknowledged as providing immanence to his talk about God's transcendence. And although Marion does not always explicitly address the ways in which particular liturgical actions function hermeneutically, he obviously assumes that such liturgical action speaks powerfully of an experience of God. This is particularly clear in his analysis of the divine kenosis in suffering and death and of the Eucharist that I examined in chapter

5. The experience of the liturgy, the participation in the life of the Church and especially in the mystery of the Eucharist, helps us to see differently, provides us with the concepts for a religious experience we could not otherwise articulate. Marion examines this in more detail in his analysis of the story of the Emmaus disciples.[71] He points out that their vision was not lacking, that intuition was present but they were unable to recognize it because they lacked concepts for it.[72]

While Marion here employs a phenomenological terminology of the adequation between intuition and signification, he is doing so both as a hermeneutic exercise (through interpreting the biblical text) and in order to point to the hermeneutic necessary for recognizing the divine. For Marion the problem is not that God is utterly transcendent or that the divine is not revealed to us, but rather that we are unable to grasp what is given: "God does not measure out stingily his intuitive manifestation, as if he wanted to mask himself at the moment of showing himself. But we do not offer concepts capable of handling a gift without measure and, overwhelmed, dazzled, and submerged by his glory, we no longer see anything"[73] (This is not to say, of course, that we could or should ever have such adequate concepts.) Christ therefore provides a hermeneutic in the story that enables the disciples to recognize (though of course not "grasp") what they are seeing. This hermeneutic is located in the action of the breaking of the bread, which is more powerful than all Christ's previous explanation and crowns the interpretation of the Scriptures. Marion concludes: "What we lack in order to believe is quite simply one with what we lack in order to see. Faith does not compensate, either here or anywhere else, for a defect of visibility: on the contrary, it allows reception of the intelligence of the phenomenon and the strength to bear the glare of its brilliance. Faith does not manage the deficit of evidence — it alone renders the gaze apt to see the excess of the pre-eminent saturated phenomenon, the Revelation."[74] When Marion speaks of the faith that sees or receives the phenomenon of revelation, he does not mean a blind faith that defies knowledge and replaces better judgment, but a hermeneutic vision that is able to recognize what it would not otherwise see.

Marion's recent paper on God as the impossible, which I examined above, does not therefore present a radical departure from his prior work (as Caputo suggested in his brief response to the original presentation at Villanova). To speak of the God who is faithful to the divine word, who does only what is consistent with the divine character, who offers infinite forgiveness, is to speak of the God who is exposed on the cross and who offers the broken body and shed blood of Christ in the Eucharist. The God of excessive love and infinite gift whom Marion's phenomenology explores as the supremely saturated phenomenon is hermeneutically grounded in the texts and experiences of the liturgy and the actions of the Eucharistic community. Marion does not speak from a "divine point of view" without hermeneutic connection to actual religious experience.[75] Rather he explores radically the phenomenological possibilities of the actual experience and action of the ecclesial community of which he is a part and of that evidenced by the writers of the Christian tradition, both East and West.

And it is precisely here where I see his own attempt to negotiate between theology and phenomenology paralleling his use of Pascal. Gabellieri says very insightfully (in a footnote): "I am alluding to *L'ontologie grise de Descartes*, the first volume of a remarkable trilogy which J.-L. Marion has devoted to the absence of the relation between ontology and metaphysics/or theology in Descartes. One perceives my question: Is this non-relation not also present in a certain manner in J.-L. Marion himself, the 'saturated phenomenon' replacing the 'white theology' and reflecting no longer the ancient ontology but only the Pascalian order of charity."[76] Marion himself frequently alludes to Pascal's distinctions between two types of rationality, one of the mind and one of the heart, but also sharpens their peculiar logic more than Pascal himself did. He thus does not merely appropriate Pascal's insights, but also modifies them. He makes this the most explicit in an interview. The passage seems so significant to me, that I will quote it in full:

> I am not a follower of Barth. I think, for example, that faith has a logic which is organized and possesses a type of rationality. The contrast between faith and reason, as Pascal sees it, seems to me absolutely detrimental [*verheerend*]. There are different types of rationalities. Yet Revelation [*die Offenbarung*], for example, presupposes a specific critical rationality in comparison with the rationality of the phenomena of the world. There is hence a phenomenality of Revelation which must be described in an ordered fashion conceptually and discursively. One point is that the phenomenality of Revelation must be distinguished from the phenomenality of phenomena of the world. In the same manner I am interested in the "theory of language" presupposed in the so-called "negative theology," a language which is not prospective [*vorausschauend*], not descriptive, and not categorical. Yet it is a language which possesses a perfect rationality. One can show in a similar fashion that there is a performative and pragmatic application which can be described conceptually, even when it is not a prospective application. One finds for example an occasion of a pragmatic use of language in negative theology. There is hence a logic.[77]

It is this different kind of "logic" or rationality that Marion seeks to explore consistently throughout his work. Sometimes he identifies this logic with Pascal's third order of charity, sometimes he calls it an evidence of the heart or a rationality of the will, sometimes a logic of love or a reflection on desire, but he does throughout insist that it is a kind of rationality, a type of logic.[78] It is not mere emotionalism, but a thinking that has its own rigor and is in fact much more appropriate for the topics of the divine or of love. And while Marion's early work explores especially the theological implications of this rationality for speaking of the divine, his more recent phenomenological work emphasizes instead the implications of such a different thinking for the topics of the self and its relation to the other in love.

PART THREE

A Self Open to the Other

INTRODUCTION

"The Sole Master and Servant of the Given"

The saturated phenomenon reformulates not only one's reflection about God but also thought about the human self. Marion often alludes to Jean-Luc Nancy's reference to the "self that comes after the subject." He strongly insists that his phenomenology of excess requires and makes possible such a different and new account of subjectivity. Again, this concern is formulated already in his work on Descartes. On the one hand, of course, the Cartesian ego is the paradigmatic account of modern subjectivity. Marion has highlighted this strong view of the Cartesian subject already in his analysis of the *Regulae*, where the Cartesian *intuitus* displaces and organizes everything else as an object of its own knowing. He summarized this as a first Cartesian metaphysical system, in which the ego becomes the ground of metaphysics by giving being to all beings as thoughts in its quasi-divine mind. On the other hand, Marion also challenges this standard interpretation of Descartes. He suggests that the Cartesian ego, although generally regarded as the paradigmatic modern account of the self-sufficient subject, already trembles in sight of its future and may even be read as being in dialogue with another. Marion argues against a monolithic reading of the Cartesian subject and goes on to interweave these insights in his phenomenological work.

Phenomenologically, Marion seeks to go beyond a Husserlian account of a transcendental subject that would be in control of all phenomena by constituting them in its own consciousness. Although Husserl always emphasized the close connection between noesis and noema, signification and intuition, consciousness and phenomenon, as we have seen in Marion's view he reduces all phenomena to mere objects. Marion takes his cue from Lévinas' critique of Husserl by enlarging Lévinas' reversal of constitution to extend to all saturated phenomena.

In rereading the modern subject and divesting it of its self-sufficient and solipsistic framework, and in giving a phenomenological account of the self's individuation, Marion also moves even more explicitly into the realm of the erotic. While the topic of love has appeared repeatedly, especially in Marion's theological work, for example in the shape of charity as the most appropriate name for the divine, it becomes paramount in Marion's phenomenological interpretations of self and other. We can see clearly how Marion's work culminates in the concern with love as its height and ultimate fulfillment.

Marion's work on self and (human) other, itself fairly recent, has received only little commentary so far but is increasingly gaining notice. A couple of general tendencies can be perceived in what literature does exist. First, Marion is again chided for not being sufficiently faithful to Husserl. James Dodd phrases this criticism particularly well: "To what extent has Marion arbitrarily exempted himself from any serious consideration of one of the essential questions of phenomenological philosophy, the constitution of the self, by simply replacing it with a description of a subject who is buffeted about in a sea of givenness, always only a partial and incomplete response to a call that can never find a genuine home in the response of one who speaks (Husserl) or one who exists (Heidegger)?"[1] Because Marion eliminates the notion of constitution in Husserl's sense and instead speaks of something like "counter-intentionality" or "being constituted" by the phenomenon, he is seen to invalidate Husserl's theory of the centrality of consciousness in phenomenology. In his consideration of a possible "phenomenon of God," Manoussakis similarly points to the difficulty of finding a balance between the need to be open to "the otherness of the Other" and Husserl's insistence that the phenomenon must appear to *me*, that it is given to my consciousness.[2]

Second (stressing one pole of the balance Manoussakis notes), Marion is criticized for an account of the self that is too passive. The self becomes a mere recipient of the incoming phenomenon and loses all constitutive function. Some (as Dodd above) have argued that the lack of constitution implies that one can no longer speak of phenomenology. Others find that the passive self becomes given over to an overwhelming divine giver and phenomenology thus becomes replaced by a (militant and fundamentalist) theology. The self no longer has any initiative and therefore becomes a passive object, manipulated at will by the (divine?) phenomenon. Zarader, for example, finds that for Marion the subject is "wholly summoned outside itself" "by making this ex-propriated subject not that which constitutes the phenomenon, but that which is dispossessed by it. It is therefore called the *Attributaire* (the 'beneficiary' or 'allottee'), understood now not as a subject having the experience of an object, but as a witness stricken by powerlessness who has the 'counter-experience of a non-object'."[3] Yet she wonders whether such a pure experience can be at all possible. She suggests that while "it is indeed possible to think without con-tradiction an experience without object" it is not possible "for an experience without subject." While Husserl can imagine an experience that does not refer to an object, it is impossible to have phenomenology without intentionality (or an intentionality without a subject): "subjectivity may well be redefined, but it remains the living nerve of every phenomenological project."[4]

Third, it has been argued that Marion's self actually is still quite Cartesian and has not freed itself enough from the modern subject. Steven Grimwood, for example, suggests that Marion's subject is not sufficiently embodied. He thinks that "only by insisting that we talk about the generation of meaning by embodied subjects in relation to the image — transcending the coded repre-sentation, the *studium* — instead of the passage of a disembodied gaze into a vacuum, is it possible to understand the relationship between the icon and the viewer in terms of creative participation within the life of the Trinity rather than mutual vaporisation."[5] Thomas Carlson also finds that "a strange trace of sovereignty" remains in Marion's unsettled subject due to "the role that he attributes to decision in the movement from givenness to phenomenality" (CE, 172). Although this criticism seems diametrically opposed to the previ-ous one, Zarader actually switches to it halfway through her reading of Marion. Although Marion tries to turn the subject into one that is "entirely empty, pas-sive, seized upon, affected, powerless, and so on," he ultimately maintains the subject.[6] She finds that "one can vary as one pleases the characteristics attrib-uted to the subject (by privileging its being-affected rather than its active being, for example), yet its *function* (which is to allow the appearing of phenomena) remains unchanged. However, if this function remains unchanged, it means that the character of subjectivity is maintained throughout, and that the prom-ised dispossession or dismissal has not taken place." She maintains that a "con-stitutive instance" is always necessary, and that thus Lévinas and Marion do not succeed in their projects. In her view, "to want the phenomenon to appear absolutely, without reference to any instance that can guarantee its appearing, is to condemn oneself to losing it as phenomenon; and to deprive oneself, as a result, of all justification by phenomenality."[7] With Janicaud, whom she men-tions in this context, she condemns "the tendency of certain post-Heideggerian authors to make the subject ever more passive[, which] follows from their at-tempt to reach the limit where it might become possible for the subject to attend, as absent, the rising up of what presents itself, which, owing to this ab-sence, would finally present itself purely."[8] For both Janicaud and Heidegger this is absurd. She concludes therefore that "if thought wishes to embrace any-thing, even a nothing, it necessarily presupposes a there that guarantees the meaning of the being of this nothing, thus causing it to escape from *pure* alter-ity."[9] The reference to Lévinas is important here. In a sense Marion can be said merely to carry further the dislocation of the self from its seat of power by the other as Lévinas has outlined it. Instead of attributing such dislocation only to the other, however, Marion applies it to all saturated phenomena. Often Lévi-nas' and Marion's projects are criticized or rejected conjointly.

For the topic of the self it seems rather obvious that Marion's analysis of the Cartesian subject would be of relevance. Of course, it is the modern Car-tesian subject that the new phenomenological self attempts to succeed. Yet Marion's work in Descartes is infinitely richer and informs his phenomenolog-ical work far more profoundly than a mere critique of the metaphysical subject found there. And, what seems far less evident, Marion's account of love (char-ity and eros) is also informed by his earlier work in a significant fashion. On the one hand, he explicitly posits his reflections on the phenomenology of eros as "six meditations" replacing those of Descartes. On the other hand, his theology and phenomenology of charity are clearly grounded in his analysis of Pascal's "third order of charity." Before examining Marion's new account of a self open to the other, then, we must again turn to his reflections on Descartes.

seven
Descartes and the Self
"The Ego and the God of the Philosopher
Evaluate Each Other from a Distance"

The status of the subject has been under discussion in much of recent philosophical thought, influenced by and responding to the challenges of Heidegger (to Husserl, Descartes, and Aristotle), Lévinas (to Heidegger), and others. And for many thinkers, not just Marion, it is the Cartesian subject that is thought to be in need of expulsion and dismissal. Marion's reading of this controversy is more subtle. Although he agrees with this criticism of Descartes in many ways, he also qualifies it in an important (and somewhat controversial) fashion. Much of Marion's recent work in phenomenology has been an attempt to rethink the modern subject and to show how its subjectivity is deeply problematic. And on this topic especially the connection between his work on Descartes and his work in phenomenology does not flow in only one direction (which of course it does not do for anything else either). Not only does his analysis of the Cartesian subject influence significantly what he wants to say phenomenologically, but his phenomenology also informs his work on Descartes in important ways (some would say it does so far too much). I will again begin by outlining Marion's work on Descartes and then go on to focus especially on his phenomenology.[1]

Marion examines not only the status of God in Descartes but also that of the ego or subject.[2] On the one hand, he points out the problems and short-comings of the definition of the Cartesian subject, such as its autarchy and solipsism. On the other hand, he challenges this account of subjectivity by reading the ego — against the common ways of interpreting Descartes — in a creative and novel way as dependent upon something prior and thus ulti-mately not self-sufficient and independent. Again Marion uses Heidegger to heighten this ambivalence of the status of the ego in Descartes by showing how Heidegger's *Dasein,* on the one hand, is painted deliberately in contradiction to Descartes' ego as its most important opponent, and, on the other hand, is dangerously close to the ego and parallels it in several respects. This explora-tion of subjectivity in Descartes thus prepares Marion's later arguments in a twofold fashion. First, it establishes the failure of the metaphysical subject and concurs with the contemporary desire to formulate a more coherent account of the self.[3] Second, it already begins to outline the shape such an account might take. By comparing Descartes' and Heidegger's definitions of the self in this manner and the ambiguous fashion in which one seeks to get beyond the other, Marion previews how he himself will attempt to overcome Heidegger's analysis of *Dasein* in his own most recent writings on the self.

I will highlight the importance of the far from monolithic stance of the ego in Descartes by grouping Marion's explications of Descartes' thinking on this subject into three different emphases. First, I will investigate Marion's interpre-tation of the ego that most clearly resonates with more standard readings. This refers to what one might call a "strong" view of the ego. Second, we will see how this leads Marion to show how this use of the ego is deeply problematic and gives rise to the need for a philosophy that comes "after the subject," a thought that challenges Descartes and goes beyond it. Third, I will put in question this first account of the ego by exploring Marion's claim that the status of the ego in Descartes is characterized by an essential ambiguity, as is particularly evident in a comparison of the *ego* and *Dasein* which Marion conducts in *Reduction and Givenness.* Finally, I will look at Marion's most recent writing on the Cartesian notion of the self that asserts, in a radically new interpretation, that the Carte-sian ego is actually addressed and affected by something prior to it and thus can become conducive to a renewed theory of the self that no longer treats it as self-sufficient and solipsistic subject. This final move obviously comes closest to the position Marion wants to maintain in his phenomenological work that is concerned to work out a novel phenomenological account of the self and of its relation to the other, in light of and departing from Descartes.

The "Strong" Self: *Ego cogito, ergo sum*

Marion compares Descartes' thought of the self to that of Augustine and Aris-totle and shows how it is unique and departs from them. Neither Augustine nor

Aristotle provides a metaphysical interpretation of the self that would see it as self-sufficient substance. Instead, "what is peculiar to Descartes consists, as he so lucidly indicates, in interpreting the certain and necessary connection of the *cogitatio* and existence as establishing a substance, and moreover a substance that plays the role of first principle" (MP, 132; PM, 141). This self-sufficient ego "that plays the role of first principle" coincides with the more common interpretation of Descartes' writings. Marion highlights several aspects of a strong Cartesian view of the self: (a) the ego as ground and originator of the code, (b) the ego as substance, (c) the ego as seat of power. This strong subjectivity leads to two troubling implications: the permanence and self-subsistence of the ego and its autonomy, self-sufficiency, and resultant solipsism. I will explicate first the three aspects of the subject which Marion does indeed find in Descartes and then consider his criticism.

Ground

We have already examined how the ego grounds the Cartesian metaphysical system in the prior chapter on that subject. Marion has argued that Descartes rereads Aristotle in a way that highlights the priority and powerful status of the self. Truth and knowledge become dependent no longer on the reality which is being examined, but rather on the subject which inspects them and the method it employs. This method is determined by the search for certainty which only becomes possible as the ego constructs its parameters in terms of order and measure as a code that organizes all objects in relation to the ego. The ego becomes the ground of all knowledge and even of its own being in a first onto-theo-logical constitution of a metaphysics of thought. (Of course, as examined earlier, another constitution of metaphysics, in which God is the supreme ground of all being, will follow in Descartes' later writings.) The ego determines the being of all other things as objects that can appear only in the way in which it allows their appearance under the rule of certainty: clear, distinct, and ultimately mathematical. A process of abstraction, deduction, and figuration makes possible a theory of perception, in which all knowledge revolves around the ego as its ground and foundation. At the same time the ego grounds its own being through its perceptions. The ego is thus at the very center of Descartes' new metaphysical system. The move from ontology to epistemology implies an emphasis on the ego as center and guarantor of knowledge.

This ego, as the only subject among its objects, attempts to be perfectly self-sufficient. As the ground for everything else, it is apparently in no need of grounding. As self-thinking thought, it provides its own ground, in a quasi-divine *causa sui*. The ego therefore controls all objects in its autonomy by bringing them into presence to itself. All objects are exposed to the ego's penetrating and constituting gaze. It provides their ground and thereby makes them present to consciousness. As *intuitus* it orders all objects into its *mathesis universalis*, grounding their being by its epistemic gaze. As Marion has shown earlier, objects only "are" as the ego grants "being" to them as objects of the cogitatio in its metaphysics of thought. The ego determines their existence and reduces any appearance (even that of other people) to an object. As ground for everything else, Marion suggests, the ego actually becomes the only self-sufficient substance for Descartes in this first constitution of metaphysics.

Substance

In an article in *Questions cartésiennes II* that compares Descartes closely to Suarez,[4] Marion at first seems to indicate that the concept of substance does not play a significant role in Descartes' thought: "The project of a *universal science* or *mathesis universalis* has no need of the concept of substance, better, it excludes it" (QCII, 87). This is the case because the *Regulae* seek to dispense with Aristotelian categories in favor of the Cartesian focus on epistemology that Marion has shown to be at work in this treatise more generally. Yet while the early works do not employ the terminology of substance, Descartes uses the term first exclusively for the ego (in the *Discourse*, where it does not yet apply to the infinite) and later in an ambivalent fashion for both the ego (as "finite substance") and for God (as "infinite substance"). Marion insists, however, that this is an equivocal use of the term that establishes neither analogy nor univocity between finite and infinite. Substance is not applied in the same fashion to finite and infinite.

Marion tries to ascertain Descartes' notion of substance in a close comparison to the meaning and use of that term in Suarez. For Suarez, *substance* means self-subsistence, the ability to exist on one's own. It includes such notions as perseity [being for oneself] and non-indigence [no need for/poverty of anything else]. Marion points out that this dual meaning of substance in Suarez becomes divided in application: one aspect of the meaning of substance (namely its primarily ontological connotation of self-subsistence) is applied only to the divine, while the other aspect of the term (namely its primarily epistemological connotation as substantiality known through accidents — in Descartes this becomes substantiality as substrate of the principal attribute) is applied only to created substances. Marion argues that Descartes employs both of the Suarezian definitions solely for human created substance and not for the divine. There is no analogy, for Descartes, between the complete substantiality of God and the conditional substantiality of human beings.[5] Marion claims that Descartes' employment of the term *substance* parallels and is grounded in his idea of the creation of eternal truths. Created substance is now self-subsisting, but it is so only because of the previous divine decision or assistance (the *concursus Dei*). It is thus an ontologically conditional substantiality, although it is epistemologically self-sufficient (paralleling the two metaphysical systems in which the ego is first the ground of all knowledge but then requires the divine causality).

For Descartes' first metaphysics consequently, the ego becomes defined as a substance that can exist by itself and can be known on its own terms. The "I think"/*cogito* establishes the primacy of the ego as a metaphysical principle. The thoughts of the ego are not things separate from it; rather, its very activity of thinking makes it into a "thinking thing," a *res cogitans*. The ego thinks both its own Being and that of all other beings; thus to a certain extent (or even to a large extent, as we will see later) it previews *Dasein*. The thought of substance is for Descartes actually deduced from the ego and determined by it. Marion therefore finds that Heidegger misinterprets Descartes' definition of being and the world. Heidegger must be "radically contested: what is problematic in the Cartesian doctrine of substance does not stem from an insufficient consideration of the specificity of the *ego* but, inversely, from the determination of substance exclusively in terms of the *ego*, a determination that then runs the risk of not being appropriate to any of the beings that cannot be reduced to the ego" (MP, 169; PM, 180). The problem is not that the ego is not sufficiently expressed in terms of substance, but rather that nothing else can now be expressed by that term without falling into the danger of univocity between equivocal beings.

Substance therefore becomes determinative of the way in which the ego apprehends other things: "The concept of substance could indeed, for Descartes, borrow all its characteristics from the ego, which even before its own substantialization as *substantia cogitans* thoroughly governs the substantiality of all substances and imposes on them its own way of Being. Before the ego is substantialized, substances must be deduced from the ego" (MP, 151; PM, 162). Substance, of course, can be thought in two different and mutually exclusive ways: as body, or extension, and as mental, or the ego's relation to its own *cogitationes*.[6]

Yet of course Descartes does also (although rarely and only late) speak of God as an infinite substance. Marion claims that Descartes apparently makes a distinction between two principal attributes, yet this amounts really to a doubling of the same attribute of "thought" which is applied to both finite and infinite substance. Although the principal attribute is that of the thinking ego, this attribute is only possible because the infinite grounds the thoughts of the ego. The second metaphysics is clearly at work here: the divine assistance makes possible human perseity as a substance (QCII, 113). Marion insists therefore that substantiality is not thought in a univocal fashion by Descartes, but that substance means something utterly different for the divine than it does for the human, although he admits that this remains ambivalent in Descartes and that he is not able to resolve the difficulties and apparent contradictions of his use of the concept of substance. Ultimately, Descartes abandons the notion of substance for anything but the *ego cogito* and, so Marion suggests, the confusion and vacillation evident in Descartes' use of this term causes it to disappear also from the history of philosophy quite quickly after that (QCII, 115). Yet, while the terminology of substance disappears, the interpretation of the self as autonomous and self-sufficient continues.

Capax / capacitas

In a later article, Marion asks about the capacities of the ego by analyzing the French translation, *capable*, of the Latin term *capax* in the Cartesian corpus.

He shows how this word underwent a change in meaning within the seventeenth century that is due to Descartes' rereading of the term. Originally, *capax* referred to a passive receptivity which designated especially one's openness to God. After Descartes the French term *capable* clearly designates an active capacity, a power that enables one to do something on one's own. It changes in a similar but reverse fashion when used for God. While it originally referred to God's infinite power, it later designates a finite capacity to be understood by humans and proven by reason. Marion describes this change:

> *Capacitas Dei* now refers to the capacity that God exercises by deploying his most intimate essence, as opposed to the receptivity of man to God. Just as man's *capacitas* becomes a power (in principle finite), God's *capacitas* becomes a capacity (in principle infinite): man thus aims to become 'lord and master of nature' . . . while *capacitas* is the means for God to have his existence proven, causally and according to the principle of reason. Power facing power, before becoming power against power, the ego and the God of the philosopher evaluate each other from a distance. (CQ, 85; QCI, 135)

In order to trace this change in meaning, Marion gives a full list of every occurrence of the term in three of Descartes' treatises and then analyzes their meaning and grammatical structure carefully. He shows that already in the *Regulae*, Descartes uses the Latin term with the new meaning and that it is thus not merely a linguistic difference between Latin and French. Descartes actively changes the meaning of *capacity* by having it designate no longer human receptivity but rather the activity of the mind and its capacity to know.[7] Knowledge thus becomes a kind of power. In order to deepen this analysis, Marion goes on to outline the medieval meaning of the term and shows how it referred instead to the human receptivity, sustained by grace, that opened itself to the divine gift and thus became enabled to participate in God.[8] This previews some of Marion's later language about the gift and one's receptivity for God in a significant fashion. He interprets the meaning of *capacity* in the medieval thinkers as the reception of a gift. It constitutes a desire for and openness toward an excess that is always beyond such human capacity:

> Receiving a gift can thus in a way always underlie the superabundance that overwhelms it and thus strive for an ever-increasing amplitude . . . here nature attempts to conform to the overabundant gift, in the epectasis of desire, instead of attempting to take its measure. Desire thus strives for a happiness that surpasses the present *capacitas*, thereby increasing it and also finally making it receptive. Thus, the constant gap, ceaselessly bridged and reopened, between the *capacitas* of the soul at a given spiritual moment and the overabundant gift that exceeds it.

He concludes that "capacity must therefore go beyond itself, in completions that will in turn become new beginnings, in order to receive the gift that exceeds it" (CQ, 87–88; QCI, 139–40).

Marion clearly censures Descartes' rewriting of this terminology and instead agrees with the medieval view of receptivity to God. His later phenomenology attempts to recover such passive capacity of openness to the gift or the revelatory phenomenon, instead of the Cartesian "power" that initiates knowledge and grasps the object of thought. While modernity from Descartes onward imagines infinite human power and a rather limited capacity for God, Marion wants to argue with the medieval thinkers that

> the unique and objectively demonstrable greatness of human nature stems from the gap between its *potentia* (finite) and its *capacitas* (infinite), whereby it cannot possess blessedness in itself, but is constrained to receive it from another. The very failure of its powers places man at the limit, where the objective lack of satisfaction of subjective desire summons him to a silent meeting with the absolutely other. This weakness of domination in fact opens up the field of participation. (CQ, 89; QCII, 141)

This medieval conception will guide Marion in his later reformulations of the "self after the subject," in that he attempts to make the self dependent upon a prior instance whom it receives and in whom it participates.

Suarez is the one who begins to change this meaning of *capacity* by presenting blessedness as a kind of power and not merely a passive receptivity. Although, according to Marion, Descartes refuses Suarez' radical answer, he does shift to a mediating position by distinguishing between different kinds of blessedness and their related capacities and powers. Due to this obscurity and his articulation of the ego in terms of power, "*capacitas* shifts from participation by means of grace to domination by means of power" (CQ, 94; QCI, 149). This turn is ultimately so successful that it is completely assimilated by later thinkers and thus becomes indiscernible. Marion concludes that "starting with Descartes, the relation between man and God is apprehended by modern metaphysics in terms of power [*pouvoir*] and capacity [*puissance*]" (CQ, 95; QCI, 151). The Cartesian ego as subject is thus deeply problematic in all of these ways: as ground of all knowledge and primary principle of the metaphysical system, as self-subsistent and autonomous substance, and as infinite power to manipulate itself, the world, and even the divine. Marion employs the language of Husserl, Heidegger, and Derrida in order to criticize this powerful subject and to point out its shortcomings.

Critique of the Metaphysical Subject

Presence and Permanence

Marion suggests that one of the largest problems for Descartes' articulation of the ego is its obsession with presence and permanence. In Heideggerian terms, the ego is not aware of its own mode of Being. For Descartes, the ego is permanently subsistent [*vorhanden*]; it is what Marion calls "a primarily subsisting permanence" (MP 173; PM, 183). This is the case because certainty, as we have seen, is possible only when the ego examines and constructs the world in terms of its clarity and through the application of abstraction and figuration in terms of order and measure. This method, the *mathesis universalis*, makes all things present to the perceiving mind which imposes order and structure upon them and thus constitutes them as objects present to the mind. Consequently, for Marion, "the ego is established in terms of constant permanence; its ontic primacy over other beings depends ontologically on the understanding of the Being of beings as subsisting, thus as persisting in remaining itself, in such a way that it can satisfy the unconditional requirement of certainty" (MP, 174; PM, 185). Furthermore, its own temporality and its evident existing in the present actually serve as proof of that existence and of its own indubitability for the ego. The *cogitatio* thus privileges presence because it seeks evidence; it needs ideas to be present and available to the mind in order to confirm its own being: "The *cogitatio* gazes only on presence, and therefore keeps watch over existence as a certain object only insofar as existence is presented in the mode of presence in the present. The *cogitatio* temporalizes its *cogitatum* exclusively in the present because it first temporalizes itself exclusively in presence" (MP, 179; PM, 190). Several of the aspects we have already examined in Descartes' metaphysics thus come together here. The ego turns everything else into an object and all science and knowing become unified in the gaze of the subject. The ego identifies things and constitutes them as objects by making them present to the mind through observation. Even the past becomes assimilated to the present through the notion of memory and imagination.[9] Thus all time is measured for the *cogito* in terms of presence, and even past and future are thought only as present. For Marion, the ego "perdures in and through the *cogitatio* as the ultimate figure of presence" (MP, 187; PM, 197).

The ego both exists in presence and is permanent in the present, where the temporality of presence is privileged by the ego because it is closely linked to the search for evidence. This implies that temporal duration, in general, depends upon the ego and is thought in terms of presence. Being and enduring together govern substance through the ego's permanence in presence. Marion concludes: "This principle must be understood as an ontological thesis concerning the way of Being of all beings, both possible and real" (MP, 191; PM, 201). The Being of the ego, then, is defined in terms of *Vorhandenheit* (as Heidegger had claimed) and inscribed into the metaphysics of presence (as Derrida and Heidegger have outlined it). Yet, not only does Marion interpret the presence and permanence of the Cartesian ego and God in light of *Vorhandenheit* and "metaphysics of presence," but he consistently reads "presence" in this Cartesian mode because the two notions have become linked (if not even equated). Thus, if God does not come into presence and permanence in a particular thought in the way in which Descartes outlines it, Marion can conclude that one has consequently escaped from the "metaphysics of presence."[10] This is one of the reasons why the language of being and causality (especially their rejection) pervades Marion's treatment so profoundly. Metaphysics is consistently defined in these ways, even in respect to the ego that founds this version of metaphysics.

Solipsism

Marion also explicates the impossibility of the ego to envision any *alter ego*, any other mind, any human being besides the ego not reduced to an object, and thus shows how Descartes' ego is indeed deeply solipsistic.[11] According to Descartes, our egoism does not depend on some kind of moral decision, but rather is intrinsic to our being as subject: "If man defines himself to himself as an ego that relates to itself constantly through its *cogitatio*, he must establish himself as the single and necessary center of any possible world" (CQ, 119; QCI, 191). Marion summarizes Pascal's criticism of Descartes on this point and agrees that Descartes' philosophy does indeed make the other inaccessible.[12] He shows how Descartes leaves out the question of other intelligences from the very beginning. He points out that the only "people" ever mentioned in the *Meditations* besides the ego are the "madmen" that have no minds (and hence imagine all kinds of crazy things) and people who are in error.[13] All others are thus immediately removed from the scene and truth is never considered as inter-subjective. Later the ego acknowledges that there might be "real men" on the square under their hats, but they might also be only automatons.[14] Marion claims that Descartes' use of other people even within his text thus resembles his use of the wax; others appear only through the decision of the ego to recognize them and are as malleable as the piece of wax: "Others may indeed enter the field of vision of the *intuitus* and find their humanity confirmed there, but they will have to undergo the treatment common to all the potential objects of the ego" (CQ, 124; QCI, 198). Marion suggests that this "treatment" consists in a kind of "stripping" that renders the other naked:

> The ego strips them of their coats and hats, and above all of their otherness; upon entering the field of the *intuitus*, they become objects, they inherit their identity from it and lose their originating phenomenal initiative — that by which they discover themselves to be what they think they are. Their humanity remains borrowed, a concession, a restoration — like a face made out of wax that lends itself to our gaze but cannot see. People have no more of a face than wax does. This is a reduction of otherness to objectivity, whereby the other becomes even more invisible insofar as it is masked by the visible evidence of its judged objectivity. Can we know others without accepting also to be acknowledged by them? Can we be acknowledged without losing control of our knowledge? Descartes does not envisage this for a single moment, which is why Pascal's attack touches him so directly. (CQ, 125; QCI, 199)

Descartes assumes that the ego knows all otherness by a combination of its own ideas. Hence, the ego is the only real person and no one else can be acknowledged as another mind. Even God does not really function as an other for Descartes, according to Marion, but more as the opening of a transcendental horizon.[15] Marion pushes this interpretation even further by concluding with a comparison of Descartes' and Pascal's thought on love. Although love is a passion for Descartes, such passions are confined to the soul. Love does not open toward other people, but rather refers the mind to itself and helps the ego to establish itself more firmly (CQ, 133; QCI, 210–11). Marion criticizes the extremely univocal terminology Descartes employs for love. It designates without distinction the desires of the miser, the drunkard, and the rapist all the way to love for God, in that love always refers to the possession of an object (CQ, 135; QCI, 212). Real charity or inter-subjectivity remains impossible for Descartes.

This view of the self-sufficient subject therefore is a deeply problematic one. Marion emphasizes several aspects of this "strong," metaphysical view of the Cartesian subject that he subsequently seeks to overcome and remedy in his own phenomenological work. First, this subject occupies a position of power and control, especially vis-à-vis God. In its attempt to ground itself and to function as a self-sufficient substance, this subject occupies the extreme metaphysical ground, approaching a kind of *causa sui*. (Marion has, of course, already shown the impossibility and inherent contradictions of this concept in regard to Descartes' third proof for God's existence.) Second, this subject brings to its height a metaphysics of presence in which the metaphysical subject attempts to survey all its objects under its controlling gaze. Finally — and maybe most importantly — this strong view of the subject is entirely solipsistic. It is unable to take account of or encounter any true other, whether human or divine. None of this, of course, is a particularly novel interpretation. Marion orients himself by the interpretations and criticisms of the Cartesian subject put forth by Heidegger, Lévinas, and Derrida. It is important to note, however, which aspects of this criticism are most emphasized by Marion, since they will serve as indicators for his own phenomenological attempt to speak of a self after the subject. The subject's connection to being, its regarding of all phenomena as objects, and its failure of inter-subjectivity are the central tenets of the Cartesian subject that must be overcome for Marion. Furthermore, he goes on to complicate this simple criticism of the Cartesian notion of the self as entirely metaphysical.

The "Ambivalent" Self: The Ego and *Dasein*

According to Marion, the Cartesian ego does not always have the clear and strong stance that we have observed in the first section. Marion maintains, instead, that its status quickly becomes ambivalent. Three aspects of Marion's treatment highlight this ambivalence especially well. The first, which we have already seen and which I will thus examine only briefly, becomes obvious in the ego's replacement with God as ultimate ground and originator of the code. Marion finds the second in the Cartesian notion of freedom toward the future which destabilizes the ego of presence and permanence we have just observed. He illustrates a third aspect in a comparison of the Cartesian ego with Heidegger's *Dasein*.

The Double Grounding of the Code

We have seen how Descartes first attempts to found the code on the human mind which constructs and constitutes it. Already in the *Regulae*, the ego puts to work its rationality, which through (de-)figuration attains the grounding and gives ontic assurance to things. Indeed the ego seems primary in the *Meditations*, in that even God is reduced to the rank of a subordinate heuristic principle. This primacy, however, is dissimulated by the ego's dependence upon a prior instance with which it is in dialogue. There is an ontic insufficiency present, because the ego itself is outside the code and thus cannot be explained by it. The ego is absolute as founding, but relative as a being. The ego recognizes itself as finite and sees an infinite as preceding it and ultimately causing it. The ego's recognition of the infinite implies its own creation. The infinite precedes the ego and marks it with finitude. Both lead to the idea of God. The ego is perfectly sufficient in regard to the code and transgresses the epistemological instance of (de-)figuration to become a being. Yet it discovers immediately its insufficiency in light of the infinite, a strange anteriority of which doubt convinces it (TB, 395). The status of the ego changes here and thus also that of the code and of grounding. At the same time the question of substance enters again into the discussion. The creature becomes the result of the Creator in the way in which a painting displays its master through a radical similarity. The ego's "sufficiency in face of the code becomes an insufficiency in face of the infinite of the divine being who reigns over it originally" (TB, 396). Both the world of matter and the ego are thus insufficient to provide final grounding for the code which enables all knowledge.

The radical doubt which assails the ego in the beginning of the *Meditations* is an example of this ambivalence. Marion had explored this with the notion of a kind of hyper-code, a rationality that humans could not discover because it exceeds the world in which we live. As the ego realizes its dependence upon a Creator, it also realizes that the rationality of the world could have been different because the world as a whole, including its geometrical construction, is dependent upon God. The ego begins to doubt its rationality because it might be deceiving itself. Marion therefore interprets the "evil demon" as a figure more for the human self than for God. We are not deceived by God, but deceive ourselves in light of God's superior wisdom. This is of course a central aspect of Marion's insistence on the importance of the doctrine of the creation of the eternal truths. Humans are not in control of mathematical or logical truths, nor are such truths in control of God (as Kepler and Galileo assumed), but both are dependent on the divine creation. Although not arbitrary, both math and this world could have been otherwise. The ego must therefore discover this divine code instead of instituting it out of its own account. The

Cartesian self thus appears as far less powerful, self-sufficient, and even rational than might appear at first glance.

Freedom and the Future

Marion argues that there is also an exception to Descartes' extreme emphasis on presence.[16] Because he reduces all time to the primacy of the present, the past and the future become impossible to think for him. Descartes attempts to think the past through the notion of memory which allows for a way of moving the past into presence, though only partially and uncertainly so. Yet, the uncertainty of the future escapes representation. Descartes thus makes this insecure future dependent upon fate or absolutely determined by God's providence. The future is closed per necessity and allows for no further possibilities. Such a conclusion, however, is of course unsatisfactory, since it eliminates all freedom of the human being. In order for moral behavior to be possible, we must behave as if the future was not yet determined, as if free choice was still possible. Descartes thus opens a space for freedom and possibility in a kind of transgression of the *Vorhandenheit* of the *cogitatio*: "In a word, the ego accedes to other modalities of Being besides presence, or to other temporalizations beside the present, by accomplishing a single and unique feat: transgressing the *cogitatio* of present evidence, such as it presents to itself the persisting presence of subsistent beings" (MP, 203; PM, 214). Marion here argues that Descartes recognizes the need for the freedom of the ego in an undetermined future and makes an attempt to open such a space. He interprets this tentative transgression of present permanence as a step that tries to overcome the metaphysics of the *ego cogito*. We thus have a first indication of how a metaphysics of presence in respect to the self can be overcome, although Marion does not really spell out this suggestions fully in this context, just as he claims it remains incomplete and insufficient in Descartes. Freedom is both essential to the ego and escapes its metaphysical constitution as grounding *cogitatio*. While Descartes' juxtaposition of these two aspects of the *ego cogito* is too stark and direct to be tenable in Marion's view, he suggests that a more subtle explication might prove fruitful. However, both a different notion of freedom and a rethinking of temporality will have to play a role in such a rethinking of the metaphysical ego.[17] Descartes' ego remains haunted by this essential ambiguity. Although it is put forth as a founding substance, permanent in presence, subsisting in itself, grounding the Being of all things around it, it also is destabilized by its past, by its responsibility for the future, by its being caused by the Creator upon whom it is dependent at every moment. This ambiguity becomes heightened in a comparison of the ego with Heidegger's *Dasein*.

Descartes and Heidegger

The ambiguity of the Cartesian ego is further illuminated by the manner in which Descartes' work gets introduced into Marion's interpretation of Heidegger, set forth in *Reduction and Givenness*. While first emphasizing the distinction between the ego and *Dasein,* Marion goes on to show in great detail how close *Dasein* actually is to the ego, despite all of Heidegger's protestations to the contrary. Marion claims that Descartes plays an extremely significant role for Heidegger throughout the latter's work. Heidegger interprets Descartes as privileging the ego and certitude and accuses him of not questioning the Being of the "sum." He is profoundly critical of Husserl's appropriation of Descartes. Heidegger asserts that precisely because of his reliance on Descartes, Husserl cannot determine the Being of the self as existing, that he is too enamored with a science of consciousness, and that by following Descartes' ideals he remains unphenomenological. Marion suggests that

> far from guiding him along the phenomenological path, as Husserl thinks, Descartes played the notable role — from Heidegger's point of view — of *holding* Husserl *back* on the phenomenological path; between Husserl and full phenomenology, thus between Husserl and Heidegger, stands Descartes, a unique obstacle and stumbling block. The "affinity" that unites Husserl with Descartes therefore designates a unique phenomenological obstacle, which phenomenology must surmount in order to remain itself; henceforth, in order to advance along the phenomenological path that Husserl leaves, Heidegger will have not only to leave Husserl but to "destroy" the one who held Husserl back — Descartes himself. (RG, 84; RD, 129; emphasis his)

Only in "destroying" the ego can there be any access to *Dasein.* An articulation of *Dasein* must thus be set within the context of a critique of Descartes' ego. In outlining his own project in *Being and Time,* Heidegger first takes Descartes to task for leaving unthought the meaning of the Being of the *sum* and for making false assumptions about certainty. For Heidegger, "the evident certitude of the ego allows Descartes only to desert any interrogation of the mode of Being implied by that very certitude and leads him to consider the meaning of its Being as self-evident, evident by itself" (RG, 88; RD, 134). Second, Descartes not only fails to think the Being of the *ego sum,* but he also degrades the Being of the world to certitude "at the expense of the phenomenality of the world" and thus fails "to think the Being of *any* being" (RG, 90; RD, 137). In contrast to the ego, "*Dasein* gives Being by determining the way of Being of the other beings, because it itself, in advance and according to its privilege, determines itself to be according to its own way of Being" (RG, 93; RD, 142). For Heidegger, *Dasein* and the *ego cogito* are radically opposed.[18] By all appearances, *Dasein* "maintains with the *ego cogito* a relation of 'destruction'" (RG, 97; RD, 147).

Yet Marion goes on to highlight how similar *Dasein* and the ego actually are. He argues that Heidegger so strongly distinguishes between ego and *Dasein* because *Dasein* in fact remains haunted by the ego and cannot really distinguish itself from it. He suggests that "*Dasein* would not have such an urgent need to destroy it if *Dasein* did not find in it, as in a delinquent outline, some of its own characteristic traits: indeed, *Dasein* cannot not recognize itself in at least four characteristics of the *ego cogito,* according to a rivalry that is all the more troubling insofar as the similitudes only sharpen it" (RG, 98; RD, 148). *Dasein* and the ego are first similar in respect to finitude. Just as *Dasein* is essentially marked by finitude and temporality, finitude serves a "quasi-ontological function for the ego." It is what provokes Cartesian doubt and the need to constitute the meaning of the *cogitata*. Secondly, both the ego and *Dasein* play or "perform" in the first person [mineness/*Jemeinigkeit*]. *Dasein* actually speaks as "I," as "ego sum" (RG, 99; RD, 149). Third, a particular notion of (im)possibility is also fundamental to the analysis of both figures. The relation to freedom for the ego in Descartes in Marion's view closely parallels Heidegger's analysis of death as the "possibility of impossibility," because in the divine determination of the ego's future it "uncovers its impossibility" and "meets the possibility of impossibility" (RG, 100; RD, 151). Finally, both ego and *Dasein* are characterized by an essential indeterminacy, in that "the indetermination that is denounced in the *ego cogito* concerns *Dasein* just as much" (RG, 100; RD, 152). For Marion, therefore, *Dasein* and the ego are much closer than might appear to be the case. He concludes:

> Everything happens henceforth as if, even in its indetermination, the ego were miming *Dasein*, in the way that the *They* mimes, in the inauthentic mode, the authentic *Dasein* to which it essentially belongs. . . . Thus ego and *Dasein* meet according to finitude, *mineness*, the possibility of the impossible, and indetermination. That their similarities remain separated, or even opposed, according to authenticity and inauthenticity does not suffice to alienate them one from the other—since this final opposition belongs entirely to the existence of *Dasein*. It does not seem so easy to decide phenomenologically between the ego and *Dasein* as strict strangers. (RG, 102; RD, 154–55)

It seems, then, that the ego is already a kind of *Dasein*, or rather, that *Dasein* has not really succeeded in overcoming the Cartesian ego.

Marion proceeds to analyze Heidegger's writing on ipseity and his repeated attempts to distinguish *Dasein* from the *cogito*. He shows that, in some contexts, the I can even function as present-at-hand, as persistent or subsistent, similar to what he has shown to be Descartes' analysis of substance (as we examined above). He thus underlines that

> the conclusion becomes unavoidable: the *I* can just as well have to be "destroyed" as to be able to be "confirmed," according to whether it is repeated by one or the other of the possible determinations of *Dasein*; either inauthentically, in the Cartesian way of the persistent and subsistent *res cogitans*; or authentically, in the way of anticipatory resoluteness, of the structure of care, of the mineness of *Dasein*. The "I think" therefore no longer appears as a metaphysical thesis to be refuted, among others, in order to free up the phenomenon of *Dasein*, but as the very terrain that *Dasein* must conquer; since no other terrain will ever be given to *Dasein* in which to become manifest. *Ego cogito, sum* states less a countercase of *Dasein* than a territory to occupy, a statement to reinterpret, a work to redo. (RG, 106; RD, 160)

The delineations between the metaphysical I (ego) and the I that seeks to overcome this very constitution (*Dasein*) thus blur to the point of confusion. And it is precisely because of this confusion, this ambiguity, that Marion seeks to overcome even Heidegger's overcoming. Heidegger's *Dasein* is not sufficiently distinguished from the Cartesian ego to serve as the new self that "comes after the subject." Both ego and *Dasein* ultimately play in the first person and thus remain solipsistic to some extent. *Dasein* does not fully free itself from the metaphysical determinations of the Cartesian subject. We will see this assertion become deepened in Marion's phenomenological analysis of the insufficiencies of previous accounts of the subject (those of Descartes, Husserl, Heidegger, and even Lévinas).

The "Affected" Self: *Ego existo et persuasus*

In his latest work on Descartes, Marion has begun to read Descartes in an even more radically phenomenological fashion. The first step occurs in an article, "Does the Cogito Affect Itself? Generosity and Phenomenology," honoring Michel Henry. Marion suggests here that the ego may be read in terms of self-affection or generosity.[19] A second step is taken in a close comparison of what Marion calls the two formulae of the Cartesian ego, one from the *Discourse*, the other from the *Meditations: ego cogito* and *ego existo*. He brings these indications together in the claim that one should really speak of an *ego persuasus* in Descartes, an ego that is dependent for its thought and existence on a prior instance.

Ego affectus

Marion begins his analysis by referring to Husserl's distinction between *noesis* and *noema* and reading them as a version of the Cartesian *cogito* and *cogitatum*. In both cases, he suggests, the objects of consciousness are in some sense separated from the ego that thinks or experiences them. This split might make it possible to interpret them as introducing a kind of alterity into the self: "The displacement that intentionality opens up — the fact that I never think without an other in my thought, therefore an other from my thought, within the depths of thought — accrues to representation by running from the *cogitatum* to its *cogito*; taking what intentionality ecstatically makes of my thought, representation runs through the displacement, as though against the grain, from the object to the thought that objectifies it" (CQ, 98; QCI, 156). What the *cogito* represents or thinks is therefore something other than it, if only a kind of alter ego. Marion suggests that while Husserl does not link his analysis as closely to Descartes as here indicated, Heidegger did indeed accuse Husserl of such schizophrenia in the ego.[20] Descartes himself emphasizes that thought is somehow prior to one's reflection on thinking. Marion here employs Henry, who claims that "consciousness thinks, and thinks of itself, fundamentally by auto-affection" (CQ, 105; QCI, 167). Marion suggests that Descartes' *cogitatio* can be interpreted as sensation in this fashion because it refers to a kind of "sensing of thought" (CQ, 106; QCI, 170). He confirms this with a brief analysis of *The Passions of the Soul*, where the soul is indeed said to excite and affect itself, and concludes: "We are therefore perfectly justified in speaking of an auto-affection of the soul, without ecstasy or displacement between cause and effect, represented and representing, intention and intuition" (CQ, 109; QCI, 174). Marion uses the passion of generosity in particular in order to combine these references to auto-affection with the ones that refer to perception nonecstatically. Generosity is a "species of wonder" for Descartes which has an ethical primacy. It repeats the acts of the *cogito* and thus is marked by "perfect auto-affection." The soul affects itself in its own experience. Generosity helps us to survive; it makes us happy and determines our well-being.[21] Marion therefore concludes that Henry's material phenomenology helps to interpret the ego in a fashion that actually protects it against the "overcoming of the subject" because it is already beyond it in some fashion. Marion employs Henry's work as license for his own re-appropriation of the Cartesian subject and untraditional reading of the Cartesian text.[22] Although this does not yet constitute a full argument against solipsism, Marion finds here at least a first step outside the ego's own mind and its dualistic restrictions. Furthermore, it justifies Marion's own readings of Descartes that often make little distinction between the Cartesian endeavor and the Husserlian one.

Ego existo

Marion goes even further in his most recent volume on Descartes, which concentrates on the subjects of God and the self. He puts forth a radically new interpretation of the ego as dependent on something prior. The ego functions as the ground of all experience for Descartes. By making such experience possible, Marion suggests, the I itself is not experienced: "In the strict sense it is excluded from experience, precisely because it makes it possible" (QCII, 5). It can only become experienced if it doubles itself as an object and posits an empirical me next to the transcendental I.[23] Furthermore, because the ego always only has relations with objects that are constituted by its vision, it cannot have relation with a real other. All others, as we have seen above, are constituted as objects and the ego apparently drowns in its own solipsism.[24] Marion challenges this standard interpretation by drawing a significant distinction between the *ego cogito* and the *ego existo*.[25] He reviews some of the interpretations of the ego as always self-transparent and referred to itself in Malebranche, Spinoza, Kant, Hegel, and Nietzsche. He summarizes the "canonical interpretation" as one that privileges the formula "ego cogito, ergo sum" (as it appears, for example, in the *Discourse on Method*) and reads it as a tautology (QCII, 12). He sees this as confirmed by both Heidegger and M. Gueroult. He points out that Gueroult especially is clearly misreading the text here, since he introduces a kind of self-reflection of the *cogito* that Descartes always rejected.[26] Marion maintains that while the *ego cogito* has been treated as the privileged definition of the ego by most of the tradition, the *ego existo* is actually Descartes' preferred and more mature definition. It appears first in the second Meditation. Marion interprets this formulation as a move from a rational to a performative statement which must justify the other one.[27] This second formulation introduces and requires an "original alterity of the ego" (QCII, 17). Already in the first moment of doubt, Descartes presents an other who might overcome this doubt before he even speaks of the ego.[28] Of course God is masked and not clearly identified at this point, but already present for Descartes at least as an hypothesis. Marion claims, therefore, that Descartes' doubt happens in a kind of "space of interlocution" that is maintained even in the hypothesis that the ego might originate its own ideas and thus assume the position of this other. The ego cannot even, in fact, attain to its own being without being caused by this other whose possibility is lodged firmly in the mind. Something must persuade me of my own existence, be that a God, an evil demon, or a second/split self. Marion suggests that the ego ultimately always finds itself involved in a dialogue, interrogated by an other: "This dialogue supposes an other speaker, who interrogates/calls [*interpellate*] the ego and precedes it: in fact, when the ego admits that it is, it admits first that it is only as second, that it comes after another" (QCII, 28). Although this other does not have a certain existence and maybe even deceives me, I receive myself through the recognition that I might be deceived.[29] The dialogue that is performed in the pages of the *Meditations* moves between myself and the possible deceiver (who might not and probably does not exist), to a dialogue that takes place within myself with myself, to a real dialogue between God and myself. Marion therefore wants to maintain that the I does not *say* the first word, for Descartes, but *hears* it.[30] Marion confirms this analysis with other passages from Descartes' works. In the third Meditation, for example, the other who precedes me is radicalized not as possibly existing deceiver but as actually existing God.[31] While I have an idea of God, I cannot be the source of that idea but there must be an other, the Infinite, outside of me addressing me and causing me. The "me" thus appears only in the dative, as recipient. The same faculty by which I perceive myself also gives me the consciousness of the idea of God: "The original dialogical situation of the *ego sum, ego existo* disengages itself finally from the fiction of a God who is supposedly deceiver (because truly all-powerful), in order to play in the clear light of the relation with the infinite, first thinker and interlocutor, in the end, first existing, certainly thinking, but especially first *thought*, because first interlocuted" (QCII, 35). At least the later account of the ego, then, is very ambivalent. The ego is interrupted and addressed by another.

There is thus a tension of inconsistency in Descartes' texts between a self-sufficient and self-identifying ego and one that is dependent upon a prior appeal and ultimately upon God. Marion shows that it is the second one which becomes authoritative and determining for Descartes. He suggests that this is also the reason why Descartes distinguishes his own formula *"ego sum, ego existo"* from a formulation by St. Augustine that is similar to the *ego cogito* and insists that he means something very different by it. What distinguishes Augustine from Descartes is precisely the difference between the two formulations: for Augustine, I deceive myself and posit my existence because of self-identity (thus resulting in tautology), while for Descartes I am deceived by an other and receive my existence from this other (thus resulting in dialogue).[32] One can hence outline a kind of Cartesian itinerary: while he begins with the canonical (Augustinian) formulation of self-transparency and tautology (*ego cogito*), he moves to a higher and better formulation that is inscribed in an interlocution of dialogue (*ego existo*).[33] Marion concludes his article by relating the two formulations to the two onto-theo-logies we have examined above. The ego as founding principle and self-identity corresponds to the first onto-theo-logy, that of the ego, which posits itself as *cogitatio*. The ego as called by a prior instance corresponds to the second onto-theo-logy, that of the *causa sui*, which causes and thinks the ego as *cogitatum*. Thus although the charge of self-identity, tautology, and solipsism holds for Descartes' first formulation of the ego (as *cogito* or *res cogitans*), it does not for the second (as *existo* or *res cogitata*). Marion suggests that this might even help us get beyond the aporia of Husserl's "Fifth Cartesian Meditation" and could overcome the scission between the transcendental I and the empirical me, although in this context he does not spell out how this might be possible.[34]

Géry Prouvost and Ruud Welten, in reviews of this final study on Descartes, find that Marion reads too much of his theological and phenomenological concerns into Descartes. Prouvost claims that "it seems as if Marion assigns himself the impossible task of reuniting Dionysius and Descartes, apophaticism and transcendental affirmation."[35] He reviews Marion's argument in detail and finds that Marion's somewhat too interpretive reading distorts history. He also points out what he sees as an inconsistent reading of Aquinas in Marion's work.[36] Welten also wonders about Marion's radical interpretations of Descartes and sees them as too closely linked with his readings of Husserl and Heidegger.[37] He suggests that Marion's rehabilitation of Descartes in terms of contemporary concerns involves too much creative re-interpretation that is not justified by the text itself.[38] Jocelyn Benoist, on the other hand, who compares Marion's book to Etienne Balibar's article on the ego which partially inspired Marion's argument, applauds Marion's attention to the detail and style of the Cartesian writings. He reviews Marion's argument overall favorably, although he is not entirely convinced that the ego can really be said to be engaged in a "dialogue."[39] He maintains that although the ego does indeed hear a voice, it is not that of another but only its own echo. Marion's interpretation is far too much influenced by Lévinas. There is no other and no "originary alterity" present in the *Meditations*. The doubling of the Cartesian cogito merely confirms its solipsism.[40] The anonymous voice Marion discovers is just that of the ego itself.[41]

Yet Marion's interpretation does not rely solely on the somewhat different formulation of the ego in the *Meditations* or the fact that the ego finds itself addressed in some fashion. In an article which focuses on the status of the "Replies" to the *Meditations*, he also shows how the Cartesian texts function structurally in a dialogue form.[42] Are the replies to be read as a mere appendage and not really important for the central argument? Or are the *Meditations* incomplete without them and are they therefore to be valued as an integral part of the work? Marion not only argues the latter, but shows how in fact all of Descartes' works presuppose the need for objections and replies to the central argument and require such dialogue. From the *Regulae*, which constitute an implicit and explicit dialogue with Aristotle, to the *Discourse*, which was followed by letters containing questions to which Descartes responded, to the *Meditations*, which were disseminated to a small group of scholars and subsequently published with their queries and Descartes' replies, all the way to the *Principles of Philosophy*, which integrate questions and replies within the text itself: all Cartesian texts display this dialogue structure. Marion shows that the *Meditations* can actually be read as a direct response to the questions concerning the "metaphysical" part of the *Discourse* which Descartes had left open: "Thus the responsorial schema was achieved completely in the scientific essays [parts 1–3 of the *Discourse*] but remained incomplete, in anticipation of replies, in the metaphysical essay [part 4 of the *Discourse*]. . . . the *Meditations* constitute, with several years' delay, replies to the[se] objections."[43] Marion also insists that Descartes fully expected and actively solicited objections and questions to his work and always intended to publish it together with these objections and their respective responses. In fact, for the *Meditations*, "the responsorial scheme is doubled, since the *Meditations* here play the part, first, of replies to the objections made to the *Discourse*, in order then to take on the role of the text to which objections are to be made."[44] Hence, so Marion concludes, it is false to read Descartes as a solitary and solipsistic thinker. Rather, as his extensive correspondence also corroborates, Descartes always thinks of the philosophical project as conducted within and for a community of scholars, rather than as a self-sufficient and solipsistic exercise: "Far from being soliloquy or solipsism, Cartesian thought, insofar as it obeys a logic of argumentation, is inscribed in its very origin in the responsorial space of dialogue."[45]

Ego persuasus

Marion appeals to this novel interpretation of the ego again in his phenomenological work and deepens the above analysis in order to maintain the priority of the appeal. Instead of *ego cogito*, he suggests, it should really be called *ego persuasus* because it depends on some anonymous substance preceding it that persuades the doubting ego.[46] The ego can never fully erase the gap between itself and the original thought that thinks it. This is confirmed, Marion asserts, by the formulation that I am only while or as long as I am thinking. The ego is not to be confused with temporality and does not exercise the role of a transcendental principle as the condition for all phenomena but depends upon time, inscribes itself into it. The ego does not even produce all of its thoughts, since those of God and of the self come to it from the outside. The ego is both deceived and assured by someone/something other (evil genius, infinite God). God alone ultimately opens and assures the finite horizon of thought in which the existence of the I can be established. The ego thus, for Descartes, becomes dependent for its existence on the infinite who thinks it. We have here a clear indication of the direction in which Marion will go in order to explicate what (or who) comes after the ego, after the transcendental subject. As we shall see, the "phenomenal self" that he attempts to articulate in his later work is indeed radically dependent upon something or someone other. It will be described as an "interlocuted" self—one interrupted and encountered by an other.

We have thus moved from a very standard interpretation of the role of the ego in Descartes to a much more radical (and contested) one. Marion's first interpretation of the ego is important in particular for the way in which he censures it. An account of the subject that interprets it as self-subsistent substance, endued with power over all things and possibly even God, he finds deeply unsatisfying. Marion shares popular critiques of such a subject, such as its being inscribed in a metaphysics of presence and unable to give an account of real alterity, reducing all others to objects of its own solipsism. Marion sees all these shortcomings as clearly connected to Descartes' project and espe-cially to his reformulation of metaphysics in terms of epistemology. The ego becomes the subject which functions as the ground for a metaphysical system precisely because of its search for certainty in terms of the method. We will see that Marion will gesture in that direction with his analysis of Pascal and take it up much more thoroughly and systematically in his most recent work on the erotic phenomenon.

Yet Marion's account of Descartes also already gives us some indication of how the subject of certainty, self-sufficiency, present permanence, and solip-sism can be overcome. It is best replaced with a theory of the self that is hidden already in some texts of Descartes: a self that is affected, persuaded, constituted by a prior instance, by an other who addresses it. The continued importance of Descartes is evident in all of Marion's more recent writings on the self and inter-subjectivity. Not only does he explicitly employ the Cartesian ego as an example of the saturated phenomenon which affects and overwhelms the self and reduces it to its dative, as the one responding to the given phenomenon. He also constructs his work on the erotic phenomenon and the encounter of the other in eros as a rewriting of the "Cartesian Meditations" (both those of Descartes and of Husserl). As I have already suggested, Marion's phenom-enology of eros is a very explicit argument against the Cartesian search for certainty and an account of the self as grounded in love, not in knowledge. Before focusing specifically on the "erotic self," let me examine how Marion's phenomenology in general seeks to counter the Cartesian subject and how this encounter is framed by the ambivalence and instability already discovered or interpreted in the Cartesian text.

eight
Phenomenology and the Self
"The Self That Comes after the Subject"

One of the most significant implications of Marion's work on donation is a dislocation and redefinition of the metaphysical subject. He begins one of his articles on this topic by insisting, "Phenomenology has perhaps never had a more pressing task to confront than the determination of what — or possibly who — succeeds the subject."[1] This endeavor is intimately linked to his work on Descartes and, as we have already seen, his phenomenological concerns are clearly evident already in his later interpretations of the Cartesian subject. On the one hand, Marion shows how the standard interpretation of Descartes is confirmed by his investigation into Descartes' metaphysical system and points to deeply troubling implications. On the other hand, Marion has argued that this strong and problematic version of subjectivity is already beginning to be challenged even by Descartes himself and that one can impose a phenomenological interpretation on Descartes' writings that uncovers an inherent dependency and dislocation of this subject. Marion has criticized the "strong" Cartesian subject most fundamentally for two reasons: (1) its obsession with permanence and self-presence displayed especially in its control and constitution of objects through the method of certainty; and (2) its insistence on autarchy leading to solipsism. In this chapter I will be concerned primarily with the first aspect, although the second will begin to emerge in the final section. The final chapter will focus specifically on the issue of inter-subjectivity.

Marion carries his critique of Descartes further by arguing that even phenomenology, especially in the shape in which it appeared in Husserl (and to some extent also in Heidegger) is unable to lead us to a new conception of the self that does not display further troubling implications. He sees four aspects of the self-sufficient subject as in need of rectification: First, the transcendental I cannot arrive at individuation or particularity. It only manages to establish its own universality, but thereby loses all identity. The "I think" cannot become a self. Second, the transcendental I is haunted by solipsism. Functioning as a kind of *causa sui*, the transcendental I has no ground and is unable to admit its own finitude. Third, Husserl's empirical I, while escaping these first two aporiae, remains dependent upon the arrival of intuition. Although it no longer has the control of the transcendental I and is instead defined by its receptivity to the impressions of consciousness, Marion interprets this as merely a reversal of the traditional subject. The "me" is still able to return to a complete and coherent subjectivity. Finally, in Husserl, the transcendental I and the empirical me become doubled by being split into subjectivity and receptivity.[2] The mode of apparition of the phenomenological I is still tied to objectness and therefore results in a phenomenology of the object in which the I assumes the poorest form of phenomenality and appears as a mere object. No phenomenological thinker has been able to escape these various aporiae: Husserl's account of the subject still amounts to a version of the transcendental ego. Heidegger's *Dasein* is inscribed in ontological difference and unable to get beyond solipsism. Lévinas' self is not sufficiently individuated.[3]

Marion's own account describes the self as the recipient of the phenomenological given, as in the dative, as the "to whom" of the phenomenological donation. Recipients give form to that which shows itself and allow it to come forth, acting like a filter or prism for the phenomenon. After the subject (and also after the phenomenon and resulting from it) comes the interlocuted, the recipient, the one devoted and given over to the phenomenological given. Ian Leask summarizes this need for the dative recipient:

> And it is precisely for this reason that reception must be a necessary operative assumption here (however "bracketable" it may be in general terms): if the interloqué is to be more than just another deconstructed subject, if it is to be reconfigured in terms of and in relation to sheer givenness, then, quite apart from its accusative and locative formations, a further, dative aspect is crucial and unavoidable. Givenness seems to require a dative subject to whom the phenomenon shows itself inasmuch as it gives itself. (GG, 187)

He continues, "as beneficiary of a givenness that is beyond the terms and domains of Being, that is outside of any ontological matrix, the dative self is a necessary medium for givenness; if givenness cannot be said to be, it can be manifest only in its (sometimes saturated) appearing to me" (GG, 188).

Marion insists that this constitutes a reversal of intentionality: the subject becomes a passive recipient instead of a constitutive actor. The interlocuted is radically displaced and submitted to an appeal and must renounce any autarchy or attempt at self-positioning. That which is received cannot be thought clearly or distinctly; one can thus not speak of a constituting subject defined by its clear thought, but only of a confused and surprised recipient who indicates the phenomenon precisely by such surprise. The phenomenon takes controlling consciousness away from the self: I find myself utterly displaced, cross-examined, questioned, unsettled. I am always already preceded by a prior call and claim. And most importantly — although we will reserve much of that for the following chapter — the new self is one called and constituted by the other. The "self after the subject" is, for Marion, a responsive self. That is not to say, of course, that there might not be situations in which the modern accounts of the subject's relation to objects would be quite appropriate. Just as Marion admits the phenomenological constitution of mathematical or "common" objects which require no hypothesis of saturation and for which Husserl's account, for example, is quite sufficient, so Marion would probably acknowledge that there are many situations where subject-object relations are the norm. But just as Marion is not concerned with mathematical objects but rather with saturated phenomena, so his new account of the self focuses entirely on the situations where the modern account of subjectivity is insufficient or simply false, such as involvement in historical events, awe before works of art, or engagements in loving relationship. Yet, so Marion will argue, this account might also alter the way we conceive of other types of relations, although he does not really explain how that is the case.[4]

Marion's explication of a revised account of subjectivity proceeds in several stages, to which he attaches different terms for the new self. Each "version" of the self gives a more thorough and deeper account. I will therefore examine these four versions in chronological fashion. Already in his preparatory work *Reduction and Givenness*, Marion outlined the new self as "interlocuted" or "dislocated" [*l'interloqué*], where the given is primary and determines or first gives rise to the one to whom it is given, its recipient or respondent.[5] Marion deepens and radicalizes this position in *Being Given*, where he distinguishes between two stages, the self in general phenomenology as the "beneficiary" or the one "to whom something is attributed" [*l'attributaire*] and the subject as being "devoted" or "given over" [*l'adonné*] to the given in a more saturated form, a self that is written in the dative and answers the question "to whom?" Finally, Marion provides fresh insight into a new account of the subject in his "erotic" reduction, which speaks of the self as the lover [*l'amant*] and constitutes Marion's clearest response to the Cartesian subject and its misguided search for certainty.

L'interloqué

Marion claims in his article on the "interloqué" that phenomenology has never decided whether to dispense with the traditional subject altogether or whether to repeat it in a new form.[6] It constantly vacillates between these two options, one outside metaphysics and one essentially remaining within it. He employs the Heideggerian figure of *Dasein* in order to illustrate this ambivalent stance. *Dasein*, he concludes after extensive analysis, does not ultimately fully "succeed the subject" but merely subverts some of its aspects, albeit important ones. In a fundamental step in the right direction, *Dasein* "no longer aims at the constitution of an object but at the opening of a world." *Dasein*, therefore, operates in this world "not as spectator, nor even in a constitutive way, but as a party possibly challenged by what it encounters" (237). Furthermore, *Dasein* also rejects substantiality and the project of grounding and self-foundation in favor of an ecstatic "exposure in person" (238). These are significant changes that liberate the self already to a great extent, although Marion does not see them as entirely sufficient. He maintains instead that the disclosedness and resoluteness[7] of *Dasein* does lead it back to a kind of self-positing autarchy. In its care, *Dasein* is directed almost entirely to itself. Marion insists that Heidegger recognized as much in the *Kehre*, where the question of Being [*Sein*] displaces that of *Dasein*. *Dasein* becomes "called" by a prior appeal, the call of Being [*Anspruch des Seins*]:

> Man answers a call that claims him for Being, instead of *Dasein* deciding about and resolving itself to its own possibility as Self. By man one must understand, against all "humanisms," the one who comes after the subject, but also after the Self, because he lets himself be claimed by the *Anspruch des Seins*. He should be called the *Angesprochene*, the one upon whom a claim is made. After the subject, even beyond *Dasein*, emerges the one who knows how to hear Being's claim.[8]

Marion derives the terminology of the "interlocuted" from this human being addressed by the appeal of Being. As Rolf Kühn argues: "The reduction of the appeal of Being by boredom for Marion has finally no other goal then opening humans for a different appeal, better: for/toward 'any possible appeal,' that is, to the 'appeal as such.'"[9] This appeal does not reinstitute the ego as a transcendental one, but rather envelopes me in an experience where I occupy only one pole of a phenomenological horizon: "No doubt, upon hearing myself interpellated, I experience an interpellated *me*, but, literally, *I* experiences a *me* orphaned of any transcendental and constitutive *I*; *I* experience *myself* means that the *I* (simple, without being double) experiences itself as a *myself/me*. I experience myself being claimed, that is, called upon in the accusative — interpellated as suspect and not as subject, named in the accusative and therefore dispossessed of any nominative function" (243). Marion outlines three essential features of this "interloqué": (a) it is always already implicated in relationships; (b) it is experienced as surprise (not ecstasy); (c) it is always already "judged," summoned to court, and put into question. This I does not posit itself but is the response to a prior appeal.

The interlocuted, then, emerges as a more originary form of *Dasein* who is displaced by the call or claim of Being. The "I" is turned into an accusative by the call: "The claim [*revendication*] calls *me*. I have not even been able to say I before the claim has already hailed me, and therefore has taken and comprehended me, because it has summoned and named me as a *me*" (RG, 198; RD, 297).[10] This is not a transcendental subject in the sense of Kant, Husserl, or Sartre, but a self outside of metaphysics that "designates an inconceivable, unnameable, and unforeseeable instance which is comprehended less than it surprises, namely the claim itself" (RG, 199; RD, 298). The self stands interrupted and accused.[11]

This "subject without subjecti(vi)ty" is not only convoked and addressed, but it suffers a surprise that dislocates any attempt to constitute itself as a subject.[12] I am defined as a self by the claim that calls upon me to identify and name it. Finally, it challenges me to an interlocutory judgment: I must answer to the claim. I am utterly unsettled by this call, cannot identify its source, have no consciousness of my (possible) subjectivity, know "neither who nor what" has called. The interlocuted is freed from its metaphysical shackles by the claim that divests it of its autarchy and self-sufficiency. It attacks and overcomes primarily the first aspect of the Cartesian self, namely the *ego cogito* of the gray ontology that serves as the ground of all knowledge and assigns all other objects their place. This self-sufficient and autonomous subject is interrupted, judged, called into question.

Marion thinks "that which comes after the subject" even more radically in *Being Given.* He first suggests the dislocation of the modern subject in thinking the aporiae of the gift and attempting to reduce the gift-object. As we have seen, he insists that the gift must be accepted and that the recipient must be conscious of a prior debt. This consciousness of an obligation that precedes me makes it impossible for me to conceive of myself as "owing nothing to anyone" and thus dislocates my self-sufficiency and autarchy. One must receive this gift in the humiliation of being indebted to someone, even to someone of whom one knows nothing. To accept the gift is to be displaced in one's subjectivity, to be challenged in one's constitution as a subject. One must expose oneself to the pure contingency of the event. To receive the gift in the attraction and prestige of its phenomenality is to sacrifice one's autarchy and to be dislocated by the decision of acceptance. Indebtedness, despite its problematic character, plays an essential role for Marion since it assures the realization of the lack of autarchy in the subject and makes the self dependent upon something or someone prior to it.

L'attributaire

Marion investigates the new status of the "subject" more particularly when speaking of the fourth saturated phenomenon, which cannot be mastered by the I.[13] The phenomenon imposes its own immediate effectivity (or actuality) on me. Not only does it suspend the relations of subjectivity between the phenomenon and the I but it inverts them. I find myself constituted by the phenomenon, become its witness or benficiary. The witness does not provide a synthesis or an analysis of what has come but remains passive. No longer does the I give meaning to the lived experience, but instead is given meaning by it. The I becomes a witness as a guardian of the paradox which controls it. Thus the I loses its anteriority as an "egogic pole" and can no longer identify itself except by admitting the primacy of the phenomenon that constitutes it. The saturated phenomenon cannot be reduced to the I that observes it, cannot be constituted as an object, but only leaves its trace in the witness. To be a witness is to be entirely passive, like the indicator of a light when information is registered or like an electrical impulse, lacking any initiative or delay. The witness finds itself so invested or even submerged in the phenomenon that it cannot but register the impulse immediately. It thus challenges Kant's and Husserl's transcendental I, by being changed from a nominative subject to a dative recipient, by answering not the question "who?" but "to whom?" (ED, 344; BG, 249). Leask wonders whether even Marion's extremely passive self can fully escape the "classic ambiguity" that seems to require the subject's priority over the objects and its determination of the phenomenon in its reception of it (GG, 189). I will examine this charge in a bit more detail later.

Marion suggests that a receptivity of sensibility may define the self more appropriately than a rational synthesis of representations in the unity of a concept that requires an act of spontaneity from the imagination. Jeffrey Kosky points out:

> Now Marion recognizes that Husserl need not understand this giving "to us" as a Kantian synthesis of the phenomenon "by us." Nevertheless, in actual phenomenological practice Husserl clearly evidences a tendency to veer from the givenness of the phenomenon *to* an I toward the synthesis of the phenomenon *by* the I to whom it supposedly gives itself. Even this given "to us," Marion argues, reinstates a condition of phenomenality—at the very least insofar as the horizon itself is defined precisely by the standpoint of the "us" that looks out toward it. . . . Nothing could appear to which I am not open or which I am not ready to receive.[14]

Therefore, instead of "I think," one should say "I am affected" (ED, 347; BG, 251). Marion thus qualifies the "witness" more particularly as the "*attributaire,*" the one to whom something is given or attributed, the one who benefits from what is given. The metaphysical transcendental I, he claims, is not able to achieve individuation and cannot liberate itself from solipsism. Furthermore, the empirical necessity of the I actually depends upon the arrival of intuition so that the subject is doubled as a transcendental I and an empirical me. I am both the me of phenomenal experience and the I who brings all these experiences together and organizes them. According to Marion, because the mode of apparition of the phenomenological I is tied to objectness [*Gegenständlichkeit*] in Husserl, the result is a phenomenology of the object that must assume its poorest form of phenomenality, in which even the I ultimately becomes an object, a phenomenon among others. Marion suggests that Heidegger recognized this insufficiency of determining the kind of Being of the I by the way of the Being of objects, and thus substituted *Dasein* for the I which no longer constitutes objects but opens a world. Although Marion judges Heidegger's achievement of positing an I that can attain individuation and ipseity "remarkable," as we have seen he also finds that *Dasein* still remains exposed to solipsism and thus is affected by a remnant of the transcendental subject of metaphysics.[15] Heidegger repeats the autarchy and self-positing of the subject in its ipseity. *Dasein* is not that which comes after the subject but is in fact "its final inheritor."

In contrast to *Dasein*, therefore, Marion speaks of the *attributaire*, who remains a kind of self but one that is devoid of all subjectivity. The phenomenon gives itself to the *attributaire* and thus originates this new self. The self acts like a filter or prism for the phenomenon by being the one to whom it appears. The *attributaire* is a kind of screen where the shock hitting it gives an indication of reception. Only in receiving what gives itself do either phenomenon or *attributaire* become visible. In the case of a saturated phenomenon, the *attributaire* turns into an *adonné* (devoted, given over) by listening to the call that cannot be identified (as either Being, the Father, or the Other). Each type of saturated phenomenon inverts intentionality in this way and makes possible an appeal. Although Marion therefore clearly takes up Lévinas' terminology of the witness and explicitly approves of Lévinas' phenomenology of the other (e.g., GG, 252), he wants to extend that role of the witness to all saturated phenomena. Any of the saturated phenomena address and call upon the self to receive and respond to the appeal.

In her contribution to Schwartz' collection *Transcendence*, which also includes her translation of Marion's article on Lévinas "From the Other to the Individual," Robyn Horner suggests in a text entitled "The Betrayal of Transcendence" that Marion "argues for an experience of transcendence that is at once resistant to rational calculation and yet able to be thought."[16] She sees two important failures in Husserl's account: subjectivity and presence, explicating their relationship as follows: "In suspending the problem of the transcendence of objects (the question of whether or not they 'exist' apart from their noematic representation in consciousness) Husserl develops a method that relies, in the end, on a self-present subject who is able to make transcendence present to itself."[17] She interprets Marion's promise in his attempt to allow phenomenology to deal with transcendence without limiting it to the "dimensions of the self-present subject." This is possible because "certain phenomena, in giving themselves to consciousness, exceed the capacity of consciousness to contain them, such as death, the idea of the infinite, or the Other. Such phenomena are therefore not constituted by consciousness but put consciousness in question. Stripping consciousness of its ability to master and understand, these phenomena reduce consciousness to the role of witness."[18]

The *attributaire*, then, designates the witnessing function of any self exposed to the impact of the self-giving phenomena. This second figure of the self hence overcomes the Cartesian subject's obsession with presence and permanence. It emerges only as a response, as a witness to the impact of the phenomenon that has always already passed. It is a witness to the past and an anticipation of the future. It is characterized by surprise and reception, not by control and certainty. It does not actively organize all data into the universal science, but rather passively receives the given that offers itself and at times even violently imposes itself. It receives its identity from the act of identifying the inbreaking phenomenon. As the beneficiary, the *attributaire* has its "being" only in connection to and relation to the phenomenon to which it is "attributed" or from which it "benefits." It does not open a world but finds itself in a world that has always already embraced it. This analysis does not only parallel Marion's somewhat untraditional interpretation of Descartes that we have examined above (and of which he reminds us frequently within *Being Given*). More significantly, this new version of the self—as a passive recipient of the phenomenon, as a witness to its exposure, as no more than the one to whom the phenomenological experience is given—constitutes a careful response to the various problems outlined in Marion's examination of Descartes' ego. This self is no longer an active *intuitus*, in full control of all objects and determining their being by arranging them into a *mathesis universalis*. No such universal knowledge or complete certainty is available to the passive self that always comes after and in response to the phenomenon. Marion carries this vision of the responsive self even further with the notion of the *adonné*.

L'adonné

Marion describes the *adonné* as one completely devoted and given over to the call that is exercised by the saturated phenomenon. He uses as paradigms again Heidegger's call of Being and in this context also Lévinas' call of the Other. Both remain limited, however, in Marion's view, because they are determined, by Being or the Other respectively (he calls them an ontological and an ethical call). Marion seeks to employ these paradigms but to free them from their respective commitments to Being or the Other. Instead, Marion insists, *any* saturated phenomenon makes an appeal to its recipient and we can be utterly devoted or given over to different calls, not merely to Being or another human face. This new self devoted to the call of the phenomenon, Marion calls the *adonné*. In *Being Given*, Jeff Kosky translates this term as "the gifted" (probably in order to retain the similarity to the other subtitles of "givenness," "the gift," and "the given"). He says about this "gifted,"

In other words, what gives itself shows itself in or, perhaps more precisely, as the response it receives from the gifted who receives himself from it. In its passive work of phenomenalizing givenness in and through its witness thereto, the "gifted" here takes on another sense: echoing Kant's theory of genius, the gifted is the one endowed or inspired with a talent or aptitude for making more of the given visible than heretofore has been seen. Receiving himself in the passivity of giving himself over to the given, the gifted registers or witnesses the appearance of the given to varying degrees depending on how gifted he or she might have been. Some gifteds are more gifted than others and so let more givenness show itself. The degree of giftedness is seen in the extent to which the gifted gives himself over to the call.[19]

Adonné, however, means to be "devoted," "given over to," or even "addicted." ("Gifted" works neither as a translation of the French term nor as a description of Marion's use of it.) In a German interview Marion wonders whether one could translate the term into German as *"der Zugegebene."*[20] While the audience rightly responds that this does not really work in German, the suggestion points to the connotations of "devotedness" or "givenness to" as particularly important to Marion.

In the same context, Marion also emphasizes that the *adonné* is not reflexive and is not to be translated in that fashion.[21] He refuses any notions of mediation or intrigue (as in Lévinas) and claims that subjectivity is a "result of the given." He also points out that what is most fundamental for him is the notion of reduction, without which phenomenology would be impossible. "Because reduction is passive, one requires reduction in order to receive passivity."[22] He uses the example that in doing high jumping [in French] one "receives oneself" as one touches down. By receiving the given, the devoted receives itself. "Consciousness is first of all only a reaction to the consciousness of another. My consciousness is formed by something else which is received."[23] He does agree that consciousness must always be consciousness of something, but insists that "it is false to say that my self-consciousness only 'accompanies' the outside world. Rather self-consciousness must itself be woken up. And this happens through the given. Hence self-consciousness always receives itself from the given. Self-consciousness does not always accompany an object — there is no empty self-consciousness — , but it is always a consciousness of a somewhat modified consciousness." And he continues immediately: "the most famous example is Descartes' *cogito*. Descartes' *cogito* is in principle a self-consciousness without object-consciousness. There is more than just objects."[24] In the following I am translating *adonné* as the *devoted*, which seems to me closest to what Marion attempts to convey with the French.

Marion emphasizes the essential anonymity of this call which proceeds from the phenomenon. The excess of intuition in a phenomenon "subverts and therefore precedes every intention that it exceeds and decenters" (BG, 267; ED, 368). The devoted therefore "receives itself entirely from what it receives" (BG, 268; ED, 370). The surrender to the phenomenon also implies surrender of autarchy, control, and self-sufficiency. It inscribes the devoted into a relation more primordial than any subjectivity. The devoted is surprised, unsettled, displaced by the coming of the phenomenon: "The call surprises by seizing the devoted without always teaching him what it might be. It reduces him to merely watching for, freezes him in place, puts him in immobile availability for what might not finally come or indeed ever begin. The devoted gives all his attention to an essentially lacking object; he is open to an empty gap" (BG, 268; ED, 370). This is an overwhelming experience which defies comprehension and thus invalidates the Cartesian *intuitus* constructing the *mathesis universalis*. This address by the phenomenon puts the devoted in an unequal, asymmetrical position. Against Lévinas, however, Marion insists that this asymmetry is not imposed by the Other. Rather, this is a general alterity "from which the Other can be lacking" (BG, 269; ED, 371). Yet since an anonymous other is still present, Marion does think that this allows the new self to escape solipsism. While that claim may not be entirely convincing, Marion does provide a fuller account of relation to the other in his work on the erotic phenomenon.[25] And of course this account clearly parallels what he has attempted to show for the ego of the *Meditations* who is interrupted and addressed by an (initially anonymous) other.

The self is not only unsettled by this prior alterity, but it also receives itself from this call. My facticity is established by realizing that I exist only because a call has preceded me: "Not only is the first word never said by the I, which can only undergo it by receiving it; not only does it not give us any objective or rational knowledge; but it opens only onto this very fact that some gift happens to *me* because it precedes *me* originarily in such a way that I must recognize that I proceed from it" (BG, 270; ED, 372). I am thus given myself by this call which individuates me through its address and gives me access to myself. The appeal gives me to me and as myself, individualizes me. It separates me from all property or possession of self. I can only anticipate my own reception of myself. Marion describes this — against Heidegger — as a kind of originary inauthenticity (I gain access to myself only as a receptive "me," not an active "I"). Authenticity seeks to mask the appeal; while inauthenticity recognizes that I am always already addressed before I find myself. Marion insists that this appeal is by definition undeniable. Although one can pretend not having heard it and refuse it, that is also already an acknowledgment. Olivier Mathieu, in a review of *In Excess*, notices some changes in terminology from *Being Given* to *In Excess*. For example, Marion no longer speaks of a "response" to the phenomenon but of "resistance" to it, which are two very different activities.[26] He complains about this confusion, which he wishes Marion had elucidated. Although Mathieu is correct to point to this ambivalence in Marion's terminology, it seems to me that, on the one hand, Marion employs the language of "response" primarily in terms of the *interloqué* or the *attributaire*, while he is more likely to use "resistance" for the *adonné*, who in the face of self-giving of the saturated phenomenon seems even more passive than the former figures of the self. The devoted clearly goes further for Marion than the interlocuted. On the other hand, Marion also seems to interpret the "bearing" of the impact (i.e., resistance) as a type of response, since it makes the given phenomenon visible in some fashion.

Marion supports this account of the self by examining the "two most canonical theories of the subject" (Descartes' ego and Kant's transcendental I) and showing how they are also already determined by an appeal.[27] He examines Descartes' notion of the ego in the *Meditations* (which I have analyzed above) that discovers itself interlocuted by an other (evil demon/God), and the Kantian notion of respect. Both, he suggests, "anticipate" the devoted (BG, 279; ED, 386). In this particular example, we see again how Marion's work on Descartes has prepared the scene for his phenomenology. Throughout this analysis he refers repeatedly to the Cartesian self and to its remarkable ambiguity that allows the self to be interpreted (in a sense against Descartes) as one affected and as dependent upon a prior appeal. The "self after the subject" is not only "novel," in that it radically rethinks the metaphysical assumptions of modern subjectivity, but it is also deeply rooted in the historical experiences of this subject, especially when it is not aware of its own dependence or seeks to ignore it by asserting its own self-sufficiency.

Marion goes on to claim that the reception of this appeal is prior to and more significant than the "existence" or "being" of this new self. Again, the language of being is important to what Marion assumes about metaphysics and therefore seeks to displace. As he attempted to think God without or beyond Being in his theological work, he now seeks to think the human self in the same fashion. The devoted is being *given* its self by that which (or who) gives *without being* (visible or identifiable). The devoted becomes visible through the claim or appeal of the saturated phenomenon. This appeal can only make itself heard by eliciting a response. The response is what makes the call visible. It responds to the appeal by acknowledging it and by answering its question. The call must be understood, received, heard, and accepted; otherwise it remains vain and empty.[28] I must allow myself to be seduced by the call and thus acknowledge its claim on me.[29] The devoted thus opens a field of manifestation by lending itself to receive the phenomenon and retaining its impact. The response makes the appeal phenomenally obvious. The appeal appears when it is heard by the first one who says: *me voici*. Marion calls this a "retardation" or delay of the appeal, because the response in a sense "terminates" it.[30] He also points out that the appeal is always excessive, while the response always remains limited: it only reveals one face of the appeal though there may be many others. Marion also explores the figure of fatigue in this context. At some point, the response tires of showing that which the appeal never tires of giving. Finally, the response is always marked by belatedness. He explicates this by interpreting even my birth as an already late arrival. My singularized identity comes to me without me and before me; I have no say in it. This lateness is reinforced and marked by inauthenticity (my origin is given to me from elsewhere; I am not in possession of myself; the equality of "I" to the "I" always remains an illusion or a lie), by the proper name (which is not actually mine and does not identify me as unique but rather connects me with many other people who carry the same [last or first] name), and by responsibility (I am responsible, not merely ethically, but even for allowing the face of the other to appear).[31] I must respond in this way to all instances of saturated phenomena: as witness to a historical event, to the affection of the flesh, before the idol which heightens my gaze. He insists that responsibility is not limited only to the face of the other, but also applies in these other moments. (One should note again that Marion is highlighting the response of the self to *saturated phenomena*, not to any type of phenomena. Our response to mathematical phenomena, for example, might be quite different and much closer to something like Cartesian subjectivity. Yet solving a math problem will probably not grant me any kind of identity.)

The appeal of the overwhelming phenomenon must elicit a response that both names the phenomenon and shapes the one responding into a particular self. The phenomenon — whether historical event, painting, or face of the other — calls me and claims me. In acknowledging this claim, I devote myself to it, make it manifest, and thus become myself for the first time. The phenomenon is always limited by my ability to receive it. The recipient becomes "devoted" to the phenomenon and receives a new (or first) identity from it. This language of receptivity and devotion does of course carry certain religious connotations.[32] In this case, these connotations or parallels are to some extent even exacerbated by the argument I have attempted to sustain throughout, namely that this proposal is grounded in Marion's analysis of Descartes. We have seen that he employs very similar terminology in his analysis of the terminology of *capax* as receptivity to the divine gift in the medieval texts and its transformation into *capable* as a kind of power in the Cartesian text. The devoted clearly seems to recover these notions of receptivity and devotion to the divine gift while eschewing notions of independence and power. Despite (or maybe due to) these apparently religious connotations, Marion insists repeatedly that the voice or origin of the call cannot be identified. It may be God (revelation), or the other (obligation), or Being (event), or life (auto-affection) or something different, but one does not know because the call is always anonymous.[33] Each of the saturated phenomena can accomplish the call and one can never identify the name of the paradox of the call. The devoted must always respond according to a pure immanence (thus one's experience of the phenomenon and not what it may be in itself). Even (and especially) the phenomenon of revelation requires the radical anonymity of that which calls. The appeal does not name itself, but has as its function only to raise up the respondent or to allow it to come to life.

Marion explains this in more detail: The *me voici* of the response gives a *te voilà!* to the call and thus attributes it a name. Only by the response does the devoted give a clear name to the caller of the appeal. In the case of one who does not want to hear, the call remains anonymous. The devoted thus lets itself be completely governed by that which it receives, whether that is a painting, a melody, the affection of anxiety, joy, or suffering: all are identified only in the response. Everything which gives itself as a call only shows itself when the devoted converts it into a phenomenon by its response; only from there does it take on visibility and eventually receive a name. Until the response has happened, it remains anonymous. If I knew beforehand who or what was calling me (Being, God, the other, life), I would no longer be devoted but in control. There would be a dialogue instead of radical interruption and passivity. Anonymity belongs strictly to the conditions of possibility of the appeal. The appeal does not need to make itself known in order to be recognized, nor must it identify itself in order to exercise itself. This poverty injures the subject and exiles it outside of any authenticity. The response only begins to say that which silences the appeal, and it never manages to say it all the way to the end. In this way its historicity opens. The appeal gives but no longer shows itself. It is an unseen sending, a veiled voice [*un envoi qui ne se voit pas, une voix qui se voile*] (ED, 417; BG, 303). The response is thus never completed; one is always attempting to catch up with it. The response always remains deficient. Carlson talks about this deficiency as a kind of debt or fault. He says:

> The role assigned to will in converting the given into the phenomenal can seem, then, to introduce into the question of revelation (and of phenomenality more broadly) an understanding of responsiveness and responsibility that entails an essential implication of debt and fault on the part of the one who manages (or not) to make the given visible — and that responsibility, along with the attendant debt or fault, would become even more pressing, more necessary and more overwhelming, as the saturation of phenomenality moves closer to revelation, where the inadequacy of my response, and hence my fault, can only grow in the immeasurable measure of what gives itself. (CE, 166)

He deeply deplores this emphasis on indebtedness and fault in Marion. He asks in conclusion: "Does it leave for us still to think the possibility (or impossibility) of receiving that which gives itself beyond obligation and fault, debt and guilt, crime and punishment — the possibility that I might be liberated to receive the given, however I might manage to receive it, without having to suffer humiliation and remonstration, without counting myself always already inadequate to the given and so forever unworthy of it?" (CE, 174). While Marion certainly speaks of deficiency in reception, the language of finitude seems more appropriate here than that of debt or guilt. This deficiency has a twofold function: On the one hand, it dislocates and destabilizes the metaphysical subject and shows that one is always dependent upon the previous address by the phenomenon. On the other hand, it also preserves the level of "saturation" of the excessive phenomenon by showing that intuition gives so much that the recipient cannot possibly grasp, hold, or contain it.

It is also important to emphasize here that although the devoted continually tries to assign a name to the call, that nomination remains a risk because transcendence can never be verified in the immanence in which the devoted must always remain. For something to become a phenomenon, I must first admit it and desire it, then receive it by being devoted or given over to it, and finally see it and agree to it. The further a phenomenon becomes saturated, the harder (and more fecund) does the decision become, because the response grows less and less adequate. The excess of the given in the case of a saturated phenomenon humiliates and withdraws any semblance of control from the devoted.[34] While the self can determine poor phenomena and be in control even of common objects, it is utterly impossible to do so in the case of saturated phenomena. Nothing which gives itself can actually arise without the devoted. The call and the recipient thus delimit each other in a certain sense. On the one hand, the devoted must receive donation in order to receive itself. Without the reception of the given, absolutely nothing comes after the subject. No self is possible without the call. On the other hand, donation is always put into play in the essential finitude of the devoted. The given can never be seen as without limit or reserve because it is always limited by our finitude. Phenomenality thus does have a finitude in the regime of donation, for that which is given does not show itself except in the measure in which it is received by the devoted. It can realize itself within the field in which the devoted receives it. In both the case of a poor and that of a saturated phenomenon, it is possible for the recipient to abandon the given because it can be no longer supported or becomes too excessive and blinding. Each saturated phenomenon can be denied, turned away from, refused articulation, and thus abandoned. Kosky rightly points out that givenness does seem restricted by the limitations of the devoted, who is not able to make all that is given appear because it exceeds his capacities.[35] Phenomenality always accepts limits precisely because the donation which transgresses them gives itself over only to my finitude. Yet, even an abandoned gift is perfectly given. The devoted thus remains "the sole master and servant of the given." This statement, which is the concluding sentence of the final part of *Being Given*, points again to the ambivalence highlighted above in Marion's treatment of the self and maybe indicates that the tension is intentional. On the one hand, the recipient is entirely passive and a mere screen for the self-giving phenomenon. On the other hand, no phenomenon can ever become visible or even possible without this reception by the consciousness of the self and thus in some fashion seems entirely dependent upon it.

Most critics of Marion's account of the self disregard one pole of this fragile tension and criticize him for going too far in the other direction. Some suggest that Marion has merely re-established a metaphysical subject, while others think his self is far too passive. Ricard combines both of these criticisms in a curious fashion by arguing that the subject reappears for Marion in a metaphysical manner *and* is too passive. He finds that Marion's reading of

Husserl is too superficial. A subject that becomes a "pure passivity: a screen or a surface without depth" is an account far too restrictive.[36] He thinks that this type of experience comes from a "universe of magic."[37] It seems he means by this that the phenomenon is anthropomorphized for Marion, since it apparently acts autonomously. He finds it not coincidental that much of Marion's imagery comes from the theater. The "assimilation" of reduction to donation goes back to an "archaic" version of mimesis and the subject becomes "a passive receptacle."[38] In his view, phenomenology cannot and should not eliminate intentionality, which is what he sees Marion doing in his account.

For Horner, on the other hand, the subject is responsive in Marion's account, even in performing the reduction: "It is not presented as *what it is* so much as signaled in its withdrawal from the scope of the reducing consciousness." She insists that "phenomenology is inevitably hermeneutics. In admitting that the reduction does not deliver the I in presence to consciousness, we also have to admit that its excessiveness can only be contextualized by an act of interpretation."[39] This is why Marion must rethink the constituting subject and turn it into a "screen" for the given, "seeking to withdraw it from any major causal or constitutional role. The transcendental function of the I can never be denied, but it seems to me that where the given totally defies comprehension, the I really has been reduced to its most basic role as witness rather than actor."[40] She does criticize this account of "counter-experience" as so extreme that the me becomes utterly undecidable. In her view, phenomenology cannot be without presuppositions: "For all that the reduction does away with every precondition, it cannot ultimately do without a horizon and a constituting I, because it must reduce to what can be known. And where Marion maintains that it does do without these conditions, the phenomenology he practices has gone beyond phenomenology. In his figure of saturation, we have the perfect example of the positive failure of phenomenology."[41] In this failure, so she contends, phenomenology opens onto theology, and she thinks that this is also Marion's intent (or at least follows neatly from his account). As the exposition of Marion's account of the phenomenological recipient surely has shown, however, he neither considers this a "failure" of phenomenology nor does he celebrate any opening onto theology in this context.

Marion himself concludes that "the phenomenology of givenness has finished radically — in my eyes, for the first time — with the 'subject' and all its recent avatars" (BG, 322; ED, 441). He admits that it may seem as if this self is a new subject that occupies a similar center in his phenomenology as *Dasein* did in Heidegger's, but insists that "it does not hold this center but is instead held there as a recipient where what gives itself shows itself, and that it discloses itself given to and as a pole of givenness, where all the givens come forth incessantly" (BG, 322; ED, 442). In the center is thus no longer a subject, but a devoted whose only function is to receive what gives itself without measure. It is important here again to recognize that Marion operates with a clear definition of what metaphysics means and what the limitations of a Cartesian metaphysical subject are. It is only these precise definitions and limitations that Marion seeks to overcome. Near the beginning of his treatment Marion emphasizes the essential passivity of the devoted by pointing to the ways in which it challenges metaphysical knowledge:

> The call surprises the devoted without always teaching him what it might be. It reduces him to merely watching for, freezes him in place, puts him in immobile availability for what might not finally come or indeed ever begin. The devoted gives all his attention to an essentially lacking object; he is open to an empty gap. Such a gap, imposed on the *self/me* without giving me knowledge of it, therefore contradicts all ecstasy of knowledge, by which the transcendental I constituted, in front of itself and in an on principle transparent evidence, the object. Surprise, this obscure and suffered seizure, contradicts intentionality, this known and knowing ecstasy deployed by the I at its own initiative. Far from surveying with its gaze the pure land of the objectivity to be known, the I transformed into *self/me* is overwhelmed by the unknowable claim. (BG, 268–69; ED, 370; transl. mod.)

While, as critics have pointed out, there may be certain ways in which this self is still necessary and even active in a certain fashion, Marion has clearly dispensed with the parameters of metaphysics which he had outlined in his account of Descartes. All attempts at autarchy and self-sufficiency have been eliminated. This new self cannot serve as the metaphysical subject grounding beings or giving them causality, because it comes after everything else and receives itself from the other. The self is neither permanent nor focused on the present. It is always in flux, always constituted anew by the phenomenon, always engaged in a dance of relation with all things. It listens to a primordial call which precedes it and shatters its obsession with presence in both temporal and spatial respects. The devotion and commitment to the phenomenon that Marion emphasizes in *Being Given* is carried to its height in his most recent work on the erotic phenomenon. Here I am not only devoted to the phenomenon and receive its impact, but I am absolutely committed as a lover to the beloved. Although in some sense the lover is a specific instantiation of the devoted recipient (not all of phenomenology is concerned with love nor is every phenomenon a beloved), in Marion's view it is the highest and most successful one, the one at the furthest remove from metaphysics.

L'amant

The lover, on Marion's account, provides the most successful overcoming of the metaphysical subject. As I have pointed out repeatedly already, Marion posits his "erotic meditations" explicitly as a response to the metaphysical ones.[42] This is particularly true in respect to the metaphysical subject. It is Marion's explicit goal to speak of an erotic self instead of a metaphysical or traditionally Cartesian one. And most of his book on the erotic phenomenon is indeed concerned not only abstractly with the topic of love, but much more concretely with what it might mean for the self to love and to approach another in love. He begins with the existential concern of the self to be loved and affirmed by another, a question he suggests defines us much more profoundly than the Cartesian search for certainty and autonomy. He engages in a phenomenological description of a search for affirmation that resembles Cartesian radical doubt — but no longer in search for certainty. This realization of the profound need for love and affirmation already begins to displace Cartesian self-sufficiency because it requires an alterity that could affirm or reassure me.[43] The metaphysical subject in its desire not to be dependent on anyone or anything else first attempts self-love, only to realize quickly that it cannot successfully or sufficiently love itself. Such attempt at self-love always results instead in self-hatred. I recognize that I cannot fulfill my own need for self-affirmation, because it is boundless and asks for an unconditional love that I am unable to give to myself: "I cannot precede myself, nor exceed myself, nor breach the distance, I can neither think nor perform the formula 'I love myself' [je m'aime moi-même]" (PE, 80; EP, 47). Marion here denies the notion of *conatus essendi* that Lévinas already challenged by showing that it is not my primary desire to remain in existence but that existence without love is meaningless and drives one to suicide. Instead of the strong subject's solipsistic autonomy, I recognize myself as fragile, insufficient, and finite. Yet while acknowledging my own unworthiness to be loved that leads to self-hatred, I also observe others who apparently do receive love even though they do not seem any more worthy of such love than I am. I envy them and demand their love. As they refuse or are unable to fulfill these demands, this desire to be loved finally leads to a hatred of all against all, a war of all against self and other: "Self-love leads only to hatred, received and given" (PE, 105; EP, 63). This vicious cycle has therefore led the self through increasingly radical self-doubt. Unlike the Cartesian doubt it does not question certainty but instead affirmation. Yet like Cartesian doubt it hits rock-bottom, a point where it cannot go any further. Somewhat later Marion makes this comparison with Cartesian hyperbolic doubt explicit and affirms it as a parallel (PE, 113; EP, 68).

Marion suggests, therefore, that I must make the first step in love. Instead of expecting to be loved by another, I must become the lover and offer myself in loving vulnerability. Instead of calculating (if you love me and give me assurance, I will return your love and assure you that you are loveable), we must give up our desire for reciprocity. Any assumption of reciprocity makes love impossible because it would confine it to metaphysics. By deciding to love, committing to love, I risk the rejection of the other and am therefore not in control. This risk of preparing the scene for the other (thus displaying an ambivalence similar to the devoted's response to the saturated phenomenon), exposing myself in the vulnerability and nakedness of my flesh, offering myself to the other, in Marion's view fully overcomes the metaphysical subject. I am not in control, have acknowledged my utter need for affirmation and assurance, and yet have relinquished even this desire. I do not organize objects, but expose my body in the vulnerability of my flesh. I am no longer obsessed with bringing into presence, but instead open in expectation toward the future, to the hope of the incoming of the other whose coming I do not control. This is an open-ended hope, one that Marion insists might always be disappointed. Instead of holding back until I am assured of complete control over all objects, I commit myself fully without any assurance. Again, therefore, the Cartesian self that reduced all things to objects of its thoughts and reigned over them in a *mathesis universalis* that established absolute order and measure, is displaced by the lover who is made fully available while ceding all ability and desire for control (even of the beloved's response).

The possible rejection, however, does not invalidate my self-giving: "For a rejected love remains a love perfectly accomplished, just as a refused gift remains a gift perfectly given" (PE, 117; EP, 71). It is the movement of love and its impact on the lover that Marion emphasizes here, not so much its import for the beloved. He insists that this perfectly reverses the Cartesian formula for the metaphysical subject and overcomes ontological language: "To love without being loved defines *love without Being*" (PE, 118; EP, 72). The lover here takes the initiative, although Marion maintains as firmly as before that this initiative does not constitute a return to self-sufficiency or autonomy: "I become myself not because I think, doubt or imagine (because others can think my thoughts which often do not even concern me but the object of my intentionality), not because I will, desire or hope (because I never know if I intervene in the first person or only as the mask which hides and support the pulsations, the passions and the needs which play in me without me). But I become definitely myself for the first time and as long as, as lover, I can love first" (PE, 125; EP, 76). The lover allows the phenomenon of the beloved to emerge and gives it visibility. The lover supports all, hopes all, believes all, endures all.[44] The lover must love to the end, even if love is never returned: "The lover loves to love for the love of love [*L'amant aime aimer pour l'amour de l'amour*]" (PE, 140; EP, 87).

John Milbank especially has objected strongly to Marion's suggestion that the self is in no need of reciprocity. He argues, for example, that Marion's claim that reciprocity always becomes onto-theo-logical "is surely residually — or even emphatically — Cartesian."[45] He makes this judgment because he sees the search for a pure gift or a phenomenological reduction to the absolutely given as fundamentally wrong-headed and still profoundly inscribed in a metaphysical project: "Marion insists on a phenomenological passivity, which far from humbling our modernity, only repeats its essence."[46] Milbank is skeptical of Marion's account of the self given itself by the phenomenon because it remains an independent and solipsistic subject in his view. For Milbank, "the gift as such involves return in some sense," something neither Derrida nor Marion want to acknowledge in his view.[47] Milbank insists that the recipient of the gift must be involved in the giving and hence that there necessarily must be some measure of reciprocity. A subject must always be involved in any reduction, because otherwise "all that would then remain of 'phenomenology' would be a shuttle from illusion to illusion. Deconstruction would have resulted, and nihilism ensued."[48] Such a result is clearly unacceptable to Milbank. Because Marion refuses to acknowledge the necessary receptivity of the subject, in Milbank's view "Marion's fundamental willing does not see at all, but blindly asserts, with the blindness of a one-way self-sacrificial charity construed as the ultimate gesture. And such 'charity' is surely more assertion than true gift, since it is a charity to no-one."[49] The gift, therefore, always requires reciprocity. He later criticizes Marion's account of eros in the same fashion.[50]

Contrary to Milbank's claims, however, Marion does emphasize the necessary receptivity of the self, although that is a passive receptivity for him. As we have seen above, Marion repeatedly points out that the self serves as the screen of the phenomenon, as the place where it becomes visible. Although he goes to great lengths to formulate this self as no longer a controlling or self-sufficient subject, the self definitely must be present for any phenomenon to become visible. Without consciousness there is no phenomenality. The phenomenon is always given to someone. And while Marion rejects reciprocity in the loving relation, he does seem to propose a sort of "mutual asymmetry," as we will see shortly. Milbank himself seems to ignore the connotations of economy in reciprocity that Marion criticizes and seeks to escape. While Milbank sees little response on the part of the beloved or the recipient in Marion's work, he fails to address how his own insistence on reciprocity and receptivity would be more successful in overcoming the metaphysical subject.

In any case, we can see that the "new self," the "self after the subject," responds to each of the metaphysical problems of the traditional subject that Marion had outlined in his work on Descartes. It becomes receptive and radically dependent upon the in-breaking of the phenomenon. Its obsession with control, presence, and permanence is displaced through the givenness of the phenomenon that comes to it from outside and constitutes the self as a witness to its own self-showing. Its search for certainty in radical systematic doubt is replaced by a search for affirmation through recognition of radical self-hatred. One aspect is still missing here, however. What has received almost no attention in this extended exploration of the new self is its openness to the other. Although Marion maintains that this self is no longer solipsistic since it is addressed by a prior instance, an account of inter-subjectivity seems to be conspicuously lacking in Marion's treatment (and to that extent Milbank might be correct in his assessment of Marion's earlier work on the self). It seems possible that the interlocuted or devoted self could be fully individuated by a historical event or a painting and would have no need of an encounter with a living being. And so far even the lover loves in isolation — loves love, commits to love as such. Since the beloved may reject the advance of the lover, we have not truly arrived at inter-subjectivity. A final avatar of the metaphysical subject, therefore, must still be overcome: its solipsism. This account Marion seeks to provide in his most recent work on the erotic phenomenon (of which I have examined only the beginning). Not only does he show that the self only becomes sufficiently individuated as the lover (as we have seen above), but the loving relationship also enables individuation of the other. This account of the self therefore does guide us to a renewed consideration of inter-subjectivity.

nine
Charity and Eros

"One Must Substitute Erotic Meditations for the Metaphysical Meditations"

We have already seen that Marion's insistence on the need for an account of the relation between self and other arises out of his critique of the Cartesian solipsistic subject. That does not necessarily explain, however, why this relation for Marion must be primarily (if not solely) an account of love. I would suggest that this connection between the topic of the other and that of love is also grounded in Marion's early work, but in this case more in his explication of Pascal than of Descartes. And in fact, as we have seen, Marion employed Pascal in order to criticize the Cartesian self as unable to open onto any other. It is Pascal, according to Marion, who charges Descartes with solipsistic egoism and who finds the Cartesian account of love deeply troubling, since it turns all others into objects of the *ego cogito*. Pascal criticizes Descartes' lack of consideration of other minds and turns his examples on him, thus exposing the solipsism of the Cartesian ego. The ego, for Descartes, loves only the self; even generosity is interpreted as self-affection.[1] The *ego cogito* makes any *alter ego* impossible.[2] In fact, for Descartes, love comes to designate not vulnerability to an other, but a desire for food, obsession with money, addiction to drink, the action of rape, and also worship of God.[3] Love is reduced to representation of

225

an object for which one feels passion.[4] For Descartes, certainty and evidence are prior and love is therefore limited, if not impossible.

Pascal attempts to overcome this metaphysical account of the ego with his notion of the three orders. I have already examined these briefly in order to show how Marion interprets Pascal as a successful displacement of the Cartesian metaphysical system. It is significant in this context, however, that the third order is one of charity. For Pascal, at least in Marion's appropriation of his work, it is love that overcomes metaphysics and provides a more successful account of God, self, and other. For Pascal, love is prior to knowledge and although that may limit certainty, it gives a superior kind of evidence. In terms of certainty or representation others appear only as objects of the solipsistic mind. In terms of love, they are able to arise as beloveds, as true others. I will briefly examine this Pascalian account of charity in order to provide the context for Marion's own work on the same topic and to show how Marion's proposal is grounded in his explication of Pascal.

Pascal and the Order of Charity

Pascal's third order is supremely defined by the vision of charity, which is one utterly different from the *cogitatio:* "Charity no longer intervenes as the pious and superfluous auxiliary to the passion of love; it opens a distinct world by opening other eyes in man" (MP, 313; PM, 332). This does not imply that charity is a mere emotion that can be dismissed easily. Rather, it is a different way of seeing the world that has its own rationality. Love opens our eyes to seeing anew, to observing and thinking differently. Charity changes our vision of the world: "Thus, charity provokes the world, seen first in its two natural orders, to be soaked, tinted, and redrawn in the unthinkable and unexpectedly visible colors of its glory or its abandon. Beneath the bright and iridescent light of charity, the world appears in all its dimensions, according to all its parameters, with all its contrasts — in short, in truth" (MP, 313; PM, 333). The order of knowing that charity constitutes is therefore not only a different way of approaching things, but, for Marion, it is a decidedly superior way. It can subvert and correct the insights received through merely metaphysical speculation. The third order of charity in Pascal hence — and most of this chapter will serve to establish that claim — previews the role of love in Marion's phenomenology, first as "third order of charity," later as "erotic reduction."[5]

The relation between second and third orders is the difference between certainty and love that we have seen above (and that is the fundamental argument of Marion's book on the erotic phenomenon). Marion, at least in his analysis of Pascal, implies a clear hierarchy of the orders in which charity is far superior to the other two: "Charity regulates the first and the second orders by theoretical necessity" but also by much greater distance (MP, 313; PM, 333). In Pascal, the three orders are fixed in a hierarchy through the gaze. The gaze must be appropriate to the order to which it seeks to correspond, thus reversing the Cartesian *intuitus* that controls its objects and imposes an order on them. Only a privileged and advanced gaze can attain the highest stage: "The more 'greatness' at work in an order, the more excellent will be the gaze that can see it" (MP, 315; PM, 335). The third order is seen as clearly superior and as only accessible to a select few: "Finally, few accede to charity, thus the third order remains invisible to the first two."[6] The third order judges the second one and serves as its standard (MP, 315; PM, 335). The second order (Cartesian philosophy) can never reach the third (the theology of charity) and is incapable of judging it. Marion will maintain the same about the erotic phenomenon: it is of a different order and rationality and provides its own kind of evidence that is superior to that of Cartesian certainty.[7]

Marion indicates that this division of orders has implications not only for metaphysics and for language about God, but also for how one might speak of the self and the other. While the ego is the fundamental and primary term in the second order, it becomes displaced and rendered insignificant in the third. We are no longer the center of attention and the sole object of love in the third order, but recognize ourselves as "strange monsters." In the move from second to third order, a radical displacement of the ego is implied:

> Passing from the second order to the third implies subverting the ego, or, more exactly, disqualifying in the order of charity the legitimate primacy that Descartes accorded to it in the order of the mind: the *ego* must be known before all else; thus it cannot be loved to the exclusion of all else. Overcoming the Cartesian figure of metaphysics consists in not loving oneself as one thinks oneself. As it is necessary to see the ego's "dignity" in the realm of thought, it is necessary to "hate" the ego in the realm of charity, such that only God remains to be loved. (MP, 321; PM, 342)[8]

While for Descartes metaphysics is identified with the ego, Pascal seeks to overcome both ego and metaphysics. Pascal replaces the I/ego with a me/self and thus moves from nominative to accusative (a move that, as we have seen, Marion will also advocate in his phenomenology of the self). Pascal therefore accomplishes what Marion seeks to do in his own work: to outline a self radically receptive instead of a controlling ego. Any attempt at egotistic self-love ends in hatred of self and other. Instead one must relinquish one's attempts to become an independent and self-sufficient subject and instead give oneself over radically to the beloved (or to God).

Certainty thus no longer becomes the operative question. Instead the self begins to ask whether it is loved. Evidence or clear and distinct knowledge are no longer of primary interest. Instead of the *I* knowing, the *me* asks whether it is loved: "In the light of the third, it falls to pieces: *I* is doubled into this *I*, which I no longer am, and a *me*, which awaits being seen in order to be; the gaze goes deeper, from evidence to love. To become a self, I need to be neither seen, nor thought, nor known, but nothing less than loved. For the Cartesian question about the conditions for exercising my *cogitatio*, Pascal has substituted an investigation into the possibility that someone loves *me, my self,* as such" (MP, 324; PM, 345). This significantly previews terminology in Marion's work on the erotic phenomenon. The need for assurance, for someone to love me, parallels exactly what Marion seeks to establish more generally. Through love the strong Cartesian ego is displaced and its desire for certainty shown to be futile and insignificant. The nature of self-love is to think of oneself as the center and to exclude others. Charity, to the contrary, is open to the other who unsettles and disturbs the self. Marion clearly outlines his later phenomenology in this summary of Pascal's objections to Descartes. Not only does Pascal point to the dislocation of the ego and its transformation into passive recipient, but he also already previews the centrality of the question of assurance and the need for love which finds its culmination in the experience of the erotic relation. Marion explicates this even more clearly in the following passage:

> Just as phenomenology performs reductions, but unto consciousness, just as Descartes performs reductions to evidence, then to the *ego,* just as Heidegger performs a reduction of beings to the Being of beings, so too does Pascal accomplish a reduction of all that happens to charity. The unconditional reduction to charity is called destitution. To leave metaphysics destitute means: to show that a superior order remains infinitely distant from it, and that, from this point of view, the evidences of the mind "are not worth the least impulse of charity" (§308/793) and thus can be judged in terms of charity. For if the inferior order cannot regulate the superior order without being guilty of some "injustice," "the order of charity" sees everything, including the inferior orders, in terms of whether or not they keep the light of charity. (MP, 336–37; PM, 359–60)

He will use precisely this distinction between reductions in order to articulate the new "erotic reduction" in his more recent work.

Pascal's "order of charity" is, as we have seen, a theological one. At times Marion even posits Pascal as a theological response to Descartes' philosophy (although he does speak of him as a philosopher at other times). Charity, for Pascal, designates both God's revelation to human beings and the appropriate human response to God. How, then, can such an "order of charity" be employed for a purely phenomenological account? When examining Marion's view of the self I did not devote a separate chapter to his more theological writings, nor will I do so for the subject of love. Yet as shown in chapter 5, the topic of love does play an important role for Marion's talk about God, even apart from the theological connotations of charity in Pascal. And indeed Marion applies the notion of "charity" first in his theological considerations, emphasizing both that God is named best by the name of love (rather than "being") and that love ought to characterize the life of a genuine believer, the one addressed by the God of charity. One might suggest, then, that Marion's more recent phenomenological exploration of the topic of eros is merely a veiled attempt to bring his theology into phenomenology and to define all of reality no longer merely as gift but as an expression of divine love. While that suggestion, despite its attractiveness to many critics, will emerge as too superficial a consideration of Marion's work, Marion does posit his accounts of love as ultimately univocal: although divine and human love can be investigated in different spheres (philosophical and theological), they play out their game according to the same paradigm. I will briefly review Marion's claims about divine love or charity but emphasize here especially how Marion contends that such a theological exposition can inform a more strictly phenomenological account. We will see that both Marion's theological explication of charity and his phenomenology of eros are deeply grounded in his interaction with the thoughts of Descartes and Pascal.

A Theology of Charity

Marion's early interpretations of charity are profoundly theological. Charity, in Marion's view, is the only appropriate language for the divine. While "being" and "causality" quickly become idolatrous and confine God to human categories, love preserves appropriate analogy by beginning from the divine and flowing toward the human. Charity is an iconic name for God because it does not limit or confine the divine, but instead is poured out in abundant givenness. All of Marion's explications at this early point are theological: charity speaks of the Christian God, of the Triune relationships within the divinity, of God's kenotic self-giving in Christ, of the sacrament of the Eucharist, and of the ideal of the Christian life as one devoted and sacrificed to God. This love appears to have few philosophical, or specifically phenomenological, connotations. And at times Marion intimates that this vision of love is one that could have not been discovered by philosophy without the aid of Christian revelation. There is something specifically "Christian" about the notion of charity. In an article entitled "What Love Knows" which was included only in the English translation of *Prolegomena to Charity*, he claims, for example: "In this context, the theology of charity could become the privileged pathway for responding to the aporia that, from Descartes to Lévinas, haunts modern philosophy — access to the other, the most faraway neighbor. It is doubtful that Christians, if they want seriously to contribute to the rationality of the world and manifest what has come to them, have anything better to do than to work in this vein" (PC, 169).

Yet in a reflection on the possibility of something like "Christian philosophy," Marion contends that insights from theology can be (and should be) appropriated by philosophy and that these can become particularly useful for phenomenology.[9] He interprets "Christian philosophy" (a term he does not really like very much and seldom uses) as a bridge between the orders of theology and of philosophy. Philosophy, in this context as in many others, for him clearly means phenomenology. What is the task of such a Christian philosophy? Marion rejects what he calls a "merely hermeneutic function" for Christian philosophy because he interprets it as subjective, secondary, and ultimately irrelevant. A Christian philosophy that would be purely hermeneutic in character would be a mere interpretive device that leaves all "real" investigation to philosophy and subsequently puts a Christian "spin" or "garb" on these prior and fundamental philosophical insights. Instead Marion proposes a heuristic function for Christian philosophy. What does that mean? It means that theology occupies its own realms where it discovers its own "theological" phenomena, specific to its realm and exercise. These are phenomena that could not have been discovered by philosophy (or any other discipline) on its own. Theology, which arises out of the liturgy and the experience of the church, is familiar with these phenomena but does not analyze them in philosophical fashion. It is the task of "Christian philosophy" as a "heuristic of charity" to formulate such concepts and the experience of such phenomena in rigorous philosophical (i.e., phenomenological) fashion and therefore to prepare them for a philosophical investigation. It bridges the gap between the two disciplines (or the two orders — Marion's language is heavily Pascalian in this context) by taking the concepts and experiences from the realm of theology, examining them with philosophical tools and then appropriating them for wider application. (Secular) phenomenology is therefore enriched by gaining new data and experiences from a realm to which it has no access. Once these phenomena have been rigorously formulated, given over to philosophical investigation, and, one might say, promulgated to this wider audience, they are available and accessible to any philosophical investigation and need no longer carry theological connotations:

> Here no confusion is possible: (a) theology deploys the discourse of charity from and about the revelata in the strict sense, that is, truths that only faith can reach; (b) philosophy discusses facts, phenomena, and statements accessible to reason and its workings; and (c) "Christian philosophy" finds and invents in the natural sphere, which is ruled by reason, phenomena and concepts that are answerable in the order of charity and that simple reason cannot see or discover. After having formalized them, "Christian philosophy" introduces them into philosophy and abandons them to it.[10]

Marion uses the language of charity heavily in this context. In fact, it is the prime example of a concept or experience that is indigenous to the task of theology but can be given by "Christian philosophy" to the realm of philosophy. It now becomes appropriated by phenomenology and can be investigated by it. It seems to me that this is clearly what Marion is doing in his phenomenological investigations (I will return to this claim in the conclusion). He takes phenomena which he has first discovered in a theological setting, formulates them with phenomenological tools, and then makes them available to a purely phenomenological investigation (although as many critics have pointed out they retain some indication of their theological heritage and origin). In *Prolegomena to Charity* he first explores what promise such a phenomenological appropriation might hold.

A Phenomenology of Charity

We receive an indication of what a more phenomenological analysis of charity might look like in a chapter from *Prolegomena to Charity* which is written in homage to Emmanuel Lévinas and repeatedly claims to remain strictly phenomenological.[11] Thus, although the book as a whole often ventures into theology, this particular article or chapter provides a good summary of Marion's thought about the role and nature of love in phenomenology. In this chapter, he rejects previous attempts to talk about inter-subjectivity as insufficient and seeks to articulate a phenomenological analysis of love. Because of its phenomenological emphasis in an overall theological context, it also provides a good transition to an examination of Marion's most recent and most strictly phenomenological work on eros and an evaluation of this work's (a)theological character.

Marion points out that phenomenology in its analysis of consciousness already opens a path toward love. Consciousness is always first aware of things outside it and affected by them. In thus being aware first and foremost of something other than itself, it is self-alienated and dependent upon another. Love might then be defined as a particularly intense state of consciousness. Yet, Marion goes on to reject this interpretation as a pathway to true inter-subjectivity. Rather, this account of love always ends up reducing any "beloved" to a state of my own consciousness, consequently to my own experience. In appropriating a person to my consciousness, I reduce him or her to an object and thus eliminate any possibility of love. The very constitution of the perception of an object forbids love. Love, thus, "appears as an optical illusion of my consciousness, which experiences only itself alone" (PC, 75; PaC, 95). A phenomenological analysis of love thus suffers a doubled aporia: Either it describes love "as such" in the abstract, but in that case it is "love in the void" and does not do any justice to the intensely personal and specific experience of love. Or it describes a personal experience of love, but in that case it remains autistic and self-idolatrous. Love as a figure of consciousness always ends up in self-idolatry. Marion therefore insists that "one must give up seeing the other as a subject, and for a radical reason. The other must remain invisible so as to offer himself to a possible love, because if, by chance, I saw him (if an intuition adequately fulfilled the intentional object), he would be ipso facto already disqualified as other" (PC, 80; PaC, 100). Obviously, such an account of solipsistic love also remains insufficient.

Marion points out that if I can reach the other only through my own intentionality, as Husserl had suggested, the other is always turned into an object. He is obviously leaning here on his earlier claims that Husserl's phenomenology defines things primarily as objects and on his criticism of the Cartesian ego that reduces all things similarly to objects of its gaze. For neither Descartes nor Husserl can one encounter the other as such or as subject. Marion thinks that this suggests that one cannot really "see" the other, because all such experience would turn the other into an object. Thus, somehow it must become possible that I allow the other his or her own intentionality. I must "face up" to the other, look only into the emptiness of his or her pupils where I cannot identify or delineate anything. I must allow for the "counter-current" of the other's consciousness and expose myself to that other consciousness which dislocates mine and renders me "unconscious" (PC, 82; PaC, 102).[12] To disclose myself in this way before the face of the other is to become a *me* that is "uncovered, stripped bare, decentered" (PC, 84; PaC, 104). Consciousness is in a sense both destroyed and retained; I am pulled outside myself, unsettled, overpowered. Love is defined by this loss of consciousness, by the crossing of two authentic gazes, in which neither is reduced to an object and neither can be located as a subject. Marion depicts this reciprocal vulnerability of gazes as follows:

> Whence comes what we will from now on consider the phenomenological determination of love: two definitively invisible gazes (intentionality and the injunction) cross one another, and thus together trace a cross that is invisible to every gaze other than theirs alone. Each of the two gazes renounces seeing visibly the other gaze — the object alone can be seen, the eye's corpse — in order to expose its own invisible intention to the invisible impact of the other intention. Two gazes, definitively invisible, cross and, in this crossing, renounce their invisibility. They consent to let themselves be seen without seeing and invert the original disposition of every (de)nominative gaze — to see without being seen. To love would thus be defined as seeing the definitively invisible aim of my gaze nonetheless exposed by the aim of another invisible gaze; the two gazes, invisible forever, expose themselves to each other in the crossing of their reciprocal aims. Loving no longer consists trivially in seeing or in being seen, nor in desiring or inciting desire, but in experiencing the crossing of gazes within, first, the crossing of aims. (PC, 87; PaC, 107)

Marion argues that although such a crossing of gazes can also denote the ethical relationship (and does so in Lévinas), the depiction of love which it makes possible is superior to that of ethics because it allows for an individuation of the other that ethics cannot accomplish. In ethics, the other is universalized and neutralized. Any "other" can offer the "face of the other" which Lévinas presupposes for the ethical relationship. Love goes beyond the neutrality of ethics and deals with the specific and particular other.[13] Only love can individualize and make concrete this face of the other. I must expose myself in ecstasy in order to shelter the nakedness of the other. The injunction of the other's gaze "enjoins me to support, with my own gaze, the unsubstitutable alterity of the gaze of the other as such. To support a gaze means to support the invisible unsubstitutable within it" (PC, 99; PaC, 119). The other summons me to love in this openness to the other's gaze.[14]

Love thus can be described phenomenologically for Marion as a "crossing of gazes" or of two currents of consciousness mutually exposing and pressing upon each other. Yet this account retains certain theological connotations. On the one hand, the erotic crossing of gazes is paralleled by Marion's explication of the crossing of gazes in prayer and becomes almost indistinguishable from it.[15] In both cases two gazes cross in a kind of reverse intentionality. Both the person at prayer and the lover become envisaged by the other, and relationship is established across that distance. On the other hand, the vulnerability of exposure in love recalls the theological account examined above. Marion's phenomenology of charity is almost as kenotic as his theology. I must abandon myself completely to the other, including facing the possibility of rejection. If not identical, the two accounts of charity are at least extremely similar. Charity always involves the exposure of the gaze and thus the willingness to become passive and abandon the position of self-sufficiency of the Cartesian ego. It also in both cases speaks of a complete self-giving to the other, thus attempting to get beyond the solipsism of the Cartesian ego and rethinking its emphasis on the present as "gift" instead of permanence. And not only are these theological and phenomenological analyses extremely parallel, but throughout *Prolegomena to Charity* Marion implies that a true account of love must take recourse to the theological.[16] He contends in the article on the possibility of "Christian philosophy," for example, that "charity discovers and introduces new phenomena into the world itself and the conceptual universe, which are saturated with meaning and glory, which ordain and eventually save the world."[17] Even the article on a phenomenology of charity he concludes, somewhat less crassly: "But to render oneself other, to surrender this gaze to the gaze of the other who crosses me, requires faith [*il faut la foi*]" (PC, 101; PaC, 120). It is only in his more recent work on the erotic phenomenon that he seeks to dispense with all such theological connotations.[18] Yet despite his attempt to keep this phenomenological account clearer of theological contamination, in some ways it actually reverts even much more explicitly to its Pascalian inspiration.

A Phenomenology of Eros

I already explored briefly in an earlier chapter how Marion conceives of his phenomenology of eros as a direct response to Descartes. This is obvious throughout *The Erotic Phenomenon*, but especially in the first chapter, which explicitly attempts to subvert Cartesian metaphysical categories. It outlines how the experience of love or assurance is opposed to the search for certainty and allows us to conceive differently of time, space, and identity. Marion seeks to open what he calls a "third reduction" that does not reduce the natural world in a way that allows phenomena to give themselves under the horizon of the Husserlian consciousness, but rather one that reduces all that is not relevant to the experience of love and the beloved. This move to a "third reduction" parallels Pascal's move to a third order, which Marion also interprets as a kind of reduction. Just as the second order (Cartesian/metaphysical) is incommensurable to the third (Pascalian/erotic) and is subject to different rules and ways of apprehending, so the third (erotic) reduction displaces and exceeds the second (the Husserlian or Heideggerian one). He chides Descartes for having prejudiced all later thinking about love by inscribing it into the metaphysical self-sufficiency of the ego. By rethinking the topic of love Marion proposes to overcome metaphysics, to "destroy" its suppression of love (PE, 20; EP, 8). Marion insists that this new reduction to eros displaces the traditional priority of ontology and metaphysics and that it requires a completely different attitude. It opens a new horizon and enters into "completely new terrain" (PE, 49; EP, 27). Although he does not mention Pascal in this context, his move to charity clearly parallels that of Pascal. He employs the figure of vanity, which he had first proposed in the context of his analysis of Pascal, in even more detail here in order to show that all other concerns (such as certainty) become irrelevant in light of the erotic reduction (PE, 48–51; EP, 26–29). I have already examined the implications of this erotic reduction for the self as the lover. I will now go on to explore how Marion's analysis of eros provides an account of inter-subjectivity.

Through the erotic reduction, Marion contends, the lover not only becomes individuated him- or herself, but also allows the other to emerge and makes him or her visible.[19] The beloved therefore emerges not as an object, but as a completely new, unique, and incomparable phenomenon. Marion describes this as a kind of saturated phenomenon, in which intuition provides more than I can grasp or contain.[20] The other can never be seen, never becomes visible, but remains a saturated phenomenon. Marion here goes beyond his analysis in *Prolegomena to Charity*, which spoke of two intuitions which cross each other. He contends that the experience of the beloved constitutes an intuition without concept, a *noesis* without *noema*. This attempt of access to the other as a phenomenon thus invalidates Husserlian phenomenology in Marion's view, in that the phenomenon does not show itself because one of my significations has been adequately filled with intuition. Signification cannot be confirmed by the intuition of an object but only by the radical alterity of the other. Signification must hence be fulfilled not by my own intentionality but by a counter-intentionality that derives from the other. The phenomenon of the other destroys the normal relation between intuition and signification in my egology. As in the earlier account of charity, the two gazes cross each other in an exchange that preserves distance, and they both appear mutually to each other through their significations.[21] Yet, beyond this earlier account, Marion suggests that this is neither a mutual phenomenon nor two phenomena mixed together, but only *one* phenomenon, what he calls a "crossed phenomenon" [*un phénomène croisé*]. Each ego provides signification to the other and gives itself fully to the other: two irreducible intuitions, one signification, and thus only one phenomenon. The erotic phenomenon thus pushes phenomenology even further. The relationship between intuition and intention becomes stretched to the breaking point. (Maybe one could say that Marion subverts the Husserlian terminology at least as much as Pascal distorted the Cartesian one when viewing it from the point of view of charity?)

Marion speaks of the mutually loving relationship in terms of an oath of fidelity: a promise fully to give each other to the other. Each ego exposes itself to the other and puts itself at the other's disposal. We are thus together converted into lover and beloved, reciprocally. The shared signification, however, must remain indeterminate: "In saying 'Here I am!' to the other, I do not tell him anything, even if eventually I assure him of something — my person" (PE, 171; EP, 107). The lover is already radically individualized and thus unsubstitutable. Marion outlines the different ways in which this is the case: First, the lover is individuated by his or her specific desire, which is tied to neither argument nor reason. A specific other "manifests to me my most secret center — that which I miss and which is still missing, that of which its clear absence has focused for a long time my obscure presence to myself" (PE, 172; EP, 108). As I discover my desire for the other, I discover myself as lover. At that moment, "I am no longer the same because I am finally myself, individualized beyond the point of return" (PE, 173; EP, 109). Secondly, I am individualized through eternity, in that any moment of love assumes that I commit myself forever and for all future. While this eternity may not last, it is certainly there in the intention. "To make love implies its irreversibility by definition (in the same way in which in metaphysics the essence of God implies his existence)" (PE, 174; EP, 109). If I engage in love only for a moment or a limited time, I belie the very activity. The promise of love, of giving myself completely, is never unsaid, even when it is later betrayed or not fulfilled completely. Finally, I individualize myself through passivity. I receive myself from the other and his or her impact on me. I do not individualize myself through affirmation or self-reflection but through being affected by the other. This takes place in a three-fold manner: The admission "Here I am" already implies passivity in which I receive the signification of love as response and therefore shared. The advance also implies passivity because it does not reach the phenomenon but only an intuition without reference. I find myself in love without apparently having decided to love, am impacted by an intuition "that arrives without yet any other" (PE, 177; EP, 111). Finally, I am passive because of the risk I take in loving and the fact that there may be no response to my love. "This risk consists in unmaking me from the activity of an ego, which poses itself by its own identity to itself, its representation of itself [keeps going] . . . to love without being loved, to make myself known without myself knowing anything" (ibid.). Even when love is returned this does not invalidate the prior disequilibrium. I thus know myself only as lover in response to the movements of the other. In the following, Marion engages in an analysis of our experience of the flesh, of erotic discourse, of various deceptive figures of love, and of the child as a witness to mutual love. Each of these carries further previous analyses of his saturated phenomenality and contributes to a recovery of an encounter with the other for the displaced self after the subject. I will summarize these descriptions only very briefly here in order to point out the continuities with previous analyses, focusing especially on the first two.

Marion first describes the erotic relationship as a meeting of the flesh that allows me to experience my flesh. Marion depicts the difference between my experience of objects and my experience of another's flesh: when I sense another body, it resists me, it is impenetrable and does not allow me access to it. Another flesh, however, acts like me: when it is touched it recedes, it does not resist but opens itself, it suffers and allows penetration, unlike other physical bodies. The rest of the world Marion describes as full of boundaries and walls that keep me out and make me fight for a place. I am in the world as a being, as something comprehended, always limited by finite horizons. Only with another flesh am I able to expand and to enter for the first time. Only another flesh welcomes me, makes a place for me, and consequently reveals me to myself. Marion therefore defines pleasure as being received by the flesh of another. This is a doubled passivity in which we each give ourselves to each other and therefore receive ourselves from the other.[22] The other gives me *my* flesh (not his) and I give the other *her* flesh (not mine). This explication of the flesh thus invalidates any metaphysical understanding which could not speak of a double passivity, but always opposes activity to passivity, and which also cannot give me an adequate idea of the other. Metaphysics speaks only of possession of bodies while only the erotic reduction makes possible an experience of the flesh that is not a possession but an opening. In Marion's view, the other thus definitely has phenomenality, not as a thing but rather as that which "phenomenalizes me as my flesh" (PE, 192; EP, 121).

Marion suggests that three "negatives" follow from this. First, the static opposition between activity and passivity is eliminated. Second, the process of erotisation is not limited or interrupted; one cannot distinguish particular erotic organs (only sexual organs, which are bodies, not flesh). Although sexual organs and sexuality certainly have a privileged place in eros, they do not exhaust it. My whole flesh is erotic and can participate in erotisation, not merely certain parts of it. Third, there is no such thing as auto-erotisation. I cannot make myself experience my own flesh. I must thus become flesh (in my entire body) in order to take possession of myself. I must give myself completely to the other in every part of my flesh, as the other also does for me without limit or measure. Marion wonders in this context whether the face has not lost its phenomenological privilege ["of the infinite noema of all my noeses"] in this analysis of the flesh, since the face emphasizes absolute transcendence, while the flesh makes possible absolute immanence. The flesh is therefore assumed in the face, and transcendence is obliterated in complete immanence. "All of his flesh becomes face, as a 'glorified body' they resume each other in one glory, that of the face" (PE, 199; EP, 127).

This analysis of the flesh therefore is able to get beyond the subject's obsession with objects which Marion has criticized in both Descartes and Husserl.[23] No longer does the ego face and constitute the world as mere objects of its consciousness, but it experiences itself as passive and is able to encounter another's experience. An analysis of the flesh allows us, in Marion's view, at least to some extent, to think of the other no longer as an object appearing on my horizon but rather as a self that experiences its flesh in the same way in which I experience my own flesh. Since my flesh is only given to me by another and I cannot experience it without the other making possible such an experience, I require the other as a real flesh even in order to "get in touch" with myself. Nothing like the *ego cogito* is therefore possible here. Instead we must posit an *ego affectus*, as Marion has attempted to uncover it even within the texts of Descartes. The self does not remain in a solipsistic self-enclosure, but only becomes a self through its experience of its own flesh, which is an experience it must receive from another flesh. And as Robyn Horner rightly points out, "Marion's decision to 'recognise' the other as this particular other always carries an element of risk: it makes us vulnerable rather than strong" (MTI, 145).

Marion goes even further here. Not only is the self always affected by another who is prior to its own experience, but this also has important implications for the ego's control over presence and permanence. This experience of the flesh cannot be controlled like an object and cannot become permanent in the presence. Marion explains that the erotic experience is different from the metaphysical one also in its duration. Not only can it never be accomplished (in the sense of finished), but it also stops suddenly and disappears in an instant instead of gradually. The erotisation of the flesh is always provisional and marked with finitude. In fact, the flesh does not necessarily have to become erotic; I can refuse to respond to the other and the other can refuse me.[24] On the one hand, Marion shows how the flesh becomes almost automatic if it is let go, if it can let itself go. The flesh begins and ends by itself without my will being able to guide it. If neither the other nor my own will resist, the flesh will take over automatically. The flesh does not need anything else in order to receive itself from the flesh of the other, and I no longer have control over it. While my will can intervene and prevent the flesh from becoming erotic, it cannot cause or control it, but instead I become its automaton. The flesh itself decides automatically when to put an end to our pleasure; neither I nor the other can prolong it. A double finitude emerges: my flesh performs the erotic reduction without me. Although it is entirely passive and dependent on the other, it takes away my intentionality and makes me its servant. I cannot make decisions over my flesh the way I do over my mind or body, but it functions by itself and without my input. The Cartesian ego here loses control not just over other objects but even over itself. Not only can I not organize these erotic experiences into a *mathesis universalis*, find a place for them according to order and measure, but I am reduced to pure reception of experience (even of myself).

Marion maintains that even the language employed to describe this experience gets us beyond metaphysical concerns. After the event I am unable to remember or to describe it distinctly. This is not a saturated phenomenon which requires endless hermeneutics because it gives too much intuition. Rather this phenomenon, although it provides an immensity of intuition that floods all concepts and horizons of manifestation, disappears immediately and cannot be explained at all.[25] One cannot speak of this phenomenon. Must one therefore be silent? No. In fact, Marion suggests, we talk in order to excite each other and in order to repeat the experience. This language does not describe or affirm or deny or transmit information, but it offers itself as a kind of performance: "they do not say what they describe, but they do what they say" (PE, 229; EP, 147). My words perform what they announce while they do so. Erotic language exercises itself and enables the flesh to enter into eros. The lovers never use words in order to describe anything or proclaim states of affairs; they are already outside the world and speak only in order to erotise each other. We are thus freed from the obligation of knowledge. The lovers speak as little as possible of the world of being and therefore transgress objectivity and carry us beyond the normal world. The discourse of lovers is therefore often considered nonsensical and even obscene or infantile. This discourse parallels the analysis Marion has provided earlier of the language of praise by envisioning a language that is purely pragmatic and not predicative. Like the person at prayer, the lovers establish relation instead of identifying objects or disseminating information. In fact, he insists that the erotic discourse must of necessity employ the language of mystical theology. Both vocabularies escape metaphysical restrictions because they are not tied to the languages of being or causality.

Marion carries this particular analysis further in his article "The Unspoken: Apophasis and the Discourse of Love." In this text he draws even more explicit parallels between the discourse of love and mystical theology, arguing that they are both perlocutionary acts of language. He spells out how a declaration of love does not make descriptive or rational statements and is not meant to convey certain facts. He no longer calls them performative, as he had done earlier in respect to the third way of mystical theology, but "perlocutionary." This means that they are meant to elicit some type of response or commitment. While they do not necessarily perform (at that moment) what they say, they do expect their words to have an effect and to cause a certain reaction and response. Marion claims that this is parallel in erotic language and the language of mystical theology. He uses examples from literature to corroborate his claims, analyzing the words of Clélia to Fabrice in Stendahl's novel *La Chartreuse de Parme*.

Marion continues this argument by further emphasizing the importance of language in the erotic experience. "Touching," for him, means to give the other his flesh, and that can be done without actual physical contact but by talking only. "I *first* make love in talking" (PE, 280; EP, 182; emphasis his). As we have seen, such talk does not speak of anything in particular and certainly not of being or predication. It first speaks to the other of the other and thus addresses the other directly and finally moves to speaking of our togetherness. The other can then hear my flesh in my words (and my willingness to give my flesh). This distance must be prior and give the other's flesh to him already, before it can become physical. I become a lover in the eyes of the other only through my words, where I express my desire and thus attain the other in person. These words are not inscribed in the same paradox and do not lie. Since they makes no predicative statements, they cannot be false. These words are performative and therefore are confirmed by the other's actually receiving her flesh through my words. If my words truly turn me into a lover, my flesh will follow. Marion concludes that this allows us to speak of love that is not sexual, including the relationships of parent and child, friends, and human with divine. He therefore is not merely exploiting a parallel between the vocabulary of theology and that of eros, but does want to bring them together in more explicit fashion. Just as the language of mystical theology is able to describe the erotic experience of the lovers, so erotic language can be extended to speak of the divine.

To become a lover through discourse makes me into a person. Marion maintains that in the erotic reduction I am individualized fully because a specific, particular me becomes the lover and experiences its own particular flesh given by the specific other. Yet this irrevocable ipseity must be given to me by another, and even its history is traced by another. "I am only insofar as I love and am loved . . . in the end I receive myself from the other, as I was born by him" (PE, 302; EP, 195). This analysis of the loving relationship therefore clearly attempts to overcome the Cartesian solipsism. I become a self only in total dependence on the other, receive myself from the other.[26] I find my identity only in my relationship to the other and discover that others have always already preceded me. Even my dignity as lover I receive from the other who always witnesses to it. Milbank paraphrases Marion well here: "Marion insists that only one's lover can provide assurance that one has been a faithful lover; this is not something one can know for oneself, for faithfulness consists finally in giving to the other that which one does not oneself have — namely, one's most basic identity as *adonné*" (CE, 261). While I can never verify the love of the other, I do indeed verify my own status as lover. I become loveable by receiving myself from the other and I thus find myself loved by another who precedes me and whom I receive:

> I discover myself loveable by the grace of the other; and if I risk myself finally in loving myself, or at least in no longer hating myself (in short, by forgiving myself), I dare it only on the word of the other, by my confidence in him and not in myself; I overcome my hatred of myself as I walk on water or advance a foot into the void — because from otherwise the voice of the other has convinced me (or almost) that I can do it and that it is worth it. I love myself mediately or rather I cease to hate myself by the mediation of the other, not by myself. (PE, 328; EP, 213)

Marion suggests that "I give myself over to the other because I receive myself entirely — as lover — from that which I receive — him" (PE, 330; EP, 214). In a sense the reduction thus precedes my advance and does not merely result from it. I become decentered and find that the other first advances upon me and precedes me in the role as lover. In my own (necessary) advance as lover

I discover that I have already been loved and that another has loved me before myself. The other awaits me and supports me "as the air supports a flight or the water a swimmer" (PE, 331; EP, 215). In the erotic reduction I search for what has already found me: "That I enter into the erotic reduction, it is required that an other lover has already preceded me and from there, calls me in silence" (PE, 331; EP, 215).

This emphasis on the other's preceding me also shows again how the erotic reduction reconceives and displaces a Cartesian or metaphysical conception of time as a series of present moments that follow each other in a linear fashion. Instead, as lover, I must live each instant as the last possibility to love. Every instant must be transformed into an ultimate, an eschatological one. I love "each moment as if for eternity" — "*sub specie aeternitatis*, under the aspect of eternity — more exactly in the light of the irrevocable" (PE, 322; EP, 209). Eternity is thus obtained in the present.[27] This experience of eternity in the present brings together past, present, and future in a fashion that defies all metaphysical conceptions of time.[28]

These various aspects of Marion's analysis of eros (and I have by no means examined all of it or summarized it in any kind of exhaustive fashion) all posit the erotic reduction as one that goes significantly beyond and displaces traditional metaphysical categories. Throughout Marion insists that love has its own logic that may seem paradoxical and irrational to a more "natural regime," but that carries its own rationality. This constitutes clearly a recovery of Pascal's notion of a third order of charity, as I have attempted to show repeatedly. Throughout Marion insists that eros has its own rationality and works within its own logic.[29] In the "regime of eros" things are possible that would not be logical in a "purely natural view." He make such comments and distinctions throughout, but let me cite one as representative: "To the contrary of what metaphysics has not finished by pretending, love does not lack reason or logic; simply, it does not admit another than its own and becomes readable only starting from it. Love does not say itself and make itself except in one unique sense, its own" (PE, 334; EP, 217). From the introduction to the conclusion, Marion insists on this "unique sense" of love (which is one of the reasons why he thinks all love must be described in a univocal fashion).[30] The erotic reduction, for all intents and purposes, does go further than the more general reduction to givenness that Marion has outlined in the rest of his phenomenological work. Although he obviously relies on previous analyses and does not invalidate his account of the gift and of givenness, he clearly sees love as the supreme instantiation of a phenomenology outside metaphysical restrictions. In the final analysis, it is love, the order of charity and its recovery in the erotic reduction, that exceeds metaphysics.[31]

More specifically, love is able to get beyond metaphysics, in Marion's view, because it displaces and invalidates the metaphysical restrictions of the doubled onto-theo-logical figure of metaphysics in Descartes. No longer is the subject a self-sufficient and solipsistic ego that constitutes all things as objects.

Rather it is a lover who abandons him- or herself in a kenotic outpouring of commitment in the vulnerability of the flesh and receives an affirmation by the beloved's response. Marion's depiction of this mutual relation and experience has responded directly to the problematic of the Cartesian subject, its self-sufficiency, its obsession with permanence in the present, but especially its solipsisim.

To what extent, then, is this depiction of erotic experience jeopardized by its parallel to Marion's earlier theological explication? Is the erotic phenomenon merely a — somewhat veiled — experience of God? And indeed, some would argue, maybe not so veiled[32]: the book clearly ends on a theological note by suggesting in the final paragraphs not only that God is the best and supreme lover and that human and divine love parallel each other, but also that all human love originates in this divine source (PE, 340–42; EP, 221–22). Yet even this somewhat more explicit reference to theology, it seems to me, is consistent with what Marion outlines in the aforementioned article on the possibility of "Christian philosophy" as the source of a (or at least his) account of love: although it has its origin in theology and the experience of the divine (possibly in a liturgical setting, maybe in a more personal spiritual setting such as prayer or meditation), now that it has been formulated phenomenologically, it can be abandoned to purely philosophical investigation. One might well apply Marion's categories to his early theological work and interpret it as a type of "Christian philosophy" that investigates theological phenomena (such as the Eucharist, the Triune relationships, or the experience of prayer) with philosophical tools (has Marion not repeatedly been chided by theologians for employing philosophical language, especially Heideggerian language and frameworks, too heavily for his theological investigations?), and one might also conclude that his more recent phenomenological project carries the task even further by investigating these same phenomena now solely (or at least primarily) in the realm of phenomenology. This phenomenology, then, need not have explicit (or even implicit) theological commitments, although its phenomena (if they indeed derive from religious experience) might well retain a flavor or slight coloration of their origin. Nor does it seem correct to bar, in any a priori fashion, the possibility for a theological project to take the phenomenological insights up again and work out their implications for its own use. Marion himself, apart from isolated hints, has so far refrained from doing so, but others have of course employed his insights for a theological exercise and agenda. The overlap between philosophy and theology in Marion's work which is deplored by so many of his critics, then, might well be read as an appropriation of phenomena derived from religious experience (within a particular theological tradition) for a primarily, if not solely, phenomenological project. While one might certainly argue that this is not the fashion in which theology and philosophy *ought* to relate and even that the notion of two orders derived from Pascal is not a particularly appropriate or insightful way of talking about their relationship, one cannot claim that Marion does not make clear

distinctions between the two disciplines or that his phenomenology, or specifically his account of love, is merely a veiled (or negative) theology that attempts
to further his theological project. (In fact, the relationship I have sought to
uncover here might even suggest the opposite, namely that Marion is using
theological insights for phenomenological purposes.) And one might also conclude, then, that Marion's account of love is the apex of his work (to date) in
more than one respect.[33] Not only does it constitute the most clearly and fully
articulated account of a phenomenology of givenness, and not only does it
carry the task of exceeding metaphysics to its height by replacing the emphasis
on being and certainty with one on love and assurance, but above all it can also
be read as the culmination of all of Marion's attempts to delineate the relationship between the theological and the philosophical exercise. More than any
other aspect of Marion's work it preserves and even articulates the distinction
between the two orders and the two types of rationality. More than anything
else it takes a concept that clearly originates in the realm of theology and appropriates it fully for an account as purely phenomenological as possible. With
the erotic phenomenon, Marion has managed to take a concern that seemed
entirely theological in origin, God as charity beyond being, and translated it
into a phenomenological account of erotic experience (including accounts of
sexual intercourse, declarations of romance, and childbirth). The residues of
theological interest evident on a couple of pages should not divert us from that
accomplishment.

CONCLUSION

"Between Evidence and
Charity One Must Choose"

In the preface I spoke of a shared "excess" and a shared "deficiency" in the commentary on Marion's work. I deplored the little attention Marion's writings on Descartes have received in the secondary literature and suggested that this early work is absolutely essential for fully understanding and appreciating Marion's more theological and phenomenological writings. This kind of thorough attention to the grounding of Marion's thought in his study of Descartes I have attempted to provide in this book. Marion's desire to "exceed metaphysics" is guided by his outline and criticism of the metaphysical system evident in Descartes: its concern with epistemology and its doubled grounding in the thinking ego and divine causality. Both Marion's theology and Marion's phenomenology seek to overcome these specific restrictions of Cartesian and contemporary metaphysics. Similarly, Marion's desire to speak of an iconic God, a God "without" or "beyond" Being, is deeply grounded in his analysis of Descartes' "white theology." Marion's own theology, I have suggested, constitutes an attempt not only to combat the modern move to univocal language for God and creatures, but also to recover a notion of analogy through a theology of the divine names. Marion's phenomenology opts for the language of saturation and excess for God, precisely because of the reduction of the divine by which late medieval and early modern drives toward univocity are characterized. Finally, Marion's phenomenology seeks to recover a notion of the self as affected, as dependent upon the in-coming phenomenon, and as erotic or inter-subjective, precisely in order to respond to the autonomy, self-sufficiency, and solipsism of the Cartesian subject. Marion's indebtedness to his own work on Descartes is, I hope, thereby firmly established.

What about the second aspect stressed so much in the secondary literature? What are we to do with the isomorphism of Marion's theological and phenomenological language? What about the "excess" of overlap between Marion's theology and his philosophy? In fact, this excess reappears even in proposals about where Marion should go next. Most of them ask Marion to say more about the relationship or distinction between theology and phenomenology. And again, these requests go in several directions, some wanting Marion to engage more in theology, others to focus on phenomenology, some to draw distinctions between the two more firmly and clearly, others to abandon such distinctions altogether. David Tracy, for example, suggests that Marion should not "return to a phenomenology of strictly theological language" but instead should "spend more phenomenological time on the original revelation itself, as witnessed in the Scriptures," especially by elaborating a "phenomenology of the voice" instead of a "phenomenology of the visible" (CE, 64). Cyril O'Regan (who is particularly interested in the absence of Hegel in Marion's thoughts) deplores the lack of firm distinction between the two disciplines in Marion's work. He insists that Marion must "secure the distinction between 'revelation' as it functions within phenomenology, and 'Revelation' within the language game of theology, or probably both" (CE, 119). He would like to see Marion be much more explicit about this distinction and therefore say much more about theology:

> Marion's silence with respect to "Revelation" is not helpful. . . . Is it possible that Revelation supplies its own content, just as it is possible that it provides its own authority? We need more clarification on what this content and authority would be. We need Marion to speak theologically and more often. We need Marion to break the silence on the negotiations between these contents and authorities. Even if meta-rules are, as I have indicated, ruled out beforehand, we could do with a sense as to what yields to what and when. We need all of this because now the issue is whether and how borders get crossed. (CE, 131–32)

Emmanuel Falque, conversely, thinks that Marion's distinctions between the two disciplines are drawn far too strictly. He asks, "in marking the distinction between phenomenology and theology too scrupulously, would one not risk, on the one hand, forbidding phenomenology its veritable right to phenomenality, and, on the other hand, forbidding theology its mode of being paradigmatic in the saturation of the phenomenon?" (CE, 182). He suggests instead that Marion's "double formation therefore ought *rightfully* authorize intersections, or even confrontations between the disciplines. But his work proceeds as if, *in fact*, he was forbidding himself from doing this, or to be more correct, as if he was refusing to do theology when pursuing a work of pure philosophy, and refusing to do philosophy when practicing theology" (CE, 183; emphases his). Falque particularly deplores the Pascalian paradigm of a third order which he thinks leads Marion to separate philosophy and revealed theology far too much. Instead he appeals to St. Thomas, who placed "the philosophical at the very heart of the theological" (CE, 187). Falque does not think that the distinctions between possibility and actuality (that Marion espouses the most often for separating phenomenology from theology) are successful. He also wonders about the apparent superiority Marion ascribes to theology in this context (CE, 190–91). He concludes by commenting on the furor created by the "theological turn":

> there is neither shame nor error in assuming and unifying what centuries of recent history have kept radically separate: the possibility of the philosophical exercise and the actuality of theological revelation. . . . Neither the distinction of the disciplines, nor that of the functions, can make thought fertile, and only those who truly possess the formation in both — and Marion by way of being a pioneer — can accomplish its work. In these new times of a possible reciprocal interaction (without confusion or separation of the orders), it comes back in this way to the philosopher to assume his or her "theological task"—or even to the theologian to seek the "philosopher's stone." (CE, 195–96)

The relationship between philosophy and theology in Marion's thought then continues to be a central concern in commentary on his work. Can one describe this "excess of overlap" between the two disciplines more successfully now with the insights gained from this examination of Marion's writings? I have already given a preliminary answer: The two are so closely related, their languages so similar, precisely because they are both so deeply and firmly grounded in Marion's work on Descartes. They both seek to overcome the same problems and therefore pursue similar paths. Yet maybe the investigation into Descartes will also shed new light on this issue. As I have already briefly suggested in the last chapter, the relationship between Marion's theology and his phenomenology is also informed in important ways by his early work, especially by his analysis of Pascal's response to Descartes. Marion has repeatedly applied Pascal's distinction between the second and third orders to a more general distinction between philosophy and theology. As we have seen, he has even explicitly proposed this as a paradigm for understanding both how theology and philosophy might relate and how we might conceive of something that would bridge the gap between them, namely something like a "Christian philosophy." Pascal — or at least what Pascal stands for — informs Marion's overall thinking in this respect maybe even more significantly than Descartes. The distinction between the orders, and the rationality of the heart that displaces that of the mind, describe well how Marion himself thinks of the relationship between theology and philosophy. And we have seen, of course, that Pascal's account of love is what overcomes Cartesian metaphysics most successfully: "Not that love dispenses with knowing or requires some sacrifice of intelligibility, but love becomes, instead of and in the place of intuitus, the keeper of evidence, the royal road to knowledge" (MP, 305; PM, 324).

Marion has uncovered in Pascal something that defines almost all of his own work, namely the claim that certain experiences or phenomena require a different kind of knowing, that they are not perceived or judged correctly by "traditional" philosophy (often that means metaphysics). Charity, according to Marion, does not imply an abandonment of reasoning or thinking altogether. Rather, it refers to a different kind of thinking or knowing. Marion stresses repeatedly that this is indeed a rationality and logic in its own right. Charity "is in no way irrational or merely affective, but . . . it promotes a knowledge; knowledge of a type that is doubtless absolutely particular, matchless, but knowledge nonetheless" (PC, 168). Or, as Murchadha puts it: "Love is not a mere affection but, Marion insists, is a form of knowledge . . . This is not a knowledge of what can be predicted, but rather a knowledge that has no object. It is, furthermore, a loving knowledge" (GG, 83).

This theme of the need to move into a different realm of understanding for such topics as God and love is not new to Marion's work. Already in 1970, as a young student at the École Normale Superieur (born in 1946, Marion was at the time 24 years old), Marion had insisted that love is the only appropriate way to characterize God and that it is the only manner in which to escape metaphysical language. In a debate with atheist student Alain de Benoist staged by the Carrefour des Jeunes, Marion argued that metaphysics and specifically its language of proofs and scientific certainty is inappropriate for speaking of the divine. God's existence cannot be demonstrated, and metaphysical presuppositions foreclose any discourse about the divine.[1] The logic of metaphysics is too limiting. A divinity that could be proven by it would not deserve the name of God: "The God one would find with proofs would precisely not be God. To pose the question of proof in regard to God is to place oneself already away from God: for one places oneself in relation to God in the position itself of God. It is perfectly normal, and I am very glad of it, that God cannot be found like that. Thus, that means that if God has a provable worth, that would mean to have no worth at all, except the worth of things that are the most common."[2] Throughout the discussion, Marion attempts to convince Benoist of another realm of reality to which the traditional language of metaphysics and the categorization and methods of the natural sciences do not have access. This is the realm of all topics that are ultimately important, among which Marion counts aesthetics, love, morality, and religion.[3] Value and meaning cannot be proven by logical verification. God manifests Godself in a divine manner; all systems of proof remain limiting and inadequate.[4] He goes on to challenge a scientific

definition of the human person as merely a certain kind of animal and emphasizes the importance of a Trinitarian understanding of creation and redemption, which for him establish two fundamental facts: God intervenes graciously
in history and thus changes the very meaning of history, and God gives Godself
as gift of absolute love and thereby allows us to enter into that game of love.[5]

These are all assertions that Marion has reiterated in his other writings. He
concludes his article "The Impossible for Man — God" by making the same
connection between God and love: "The radical and non-metaphysical transcendence for which we have been seeking thus reveals itself with great clarity
in the impossible — but in the only [im-]possible worthy of God, which is charity. Only with love, and therefore with 'God [who] is love' (1. John 4:8 and 16),
is nothing impossible. God's transcendence manifests itself in charity, and only
thus does transcendence reveal itself to be worthy of God." In this article, as we
have seen above, Marion explores the notions of the impossible and of transcendence and evaluates their adequacy for expressing an idea or experience
of the divine. After showing that the language of being/existence or even that
of personal belief is insufficient to speak of God, he suggests that such does not
imply the complete impossibility of articulating divinity within phenomenology.[6] Rather, God enters into phenomenology precisely as the "impossible" phenomenon, as the question that eternally returns to haunt us.[7] God, as the one for
whom nothing is impossible, transcends any human possibilities and inverts any
human understandings of possibility and impossibility. God's radically transcendent possibility is not metaphysical omnipotence, but instead God's continually
faithful word that comes to us as an overture of love and forgiveness.[8]

As the juxtaposition of these two pieces — the 1970 debate and the 2003
paper — suggests, Marion's thinking has been guided by similar concerns
for more than three decades. One might even say that his published work is
framed by this question phrased in an almost identical fashion. In the first few
lines of the debate he asserts: "We have the tendency to await God at the end of
the question without realizing that he is already there before the question has
even been posed. That is one way, among an infinity of others, of understanding that God always loves first."[9] His recent book, which attempts to develop a
phenomenology of eros, concludes on a very similar note: "God precedes us
and transcends us, but first and foremost in that he loves us infinitely better
than we love ourselves and him. God surpasses us as the best lover" (PE, 342;
EP, 222). God, our desire but incapacity to speak of God, and God's love for us
are constant themes in these quotations. Indeed, these topics of the inadequacy
of metaphysics, of a language appropriate to speak of God, and of the importance of love permeate all of Marion's writings. All three of these topics come
together in what we have seen above in Marion's analysis of Pascal. Marion explicates the distinction between a metaphysical discourse and a discourse more
appropriate to God in his examination of Pascal. His suggestion of a different
order, defined by love or desire and having its own logic, is rooted in Pascal.

Marion reiterates such statements when he speaks of the distinction between revealed theology and phenomenology throughout his work. As indicated above, he uses precisely this distinction between second and third order repeatedly in order to designate the boundary between philosophy and theology. Let me cite three examples. First, in his article "Metaphysics and Phenomenology: A Relief for Theology" he argues in respect to phenomenology's treatment of more traditionally theological topics, that even if phenomenology can "in a strict sense make the face one of its privileged themes, it cannot and must not understand that face as a face of charity; when the being-given turns to charity (the loved or loving being, the lover in the strict sense), phenomenology yields to revealed theology exactly as the second order, according to Pascal, yields to the third" (590–91). The distinction between second and third order in Pascal here also determines the boundary between metaphysics and theology for Marion.

Second, in the consideration of the possibility of "Christian philosophy," he suggests that charity "determines the domain of theology."[10] He appeals explicitly to Pascal in outlining the way in which theology might have an impact on philosophy (or specifically phenomenology):

> The order of charity, which concerns love in all its facets, dominates the other two and, for that reason, remains less visible and known than they do; indeed, according to an essential paradox, no order can know, or see, a superior order (even if an order knows itself and can see all inferior orders). Charity, the supreme order, thus remains invisible to the flesh and to the spirit, to powers and sciences. The result is that charity opens a field of new phenomena to knowledge, but this field remains invisible to natural reason alone. That is why philosophy needs an "indispensable auxiliary" in order to gain access to it, revelation: because it is revelation, as the revelation of charity, which offers perfectly rational phenomena to philosophy, although they belong to charity and are as new as it is.[11]

Marion goes on to employ this notion of the orders to speak of the task of Christian philosophy as introducing certain phenomena of revelation into the philosophical discourse. As examples of such phenomena he offers similar ones as in the 1970 interview: a clear concept of (salvation) history, love, the human face, faith. Marion here clearly distinguishes philosophy, as having only "natural light" and discussing "facts, phenomena, and statements accessible to reason and its workings," from theology, as revelation and discourse about "truths that only faith can reach."[12]

Third, in *Prolegomena to Charity*, he appropriates Pascalian terminology in a recovery of "apologetics" as a move to another order that instead of "convincing" our minds would "constrain" or convert our will.[13] Such a renewed apologetics would not try to conquer by reasons and logic, but would rather attempt to move us from "evidence" to "love."[14] Instead of trying to convince our reason, theology would address our will or our heart. To get to love one must thus proceed to another order. One deals no longer with reason or philosophy but with the heart, the will, ultimately with a personal decision of loving commitment to God. When dealing with love, the will is paramount and reason superseded: "The will alone can love, and reasons cannot in any way, by their superabundant constraint, exempt the will from deciding. In short, because 'there is a great distance between the knowledge of God and loving him' . . . only the will can love that which reason knows, without, by definition, being able to do better than knowing. Rigorously, if 'God is love' (John 3:8), then love alone — and thus the will — will be able to reach him" (PC, 61; PaC, 79). In order to reach God, in order to speak adequately of love (God and love being ultimately the same), one must transgress reason and philosophy and move on to something higher and different, to another order. In this order, the self is dislocated by the divine gaze, who envisages it in love, and only in responding to this love does it become a person.[15] In love one surrenders to and ultimately imitates God. Just as in Pascal, to whom Marion again explicitly appeals in this context, love is a different kind of understanding, a different kind of sight: "Love opens the eyes. Opens the eyes: not in the way violence opens the eyes of the disabused, but as a child opens his eyes to the world, or a sleeper opens his eyes to the morning" (PC, 69; PaC, 87–88). Love alone makes it possible to know the other as such. Phenomenology abandons us here and theology must go further: "In short, in order for the other to appear to me, I must first love him. If phenomenology is able to lead up to this point, it does so only at its limit and aporia. Only a thinking of charity can advance further" (PC, 164). In order to think love truly, one must think it outside of metaphysics or even phenomenology, one must think it with the heart.

Finally, in a recent interview Marion links this different account of knowledge to an overcoming of metaphysics by claiming that

> desire is prior to the philosophical intention to know and is to be taken seriously as such. . . . But the question is whether desire does not claim far more than mere philosophy understood as a theory of knowledge. Perhaps the question of desire is too serious to be explained within the same horizon as the question of knowledge. Perhaps the question of desire can not only not be answered, but not even be asked in the horizon of Being. So this is a reason why I think desire is the "backstage" of metaphysics, something never enlightened by metaphysics (which is unable to do so). And so we have now, perhaps, to open a new horizon where the question of desire may be taken seriously.

After pointing to the insufficiency of psychoanalysis to deal with this question, he insists again: "But there is perhaps a deep rationality and consciousness of desire which is other than, and goes far beyond, mere unconsciousness. To open this new horizon, we have to get rid of the horizon of Being, which is, at the end of metaphysics, quite unable, because not broad enough, to do justice to desire."[16]

In all these cases (except the final one that does not make it explicit) Marion identifies theology with a rationality of the "will" while philosophy is a rationality of the "mind." We have seen that he carries these distinctions into his account of eros, by speaking of it as a reduction to loving or choosing, instead of thinking or being certain. The rationality of love is therefore, by all appearances, a theological transgression of philosophy. Theology and philosophy are two distinct rationalities, one concerned with and dependent upon the mind, the other concerned with and dependent upon the heart.[17] And when Marion does not attempt to keep them separate but envisions a possible interaction between them, it is always one in which philosophy describes possibilities and theology is convinced of actualities, one in which theology gives content to philosophy, which functions as a method to deal with the phenomena given by theology. In order to have any sense of God, then, one must move into a different regime of rationality. One must approach God with the heart and not with the mind. God is known in love, not in certainty. What Marion says about Pascal perfectly defines also the central thrust of his own work:

> Metaphysics is widowed of the thought of God—less on account of the insufficiency of its procedures and the unadaptability of its concepts . . . than by its epistemological and methodological failing: it still claims to base itself on a method of evidence when it aims to elevate itself, as if by a theoretical Jacob's ladder, to God. But from the moment the question of God is opened, the method and, more radically, the gaze on evidence lose all efficacy. Better, the "Christian's God" would not become accessible to charity alone, if he were not exhausted in it. To have the pretense of knowing him without loving him amounts to missing, from the outset and on principle, both the destination and the road. *Metaphysics is closed to God precisely because it wants to reach him with full certainty and total evidence. Between evidence and charity, one must choose.* What separates Pascal and Descartes is nothing less than this choice. And this choice separates them infinitely, for "What a long way it is between knowing God and loving him!" (§377/280). (MP, 305–306; PM, 324; emphasis mine)

The question of God requires a prior commitment of love because otherwise our eyes remain blind to its vision. In a similar way, the question of love also requires a different way of thinking or knowing, another regime of rationality, precisely another kind of "reduction."[18] Marion wants to exceed metaphysics with a thought of love precisely because of this choice. Exceeding metaphysics through and because of the givenness of charity—this characterizes all of Marion's thought from his early writings on Descartes to his most recent statements about the erotic phenomenon. And in the final count this is what Marion's work is all about: the generous givenness that pours itself out in abandon for the other as in Meyer's three-bowled fountain, where each basin ceaselessly empties itself into the one below while being filled from above and where the gap between them is traversed through the cascade of shared givenness.[19]

NOTES

Preface

1. Marion indicates in both *On the Metaphysical Prism of Descartes* and *In Excess* that these works conclude the respective trilogy (DS, vii; IE, xxii). In fact, he refers to the *Metaphysical Prism* as "the conclusion of a double Cartesian Triptych" (MP, xv; PM, v). For a delineation of the three projects see also Kevin Hart's introduction to *Counter-Experiences: Reading Jean-Luc Marion* (South Bend, Ind.: Notre Dame University Press, 2007).

2. For an outline of Marion's life and philosophical career so far, see the first chapter of Robyn Horner's theological introduction to Marion: Robyn Horner, *Jean-Luc Marion: A Theo-logical Introduction* (Burlington, Vt.: Ashgate, 2003), 3–12. See also the brief bibliographical entry in Alan D. Schrift, *Twentieth-Century French Philosophy: Key Themes and Thinkers* (Oxford: Blackwell Publishing, 2006), 165.

3. Thomas A. Carlson, "Converting the Given into the Seen: Introductory Remarks on Theological and Phenomenological Vision," in ID, xi–xxxi.

4. Wayne J. Hankey, "'Theoria Versus Poesis': Neoplatonism and Trinitarian Difference in Aquinas, John Milbank, Jean-Luc Marion and John Zizioulas," *Modern Theology* 15.4 (1999): 389.

5. Hankey, "Theoria," 394.

6. Kenneth L. Schmitz, "The God of Love," *Thomist* 57.3 (1993): 495.

7. Arthur Bradley, "God *sans* Being: Derrida, Marion and 'a paradoxical Writing of the word *without*,'" *Literature and Theology* 14.3 (2000): 300.

8. Derek J. Morrow, "The Conceptual Idolatry of Descartes's Gray Ontology: An Epistemology 'Without Being,'" in GG, 11.

9. In English treatments he is usually referred to as Pseudo-Dionysius or as the Pseudo-Areopagite, a label which Marion disdains (e.g., IE, 134–35, note 1; DS, 162, note 12). Unfortunately, several of the translations of Marion's works neglect to translate his name into English and refer to Dionysius with the French term "Denys."

Part 1 Introduction

1. Bruce Ellis Benson, "Love Is a Given," *Christian Century*, 8 Feb. 2003: 22.

2. Marion remarks in the preface to the English edition that "curiously, its theses were better received by the philosophers and academics than by the theologians and believers" (GWB, xix).

3. Hankey, "Theoria," 389.

4. In fact, there have been many harsh words over Marion's treatment of Aquinas. Marion included several comments about Aquinas' close affinity with the idolatry of

being in *God without Being,* and, after a general outcry of Thomistic theologians in France, revised his stance in an article on Aquinas' onto-theo-logy ("Saint Thomas d'Aquin et l'onto-théo-logie," *Revue Thomiste* 95.1 [1995]: 31–66. He actually included this article in the most recent [third] edition of *Dieu sans l'être,* DSL, 279–332. English translation: "Saint Thomas Aquinas and Onto-theo-logy," trans. B. Gendreau, R. Rethty, and M. Sweeney, in *Mystic: Presence and Aporia,* ed. M. Kessler and C. Sheppard [Chicago: University of Chicago Press, 2003]). Some commentators claim that his "recantation" has been very half-hearted and does not actually alter his position while others find that he concedes far too much and has radically compromised his position. Georges Kalinowski strongly criticizes Marion's treatment of Aquinas and finds that he has not read him properly and that his modification of his position in the later article is negligible and thoroughly insufficient. Georges Kalinowski, "Discours de louange et discours métaphysique: Denys l'aréopagite et Thomas d'Aquin," *Rivista di Filosofia Neo Scolastica* 73 (1981): 399–404. See also Kenneth Schmitz's similar criticism: Schmitz, "God of Love," 507. Michael B. Ewbank, on the other hand, finds Marion's treatment of Aquinas eminently useful. Michael B. Ewbank, "Of Idols, Icons, and Aquinas's Esse: Reflections on Jean-Luc Marion," *International Philosophical Quarterly* 42.2 (2002): 161–75. See also Marcel Duquesne's review of *God without Being,* "A propos d'un livre récent: Jean-Luc Marion «Dieu sans l'être»," *Mélanges de Science religieuse* 42.2 (1985): 57–75 and 42.3 (1985): 127–139; and Fergus Kerr's article on this topic: "Aquinas after Marion," *New Blackfriars* 78 (1995): 354–64. For a more thorough review of this controversy, see MTI, 93–99.

5. Jean-Yves Lacoste, "Penser à Dieu en l'aimant: Philosophie et théologie de J.-L. Marion," *Archives de Philosophie* 50 (1987): 256, 260ff.

6. Schmitz, "God of Love," 506–507.

7. Milbank's most detailed criticism is found in the chapter "Only Theology Overcomes Metaphysics" in his work *The Word Made Strange: Theology, Language, Culture* (Oxford: Blackwell Publishers, 1997). All page references within the next paragraphs refer to this text unless indicated otherwise.

8. See also Paul Lakeland's interesting comparison of Milbank's and Marion's work, in which he claims that Milbank desires to reclaim a certain kind of metaphysical speculation (or a "metaphysics of desire") for ecclesiological purposes. Paul Lakeland, "Is the Holy Wholly Other, and Is the Wholly Other Really Holy? Reflections on the Postmodern Doctrine of God," in *Divine Aporia: Postmodern Conversations about the Other,* ed. John C. Hawley (Lewisburg, Pa.: Bucknell University Press, 2000), 57–69.

9. Bernard G. Prusak criticizes Milbank's evaluation of Marion's work in a footnote in his introduction to the translation of the "Theological Turn." He finds that his "criticism is, at least, highly questionable, if not simply empty. . . . In the end, Milbank's criticism ignores the whole problematic of the constitution of the ego and seems to reduce phenomenology to a kind of psychology." Translator's introduction in *Phenomenology and the "Theological Turn": The French Debate* (New York: Fordham University Press, 2000), 11.

10. Milbank spells this criticism out in much more detail in his article "Can a Gift Be Given? Prolegomena to a Future Trinitarian Metaphysic," *Modern Theology* 11.1 (1995): 119–61. I will look at this criticism more carefully in chapter 3.

11. Patripassianism is an early third-century Christian heresy that claimed that

the Father suffered in the Son. It is usually rejected because it reduces the Trinitarian distinctions between the divine persons and identifies Father and Son too closely with each other.

12. The book was discussed in an issue of the *Revue de Métaphysique et de Morale* 96.1 (1991). It included articles by Michel Henry, "Quatre principes de la phénoménologie," 3–26; François Laruelle, "L'Appel et le Phénomène," 27–41; and Jean Greisch, "L'herméneutique dans la «phénoménologie comme telle»: Trois questions à propos de Réduction et Donation," 43–63. It was followed by a response and an article by Marion: "Réponses à quelques questions," 65–76; "Le sujet en dernier appel," 77–95.

13. Emmanuel Gabellieri, "De la métaphysique à la phénoménologie: une «relève»?" *Revue Philosophique de Louvain* 94.4 (1996): 641.

14. Ibid., 642–44.

15. Vincent Holzer, "Phénoménologie radicale et phénomène de revelation," review of Jean-Luc Marion, *Étant donné*, in *Transversalités: Revue de l'institut catholique de Paris* (1999): 56.

16. Ibid., 65.

17. Marie-Andrée Ricard, "La question de la donation chez Jean-Luc Marion," *Laval théologique et philosophique* 57 (2001): 88.

18. See also Robyn Horner's analysis of Janicaud's criticism of Marion (RGG, 102ff.).

19. Janicaud interprets even the late work of Heidegger as implicated in such theology. It "has nothing to do with the Husserlian enterprise of constitution" and it is exposed "to the disaster or catastrophe of abandoning the phenomena" (TT, 30). He asserts that this move in Heidegger actually opens the way for the theological turn: "If the 'phenomenology of the unapparent' finally makes all rule-based presentation of phenomena vacillate in favor of a hearkening to a word whorled with silence, here — against all expectations — is a line extended toward the originary, the nonvisible, the reserved. Ready to renounce a thematic phenomenology, the candidates to the theological heritage will content themselves with a phenomenology of points and dots" (TT, 31). Heidegger's suggestions thus permit "the most audacious soundings"; in fact, "without Heidegger's *Kehre*, there would be no theological turn" (TT, 31).

20. Janicaud is not alone in seeing Marion particularly influenced by Lévinas. James K. A. Smith suggests the same and criticizes Marion's consequent refusal to allow the transcendent to become immanent in incarnation and revelation. See Smith, "Between Predication and Silence: Augustine on How (Not) to Speak of God," *Heythrop Journal* 41.1 (2000): 77.

21. "In Marion's work, there is no respect for the phenomenological order; it is manipulated as an ever-elastic apparatus, even when it is claimed to be 'strict.' In the same way, his response concerning 'givenness' [*donation*] makes use of the term's very ambiguity to avoid truly responding to the question posed" (TT, 65).

22. Janicaud, *Phénoménologie éclatée* (Combas: Édition de l'Éclat, 1998), 44–70, especially 48–52. Translated as *Phenomenology "Wide Open": After the French Debate*, trans. Charles N. Cabral (New York: Fordham University Press, 2005).

23. Anthony J. Godzieba, "Ontotheology to Excess: Imagining God without Being," *Theological Studies* 56.1 (1995): 4–5.

1. Descartes and Metaphysics

1. English translation: René Descartes, *Rules for the Direction of the Mind*, in *The Philosophical Writings of Descartes*, vol. 1, trans. John Cottingham, Robert Stoothoff, and Dugald Murdoch (Cambridge: Cambridge University Press, 1985). I provide references to this English translation and to the French: *Oeuvres de Descartes*, ed. Charles Adam and Paul Tannery (Paris: Vrin, 1887–1913), abbreviated as AT.

2. Brandon Look, review of Marion's *Cartesian Questions*, in *Review of Metaphysics* 54.1 (2000): 161.

3. For a more detailed examination of the notion of metaphysics in Aquinas, see John Wipple's *The Metaphysical Thought of Aquinas: From Finite Being to Uncreated Being* (Washington, D.C.: The Catholic University of America Press, 2000). He shows that Aquinas' definition is grounded in his explication of Aristotle and Boethius. He argues that for Thomas "this science is named theology or divine science because foremost among the things considered is God. It is known as metaphysics because it comes after physics in the order of learning. This is so because we must move from a knowledge of sensible things to an understanding of things which are not sensible. This same science is also known as first philosophy insofar as the other sciences take their principles from it and therefore come after it. As I have explained in some detail elsewhere, Thomas does not always offer this same reason for describing metaphysics as first philosophy. In his commentary on the *Metaphysics* he will say that it is so named because it deals with the first causes of things" (8). This essentially corresponds to what Marion claims about Aquinas. Wipple assures us that "for Aquinas being as being or being in general is the subject of metaphysics . . . In metaphysics . . . one studies being taken as such (rather than as restricted to a given kind of being). And one studies it *as* being" (9–10). He goes on to show how Aquinas reconciles these various notions of the meaning of metaphysics by identifying divine science with the science of being as being (12). He consequently outlines a distinction between two kinds of theology in Aquinas: "Thomas concludes that theology or divine science is of two sorts. One kind considers divine things not as the subject of the science, but only as principles of that subject. This is the theology which the philosophers have pursued and which, Thomas comments, is also referred to as metaphysics. Another kind of theology considers divine things for their own sake as its very subject. This is the theology which is based on (*lit.*, 'handed down in') sacred Scripture" (17). Marion will make a similar point later on, although he does not draw the distinctions out as explicitly as Wipple does.

4. Marion argues this for the following thinkers in greater detail: Peter de Fonseca, Scipion DuPleix, Abra de Raconis, and Eustache de St. Paul.

5. Marion calls him a "privileged witness" for measuring Descartes' originality (QCII, 370). He treats Mersenne's concept of metaphysics in the final chapter of QCII (369–91). This chapter is not included in the English translation of the book.

6. QCII, 391.

7. He suggested "first philosophy" as an appropriate subtitle for his *Meditations*, rejecting the term "metaphysics" that the French translator later appended to this work, since he saw its intent as larger than "metaphysics" (i.e., dealing with the first principles of human knowledge and not merely with the "objects" of "God" and the "soul").

8. "The Idea of God," in: *The Cambridge History of Seventeenth-Century Philosophy*, ed. Daniel Garber (New York: Cambridge University Press, 1998), 24. Marion reads the *Regulae* as an explicit conversation with Aristotle (not as a commentary on

the *Discourse* or a preview to the *Meditations*). He shows how Descartes reformulates Aristotelian notions and formulates a program that could replace the Aristotelianism in the Scholastic schools (OG, 21). Descartes does not criticize Aristotle explicitly, but instead institutes a kind of metaphor in which Aristotle is reread and displaced. See Derek Morrow's useful summary of Marion's argument regarding Descartes' "deconstruction" of Aristotle in the *Regulae* (GG, 12–18).

9. Foreword to CQ. Robyn Horner also points this out in her introduction (MTI, 3).

10. Although what follows is surely not a very complete summary of *Ontologie grise*, I do lay out Marion's argument in this book in more detail than that of the *Metaphysical Prism*, for example, since *Ontologie grise* is still in the process of translation and thus has not been as accessible to English-speaking readers.

11. Rule 1 asserts: "The aim of our studies should be to direct the mind with a view to forming true and sound judgements about whatever comes before it" (CSM I:9; AT X:359).

12. Rule 2 emphasizes: "We should attend only to those objects of which our minds seem capable of having certain and indubitable cognition" (CSM I:10; AT X:362); while Rule 3 points out: "Concerning objects proposed for study, we ought to investigate what we can clearly and evidently intuit [to look, gaze at] or deduce with certainty, and not what other people have thought or what we ourselves conjecture. For knowledge [*scientia*] can be attained no other way" (CSM I:13; AT X:367).

13. OG, 41.

14. Rules 4–6 are Marion's guidelines here: Rule 4: "We need a method if we are to investigate the truth of things" (CSM I:15; AT X:371); Rule 5: "The whole method consists entirely in the ordering and arranging of the objects on which we must concentrate our mind's eye if we are to discover some truths. We shall be following this method exactly if we first reduce complicated and obscure propositions step by step to simpler ones, and then, starting with the intuition of the simplest one of all, try to ascend through the same steps to a knowledge of all the rest" (CSM I:20; AT X:379); Rule 6: "In order to distinguish the simplest things from those that are complicated and to set them out in an orderly manner, we should attend to what is most simple in each series of things in which we have directly deduced some truths from others, and should observe how all the rest are more, or less, or equally removed from the simplest" (CSM I:21; AT X:381).

15. Rule 7 reads: "In order to make our knowledge complete, every single thing relating to our undertaking must be surveyed in a continuous and wholly uninterrupted sweep of thought, and be included in a sufficient and well-ordered enumeration" (CSM I:25; AT X:387).

16. Rule 12 reads: " Finally we must make use of all the aids which intellect, imagination, sense-perception, and memory afford in order, firstly, to intuit simple propositions distinctly; secondly, to combine correctly the matters under investigation with what we already know, so that they too may be known; and thirdly, to find out what things should be compared with each other so that we make the most thorough use of all our human powers" (CSM I:39; AT X:410). In the explication of the first aspect of this rule, Descartes insists: "As for simple propositions, the only rules we provide are those which prepare our cognitive powers for a more distinct intuition of any given object and for a more discerning examination of it. For these simple propositions must occur to us spontaneously; they cannot be sought out" (CSM I:50; AT X:428).

17. Rule 14 introduces the notion of *figura*: "The problem should be re-expressed in terms of the real extension of bodies and should be pictured in our imagination entirely by means of bare figures. Thus it will be perceived much more distinctly by our intellect" (CSM I:56; AT X:438). Rules 15 and 16 carry this further.

18. "Quelle est la méthode dans la métaphysique?" (QCI, 75–109).

19. Wolfgang Röd, review of *Sur le prisme métaphysique*, in *Archiv für Geschichte der Philosophie* 75 (1993): 230.

20. Josef Wohlmuth, ed. *Ruf und Gabe: Zum Verhältnis von Phänomenologie und Theologie* (Bonn: Borengässer, 2000), 68, 66. Henceforth abbreviated as *Ruf und Gabe*.

21. Marion's clearest outline of this is in his aforementioned article on Aquinas where he employs it in order to evaluate the metaphysical status of that thinker: "Saint Thomas d'Aquin et l'onto-théo-logie" (DSL, 279–332).

22. Martin Heidegger, *Identität und Differenz* (Pfullingen: Verlag Günther Neske, 1957); *Identity and Difference*, trans. Joan Stambaugh (New York: Harper Torchbooks, 1969), 71.

23. DSL, 287. On the topic of the *causa sui* see especially chapter 4.

24. Paul DeHart, "The Ambiguous Infinite: Jüngel, Marion, and the God of Descartes," *The Journal of Religion* 82.1 (2002): 83.

25. "Metaphysics and Phenomenology: A Relief for Theology," trans. Thomas A. Carlson, *Critical Inquiry* 20 (Summer 1994): 577.

26. Especially in section 2 of the second part, entitled "The Founding in Question" (TB, 345–426).

27. No temporal condition is indicated in the *Discourse* ("as long as I am thinking . . ."); therefore the ego in the *Meditations* is actually more fragile on Marion's reading. Furthermore, in the *Discourse* the ego is stated clearly as a substance, while Descartes is later more ambivalent about the terminology of substantiality. This shows that the ego *cogito* is altogether much stronger in the *Discourse* than in the later *Meditations*. The ego exercises this metaphysical status "according to the figure of a metaphysics of representation" (CQ, 35; QCI, 62). The "I think" as first principle and substance does make "Being of beings" an issue in two senses: "The validation of my thought as a substance rests on the general and unconditional equivalence between the act of thinking and the fact that I exist" (CQ, 35; QCI, 63). "The act of thinking already performs the being" in and as actuality. Descartes does equate thinking and existence when both are introduced by the "I": "Existing, like thinking, emerges only through the intermediary of an *I*, and thus, the first thesis of the metaphysics is established through a protology of the ego" (CQ, 36; QCI, 64).

28. "Therefore, the *Discourse* cannot present a perfectly elaborated metaphysics of the proofs of the existence of God, not only because of the unilateral privilege granted to perfection against the infinite in divine essence, but also, and in equal part, because it neglects causality as a metaphysical principle for existence, as it can be applied 'in the case of ideas' (41, 3), and therefore even to the idea of the infinite, thus 'even God himself' . . . , and therefore to the idea and the existence of God." (CQ, 30; QCI, 55.)

29. MP, 115; PM, 122.

30. "Metaphysics and Phenomenology," 578.

31. MP, 7; PM, 8.

32. He spells this out in detail in §15, "The Ego Outside Subsistence," in part 3 (on the ego) of the *Metaphysical Prism* (MP, 193–205; PM, 203–16).

33. Marion does point out that neither Heidegger nor Derrida articulates fully what they mean by that expression. See *Ruf und Gabe*, 57.

34. Charles Matthew Stapleton, "The Derrida-Marion Debate: Performative Language and Mystical Theology," *Kinesis* 31.2 (2004): 4.

35. He spells this out in detail in §20, "The Exceptional Name," in part 4 (on "God") of the *Metaphysical Prism* (MP, 261–76; PM, 276–92).

36. This constitutes the final section (part 5, "Overcoming") of his *Metaphysical Prism* (MP, 277–345; PM, 293–369).

37. David Tracy also comments on the significance of Pascal for Marion's work (CE, 61).

38. See the first part of his article on Pascal (QCII, 339–50) and the almost identical introduction to the last part of the *Metaphysical Prism* (MP, 277–89; PM, 293–306).

39. "Pascal et la 'règle générale' de vérité" (QCII, 339–68).

40. QCII, 341.

41. QCII, 347.

42. QCII, 348.

43. QCII, 353.

44. QCII, 355.

45. QCII, 357.

46. QCII, 359.

47. QCII, 363.

48. QCII, 364.

49. "Evidence and Bedazzlement" (PC, 53–70; PaC, 69–88).

50. Increasingly, more commentators are beginning to realize this. See several of the chapters in Hart's *Counter-Experiences*. I will deal with some of these in the final chapter, on love.

51. "Charity achieves the rank of hermeneutic principle: once its point of view is admitted — that is to say, once the mind succeeds in reaching it, another world, or other dimensions of the old world, is disclosed to the gaze."

52. "For Descartes, the knowledge of God is accomplished in the evidence because first of all it accomplishes the evidence itself: in order to know God, one must first, always, and only know; and if it is then fitting to worship him, indeed to love him, this will be possible only and justified only on the basis of a knowledge that is certain because it is clear and distinct. Here resides the blasphemy and the idolatry in the eyes of Pascal, for whom the love of God precedes and renders knowledge of him possible, since whoever reasons with regard to God thinks, whether he knows it or not, in a theoretical situation affected by the 'wretchedness' of sin . . . Not that love dispenses with knowing or requires some sacrifice of intelligibility, but love becomes, instead of and in the place of *intuitus*, the keeper of evidence, the royal road to knowledge" (MP, 305; PM, 324).

2. Theology and Metaphysics

1. Tobias Specker draws a careful distinction between three different meanings of the word "theology" in Marion. Marion himself distinguishes between theo-*logy* and *theo*-logy. The introduction to part 2 will consider these distinctions more carefully.

2. ID, 16; IeD, 31.

3. ID, 16–17; IeD, 31.

4. John Martis, "Postmodernism and God as Giver," *The Way* 36 (1996): 238–39. In a comparison of Marion with Walter Kaspar, Anthony Godzieba speaks similarly of Heidegger's insights: "According to him [Heidegger], philosophy's intrinsic metaphysical identity reveals itself in the obsessive search for the unifying 'ground,' or arche, which makes beings possible, the place 'from which' the beings of our experience derive and 'upon which' they are grounded. Such a 'grounding' reality has been conceived and named differently in different historical epochs, but no matter how the ground has been conceived, no matter what style metaphysical thinking has taken, 'what characterizes metaphysical thinking which grounds the ground for beings is the fact that metaphysical thinking departs from what is present in its presence, and thus represents it in terms of its ground as something grounded.' Right here is Heidegger's indictment of metaphysics: it ignores the phenomenality of beings, their sheer givenness as modes of presencing, and persists in formatting reality along the lines of dualistic oppositions (ground/grounded, source of presence/what is present)." Godzieba, "Ontotheology to Excess," 6.

5. GWB, 10–14; DSL, 20–23. See also his elucidation of the idol in ID, 5–9; IeD, 15–24. For a good introduction to how the terminology of idol and icon functions in Marion's work, see Ruud Welten, *Fenomenologie en beeldverbod bij Emmanuel Levinas en Jean-Luc Marion* (Budel: Uitgeverij Damon, 2001), especially 124–52.

6. Merold Westphal, *Overcoming Onto-Theology: Toward a Postmodern Christian Faith* (New York: Fordham University Press, 2001), 267.

7. "The divine appears thus only in ontological difference unthought as such, hence also in the figure of the founding funds required for the securing of beings, funds having to be placed in security, hence to be found. Onto-theo-logy disengages, of itself, a function and hence a site for every intervention of the divine that would be constituted as metaphysical: the theo-logical pole of metaphysics determines, as early as the setting into operation of the Greek beginning, a site for what one later will name 'God' . . . The advent of something like 'God' in philosophy therefore arises less from God himself than from metaphysics, as destinal figure of the thought of Being" (GWB, 34; DSL, 53).

8. This distinction provides the framework for Specker's analysis, which is occupied with the possibility of thinking God in a manner that would preserve the divine transcendence and employs Marion to outline an "idolic" and an "iconic" way of "thinking God." The analysis of the idol occupies part 2 of the work (AGD, 75–198).

9. Tobias Specker shows this especially for the case of Heidegger, emphasizing how Marion sees Heidegger's philosophy as absolutely determinative of contemporary thought and yet criticizes its limitations for thinking about the divine.

10. Marion argues that this is true both for attempts to "prove" God's existence and similarly for attempts to refute such proofs: "In order to establish an atheism in the modern sense of the term, that is, a doctrine that denies existence to any 'supreme Being' (or the like), one requires a demonstration, and a rigorous one. One requires, therefore, a conceptual thinking that is compelling. And thus a concept of 'God' is necessary here, a concept that would enter into the demonstration to provide the ultimate point on which it rests . . . In its conclusion of exclusion, that demonstration is worth as much as the concept of 'God' that sustains it. . . . that atheism, conceptual of course, is only ever valid as far as the concept of 'God' that it mobilizes extends . . . If, then, 'God' covers a particular semantic terrain, the refutation will not eliminate God

absolutely but only the meaning of God that its initial 'God' offers to be disputed" (ID, 2; Ied, 16–17).

11. ID, 30; IeD, 48.

12. The famous "Parable of the Madman" can be found in Nietzsche's *Gay Science*. English translation: Walter Kaufman, ed., *Existentialism: From Dostoevsky to Sartre* (New York: Penguin, 1975), 126–27.

13. ID, 32; IeD, 51; GWB, 57; DSL, 87.

14. Godzieba, "Ontotheology to Excess," 8.

15. ID, 31–33; IeD, 49–51.

16. He points out that even Heidegger calls Nietzsche the last metaphysician.

17. "The Being of each being (the valuation of value) calls for the completion of a totality, where the being is absorbed in its completeness: the ultimate accumulation that capitalizes nothing but, if one wishes to recognize in it the other dimension of onto-theology, announces something like being in its supreme figure" (ID, 43; IeD, 63).

18. See also GWB, 29ff., 38f., 59f.; DSL, 44ff., 59f., 90f.

19. Martin Heidegger, "Phenomenology and Theology," trans. James G. Hart and John C. Maraldo, in *Pathmarks*, ed. William McNeill (Cambridge, Mass.: Cambridge University Press, 1998), 39–54.

20. Heidegger said this in a seminar in Zürich in 1951 (when asked whether Being and God were the same). Marion cites Heidegger's full response [both German and French] in DSL, 92–93; GWB, 61, 211–12.

21. GWB, 41; DSL, 64.

22. GWB, 44; DSL 69.

23. Jeffrey Bloechl, "Dialectical Approaches to Retrieving God after Heidegger: Premises and Consequences (Lacoste and Marion)," *Pacifica* 13 (2000): 291.

24. Emilio Brito considers Marion's reaction to Heidegger too extreme. He interprets Marion as representative of one particular type of religious reception of Heidegger, namely one that attempts to separate the divine from all ontotheological construction and interprets even Heidegger himself as engaged in an idolatrous project. He thinks that Marion is wrong here, because Heidegger's "final god" is supposedly neither a being nor can be identified with Being. Emilio Brito, S.J., "La réception de la pensée de Heidegger dans la théologie catholique," *NRT* 119 (1997): 371–72.

25. For a more detailed analysis of Marion's relation to Heidegger, see Specker's treatment in AGD, 161–198.

26. Felix Ó Murchadha, "Glory, Idolatry, Kairos: Revelation and the Ontological Difference in Marion," GG, 70–71.

27. Béatrice Han, "Transcendence and the Hermeneutic Circle: Some Thoughts on Marion and Heidegger," in *Transcendence in Philosophy and Religion*, ed. James Faulconer (Bloomington: Indiana University Press, 2003), 122–23.

28. Ibid., 138.

29. Henry, "Quatre principes," 21.

30. This explication is pursued in §18 of *Idol and Distance:* "The Other Différant."

31. "Beyond onto-theology and Being/beings (ὄν), difference differs/defers (itself) indifferently (in) their difference, without having to grant it the least privilege, and above all not that which it would refuse to itself. The ontological difference would thus constitute only a particular case of a *différance* that, before and around it, differs/defers

in an indefinite, insignificant, and bottomless chassé-croisé. To a regional ontological difference, one must not prefer any more essential instance; one must only adjoin
thereto, in order to surround it, situate it, traverse it, and pass beyond it, the indefinite
network of differences where *différance* differs/defers (from) (itself) without privilege,
priority or dominance. Being/beings can be located as one of the possible centers, equal
to all the others within the differing/deferring network, whose indefiniteness can admit,
at every point, another center. To disappropriate the ontological difference of difference, to reappropriate difference in a perfect indifference to *différance*" (ID, 225–26;
IeD, 274–75).

32. Stapleton, "Derrida-Marion Debate," 5, 6.

33. *Ruf und Gabe*, 55.

34. Victor Kal, "Being Unable to Speak, Seen as a Period: Difference and Distance in Jean-Luc Marion," in *Flight of the Gods*, ed. Ilse N. Bulhof and Laurens ten
Kate (New York: Fordham University Press, 2000), 154.

35. Thomas Guarino, "Postmodernity and Five Fundamental Theological Issues," *Theological Studies* 57.4 (1996): 676.

36. In fact, Marion insists repeatedly in *God without Being* that he intends to
remain "strictly theological" or that he is engaged in a theological evaluation of philosophy (e.g., GWB, 80, 109, 171; DSL, 120, 158, 241).

37. *Ruf und Gabe*, 46. He continues by saying: "The provocation was real. Today
I would no longer act like this. But at the time of *God without Being* I couldn't do it any
better." Ibid.

38. Jeffrey L. Kosky, "Philosophy of Religion and Return to Phenomenology in
Jean-Luc Marion: From *God without Being* to *Being Given*," *American Catholic Philosophical Quarterly* 78.4 (2004): 630.

3. Phenomenology and Metaphysics

1. The subtitle of the work is "Six Meditations," and Marion makes it clear that
the reference to Descartes and Husserl is intended.

2. Marion insisted on "givenness" (instead of "donation") in the English translation (IE, xi). As I will outline below, there is a whole controversy surrounding even his
translation of the German *Gegebenheit* to the French *donation*.

3. RG, 3; RD, 9–10.

4. Husserl's breakthrough consisted in a broadening of intuition to the point of
claiming to free it from all limits. According to Marion's reading of Derrida, however,
Husserl consigns phenomenology radically to the metaphysics of presence of intuition.
Husserl reduces thought "to the evidence of the given" (RG, 18; RD, 31). Marion criticizes Derrida for equating intuition and presence, for assuming that Husserl does not
separate intuition and signification. For Husserl, signification is sufficient to present
something to presence without the corresponding intuition. In fact, signification and
intuition are in competition over the fields of what is given to be seen. Givenness su-
persedes them both in what it gives to appearing in presence. Marion thus ultimately
justifies Derrida's critique of Husserl as the "last figure of the metaphysics of presence"
but interprets it differently.

5. According to Marion, Heidegger also criticizes Husserl for not thinking Being
or givenness radically enough. For Heidegger, "givenness broadens presence in that it
frees it from any limits of the faculties, as far as to let beings play freely — eventually be-

ings in their Being. And only such a liberating broadening will be able to claim to surpass the 'metaphysics of presence,' which, in fact, does not cease to *restrain* the present and to *hold back* its givenness" (RG, 37; RD, 60–61). After a close examination of this question Marion finds that Heidegger does do justice to both Husserl and Derrida.

6. There is no agreement in the present English translations on whether to employ *objectity* or *objectness*. Although I prefer objectity, since it is closer to Marion's French term [*objectité*], I have decided to use objectness for clarity's sake.

7. Marion often seems to employ these two Husserlian concepts interchangeably.

8. Martin Gagnon, "La phénoménologie à la limite," *Eidos* 11.1–2 (1993): 114, 121.

9. Chapter 4, "Question of Being or Ontological Difference" (RG, 108–140; RD, 163–210).

10. See the discussion of this comparison in his third chapter (RG, 77–107; RD, 119–161).

11. Marion will explicate this argument further in the latter part of *Being Given* (ED, 259–262; BG, 185–187).

12. ED, 49ff.; BG, 32ff. As pointed out above, Marion distinguishes between "objectivity" [*Objektivität*] and "objectity" or "objectness" [*Gegenständlichkeit*].

13. James Dodd, "Marion and Phenomenology," review of Jean-Luc Marion, *Being Given*, in *Graduate Faculty Philosophy Journal* 25.1 (2004): 163.

14. ED, 57; BG, 37.

15. The given must be utterly reduced to itself; everything else must be put in reduction. Marion explains this by using a painting as example. A painting can only appear when it is limited not by its being or exposure but only by its "being given" to the gaze of the observer. Its reductions to subsistence [*Vorhandenheit*], use [*Zuhandenheit*], or thing [*Seiendes*] are all insufficient (ED, 62–70; BG, 40–45). Painting (and other "art") requires a kind of liturgy, has the effect of "melody" on the observer (ED, 72; BG, 48). Paintings do not show objects or present themselves as beings but accomplish themselves as effects in the sense of a shock of emotion or meaning. Marion claims that what is at issue in the painting is neither perception nor even emotion, but passion: the painting "speaks to my soul" and "causes it to vibrate" (ED, 75; BG, 51). The point in the appearing of the phenomenon is thus not visibility, but its self-giving as act and effect. Many other phenomena give themselves in this way without objectness and without being "objects."

16. Benson, "Love Is a Given," 25.

17. Gerhard Höhn, "Suche nach Ursprünglichkeit: Die Wiedergeburt der Metaphysik aus dem Erbe der Phänomenologie," *Frankfurter Rundschau*, 29 November 1994, n.p.

18. Natalie Depraz, "Gibt es eine Gebung des Unendlichen?" in *Perspektiven der Philosophie*, ed. Rudolph Berlinger (Amsterdam: Rodopi, 1997). All page numbers within the next paragraph refer to this article, unless indicated otherwise.

19. Jocelyn Benoist criticizes Marion in a similar fashion. He also sees a problem of language and silence, in that Marion does not acknowledge the function of language sufficiently. Benoist is bothered by the concept of donation/givenness, because in Husserl donation does not designate the signified object but intuition, and thinks that intuition and signification are too often too quickly identified with each other in Marion. The given in Husserl, according to his interpretation, refers to an act of consciousness,

not to the object. He thinks that finally "donation" is an empty concept because it really has no relation with the object that is given but refers to the significations themselves, and he insists that Marion combines intuition and signification into one concept of donation, but that since he never explicitly analyzes the notion of signification his treatment remains "linguistically naive" (82) because he never specifically addresses the deeply linguistic character of all existence that allows distinctions between types of phenomena. He suggests that Marion confuses the Husserlian term *donation* with the Lévinassian and Ricoeurian (and possibly Heideggerian) term of the *appeal/call*. In his excess he is entirely metaphysical. It is false to say that for Husserl "signification is a 'richer' domain than intuition" (85). He admits that to some extent Husserl himself is ambiguous on this point [of fulfillment of intention], but in Benoist's view a simple inversion of Husserl's relation does not work. "To the contrary, Marion parts company with Husserl (a simplified and so to say reduced Husserl, in that the true place of the difference between intuition and signification — presence or not — is no longer visible) in the belief that there is something in common between intuition and signification, and hence, against Husserl, believes himself authorized to think that the one can surpass the other" (88). For him, this is properly metaphysical. He desires contingency where Marion introduces the "unconditioned" and does not think that Marion can get rid of the horizon in order to introduce something absolute. Marion commits several grammatical errors; his phenomenological structure cannot be supported. Benoist criticizes Marion's notion of saturation in detail and objects to Marion's "counting" of horizons. He does not think that the "infinite" can have a phenomenological sense. Intuition and signification must only be "distinguished" but not opposed; since Marion does so (falsely) he introduces phantom phenomena. Because Marion does not distinguish concepts at the beginning clearly enough, he goes too far in a direction in which one cannot go because it has no meaning or sense. Jocelyn Benoist, "L'écart plutôt que l'excédent," *Philosophie: Jean-Luc Marion* 78 (2003): 77–93. See also Paul Gilbert's analysis, which compares the terminology of substance in Derrida's and Marion's phenomenology. Paul Gilbert, "Substance et présence: Derrida et Marion, critiques de Husserl," *Gregorianum* 75.1 (1994): 95–133.

20. Ricard similarly insists that the reduction is not an "exclusive" operation for Husserl. It does not close but open. Marion therefore misreads Husserl because he sees him as restrictive, as distinguishing between phenomena and rejecting some as inauthentic. Ricard, "Question de la donation," 86–87.

21. Depraz, "Gebung des Unendlichen," 112–13. She wonders whether Marion's project is possible and whether it does not return to an entirely ontotheological metaphysics. She thinks that Marion's and Henry's thought are mere constructions of phenomena, not descriptions of actual or possible experiences (129). She briefly summarizes Marion but in that context does not criticize him (145–47).

22. Depraz has recently reviewed Marion's work in a much more favorable manner in her "The Return to Phenomenology in Recent French Moral Philosophy" in *Phenomenological Approaches to Moral Philosophy*, ed. John Drummond (Dordrecht: Kluwer Publishing, 2002), 517–32.

23. Claude Piché, review of Jean-Luc Marion, *Réduction et donation*, in *Philosophiques* 20 (1993): 224.

24. Rolf Kühn, "Intentionale und materiale Phänomenologie," *Tijdschift voor Filosofie* 54.4 (1992): 694.

25. Ibid., 713.

26. Jeffrey A. Bell, review of *Reduction and Givenness*, in *International Studies in Philosophy* 35 (2003): 356.

27. Ibid., 357.

28. Marion also wonders why Heidegger did not carry this hypothesis further. He suggests that examining the Being of *Dasein* remains unsuccessful in thinking the Being of beings as such. After analyzing several of Heidegger's attempts to think Being as such (e.g., by the experience of the Nothing, of boredom, of anxiety), Marion ultimately concludes that Heidegger is unsuccessful in thinking Being. Heidegger must reinterpret his own writing in order to discover Being within it. Thus "since the 1929 lecture does not manage to refer to the Nothing opened up by anxiety to the 'phenomenon of Being,' it is necessary, in an a posteriori reprise that is all the more frantic in the measure that the initial failure is serious, not only to frame the weak text with a preface and a postscript, but to reinforce it through accentuations, substitutions, and additions. This work, never interrupted over the course of at least twenty years (from 1929 to 1949), would not have made any sense if Heidegger had not himself admitted that, with the appearance of the Nothing, the 'phenomenon of Being' was nevertheless not attained. Between the one and the other a hermeneutic has to intervene" (RG, 181; RD, 272). Pure donation has not been thought. *Dasein* must still allow itself to hear the call of Being or its claim which is assimilated into the *Ereignis*, but can never be fully identified. Marion thus suggests that *Dasein* must become what he calls the *interloqué*/interlocuted. An analysis of boredom again allows Marion to think further the claim of Being or any other claim that might transgress ontology into a new reduction. Boredom leaves all beings in their place, does not evaluate, affirm, or love them, ignores any call, claim, wonder, or ecstasy, refuses any kind of response. Boredom renders the Being of the beings of the world insignificant and can disqualify even the call of Being.

29. "It is obviously not a question here of invoking revealed authority in order to broaden the field of phenomenology, but of confirming that another call — no doubt the call of the other — might dismiss or submerge the first call issued by the claim of Being. . . . The call itself intervenes as such, without or before any other 'message' than to surprise the one who hears it, to grab even the one who does not expect it. The model of the call exerts itself before the simple claim of Being, and more fully. Before Being has claimed, the call as pure call claims" (RG, 197; RD, 295–96).

30. He feels himself justified in doing that based on Michel Henry's confirmation of this as a fourth principle of phenomenology in Henry's review of Marion's *Reduction and Givenness*. Henry, "Quatre principes."

31. For the most detailed exposition of this argument, see Janicaud, *La phénoménologie éclatée*, 54–56.

32. Dodd, "Marion and Phenomenology," 161.

33. Ibid., 162. He approves far less of the theological connotations of the work, which he does not find compelling and which "are in the end not what is interesting about this book." Ibid. He concludes his review in the same tenor: "Marion has clearly taken a bold move in this direction, but to date it remains somewhat in methodological limbo, since it studiously evades the possibility that theology cold prepare us for phenomenology. Which is understandable, since it probably is not the case" (183).

34. This is outlined in section 3 of *Being Given* (ED, 169–250; BG, 119–78).

35. Jeff Kosky translates this as "unpredictable landing" and justifies this somewhat awkward terminology as follows: "'Unpredictable landing' here translates the French 'arrivage,' a term from everyday, colloquial usage. This French term appears

in everyday life when one dines at a restaurant featuring fresh fish. A literal translation would be something like 'catch of the day' or 'according to the market,' which lose too much of the meaning Marion here intends. The unpredictability and uncertainty of what will arrive to market each day is, as any traveler knows, mirrored in the guesswork that surrounds the landing of a jet at any major airport. I have therefore chosen to shift the register from dining out to air travel and render *arrivage* as *unpredictable landing* — intending no slight, or homage, to the airline industry" (BG, 351).

36. Dodd criticizes Marion strongly for having "succeeded in writing two elegant books on the problem of givenness in which he maintains an almost complete silence on the significance of the problem of time for Husserl's phenomenology. This is problematic, for the problem of time in Husserl is nothing less than the problem of the phenomenality of consciousness itself, a decisive issue if he is to be able to maintain his understanding of phenomenology as the science of intentional lived experience" ("Marion and Phenomenology," 169). He elucidates this criticism in detail by showing the importance of time for Husserl. One can certainly argue that Marion's analysis of the arrival does imply a consideration of temporality. For Dodd, however, this is not sufficient: "This is not because of a lack of initiative (the present moment, after all, always has the initiative). The argument has to do with the manner in which a lived experience (*Erlebnis*) is originally constituted as temporal. In other words, for Husserl, thanks to the temporality of consciousness, the experiencing subject is never taken completely by surprise, overwhelmed, or submerged in a givenness that passes beyond all confines of what can be anticipated. Not because everything is anticipated, projected in a horizon of intentional determinability in advance; rather, it is because the unanticipated, the radical moment, is embedded in a temporal density that structurally resists all saturation, that always enacts phenomenality itself in such a way that an intrinsic, thoughtful distance is maintained that refuses to be surpassed" (173). It certainly is true that the topic of time does not figure significantly in Marion's phenomenological writings (although he does include a brief reconsideration of temporality in the first reflection on the erotic phenomenon [PE, 56–64]).

37. Marion thus suggests that facticity must be enlarged to include all phenomena, not merely *Dasein* as Heidegger would have maintained (ED, 203ff.; BG, 144ff.).

38. He is relying in particular on Jacques Derrida's *Given Time: I. Counterfeit Money*, trans. Peggy Kamuf (Chicago: University of Chicago Press, 1992). The entire second part of the book deals with this subject of the gift (ED, 103–68; BG, 71–118).

39. "The consciousness of owing (oneself) to the missing giver makes the self, the debt, and the consciousness of all these coincide. The givee is found to be originally insolvent in and through the recognition of the irreparable anteriority of the debt to all response — the anteriority of the gift of self given to the self over and above the self itself. The debt therefore designates not so much an act or a situation of the self as its state and its definition — possibly its way to be" (BG, 99; ED, 142–43).

40. BG, 115–17; ED, 164–67.

41. It is unclear to me what she means by that besides maybe the insistence in both of the need for a response to grace (which certainly is not a heretical notion, even if Pelagius held it). She merely warns of this threat, but does not explain why indebtedness would "run the risk of entering into Pelagian waters" (RGG, 183).

42. Caputo, "Apostles of the Impossible," GGP, 210–15.

43. Milbank lays out this argument in detail in "Can a Gift Be Given? Prolegomena to a Future Trinitarian Metaphysic," *Modern Theology* 11.1 (1995): 133–38.

44. Ibid., 134.

45. He suggests that "an absolutization of gift 'without being' reduces to an absolutization of empty subjectivity, whose apparent kenosis is almost indistinguishable from demonic self-enclosure. The gift without being is not a gift 'of' anything, and so is not a gift. . . . Marion's extra-ontological gift does not, therefore, I contend, capture the logic of Creation, which demands, indeed, another ontology, perhaps precisely an ontology of the gift, but all the same an ontology." Ibid., 137.

46. Idem, *Being Reconciled: Ontology and Pardon* (New York: Routledge, 2003).

47. See especially PE, 114–16; EP, 69–70.

48. ED, 244ff.; BG, 173ff.

49. John Caputo compares Derrida's and Marion's use of Husserl in terms of their treatment of the relationship between intuition and intention. He claims that Derrida's "hyperbolic desire" carries Husserl's "intention" to infinity, while Marion's "hyperbolic givenness" carries "fulfillment" to an extreme. "The Hyperbolization of Phenomenology: Two Possibilities for Religion in Recent Continental Philosophy" (CE, 68).

50. Benson, "Love Is a Given," 23.

51. Ruud Welten, "Saturation and Disappointment: Marion According to Husserl," *Tijdschrift voor Filosofie en Theologie/International Journal in Philosophy and Theology* 65.1 (2004): 85.

52. Ibid., 90.

53. Ibid., 92.

54. Richard Kearney, *Debates in Continental Philosophy: Conversations with Contemporary Thinkers* (New York: Fordham University Press, 2004), 24.

55. Depraz, "Gebung des Unendlichen," 116–17. She does not approve of Marion's (or anyone's) move to the extreme boundaries of phenomenology. The expression of a "flat" or "common" phenomenon makes no sense to her, since such a superficial phenomenon would lose all phenomenal dimension (116). She thinks a so-called "saturated" phenomenon would "harbor the same danger" because it becomes visible and thereby loses its infinity (116). She insists: "In short, there is no such thing as a flat phenomenon. The expression is non-sense, which destroys the real sense of the phenomenon. Every phenomenon is worthy of this name, as soon as it saturates itself by negating itself and negates itself by saturating itself: its phenomenality is only proper at this prize" (117).

56. Ricard, "Question de la donation," 89, 92.

57. The first four phenomena invert each one of Kant's categories. The fifth, on the other hand, inverts all four at the same time and is thus doubly saturated. Marion proposes these phenomena briefly in *Being Given* (ED, 318–25; BG, 228–33) and then devotes most of *In Excess* to a more thorough explication.

58. Some commentators have also criticized Marion's use of Kantian categories in this context and claim that these are not truly phenomenological and therefore should not provide the parameters for the appearing of a phenomenon. Emmanuel Falque, for example, finds that to escape from Kant or metaphysics it is not sufficient simply to invert them and objects to the saturated phenomenon being the paradigm for all phenomenality. "Phénoménologie de l'extraordinaire," *Philosophie* 78 (2003): 72. Dodd is similarly surprised by the use of Kant in this context: "The reliance on Kant in these pages to frame the description of temporality is telling, and characteristic of much of Books IV and V of *Being Given*. The 'excess' of saturated phenomena, and of the givenness of the given in its non-containment in phenomenality, is presented as an exception

to a very Kantian conception of phenomenality, not necessarily to a Husserlian or for that matter Heideggerean. This is surprising, given the ground laid by Marion's investigations in *Reduction and Givenness*. There would seem to be little reason to turn to Kant, for whom phenomena are defined as appearances insofar as they are thought as objects in accordance with the categories. But it is precisely the problem of originary constitution that ultimately bars ascribing this Kantian paradigm to Husserl — the mark of pure phenomenality for Husserl is not only, perhaps not even primarily, the regulation of an appearing through categoriality" ("Marion and Phenomenology," 170). Tobias Specker also comments repeatedly on Marion's "turn-about" in regard to Kant. As summarized above, Marion does provide some justification for his turn to Kant here. Welten justifies this use of Kant (correctly, in my view) as a mere "classical model." Marion neither tries " to refute Kant nor to substantiate him. Where Kant marks out the limits of our capacity for thought, there the saturated phenomenon breaks in through this very demarcation." Kant's four-fold categories serve merely as "a point of orientation" that enables the description of its excess. Welten, *Fenomenologie*, 197.

59. He gives various examples: a short analysis of the causes of WWI, the Battle of Waterloo, the room in which he is giving his address, Montaigne's friendship, the death of another person, my own death, time, my birth (DS, 37, 44, 46, 48, 49; IE, 31ff.).

60. Marion here introduces explicitly a positive notion of hermeneutics for the first time. In his early work, hermeneutics was either neglected or had negative connotations. Several thinkers have criticized him for this. Jean Greisch, in a special issue of the *Revue de Métaphysique et Morale* devoted to *Réduction et donation*, for example, particularly censored the apparent lack of hermeneutics in Marion's work. He wonders about the transition from being to Being which is a hermeneutic move in Heidegger lacking any recognition by Marion ("L'herméneutique dans la «phénoménologie comme telle»," 45). Thus, the phenomenon does not bring with itself its proper visibility and impose it upon consciousness; rather consciousness is required to interpret this appearance. The phenomenon is therefore "unapparent" (45). He applauds Marion's analysis of Husserl's hesitant concept of ontology. Heidegger's hermeneutics of facticity is crucial and overlooked by Marion (46). Phenomenology must be a possibility and a mode of research and therefore be a hermeneutics of facticity (48). Secondly, Greisch desires a hermeneutics of the self which he misses in Marion. This criticism will become significant in chapter 7. Jean Grondin also criticizes the lack of hermeneutics in Marion. He calls Marion's work "superbly written" and "ambitious" but wonders whether it really remains phenomenology ("La tension de la donation ultime et de la pensée herméneutique de l'application chez Jean-Luc Marion," *Dialogue* 38.3 [1999]: 548). Real phenomenology (as in Sartre and Merleau-Ponty) must remain concerned with the "things themselves" (548). He shows how although Marion tries to open a new realm to phenomenology, he also is very much indebted to Husserl and Heidegger (549). He thinks that richest inspiration comes from Heidegger's *es gibt* and wonders why it does not appear more (549). Emmanuel Gabellieri acknowledges Marion's improved emphasis on hermeneutics, but wonders whether not more hermeneutics should be at work in the other saturated phenomena (not merely the historical one). He does not think that one can draw a clear line of demarcation between saturated phenomena and everyday ones ("De la métaphysique," 639). He asks whether not anything (any being or reality) "can open me to the enigma of being or to the contemplation of God" (639).

61. In his two phenomenological works Marion focuses mostly on the idol as a

painting. Various examples (strewn over the whole history of painting) are analyzed. Unlike all other presences, the painting has no shadows and no absence: it presents the visible fully without promising anything more to see than what offers itself already. It thus shows a reduced visible that is presented in a pure state without any leftover appresentation and comes to such an intensity that it saturates the capacity of my gaze or even exceeds it. In a painting, we see not objects but the vision of the painter: "Painting excludes absence and the deception of the gaze: all is there to see, nothing withholds itself here in absence or refuges itself into appresentation; it carries presence, to the point of carrying even absence (appresentation) to direct visibility. Painting adds presence to presence, there where nature preserves space" (DS, 79; IE, 66). The painter produces and adds visibles to the world, metamorphoses unseens that would remain inaccessible without this creation. At each new epoch, these new visibles fascinate our gaze and make us see the world through their paradigm. They are idols that obligate us; we cannot ignore paintings. We can never see a painting once and for all as we can objects of the world; rather we must always return to see it, must always go to see it. A painting does not come to me but constrains me to go to it. Paintings require an ever new encounter, each unrepeatable and unsubstitutable. It is never a closed object, never exhaustively seen, but is different every time. It is so intense that we need to keep re-seeing it; it has the quality of an event. We are saturated with the feeling of a work of art; it absorbs us, "arises before us, silent, irresistible, to be adored" (DS, 90; IE, 74).

62. Marion reminds us that Husserl already distinguished between my body and my flesh. My flesh is the only thing that can sense before being sensed, see before being seen, appear to myself before making other things appear. My flesh is my soul or what Marion calls "my psychosomatic unity." Only the flesh can suffer. I can experience other people's bodies, but never their flesh. One does not feel one's flesh except by feeling with it. The flesh can take on a body, but the body can never take on flesh. The flesh can never become visible, just as the body which is visible and appears can never feel. The flesh is not a faculty, but it alone turns the world into apparition, the given into phenomenon. Marion claims that not only can one speak of a kind of spiritual flesh, but the flesh alone spiritualizes. Before the ego proves itself, it is already established by the sensing body. I cannot separate myself from my flesh; it designates my "here," my only means of phenomenalization, the only origin of the phenomenological I. The ego thus takes its self in its flesh. Marion usually associates this analysis with Michel Henry (almost never with Maurice Merleau-Ponty).

63. Marion analyzes each of these figures briefly (DS, 110ff.; IE, 91ff.).

64. I will explore this new subjectivity further in chapter 8.

65. Ruud Welten explains the influence of Henry on Marion's thought in very helpful fashion in two excursus, first highlighting the importance of the invisible and then showing the parallels between Henry's reading of Descartes and Marion's readings of both Descartes and Henry. Welten, *Fenomenologie*, 130–42 and 171–80. See also his comments on 226.

66. ED, 299; BG, 214.

67. ED, 323; BG, 232. He does refer briefly to Lévinas in his analysis here. The face cannot be given to be seen, but rather envisages us. We fix only on the emptiness of the pupils in the face of the other, the one place precisely where nothing is seen but from where the gaze of the other proceeds. The phenomenality proper to the face is one of speech; the face opens ethical discourse by its injunction: "Thou shalt not kill!" (DS, 140; IE, 126). The face cannot be possessed, produced, or constituted as

an object. Overall, however, Marion wants to move beyond a "mere" emphasis on ethics. I criticize this desire in my article "Praise — Pure and Personal? Jean-Luc Marion's
Phenomenologies of Prayer," in *The Phenomenology of Prayer*, ed. Bruce Ellis Benson
and Norman Wirzba (New York: Fordham University Press, 2005), 177–78. Gerald Mc-
Kenny criticizes Marion's neglect or even explicit marginalization of ethical concerns
even more strongly. He wonders (in response especially to *The Erotic Phenomenon*) why
love would be the "privileged route of access to the other" (CE, 340). While Marion
is able to talk about individuation, he neglects the universality of justice (CE, 351).
Michael Kessler concurs with this by criticizing Marion's neglect of the political (CE,
357–79).

68. ED, 342; BG, 246. It is clear here that although Marion avoids proceeding
into the realm of theology (for good reasons), his phenomenology does prepare the
ground for its possibility. Saturated phenomena are of such great interest to him precisely because they push phenomenology as far as possible in the direction of theology while remaining separate from it. Marion does not deny the phenomenological
possibility of examining common and "everyday" phenomena. Yet he is profoundly
interested in the limit-cases of saturated phenomena because they open the space that
makes a thought of something beyond strictly philosophical phenomenology possible.
Marion does not explicitly think the phenomenon of Revelation, but he seeks to show
that it is not unreasonable, that its possibility constitutes a coherent thought for phenomenology. I will examine this more carefully in the next chapter.

69. "Le temps de l'attente ne passe pas, car rien ne s'y passe" (PE, 58; EP, 33).
Throughout this section Marion plays on the double meaning of "passer."

70. In this case, it is consequently not only God or religion or revelation that overcomes metaphysics. All four saturated phenomena are in that part of the realm of phenomenology which no longer coincides with metaphysics. Marion's radical reduction
claims to have accomplished what his theology already proposed, namely to proceed
beyond the restrictions of being, grounding, and causality. No longer is it apparently his
primary concern to speak only of God non-idolatrously; rather, the phenomenological exercise has led us to refuse no purity or excess. Just as God is completely given to
human immanence in self-abandonment and kenotic sacrifice, so all phenomena are
described as gifts arriving from a transcendent "otherwise" to the immanent experience
of the dislocated recipient.

Part 2 Introduction

1. Specker outlines these paradigms in AGD, 45, and employs them throughout
his work.

2. He examines this topic especially in the chapter "Of the Eucharistic Site of
Theology" (GWB, 139–58; DSL, 197–222).

3. Marion added two chapters as "hors-texte" ("outside the text" — as many readers have pointed out, a title probably in defiance of Derrida's statement that there is
"nothing outside the text"), thus indicating that in some sense they do not belong to the
text proper. They are also heavily theological. The first concerns again the Eucharist,
the other faith.

4. In retrospect, Marion himself identified especially the final two chapters of
God without Being as theological in nature. He says that although "the critical portion
of this essay was accomplished within the field of philosophy" he "could not, at that

time, glimpse its constructive side (access to charity) except through recourse to theology" (BG, x). David Tracy is quite emphatic, however, that *God without Being* is *not* a theological text, but what he calls "a phenomenology of theological language and iconic image" (CE, 62).

5. "The simple comprehension of the text — the function of the theologian — requires infinitely more than its reading, as informed as one would like; it requires access to the Word through the text. To read the text from the point of view of its writing: from the point of view of the Word. This requirement, as untenable as it may appear (and remains), cannot be avoided" (GWB, 149; DSL, 210).

6. Kraftson-Hogue considers Marion's writing on the gift and on the language of praise in a comparison with the theology of Augustine. He says: "To claim that it is possible for a reader to move beyond the text and to interpret from the point of view of the text's referent is certainly a radical claim. As Marion writes, it may even return the discussion of God without Being to another form of idolatry, the idolatry of the interpreter who reduces the referent to his or her own interpretive rationale." Mike Kraftson-Hogue, "Predication Turning to Praise: Marion and Augustine on God and Hermeneutics — (Giver, Giving, Gift, Giving)," *Literature and Theology* 14.4 (2000): 408.

7. See his more extensive analysis of this parable, discussed near the end of chapter 6.

8. Graham Ward, "The Theological Project of Jean-Luc Marion," in *Post-Secular Philosophy* (London: Routledge, 1998), 229–39. All references in the next paragraph refer to this article.

9. Ward finds this even more exacerbated in the somewhat later *Le croisée du visible*; Ward, "Theological Project," 230.

10. Peter-Ben Smit, "The Bishop and His/Her Eucharistic Community: A Critique of Jean-Luc Marion's Eucharistic Hermeneutic," *Modern Theology* 19.1 (2003). Further references in this paragraph are to this article.

11. John D. Caputo, "God Is Wholly Other — Almost: *Différance* and the Hyperbolic Alterity of God," in *The Otherness of God*, ed. Orrin F. Summerell (Charlottesville: University Press of Virginia, 1998), 190–205. All page references within this section refer to this article, unless indicated otherwise.

12. Caputo finds that in this text "the relationship with God is absolute, not relative, a paradoxical non-relative, perhaps even nonrelational relation, completely unconditioned by any horizon, unscreened by any human construct, absolutely unmediated by anything human, finite, idol-like. This is a very hard saying indeed; and, in the end, it asks too much" (194).

13. "Marion loves another discourse, a better, more iconic and less idolic one, but one that is no less a frame, screen, horizon, or textual condition" (195).

14. Caputo has made this claim about Marion's apparent "terrorism" and "violence" already in an earlier article dealing specifically with *God without Being*. ["How to Avoid Speaking of God: The Violence of Natural Theology," in E. Long, ed., *Prospects for Natural Theology* (Washington, D.C.: Catholic University of America Press, 1992), 128–50]. In this article he defines "the violence of the wholly or absolutely other" as a "violation of the human order by a kind of otherness or transcendence that just comes crashing in upon it." He calls this kind of thinking "a dangerous illusion" that "abandons philosophy, thinking, all responsibility" (129). He insists that "what we always get — it never fails — in the name of the Unmediated is someone's highly mediated Absolute:

their jealous Jahweh, their righteous Allah, their infallible church, their absolute Geist that inevitably speaks German" (130) (French, in this case). Caputo claims that Marion "wants a hermeneutic free of the limits of the hermeneutic situation, of hermeneutic conditioning. He wants a hermeneutics that is no hermeneutics at all, because the interpretation is not an interpretation but a kind of absolute deliverance that delivers us from the conflict of interpretation that arises if you admit that you really have a text on your hands" (145). Caputo concludes: "Now if onto-theo-logic is always also onto-theo-politics, if metaphysics always implies a metaphysical power structure, a seat and site of power and authority, if metaphysical binarity has always meant rigorous hierarchical distinctions and massive powers of exclusion, then Marion has done very little to overcome paganism and metaphysics in *Dieu sans L'être*. Indeed, I would say that he has done a great deal to reinstate it, that this theology of docile abandon to the Logos lends onto-theo-political power a helping hand in its most violent form" (147). Caputo's strong dislike of Marion's Roman Catholicism is evident throughout the article — for example, in speaking of the "immaculate conception" of Marion's discourse (150).

15. James K. A. Smith, "Liberating Religion from Theology: Marion and Heidegger on the Possibility of a Phenomenology of Religion," *International Journal for Philosophy of Religion* 46.1 (1999). Apart from the fact that Smith has recently changed his stance on this particular issue, it seems to be mostly the genre of Marion's examples to which he objects (especially their Roman Catholicism). In fact, some of the more philosophical critics of Marion may be motivated by a similar antipathy to Marion's specific allegiances rather than the fact of any religious commitments per se. When speaking of theology, it seems to me, Marion should be free to employ whatever tradition he wishes to explicate. Particular theological commitments do not necessarily jeopardize a *theological* project, but may in fact be necessary for its coherence.

16. Ibid., 23–24.

17. Ibid., 27–28.

18. As pointed out in note 15 above, Smith has come to concur with this judgment. In a presentation on Derrida, "Hope without Hope? A Phenomenological Critique of Derrida's 'Messianic' Expectation," at the AAR/SBL conference in Toronto, 23–26 November 2002, he criticizes Derrida for being too indeterminate and finds that thought about God must ultimately acknowledge some type of positive content. The only discomfort he expressed with Marion's project was in regard to its Roman Catholicism.

19. Kearney, *The God Who May Be: A Hermeneutics of Religion* (Bloomington: Indiana University Press, 2001), 6. All page references in the next paragraph refer to this work, unless indicated otherwise.

20. As noted above, Jean Greisch and Jean Grondin have also pointed to a lack of hermeneutics in Marion. Greisch, "L'herméneutique," 43–63; Grondin, "La tension de la donation ultime," 547–59.

21. Emphases are his.

22. John P. Manoussakis, "Thinking at the Limits: Jacques Derrida and Jean-Luc Marion in Dialogue with Richard Kearney," *Philosophy Today* 48.1 (Spring 2004): 16; reprinted in Richard Kearney, *Debates in Continental Philosophy: Conversations with Contemporary Thinkers* (New York: Fordham University Press, 2004), 21–22.

23. Kevin Hart interprets Marion's statement in a very similar fashion (CE, 26).

24. Manoussakis, "Thinking at the Limits," 23–24; Kearney, *Debates*, 29. Emphasis mine.

25. He spells this out the most carefully in his introduction to his English translation of Marion's *Idol and Distance:* Thomas A. Carlson, "Converting the Given into the Seen: Introductory Remarks on Theological and Phenomenological Vision" (ID, xi–xxxi).

26. "To free the absolute and unconditional (be it theology's God or phenomenology's phenomenon) from the various limits and preconditions of human thought and language (signaled especially by the thought and language of Being) will imply a thoroughgoing critique of all metaphysics, and above all of the modern metaphysics centered on the active, spontaneous subject who occupies modern philosophy from Descartes through Hegel and Nietzsche" (ID, xii).

27. "If it is true, then, that Marion's phenomenology is not, or does not intend to be, in any straightforward way a theology, it is also true that his theology and phenomenology inform one another more or otherwise than Marion himself might allow, for the former already operates in a quasiphenomenological manner, and the latter in fact accepts the understanding of revelation set out in the former (to the exclusion of other historically actual, and therefore possible, understandings of revelation)" (ID, xv).

28. "This concern to free the unconditional from any and all conditions that human thought might set upon its appearance, a concern central to Marion's theological project overall and to its core treatment of idol and icon specifically, defines also the starting point of his phenomenological work. Indeed, Marion's central phenomenological aim — to free phenomenality from the metaphysical preconditions set either by subjectivity (as with transcendental apperception in Kant) or by God (as with the principle of sufficient reason in Leibniz) — can be taken to mark a generalization of the specifically theological concern to free the appearance of the Christian God from idolatry" (ID, xviii).

29. "To a theological vision, 'everything' is given by God through the infinite kenosis of charity, just as to phenomenological vision, 'everything' without exception must obey the law of givenness (including nothing), since the given 'such as it gives itself' is finally 'without limit or reserve' (ED, 425). The reception of that gift, then, both theologically and phenomenologically, is a question of repetition and responsibility" (ID, xxvii).

30. E.g., "just as the phenomenon 'in its fullest sense' shows itself of itself and starting from itself, without precondition, even to the one who does not yet see it, so here in Marion's theology, God loves even those who do not love him, shows himself even to those who do not yet see him. And just as my will to see phenomenal givenness would itself be a function of that givenness itself, so here my eventual capacity to love and to see God would be given first and only by God's love for me. At this level the structure of Marion's phenomenological vision and the structure of his theological vision are strikingly similar, if not isomorphic: if I see the givenness of the phenomenon, which means if I give myself to it by repeating the act of giving, this is only because that givenness first gave me to myself and moved me to receive givenness in my very being; if I love God, which means if I give myself to him in the love that gives me to others, this is only because God first loved me even when I was not, and moved me to love in my very being" (ID, xxx–xxxi).

31. For example, DSL, 36, note 18, and 122, note 36; GWB, 202, note 21, and 217, note 65.

32. "The Impossible for Man — God," in John D. Caputo and Michael Scanlon, eds., *Transcendence and Beyond: A Postmodern Inquiry* (Bloomington: Indiana University Press, 2007), 17–43.

4. Descartes and God

1. DeHart, "Ambiguous Infinite," 95.

2. Marion quotes this text often. It is found in Descartes' letter to Mersenne written on 15 April 1630. The conclusion of the letter reads:

"Your question of theology is beyond my mental capacity, but it does not seem to me outside my province, since it has no concern with anything dependent on revelation, which is what I call theology in the strict sense; it is a metaphysical question which is to be examined by human reason. I think that all those to whom God has given the use of this reason have an obligation to employ it principally in the endeavour to know him and to know themselves. That is the task with which I began my studies; and I can say that I would not have been able to discover the foundations of physics if I had not looked for them along that road. It is the topic which I have studied more than any other and in which, thank God, I have not altogether wasted my time. At least I think that I have found how to prove metaphysical truths in a manner which is more evident than the proofs of geometry — in my opinion, that is: I do not know if I shall be able to convince others of it. During my first nine months in this country I plan to write something of the topic; but I do not think it opportune to do so before I have seen how my treatise on physics is received. But if the book which you mention was very well written and fell into my hands I might perhaps feel obliged to reply to it immediately, because if the report you heard is accurate, it says things which are very dangerous and, I believe, very false. However, in my treatise on physics I shall discuss a number of metaphysical topics and especially the following. *The mathematical truths which you call eternal have been laid down by God and depend on him entirely no less than the rest of his creatures. Indeed to say that these truths are independent of God is to talk of him as if he were Jupiter or Saturn and to subject him to the Styx and the Fates.* Please do no hesitate to assert and proclaim everywhere that it is God who has laid down these laws in nature just as a king lays down laws in his kingdom. There is no single one that we cannot grasp if our mind turns to consider it. They are all inborn in our minds just as a king would imprint his laws on the hearts of all his subjects if he had enough power to do so. The greatness of God, on the other hand, is something which we cannot grasp even though we know it. But the very fact that we judge it beyond our grasp makes us esteem it the more greatly; just as a king has more majesty when he is less familiarly known by his subjects, provided of course that they do not get the idea that they have no king — they must know him enough to be in no doubt about that. It will be said that if God had established these truths he could change them as a king changes his laws. To this the answer is: Yes he can, if his will can change. 'But I understand them to be eternal and unchangeable.' I make the same judgement about God. 'But his will is free.' — Yes, but his power is beyond our grasp. In general we can assert that God can do everything that is within our grasp but not that he cannot do what is beyond our grasp. It would be rash to think that our imagination reaches as far as his power. I hope to put this in writing, within the next fortnight, in my treatise on physics; but I do not want you to keep it secret. On the contrary I beg you to tell people as often as the occasion demands, provided you do not mention my name. I should be glad to know the objections which can be made against this view; and I want people to get used to speaking of God in a manner worthier, I think, than the common and almost universal way of imagining him as a finite being. With regard to infinity, you asked me a question in your letter of 14 March, which is the only thing I find in it which is not in the last letter. You said that if there were an infinite line it would have an infinite number of feet and of fathoms, and consequently that that the infinite number of feet would be six times as great as the number of fathoms. I agree entirely. 'Then this latter number is not infinite.' I deny the consequence. 'But one infinity cannot be greater than another.' Why not? Where is the absurdity? Especially if it is only greater by a finite ratio, as in this case, where multiplication by six is a finite ratio, which does not in any way affect the infinity. In any case, what basis have we for judging whether one infinity can be greater than another or not? It would no longer be infinity if we could grasp it. Continue to honour me by thinking kindly of me." CSMK III:22–23; AT I:144–47. Emphasis mine.

3. Marion's most careful outworking of Descartes' "theology" can be found in *Théologie blanche*. He summarizes a large part of his argument in a chapter entitled "The Idea of God," in *The Cambridge History of Seventeenth-Century Philosophy*, ed. Daniel Garber (New York: Cambridge University Press, 1998), 265–304, that was also included in *Cartesian Questions II* (QCII, 221–79). While Marion analyzes the first part of this quote in great detail in *Théologie blanche*, he deals with the second, more poetic, part of the statement in a later article entitled "Dieu, le Styx et les destinées" (QCII, 119–41).

4. The movement of univocity implies, first, that the eternal truths are independent of God. Marion claims that "the univocity of knowing constitutes the radical epistemological condition of the independence of the eternal truths" (TB, 69). This independence then leads to God's subjection to these truths.

5. In the article mentioned above, "Dieu, le Styx et les destinées" (QCII, 119–41).

6. I will skip the middle move. Suffice it to say in this context that although Bérulle admits, unlike Suarez, that the eternal truths might be dependent upon God in some fashion, he sees them as uncreated and suggests a doctrine of emanation or exemplarism in order to describe their relationship to God. This solution Descartes finds eminently unsatisfactory and contests directly (TB, 142). Bérulle establishes a kind of emanating relationship between God and creatures that Descartes conceives only between creatures. No such easy continuity can apply to God. God cannot be subject to essence or be its source in a simplistic fashion (TB, 146). For Bérulle, all this is connected to a theology of the Trinity. This is particularly evident in his exemplarism (TB, 150). Thus, although Bérulle and Descartes met repeatedly and Bérulle was his spiritual director for a time, Marion insists that there is no positive theological influence from one to the other (TB, 158).

7. For Suarez on the notion of analogy, see E. J. Ashworth, "Suárez on the Analogy of Being: Some Historical Background," *Vivarium* 33.1 (1995): 50–75; and Alain Guy, "L'analogie de l'être selon Suarez," *Archives de Philosophie* 42 (1979): 275–94. Guy especially sees the analogy of Being in Suarez as more complicated than Marion's analysis seems to indicate. While he admits that Suarez often uses the term "being" in univocal fashion and does indeed see it as applied more properly to creatures, he continues to maintain metaphysical analogy (instead of univocity).

8. Marion briefly points out several other options here: on the one hand Vasquez, for whom eternal truths are also created, but who still insists that God cannot change logic and thus erases divine distance and freedom; on the other hand Saint-Paul, Du-Pleix, and Goclenius, who see the eternal truths as somehow located in God but only in terms of exemplarism. For all thinkers in this context, the eternal truths are ultimately independent of God or God even submitted to them. Truths are determined autono-

mously; they are perfectly neutral and not affected by God. According to Marion, Descartes judges this — rightly so — as blasphemous because the intelligibility of eternal truths is no longer measured according to God's incomprehensibility but thought in terms of evidence and therefore made dependent upon human, not on divine, knowing. Truth becomes univocal, in that the same logical identity is imposed upon both God and creatures (TB, 69). The debate over the creation or the independence of eternal truths is therefore clearly linked to the debate over univocity.

9. The notion of substance is a special case that I will examine later.

10. Furthermore, Marion points out that Descartes and Kepler also read and probably even met each other and that Descartes' work on optics is influenced by many of Kepler's insights (TB, 196).

11. TB, 179.

12. TB, 181.

13. TB, 182.

14. TB, 194.

15. TB, 209–13.

16. TB, 213.

17. Marion suggests that this assertion played a significant role at Galileo's trial and ultimate condemnation: "Nevertheless, the boldness of such an equality between the human understanding and divine wisdom might well threaten the omnipotence of the creator; one presumes that this played some role in the accusations made against Galileo in his second trial" ("Idea of God," 269; QCII, 231). Galileo is actually condemned for assuming an equality between divine and human knowing and for being unable to establish any notion of divine omnipotence satisfactorily (TB, 218). Barberini and others perceive a contradiction between Galileo's insistence on the mathematical model of creation which subjects all rationality to its rules — a notion which played a large role in Galileo's *Dialogo* — and God's omnipotence. On pressure Galileo actually adds a clause to his preface that emphasizes God's omnipotence and the finitude of human knowing in order to eliminate the univocity that he has established. Marion claims that this trial is then actually an example of the crisis of analogy. What threatens Christian theology here is not "the strictly rational interpretation of the created world," but rather "the direct attribution of this interpretation to God himself" (TB, 220). The issue is not contesting whether Galileo is right about astronomy or even his Scriptural exegesis. Rather the issue is one of theology: his affirmation of univocity and denial of analogy.

18. TB, 216.

19. TB, 224.

20. TB, 225.

21. TB, 226.

22. I quoted extensively from the Letter to Mersenne of 15 April 1630 above. Two of the following letters are also significant.

On 6 May 1630, Descartes writes to Mersenne: "As for the eternal truths, I say once more that they are true or possible only because God knows them as true or possible. They are not known as true by God in any way which would imply that they are true independently of him. If men really understood the sense of their words they could never say without blasphemy that the truth of anything is prior to the knowledge which God has of it. In God willing and knowing are a single thing in such a way that by the very fact of willing something he knows it and it is only for this reason that such at thing is true. So we must not say that if God did not exist nevertheless these truths would be true; for the existence of God is the first and the most eternal of all possible truths and the one from which alone all others proceed. It is easy to be mistaken about this because most people do not regard God as a being who is infinite and beyond our grasp, the sole author on whom all things depend; they stick at the syllables of his name and think it sufficient knowledge of him to know that 'God' means what is meant by Deus in Latin and what is adored by men. Those who have no higher thoughts than these can easily become atheists; and because they perfectly comprehend mathematical truths and do not perfectly comprehend the truth of God's existence, it is no wonder they do not think the former depend on the latter. But they should rather take the opposite view, that since God is a cause whose power surpasses the bounds of human understanding, and since the necessity of these truths does not exceed our knowledge, these truths are therefore something less than, and subject to, the incomprehensible power of God. What you say about the production of the *Word* does not conflict, I think, with what I say; but I do not want to involve myself in theology, and I am already afraid that you will think my philosophy too free-thinking for daring to express an opinion on such lofty matters" (CSMK III:24–25; AT I:148–50).

On 27 May 1630 he writes: "You ask me by what kind of causality God established the eternal truths. I reply: by the same kind of causality as he created all things, that is to say, as their efficient and total cause. For it is certain that he is the author of the essence of created things no less than of their existence; and this essence is nothing other than the eternal truths. I do not conceive them as emanating from God like rays from the sun; but I know that God is the author of everything and that these truths are something and consequently he is their author. I say that I know this, not that I conceive it or grasp it; because it is possible to know that God is infinite and all powerful although our soul, being finite, cannot grasp or conceive him. In the same way we can touch a mountain with our hands but we cannot put our arms around it as we could put them around a tree or something else not too large for them. To grasp something is to embrace it in one's thought; to know something, it is sufficient to touch it with one's thought. You ask also what necessitated God to create these truths; and I reply that he was free to make it not true that all the radii of the circle are equal — just as free as he was not to create the world. And it is certain that these truths are no more necessarily attached to his essence than are other created things. You ask what God did in order to produce them. I reply that from all eternity he willed and understood them to be, and by that very fact he created them. Or, if you reserve the word created for the existence of things, then he established them and made them. In God, willing, understanding and creating are all the same thing without one being prior to the other even conceptually. As for the question whether it is in accord with the goodness of God to damn men for eternity, that is a theological question: so if you please you will allow me to say nothing about it. It is not that the arguments of free thinkers on this topic have any force, indeed they seem frivolous and ridiculous to me; but I think that when truths depend on faith and cannot be proved by natural argument, it degrades them if one tries to support them by human reasoning and mere probabilities" (CSMK III:25–26; AT I:151–54).

23. David J. Marshall, Jr., "Werke zu Descartes," review of Jean-Luc Marion, *Ontologie grise* and *Théologie blanche*, in *Philosophische Rundschau* 31 (1984): 134. Further page references in this paragraph are to this review. Marshall also argues that Marion's interpretation of the development of philosophical thinking is too limited and one-sided. If he had considered German Dominicans (Meister Eckhart, Tauler, Cusa-

nus, Luther, etc.) instead of merely English Franciscans Marion's review, his evaluation of the demise of analogy, and the importance of Descartes in this development would have been tempered. Overall Marshall objects particularly to the strong influence of Heidegger on Marion's Descartes interpretations.

24. TB, 109. Marion repeatedly points out how very often the two movements of increasing univocity and loss of a language of analogy correspond. He says of Galileo, for example, that "his response affirms univocity without ambiguity and neglects analogy without scruple" (TB, 221).

25. The various connotations of Marion's use of the term "blanche" really come out only in the French. I will therefore leave this citation in the original to capture Marion's use of terminology in this context: "Descartes déploie donc une théologie, pour satisfaire à l'instance théiologique de sa métaphysique, bref pour assurer un fondement à l'ontologie grise. Cette théologie, nous la qualifierons de théologie blanche. Blanche parce que anonyme et indéterminée, comme un blanc-seing, qui qualifie son bénéficaire sans spécifier pour quelle entreprise, ou comme un chèque en blanc, qui ne précise pas le montant du crédit que pourtant il accorde. La théologie de la métaphysique cartésienne reste blanche d'abord parce que son bénéficaire (ou son porteur) reste, finalement, anonyme" (TB, 450). He later indicates that the "whiteness" of Descartes' theology also stands for a kind of innocence. Descartes does not "quite know what he is doing" (TB, 453).

26. TB, 19.

27. For the doctrine of analogy in Aquinas, see Ralph McInerny's *The Logic of Analogy* (The Hague: Martinus Nijhoff, 1961) and *Aquinas and Analogy* (Washington, D.C.: The Catholic University of America Press, 1996); Philip Rolnick, *Analogical Possibilities: How Words Refer to God* (Atlanta: Scholars Press, 1993); and George Klubertanz, *St. Thomas Aquinas on Analogy: A Textual Analysis and Systematic Synthesis* (Chicago: Loyola University Press, 1960).

28. TB, 89.

29. TB, 90. Rolnick qualifies this slightly. He claims that "from the point of view of what the word means it is used primarily of God and derivatively of creatures, for what the word means — the perfection it signifies — flows from God to the creatures. But from the point of view of our use of the word we apply it first to creatures because we know them first. That . . . is why it has a way of signifying that is appropriate of creatures." *Analogical Possibilities*, 80 (§I.13.6). See also Wippel, *The Metaphysical Thought of Thomas Aquinas*, 74–93. One might suggest that Marion recovers the second move (from creatures to God) more strongly in his phenomenological work, where he describes our *experience* of revelation.

30. Marion links this to the notion of the series elaborated above. God can become inscribed in the series for Descartes while remaining outside of it as transcendent. There is thus both reference and distance.

31. Ralph McInerny especially chides Cajetan for his complete confusion of St. Thomas' doctrine of analogy. He remarks, for example, about Cajetan's explication of one of Thomas' most famous passages on analogy: "If some analogous names have feature X and other analogous names do not, feature X is accidental to their being analogous names. To underscore this point, Thomas notes that you can find the same variation *secundum esse* in univocal terms. In short, the objection is based on a fallacy, and the reply points out the fallacy and rejects the conclusion drawn. What Cajetan did was to take the distinctions introduced to make this point as if they were members

of a threefold division of analogous names. Missing the point of the reply, which is that different situations *secundum esse* are compatible with names being analogous, he built those accidental differences into 'types' of analogous name, a fateful move which continues to haunt Thomistic interpretation." *Aquinas and Analogy*, 11. He draws the following scathing conclusion: "It would perhaps be unkind to draw attention to the glaring weaknesses of Cajetan's *opusculum* [Cajetan's early treatise on the notion of analogy in Aquinas] if it had not held in thrall not only its author but also countless others throughout subsequent centuries. That it is a hopelessly confused account almost from its opening page is clear enough. We want to know what analogous names are, and we are told that they are of three kinds. It emerges that the first kind is not an analogous name at all and the second is so only abusively; and, when we turn to what an analogous name is in the proper sense, we are told that it comes in two kinds, metaphorical, that is, improper, and proper. What is a metaphor? A term is used metaphorically when it is used metaphorically. What then is proper proportionality? When the common term is said non-metaphorically of its analogates, that is, then it is said of them proportionally. That is what we have learned after looking carefully at twenty percent of Cajetan's *opusculum*, and what we have learned is nothing" (ibid., 23–24).

32. TB, 94.

33. Ibid.

34. On Suarez and analogy see the articles mentioned above. Another very detailed analysis is provided by John P. Doyle, "Suarez on the Analogy of Being," *Modern Schoolman* 46 (1969): 219–49, 323–41.

35. TB, 76.

36. TB, 77.

37. TB, 96.

38. TB, 100.

39. TB, 103.

40. A summary of this argument may be found in his article "The Essential Incoherence of Descartes' Definition of Divinity" in *Essays on Descartes' Meditations*, ed. Amélie Rorty (Berkeley: University of California Press, 1986): 297–338.

41. Since the context here is that of the "doubled onto-theo-logy," thus of Descartes' fullest metaphysical articulation, Marion's explication relies almost entirely on an analysis of the *Meditations*. As we have seen above, he argues that the proofs for God's existence and the related metaphysical proposal are not yet fully developed in the *Discourse on Method*. David Tracy points out that "before Marion's groundbreaking work on Descartes, there was a virtual ignoring of Descartes' *Third Meditation* and its recognition that the category of the Infinite is ontologically prior to the category 'finite' and thus breaks all our finite categories and disallows the univocity and 'common being' that Descartes elsewhere . . . employed in the *Meditations*" (CE, 59).

42. Marion summarizes Dionysius' theology of the divine names most succinctly in the last chapter of his work *In Excess* (DS, 155–74; IE, 128–45). A longer explication enters into both *God without Being* and especially the third part of *Idol and Distance*.

43. For a closer analysis of the terminology of substance in Descartes, see chapter 7, on the ego.

44. Wolfgang Röd, review of *Sur le prisme métaphysique*, 230.

45. MP, 237; PM, 250.

46. MP, 240; PM, 253.

47. MP, 242; PM, 255.

48. Kenneth P. Winkler, "Descartes and the Names of God," *American Catholic Philosophical Quarterly* 67.4 (1993): 451–66.

49. Philip Clayton, "Descartes and Infinite Perfection," *Proceedings of the American Catholic Philosophical Association* 66 (1992): 143.

50. Prouvost, "Tension irrésolue," 101.

51. Röd, review of *Sur le prisme métaphysique*, 230.

52. See the more detailed analysis of the *causa sui* in QCII, 143–82.

53. In his article "The Idea of God," however, he compares the second definition (in terms of perfection) to the affirmative way and the *causa sui* to the way of eminence (276–78). Specker also points to this inconsistency and argues that it shows the inherent ambivalence of the idea of infinity (AGD, 234–35).

54. Jean-Marc Narbonne, "Plotin, Descartes, et la notion de *causa sui*," *Archives de Philosophie* 56 (1993): 180.

55. QCII, 148f.

56. QCII, 150.

57. Ibid.

58. QCII, 151–53.

59. QCII, 154–55.

60. QCII, 157–59.

61. QCII, 167–69.

62. QCII, 171.

63. QCII, 178.

64. QCII, 181. This contention also lies at the heart of Marion's article on Aquinas where he revises his earlier position in *God without Being* (that Aquinas is implicated in onto-theo-logy by making the name of "being" superior to that of the good) by arguing that Aquinas escapes onto-theo-logy because he does not claim to have full knowledge of the divine and because he rejects the concept of *causa sui*. See DSL, 279–332.

65. TB, 428.

66. TB, 429–30.

67. TB, 432.

68. MP, 244; PM, 257.

69. MP, 267–68; PM, 281–82.

70. Marion spells out in detail how Descartes' followers show the tension in his conceptions of God: Louis de la Forge takes up all three definitions while Johann Clauberg reviews them and then eliminates their complexity in favor of a simple perfection and causality. Dom Robert Desgabets simply reproduces Descartes but does not reconcile the names, nor does Spinoza add anything new. For Nicolas Malebranche God is primarily defined as being, and infinity becomes a mere attribute of perfection. Leibniz embraces Malebranche's duality and divides it into two causalities: two distinct conceptions of divine essence which ground two great principles (non-contradiction — God's perfection and sufficient reason — and causality): Leibniz "offers a justification for this duality in terms of the irreducible duality of the principles of metaphysics; neither the exclusively metaphysical status of the divine names nor their submission to metaphysics ever appeared so clearly" ("Idea of God," 283; QCII, 260–61). Others also define the divine essence in terms of causality. Marion claims that Thomas Hobbes, for example, has no conception of God's essence at all: "By reducing natural theology to causality and by sacrificing infinity (and even perfection), Hobbes opens a wide path that many

will follow. But in this way he exposes metaphysical discourse on God to the danger of collapse, when Hume undermines causality itself" ("Idea of God," 285; QCII, 265). Marion goes on to speak of John Locke, Henry More, Ralph Cudsworth, and Isaac Newton in similar fashion ("Idea of God," 286–89; QCII, 267–74). He considers the most problematic that "after Descartes (and Duns Scotus), infinity is not found among the central notions that make up the idea of the divine essence. This demotion can be compared to the parallel and contemporary abandonment of the doctrine of the creation of the eternal truths" ("Idea of God," 292; QCII, 276).

71. Röd, review of *Sur le prisme métaphysique*, 231.

72. Marion will take this up in an examination of the terminology of *capax/capable* in Descartes' work which I will examine in chapter 7.

73. "Pascal does not reproach Descartes for ignoring God, but for knowing him only for the purpose of using him to regulate the machine of the world, far from submitting to him . . . What makes Descartes useless — for salvation — is that he puts God at the service of knowing, instead of knowing God in order to put himself at his service" (MP, 298; PM, 316).

74. Furthermore, according to Marion, Pascal makes it clear in his analysis of charity that theology and metaphysics or philosophy must remain distinct. None of Pascal's followers recognizes this. Marion even suggests that Pascal and Kierkegaard are ignored by the tradition of philosophy, precisely because they already get beyond metaphysics and onto-theo-logy by disqualifying them (MP, 336; PM, 359).

75. He also remarked to me in personal conversation that he was hesitant to continue employing such metaphysically loaded language. My argument about a recovery of the notion of analogy in his work obviously refers only to his particular definition and interpretation of it and not to the entire (metaphysical) heritage of the doctrine.

5. Theology and God

1. Ruud Welten, "The Paradox of God's Appearance: On Jean-Luc Marion," in *God in France: Eight Contemporary French Thinkers on God*, ed. Peter Jonkers and Ruud Welten (Leuven: Peeters, 2005), 188–89.

2. Steven Grimwood compares Marion's analysis of icon and idol to Baudrillard's notion of the simulacrum and observes important parallels between simulacrum and idol (although he seems to collapse icon and idol into each other, describing even God as a mere simulacrum). Relying on Ward's (rather tendentious) summary of Marion, he suggests that the idol is life-denying and thus cannot present a "lower-water mark of iconicity," as Marion says without jeopardizing his analysis significantly. Although his comparison to Baudrillard is interesting and enlightening regarding the idol (less so the icon), he disregards Marion's important reflections on the idol in *The Crossing of the Visible* and his criticism therefore remains necessarily incomplete. He goes on to give an analysis of space and time in terms of both Orthodox liturgy and postmodern architecture, although it is somewhat unclear how he sees his analysis relating to his criticism of Marion. He claims that "The insistence that any consideration of iconography should allow for the subject to 'speak' at once distances it from Marion, for in *God without Being* such a subject is curiously absent. At first, this seems almost paradoxical, because in Marion's scheme it is the 'gaze' which determines iconicity, and where there is a gaze there must be an observer. Marion, however, considers the gaze without any consideration of the gazer or his context; furthermore, in the case of the icon, the

gaze of the viewer is actually overwhelmed by the intention of the gaze of the icon itself (which summons the viewer's gaze towards the invisible)." Steven Grimwood, "Iconography and Postmodernity," *Literature and Theology* 17.1 (2003): 88.

3. See also Victor Kal's summary of the distinctions between idol and icon in Marion ("Unable to Speak," 157ff.).

4. Welten, *God in France*, 192.

5. Ibid., 194.

6. In a review of *God without Being*, Charles Lock remarks that "on the icon Marion writes, as elsewhere, in full if obliquely acknowledged awareness of Orthodox theology." "Against Being: An Introduction to the Thought of Jean-Luc Marion," *St. Vladimir's Theological Quarterly* 37.4 (1993): 373.

7. Welten, *God in France*, 193.

8. Stijn van den Bossche, "God Does Appear in Immanence after All: Jean-Luc Marion's Phenomenology as a New First Philosophy for Theology," in *Sacramental Presence in a Postmodern Context*, ed. L. Boeve and L. Leijssen (Leuven: Leuven University Press, 2001), 326. All page numbers in the next paragraph refer to this article, unless indicated otherwise. The article had its origin as "God verschijnt toch in de immanentie. De fenomenologische neerlegging van de theologie in Jean-Luc Marions *Étant donné*," in GD, 128–53.

9. To "carry further" is here not meant in a temporal sense, since *Idol and Distance* (where the terminology of distance is most prominent) was published before *God without Being* and the *Crossing of the Visible* (where the terminology of the icon is more prominent). In all cases, the terminology of distance and icon are closely related and often employed together. I should also emphasize again that Marion himself does not employ the terminology of analogy in the context of his analysis of distance. Others have pointed primarily to Marion's criticism of analogy (see for example Fergus Kerr's article that is primarily concerned with Marion's critique of Aquinas). He says of Marion: "With a deep-seated suspicion of the very idea of analogy, apparently, which Aquinas would not have shared, he seems to back away, in the preface, from accusing him of turning the God of self-giving love into the metaphysical idol of the Supreme Being" ("Aquinas after Marion," 363). I do not think that this negative interpretation can be sustained after a careful reading of *Théologie blanche*, where Marion clearly deplores the demise of the doctrines of analogy (if they are rightly interpreted). See the section of chapter 4 above outlining this move.

10. See chapter 2 for a more detailed analysis of Marion's critique of these thinkers on this particular issue.

11. He explains, "Thus one could speak of an asymmetry of distance: its definition concerns two poles, or better, it gives rise and guarantees them. But this definition is stated only on the basis of one of the two poles — our own, which is humanly defined. The separation that unites will therefore affect the other term with a lack of definition all the more insofar as, precisely, that lack of definition properly qualifies, within distance, the intimate alterity of the terms" (ID, 199; IeD, 249).

12. Bloechl, "Dialectical Approaches," 295.

13. Ibid.

14. Ibid., 297.

15. For a closer analysis of Marion's view of the performative use of language in *Idol and Distance*, see Kal, "Unable to Speak," 161. Marion's analysis of the discourse of praise in Dionysius is reproduced in a very similar fashion in his response to Derrida's

"negative theology" in his later phenomenological work (DS, 171–74; IE, 142–45). Again one may wonder what this extreme similarity of his theological and phenomenological use of "praise" may indicate. James Smith evaluates especially the later analysis in "Between Predication and Silence."

16. While this is the way in which Marion usually describes the two ways, Dionysius seems to see the apophatic way primarily as a denial of names that are quite apparently false. Most of his examples refer to inappropriate imagery for God or extreme anthropomorphisms.

17. Marion seems to be thinking of such Dionysian statements as the following from the treatise on *The Divine Names:* "Nor can any words come up to the inexpressible Good, this One, this Source of all unity, this supra-existent Being. Mind beyond mind, word beyond speech, it is gathered up by no discourse, by no intuition, by no name. It is and it is as no other being is. Cause of all existence, and therefore itself transcending existence, it alone could give an authoritative account of what it really is" (*Divine Names,* 50). Later Dionysius maintains that "what happens is this. We use whatever appropriate symbols we can for the things of God. With these analogies we are raised upward toward the truth of the mind's vision, a truth which is simple and one. We leave behind us all our own notions of the divine. We call a halt to the activities of the mind and, to the extent that is proper, we approach the ray which transcends being. Here, in a manner no words can describe, preexisted all the goals of all knowledge and it is of a kind that neither intelligence nor speech can lay hold of it nor can it at all be contemplated since it surpasses everything and is wholly beyond our capacity to know it. Transcendently it contains within itself the boundaries of every natural knowledge and energy. At the same time it is established by an unlimited power beyond all the celestial minds. And if all knowledge is of that which is and is limited to the realm of the existent, then whatever transcends being must also transcend knowledge" (*Divine Names,* 53). Marion affirms that for Dionysius the good is more important than being, as is obvious both in his organization, which posits the good as a higher and better name for God than being, and in such passages as the following: "Given that the Good transcends everything, as indeed it does, its nature, unconfined by form, is the creator of all forms. In it is nonbeing really an excess of being. It is not *a* life, but is, rather, superabundant Life. It is not *a* mind, but is superabundant Wisdom. Whatever partakes of the Good partakes of what preeminently gives form to the formless. And one might even say that nonbeing itself longs for the Good which is above all being. Repelling being, it struggles to find rest in the Good which transcends all being, in the sense of a denial of all things" (*Divine Names,* 73). All references are to Pseudo-Dionysius, *The Complete Works,* trans. Colm Luibheid, in *The Classics of Western Spirituality* (New York: Paulist Press, 1987).

18. ID, 142; IeD, 180.

19. Dionysius himself claims of this process, in particular of the result of its *apophatic* stage: "But my argument now rises from what is below up to the transcendent, and the more it climbs, the more language falters, and when it has passed up and beyond the ascent, it will turn silent completely, since it will finally be at one with him who is indescribable" (*Mystical Theology,* 139).

20. Kal, "Unable to Speak," 162.

21. ID, 153; IeD, 192.

22. Guarino, "Fundamental Theological Issues," 659.

23. Ibid., 677.

24. Guarino concludes in a similar vein: "Jean-Luc Marion, with his concern for the conceptual reification and idolic tendencies within the tradition, invites us to examine carefully our linguistic usage. He offers a salutary warning that deserves repeating: To write theology is to deal with the Other, not the same. Theology has a natural congruency with postmodern anxiety about naively referential semiotic systems. Willingly it speaks of the 'deferring' character of theological signs and the 'undecideability' of language. At the same time, only a qualified appropriation of postmodern thought on the nature and function of signifiers seems called for. Marion minimizes the extent to which the tradition has already understood and defended the surplus of intelligibility proper to the Godhead, while still preserving a positive moment within revelation. Must language be completely nonobjectifying to protect God's otherness?" Ibid., 679–80.

25. Gerald McKenny criticizes this conception of love as a type of knowledge by insisting that love should be a "deed" instead and must be expressed in ethical action (CE, 351–52). While Marion certainly does not place much emphasis on the ethical dimension, it is not true that there is no action involved in love. Rather this "knowledge" of the will is a practical kind of knowing that precisely moves us to loving action, as his analysis of kenotic giving indicates.

26. This new dimension actually has been suggested already by Hans Urs von Balthasar, by whom Marion is deeply influenced, who distinguishes between four orders or differences "of the miracle of being" (referring, among others, to Heidegger). Marion seems to follow him repeatedly in these distinctions. See, for example, Hans Urs von Balthasar, *Im Raum der Metaphysik*, vol. 3.1 of *Herrlichkeit: Eine Theologische Ästhetik* (Einsiedeln: Johannes Verlag, 1965), 843–957. See the interview in *Ruf und Gabe*, 35–39, and Horner's account (MTI, 4, 51–53) for further information on this influence.

27. ID, 234–38; IeD, 284–88.

28. ID, 248, 250; IeD, 297, 299.

29. For criticisms of this contention see the discussion below.

30. GWB, 135; DSL, 193–94.

31. GWB, 137; DSL, 194.

32. Kurt Wolf, *Religionsphilosophie in Frankreich: Der 'ganz Andere' und die personale Struktur der Welt* (München: Wilhelm Fink Verlag, 1999), 156–57.

33. Provoust, "Tension," 101.

34. Jean-Yves Lacoste, "Penser à Dieu en l'aimant: Philosophie et théologie de J.-L. Marion," *Archives de Philosophie* 50 (1987): 245–70.

35. Ibid., 267.

36. Ibid., 270.

37. Bradley, "God *sans* Being," 302.

38. E.g., ID, 71; IeD, 90.

39. ID, 172; IeD, 211.

40. Marion also emphasizes the dichotomy of God's absence and presence in an article on the ascension. Throughout the article he plays on the dual meaning of "present" as designating both presence and gift. "The Gift of a Presence," PC, 124–52; PaC, 147–78.

41. "Because, as opposed to the concept that, by the very definition of apprehension, gathers what it comprehends, and, because of this, almost inevitably comes to completion in an idol, love (even and especially if it ends up causing thought, giving rise — by its excess — to thought) does not pretend to comprehend, since it does not

mean at all to take; it postulates its own giving, giving where the giver strictly coincides with the gift, without any restriction, reservation, or mastery. Thus love gives itself only in abandoning itself, ceaselessly transgressing the limits of its own gift, so as to be transplanted outside of itself" (GWB, 48; DSL, 75).

42. Marion plays out the counterpart to this argument in his analysis of evil in *Prolegomena to Charity*. Here he also suggests that only by loving can we become persons. Hatred, including self-hatred all the way to suicide, or indifference dissolve who we are because they separate us from others. He describes hell as the impossibility of further relationship. To be cut off from all others, betrayed to the point of self-loss, is to stop being human. "Evil aims only to universalize what its reality — on the extreme fringe of nothingness — amounts to: a person bereft of all personality, an eternal absence inhabited only by this minimum of consciousness, which allows him to hate his inexistence" (PC, 29; PaC, 41). In order to defeat evil, one must become a person. It appears from this that even personhood is dependent upon love of other people.

43. GWB, 197; DSL, 276–77.

44. He does so in the first chapter, "Evil in Person" (PC, 1–30; PaC, 13–42).

45. Marion plays throughout the article on this dual meaning of *"faire mal,"* which designates both being in pain and inflicting pain.

46. "The severity of evil consists, precisely, in the way in which it imposes its logic on us as though it were the only logic feasible: our first effort at deliverance retains evil as its sole horizon. Counter-evil remains an evil, just as a backfire is still a fire — destructive, first and always" (PC, 5; PaC, 17).

47. "In its logic, then, evil in no way forbids what we so often call the search for justice. Rather, it sets out to give the search for justice a rigorous conceptual status and the means to develop itself. Thus the worst thing about evil is perhaps not the suffering, nor even the innocent suffering, but rather that revenge appears to be its only remedy; the worst thing about evil [*le mal*] is not, in a sense, the hurt [*le mal*], but the logic of revenge that triumphs even in the (apparent) reestablishment of justice, in the (temporary) cessation of suffering, in the (unstable) balance of injustices" (PC, 7–8; PaC, 20).

48. PC, 9; PaC, 21.

49. One may wonder how this explication squares with Marion's admiration for and use of Nietzsche. I have been unable to find any reference in Marion to Nietzsche's scathing denunciation (e.g., in the second essay, "'Guilt,' 'Bad Conscience,' and the Like," of his *Genealogy of Morals*) of the Christian view of the atonement in which God suffers in place of the sinner.

50. CV, 131; CoV, 73.

51. Marion calls this "the agony of the invisible holiness in the horror of the visible sin" (CV, 149; CoV, 84).

52. "The Impossible for Man — God," in Caputo and Scanlon, *Transcendence — and Beyond*, 17–43. All page numbers within the next couple of paragraphs refer to this text, unless indicated otherwise.

53. "Only God has the power, precisely, to forgive, because only love is able to forgive and has the right to do so. . . . Man cannot forgive because he has neither the power to forgive (in his heart, he remains a murderer) nor the right to forgive (every sin is ultimately against God). Evil remains imprescribable for man, who is powerless to forgive it and therefore must recognize himself to be its prisoner . . . it is impossible in principle for man to forgive or even to ask for forgiveness, and that on the contrary this is possible only with God, as the prerogative of his radical transcendence. Only God has

the power to forgive sins — which is to say the sins that all of us (who alone sin) commit in the final analysis against God (even when we inflict them first on other human beings). The impossible for man has the name God, but God as such — as the one who alone forgives the trespasses made against him" (37–38).

54. Kraftson-Hogue, "Predication Turning to Praise," 410.

55. See his article "They Recognized Him; and He Became Invisible to Them," *Modern Theology* 18.2 (2002): 145–52, where Marion argues that "precisely that very evening, in which he [Christ] is again eating it [the Passover/Eucharist], is already part of the Kingdom of God fulfilled in spirit and truth" (150).

56. "They Recognized Him," 150–52.

57. Ibid.

58. As we have seen, Marion repeatedly emphasizes his faithfulness to the traditional theological message and rejects the idea of any "innovation" in theology (GWB, 156–58; DSL, 218–22). Theology, in fact, must be exercised within a strict ecclesial hierarchy and in obedience to one's bishop (GWB, 149–56; DSL, 210–18). See the opening section of this part.

6. Phenomenology and God

1. Gabellieri points out, interestingly enough, that Marion by dividing theology and phenomenology so clearly in terms of actuality and possibility in fact introduces limits and boundaries, although he emphasizes so strongly that his phenomenology is without boundaries or limits. Gabellieri, "Métaphysique," 641.

2. Particularly in *Sauf le Nom* (Paris: Éditions Galilée, 1993) and "How to Avoid Speaking: Denials," in *Derrida and Negative Theology*, ed. Harold Coward and Toby Foshay (Albany: SUNY Press, 1992), 73–142.

3. He spells this argument out in more detail in his recent article "The Unspoken: Apophasis and the Discourse of Love," *Proceedings of the American Catholic Philosophical Association* 76 (2003): 39–56, reworked as "Ce qui ne se dit pas — l'apophase du discours amoureux," in VR, 119–42.

4. *Ruf und Gabe*, 41.

5. ED, 328; BG, 236.

6. ED, 329ff.; BG, 236ff. John Caputo recently deplored Marion's use of this particular example. "Hyperbolization of Phenomenology," 78, 81.

7. Welten, *God in France*, 202. Emphasis his.

8. Ibid., 206. He spells this out even more fully in his work *Fenomenologie en beeldverbod*, where he argues (in conclusion) for a "radical difference" between Marion's notions of the (theological) actuality of Revelation and the (phenomenological) possibility of revelation. Welten speaks of Marion's work as a "theo-phenomenology" that is able to examine the special status of the unique phenomenality of "religious experience." See Welten, *Fenomenologie*, 209.

9. For example, ED, 329; BG, 367; and "Metaphysics and Phenomenology," 590–91. See also Tanner's criticism of this that I explicated above (CE, 201–231).

10. This analysis appears in the final chapter of *In Excess*: "In the Name: How to Avoid Speaking of it" (DS, 155–95; IE, 128–62). It is a revision of his earlier paper at the Villanova conference (GGP, 20–53).

11. DS, 162; IE, 134.

12. Caputo objects to Marion's use of this word (or rather finds it very appropriate

in light of his own criticism) because in English it refers to a confessional denomination and also has a monetary meaning. He points out: "Hence to say in English that mystical theology deals in 'denomination' would implicate it in economics and currency, in good investments and bad, and also implicate it in various confessional, denominational conflicts, in religious communions and excommunications, the wars, figurative and literal, among what Derrida calls the concrete messianisms" (GGP, 190). I will examine Caputo's criticism of Marion in more detail later.

13. More recently, Marion has qualified this as a "perlocutionary act," accomplishing something similar to the statement "I love you!" "The Unspoken," 49–54.

14. Martin Laird, "'Whereof We Speak': Gregory of Nyssa, Jean-Luc Marion and the Current Apophatic Rage," *Heythrop Journal* 42 (2001): 9.

15. Marion briefly takes up this reflection on the divine names in his most recent work on the erotic phenomenon. He suggests that the language of love must use the vocabulary of mystical theology because it becomes performative and not predicative (PE, 232–34; EP, 149–50).

16. By extension, Derrida's critique of mystical theology is false. Bradley concedes that if "Marion is right to claim that 'without being' carries a negative sense and means 'otherwise than being,' then it follows that—contra Derrida—negative theology exceeds the orbit of presence. And, upon this interpretation, negative theology begins to look more like a subject, rather than an object of deconstruction." He goes on to argue, however, that neither Marion's nor Derrida's interpretations of Dionysius' term *hyperousious* is correct, but that instead it implies an essential ambiguity that cannot be limited to either purely positive or negative connotations. Bradley, "God *sans* Being," 306. Stapleton speaks of both Marion's and Derrida's critiques of the other as "absurd" and superficial. He asks: "Might one reason for Marion's rash critique of Derrida be that he has not recognized the performative aspect of language at play, at work, because he only knows how to characterize the third way by what it is and is not, falling back, however much he may want to, on the old metaphysical divisions of true and false?" ("Derrida-Marion Debate," 13). He finds that the "thesis that prayer and praise speak to God, as opposed to speaking about or of God, is problematic" because it still implies things about God (at very minimum his existence). He explains Marion's response to this through his use of God's "hyper-name," which "inscribes God's adherents within the name, and accordingly, names them, speaking new existence into them. From this new perspective, prayer and praise do not so much speak *to* God, as they speak *from* God" (Ibid., 14).

17. DS, 195; IE, 161f.

18. Caputo and Scanlon, *Transcendence and Beyond*, 17–43. All references in this section refer to that article, unless indicated otherwise.

19. "Thus the two chief meanings of transcendence in philosophy, different as they are, share a common feature: Neither one transcends the horizon of entity, much less the horizon of being. Transcendence, in philosophy, even and especially the transcendence that we would like to assign to God as his proper mark, is defined as what does not rise beyond being—into which it runs, instead, head on, as the ultimate transcendental" (19).

20. "This twofold impossibility of entering intuition rests neither on any doctrinal preference nor on any arbitrary negativity, but results from the unavoidable requirements of the simple possibility of something like God. The most speculative theology agrees with the most unilateral atheism to postulate that, in God's case, all formal con-

ditions of intuition must be transgressed: if intuition implies space and time, then there can never be any intuition of God because of the even more radical requirement that there must not be any intuition if God is ever to be considered" (21).

21. "Incomprehensibility, which in every other case attests either to the weakness of my knowledge or to the insufficiency of what is to be known, ranks, here and here only, as an epistemologic requirement imposed by that which must be thought — the infinite, the unconditioned, and therefore the inconceivable" (22).

22. See the discussion of this (more explicitly theological) part of the article at the end of chapter 5.

23. Caputo claims that for Marion intention is always larger than intuition, except in the sole case of God, where intuition overflows in intention (obviously such a claim cannot hold in light of *Being Given* and *In Excess*, which clearly argue this reversal for many other phenomena besides God). Caputo pursues this claim (regarding Marion's emphasis on overflowing intuition) in greater detail in his recent paper mentioned above ("Hyperbolization of Phenomenology," CE, 67–93).

24. Against Marion, Caputo claims that Derrida's deconstruction is not atheistic, but is a certain way of acting or thinking about things which emphasizes contingency and which "is through and through a messianic affirmation of the coming of the impossible" (GGP, 197). While Marion seems to advocate a Messiah *"already given, a figure of transfiguring glory, the icon of the invisible God, an impossible gift of God,"* Derrida sees a "darker figure of a Messiah still to come, unimaginable, unprefigurable, who is *never to be given"* (GGP, 186). Because this Messiah never appears and cannot be identified, Derrida is said to generalize the content of religion in a way that is no longer determined by any particular religion or God. "What Derrida tries to do in *Sauf le nom* is to examine what that means and what significance mystical theology holds for everyone, even if one is not a card-carrying, service-attending member of one of the religions of the Book. What is the *general import* even if one has not seen the inside of a church or synagogue or temple since childhood?" (GGP, 198). Therefore "Derrida is not a learned despiser of religion but a lover of a religion without religion" (GGP, 198). This religion without religion refers to a religion "which is informed by the general and translatable structure of the religious without taking up the determinate content of any of the specific religious translations or 'denominations.' . . . Derrida's religion, then, is very un-denominational, by keeping a safe distance not only between itself and any of the concrete messianisms (Christian, Jewish, Islamic) of the religions of the book, but also between itself and any monetary denominations, that is, economies — whereas Marion is interested in a very Christian economy" (GGP, 198). Derrida only employs the general and abstract structure of religion, but never determines its content in any way. The name of God cannot be translated, for Derrida, and its ambiguity can never be resolved. "For Marion the signifier 'God' is flooded by givenness [which Caputo calls a "narrow sense of conceptual presentation"]; for Derrida it is a dry and desert aspiration for I know not what" (GGP, 199). For Derrida, the name of God designates that which structurally cannot come, is always to come, never given, an unadulterated promise or hope that always remains in the future. The Messiah is reduced to a pure idea of hope, never refers to anything actual. According to Caputo, "for Derrida, the 'presence of God' does not mean, on the one hand, either God's historical givenness made flesh in a man or God's mystical givenness beyond intention in the soul, but neither does it mean, on the other hand, a cold and heartless atheism" (GGP, 199). While

this atheism may be neither "cold" nor "heartless," it is not entirely clear in what way it might be "warm" or have "heart," since it can never receive any content.

25. Caputo, "Wholly Other," 196.

26. "Hence, in the guiding thread of the saturated phenomenon, phenomenology finds its ultimate possibility: not only the possibility that surpasses actuality, but the possibility that surpasses the very conditions of possibility, the possibility of unconditioned possibility—in other words, the possibility of the impossible, the saturated phenomenon" ("Wholly Other," 197).

27. "The impossible is given in the conflict with the conditions, in the disagreement, and so on the margins between ordinary possibility and the absolutely impossible or absolutely unconditioned. The impossible is possible under the condition of the conditions of possibility that it stresses and strains to the limit" ("Wholly Other," 198).

28. "Is not the transgressive phenomenon that Marion seeks to salvage from metaphysics possible only under the condition of the very form of transgressiveness, the amorphous form, of différance itself? Is not différance a different sort of condition, namely, a condition that allows for escape, a possibility that is interested in the im/possible, and hence a certain condition of impossibility? Does it not turn out that the saturated phenomenon—the impossible—is possible only under the condition of im/possibility called différance? Is it then not better to say that différance is not idolatry, not even a higher and more subtle one, but an open-endedness that makes it possible for divergent, exotic, overcharged phenomena, or quasi-phenomena, to slip free of the normalizing, regulating conditions imposed by the multiple varieties of normalization under which we labor, be they social, intellectual, or religious?" ("Wholly Other," 200).

29. "Wholly Other," 201.

30. Caputo insists that he "finds it necessary to deny the saturated phenomenon in order to make room for faith; and if not exactly to deny, then at least to displace it, to expose it to a certain undecidability and an other saturation. . . . The believer believes, that is, construes dark shadows, reads traces, hopes without seeing, trusts in an operation that is *no less* a poverty of intuition than a surfeit of intuition, *no less* a desert aridity than an intuitive flood, *no less* a dark night than a bedazzling light" (ibid., 203; emphasis his).

31. Ibid., 204.

32. John Caputo, "Marion's Line," presentation to the Society for Phenomenology and Existential Philosophy, Philadelphia, October 2006. I want to thank Dr. Caputo for sending a copy of his presentation to me after the conference.

33. Eric Boynton, "Enigmatic Sites and Continental Philosophy of Religion: Must Philosophy Once Again Yield to Theology?" in *Explorations in Contemporary Continental Philosophy of Religion*, ed. Deane-Peter Baker and Patrick Maxwell (New York: Rodopi, 2003), 50–51.

34. Ibid., 62.

35. Marlène Zarader, "Phenomenality and Transcendence," in *Transcendence in Philosophy and Religion*, ed. James Faulconer (Bloomington: Indiana University Press, 2003), 106.

36. Ibid., 109.

37. Ibid., 117.

38. Thomas A. Carlson, "The Naming of God and the Possibility of Impossibility:

Marion and Derrida between the Theology and Phenomenology of the Gift," in *Indiscretion: Finitude and the Naming of God* (Chicago: University of Chicago Press, 1999), 190–236. All page references within the next few paragraphs refer to this work, unless indicated otherwise.

39. He points out that "the relation between theology and philosophy becomes a question here precisely because, on the one hand, Marion wants to make claims about the gift as such, or the 'very essence of language' as gift, while, on the other hand, he makes those claims by speaking more specifically about the gift of God in Christ and by using the language of a determinate theological tradition issuing from that gift. Perhaps recognizing the difficulties of thinking givenness as such, in its unconditional character, in and through a determinate tradition with determinate content, Marion will later seek to advance his thought on givenness by means of a phenomenology that would be free of all such determinations. This second approach, however, is not without its own ambiguities, for just as Marion's theology seeks already to be phenomenological, so his later phenomenology . . . continues to bear traces of his theology" (202–203).

40. Carlson finds that "the separation between phenomenology and theology in Marion is not absolute and the distinction not entirely stable: while seeking to think givenness — and even revelation — in purely phenomenological terms, Marion will still seem to draw on the thought of givenness and revelation that are given first in his theology. Likewise, conversely, his theology of the gift can often seem already to be drawing on a phenomenology that extends beyond the limits of theology" (208).

41. "In sum, the God of phenomenology gives without reserve, in an excess so extreme that that God is present only as absent, to the point of remaining unavailable. But at precisely this point, the question becomes unavoidable: how should we understand the relation between, on the one hand, a God who appears historically, is really experienced and supports (or is supported by) a community and a tradition, and, on the other hand, a God who, in the unconditional givenness that Marion so rigorously defines, does not appear and remains radically unavailable? Are real experience, historicity, community, and tradition actually compatible with such an unconditional givenness? Or, on the contrary, might experience, history, community, or tradition contradict the very definition of the unconditional as unforeseeable, nonrepresentable, and nonrepeatable?" (212–13).

42. Carlson asks about a double bind in Marion: "on the one hand, if Marion's theology pushes the absence and unknowability of God to an extreme, then the theology loses its distinctively Christian content. On the other hand, his phenomenology, which seems able to articulate the absence and unknowability of God even more effectively than can his theology, at the same time seems to bear traces of that theology's distinctive shape and content. What might be the significance of the parallels just noted between the theological and phenomenological in Marion, and what would be at stake in maintaining the distinction between an identifiably Christian God the Father and a completely indeterminate God of phenomenology?" (214).

43. "Religion as such, negative and affirmative theologies, would move within this space of oscillation between the unicity of pure appeal, on the one hand, and the repetition of code, language, or rite, on the other. The pure appeal to which a nonpredicative discourse (such as Marion's) might aspire could render a determinate theology unnecessary or even impossible. Conversely, the very notion or possibility of pure appeal or nonpredicative discourse could not arise without such a theology" (220).

44. According to Carlson, "death resembles the mystical union of the speaking

self with God, a union in which that self is dispossessed of itself, deprived of its capacity for thought or speech and, to that degree, of its capacity for 'experience.' The articulation of that union from within thought and speech occurs in a discourse whose referent remains inaccessible, a discourse that enacts a circling of the possible around the impossible. 'The impossible,' then, might be understood either in terms of mystical union with the Good or in terms of death — or in terms where death and the Good would illuminate one another" (230).

45. I would say, conversely, that Marion's account of death and (im)possibility closely parallels that of Heidegger (as we will see below, he formulates it thus as a deliberate choice against Lévinas' less "generous" account). Marion precisely capitalizes on the themes of generosity in Heidegger.

46. "This interplay seems to me precisely what needs to be articulated and exploited in a contemporary philosophy of religion — that is, in a philosophy of religion where the philosophical and the religious might betray a common debt to that which exceeds them. The 'philosophy of religion' in this context would have not to avoid or resolve but rather to explore and exploit the incalculable ambiguities that would mark the indiscrete interplay of two fields which, via the apophatic analogy, remain neither wholly distinct nor ever yet identical. The one could always prove both greater and smaller than the other" (RGG, 261–62).

47. Since this more or less amounts merely to a thorough summary of the first four parts of that work, I will skip this part of her treatment.

48. She asserts that "ultimately, his attempt to withdraw the gift from the realm of causality cannot work in the way he intends. That is not because he suspends the donor and the recipient, but because he eventually needs to reinstate them in some fashion if he is going to determine a given as a gift. It is not the complete loss of the donor and the recipient that counts, but their intrinsic undecidability" (RGG, 182).

49. "God's revelation in Christ is a phenomenon that can be seen by those who, allowing themselves to be determined by the phenomenon instead of determining it for themselves, learn to see it for what it is" (RGG, 175).

50. Horner's recent book on Marion does not really add much to her earlier argument (although it certainly provides a very useful introduction to Marion's work).

51. Ruud Welten, "Saturation and Disappointment: Marion according to Husserl," *Tijdschrift voor Filosofie en Theologie/International Journal in Philosophy and Theology* 65.1 (2004): 80.

52. Ibid., 80–81.

53. Ibid., 93

54. Ibid.

55. Ibid., 95.

56. Ibid., 96.

57. Kearney, *God Who May Be*, 31. All page numbers within the next paragraph refer to this work, unless indicated otherwise.

58. He closes his introduction by saying: "Religiously, I would say that if I hail from a Catholic tradition, it is with this proviso: where Catholicism offends love and justice, I prefer to call myself a Judeo-Christian theist; and where this tradition so offends, I prefer to call myself religious in the sense of seeking God in a way that neither excludes other religions nor purports to possess the final truth. And where the religious so offends, I would call myself a seeker of love and justice *tout court*" (*God Who May Be*, 5–6).

59. See, for example, "Can a Gift Be Given?" 135–37.

60. Ibid., 136. It is somewhat ironic, in light of the discussion with which I began this part, that in a recent book Milbank affirms Marion's insistence on the bishop as primary theologian (which is one of the very few positive statements he makes regarding Marion's work). John Milbank, *Being Reconciled: Ontology and Pardon* (New York: Routledge, 2003), 123.

61. Milbank, *Being Reconciled*, 156.

62. Bruce Ellis Benson, *Graven Ideologies: Nietzsche, Derrida and Marion on Modern Idolatry* (Downers Grove, Ill.: InterVarsity Press, 2002), 169. All references in the next paragraph refer to this work, unless indicated otherwise.

63. Benson, "Love Is a Given," 25.

64. He even comments on the almost identical spelling of their names.

65. It is a little ironic that Benson employs the term "Orthodox" so heavily in his work, although his interpretation of Christianity is extremely Protestant and he often fails to appreciate the Eastern Orthodox imagery and terminology in Marion's work.

66. John Panteleimon Manoussakis, "The Phenomenon of God: From Husserl to Marion," *American Catholic Philosophical Quarterly* 78.1 (2004): 55.

67. Ibid., 61.

68. Ibid., 62, 64.

69. Ibid., 68.

70. It is not incidental, of course, that Manoussakis is a student of Richard Kearney and has assisted in and even edited some of the latter's work.

71. Shane Mackinlay in "Eyes Wide Shut: A Response to Jean-Luc Marion's Account of the Journey to Emmaus," *Modern Theology* 20.3 (2004), provides a stinging criticism of Marion's account of this story. He thinks that Marion completely misinterprets the story and that the phenomenological parameters he applies to it miss the point. The disciples do not operate with a lack of understanding, nor do they confront an overdose of intuition. He also criticizes Marion's concept of faith: "The disciples' lack of faith is not simply a lack of concepts to understand the excess of Jesus' revelation, but rather a lack of openness to his revelation as such, which prevents them from seeing it as either revelatory or excessive. When the disciples finally recognise Jesus, it is not because his action of breaking the bread gives them a signification, as Marion claims, or at least not because they receive a signification in the conceptual sense that Marion has been using" (451). Overall, he seems to disagree more with Marion's use of this particular story than his phenomenology in general. He says, for example: "Contrary to Marion's account, the journey to Emmaus is not a story of the previously invisible and dazzling becoming visible. Rather, it is a story of that which was visible only because it was misunderstood being revealed in its dazzling and saturated excess, which is beyond the disciples' capacity to grasp as a visible, constituted phenomenon" (452). He seems to think that Marion is arguing that somehow the disciples are provided with concepts in the breaking of the bread and can now "grasp" the divine phenomenon. That is clearly mistaken. For Marion, the saturated phenomenon (especially the doubly saturated phenomenon of revelation) can never be grasped even when it is received in its blinding appearing.

72. "What concrete sign, what sensible perception, what intuition was lacking? None whatsoever, clearly. In fact, they kept themselves from recognizing him. Why were they denying the evidence? Not because it was deficient — it wasn't lacking in the slightest — but because it contradicts their entire comprehension (their miscomprehen-

sion, or at the least, their pre-comprehension) of a phenomenon that is nevertheless patently beneath their eyes, and in their ears. They do not recognize him because they cannot even imagine that this is really him, Him, who has rejoined them, so far do their poor, cobbled-together, honest-to-goodness concepts find themselves outstripped by 'events' that leave them petrified within a matrix of irrefutable prejudices. Not that they would not want to believe: they simply do not even imagine the other hypothesis, it never crosses their minds, even for an instant. The dead man is dead, period. Every other possibility finds itself completely excluded, not even considerable. They see nothing — in the sense that one sees nothing in a game of chess if one does not know how to play; they hear nothing — in the sense that one hears nothing (except noise) in a conversation if one does not know the language in which it is being conducted. . . . Every intuition gives itself to them, but their concepts catch nothing of this" ("They Recognized Him," 147).

    73. Ibid., 148.

    74. Ibid., 150.

    75. Marion actually does mention the importance of hermeneutics in the context of an interview with Richard Kearney: "Together with the crisis in metaphysics, or as a consequence of this very crisis, the question of revelation per se was reopened. Under this light, the experience of a Buddhist, for example, faces the same problem and the same critique as the question of experience of the (Judeo-Christian) revelation. Neither can be taken as 'rational' by the standards of philosophical and scientific rationality. On the other hand, Buddhists as well as Christians think that they have the right to be taken as reasonable and capable of performing sound reasoning and philosophical questioning, regardless of their faith. *Obviously, a broader and less rigid concept of rationality is in order here.* If you want to focus on the interreligious discourse (understood not in the sense of ecumenism, but as the question of what constitutes, or not, revelation), such a matter can only be addressed when you assume that revelation nullifies any natural experience. But to assume that you must already know what revelation is or does is the same as saying that the hermeneutics of revelation is now over, that revelation has nothing to reveal any more, and thus, by definition, that there is no revelation. *If we speak of revelation, then, we have to accept that hermeneutics is still going on,* that revelation is open, as history is still in the making. There is no contradiction in saying that everything was fully revealed and achieved but that, even today, we don't know, we can't know, how far it reaches." Kearney, *Debates,* 20–21; emphases mine.

    76. Gabellieri, "Métaphysique," 641.

    77. *Ruf und Gabe,* 45.

    78. He explores this last possibility (of reconceiving and taking seriously the notion of desire as a kind of rationality) also in an interview with Richard Kearney. Kearney, *Debates,* 24–25.

Part 3 Introduction

    1. Dodd, "Marion and Phenomenology," 176.

    2. Manoussakis, "Phenomenon of God," 57.

    3. Zarader, "Phenomenality and Transcendence," 112.

    4. Ibid., 114.

    5. Grimwood, "Iconography and Postmodernity," 89.

    6. Zarader, "Phenomenality and Transcendence," 115.

7. Ibid., 116.
8. Ibid.
9. Ibid.

7. Descartes and the Self

1. Although his more theological works certainly have things to say about the human subject, this topic is explored in far less detail and it is a particularly prominent topic of his phenomenology. I will focus primarily on his phenomenology in this context, supplementing it with occasional references to his more theological writings.

2. In fact, in terms of Marion's argument regarding Descartes it would actually have made more sense to examine the ego first and God second, since Marion wants to show that Descartes moves from a first metaphysical onto-theo-logy of the ego to a second metaphysical onto-theo-logy grounded in God. Yet since overall he is much more interested in the role played by God than that of the ego and since the status of God in Descartes prepares Marion's (earlier) theology and that of the ego has more implications for his (more recent) phenomenology, it seemed more appropriate to examine the two in that order.

3. This desire is exemplified, for example, in a recent collection, *Who Comes after the Subject?*, ed. Eduardo Cadava, Peter Connors, and Jean-Luc Nancy (New York: Routledge, 1991). Marion contributed a chapter, entitled "L'Interloqué," to this collection (236–45), which was reprinted (in slightly expanded form) as "The Final Appeal of the Subject" in John Caputo's anthology *The Religious* (Oxford: Blackwell, 2002), 131–44.

4. "Substance et subsistance. Suarez et le traité de la *substantia—Principia Philosophiae I, §51–54,*" QCII, 85–115.

5. QCII, 98.

6. MP, 162; PM, 172–73.

7. CQ, 83; QCI, 132.

8. "In this investment of himself, man's only task is to let God occur, by offering him the largest possible capacity. Hence . . . the constant opening up of capacity toward God; this stretching of the inner space has to be accomplished by desire — that is to say, by the infinite, the infinity of desire, which only God can create" (CQ, 87; QCI, 137–38).

9. "The horizon of presence exceeds the present because the *cogitatio*, being redoubled by a *motus cogitationes*, leads back to the present what appeared to have escaped it definitively. Since the *cogitatio* has been put into motion, the sway that presence exerts over temporality will exceed the present and prolong it into the fields of the past" (MP, 181; PM, 191).

10. This is particularly true of his response to Derrida in the final chapter of *In Excess*.

11. CQ, 118–31; QCI, 189–219.

12. QCI, 189–219.

13. These "people" (madmen/people who are in error) are mentioned in the first Meditation.

14. This passage occurs in the second Meditation, as a further example right after the analysis of the piece of wax.

15. CQ, 130; QCI, 206.

16. He outlines this in sections 14 and 15, "The Subsistent Temporality of the Ego" and "The Ego outside Subsistence," in MP, 169–205; PM, 180–216.

17. Marion attempts both in various places in his work. See, for example, the chapter "The Freedom to Be Free" on freedom and morality (PC, 31–52; PaC, 43–67), or his discussion of temporality in *Being Given* (ED, 185–212; BG, 131–50).

18. "*Dasein* maintains with itself a surprising relation of uncertainty: far from assuring itself of itself in knowing itself as such, it knows itself only in admitting what play is at play in it—the play of its Being or more exactly the play of Being put into play, always to be decided in the case of this privileged being. *Dasein* knows itself authentically only by recognizing itself as an undecided and all the more uncertain stake, which will never and must never be rendered certain. *Dasein* plays—in the sense that wood has play: it maintains a gap, an articulation, a mobility, in order that the fold of Being, everywhere else invisible, should unfold, turning on that being like a panel on a hinge. Such a play, in the end beyond both incertitude and certitude, decidedly opposes *Dasein* to the *ego cogito*" (RG, 95; RD, 145).

19. CQ, 96–117; QCI, 153–87.

20. CQ, 100; QCI, 158.

21. "Therefore, generosity concerns the manner of the being, the survival of the being, and the perfection of the being of the ego, for which it thus explicitly sanctions the sum" (CQ, 116; QCI, 186).

22. Marion suggests that Henry's interpretation "gives access to an original and powerful understanding of the *cogito, ergo sum,* and not only that its phenomenological repetition pulls the Cartesian ego out of its aporias for which the greatest interpreters—Kant, Nietzsche, Husserl, Heidegger—had opposed it, but above all that this line opens absolutely new perspectives on the whole of Descartes' work. In particular, it would in this way seem possible to reestablish, in the 'I think, therefore I am,' that generosity finally effects the unity long missing between the love of wisdom and the search for truth" (CQ, 117; QCI, 187).

23. This is an argument he will later make against Husserl.

24. QCII, 6.

25. QCII, 3–47.

26. QCII, 14.

27. QCII, 16. He had already spoken of such a move to performativity in his original interpretation of the ambivalent role of the ego in the establishment of the code (TB, 380ff).

28. QCII, 21.

29. "Existence follows here neither from a syllogism, nor an intuition, nor an autonomous performance, nor an auto-affection, but from my affection by an other Other than me [*an autre autrui que moi*]" (QCII, 29).

30. QCII, 31.

31. QCII, 34.

32. QCII, 41.

33. QCII, 43.

34. QCII, 46.

35. Géry Prouvost, "La tension irrésolue: Les *Questions cartésiennes, II* de Jean-Luc Marion," *Revue Thomiste* 98.1 (1998): 98.

36. Ibid., 99.

37. Ruud Welten, "Het andere ego van Descartes," *Tijdschrift voor Filosofie* 60.3 (1998): 572–79.

38. Ibid., 579.

39. Jocelyn Benoist, "Les voix du soliloque," *Les études philosophiques* 4 (1997): 550.

40. Ibid., 551–52.

41. Ibid., 554–54.

42. "Le statut responsorial des Meditationes," QCII, 317–37, reprinted as "The Place of the Objections in the Development of Cartesian Metaphysics" in *Descartes and His Contemporaries: Meditations, Objections, and Replies,* ed. Roger Ariew and Marjorie Grene (Chicago: University of Chicago Press, 1995).

43. "Place of Objections," 15; QCII, 330.

44. "Place of Objections," 17; QCII, 333.

45. "Place of Objections," 20; QCII, 337.

46. ED, 374–83; BG, 271–78.

8. Phenomenology and the Self

1. "L'Interloqué," 236.

2. These criticisms are outlined in ED, 348–53; BG, 252–56.

3. I will leave aside here Marion's criticism of Lévinas, which I have examined in detail in my article "Ethics, Eros, or Caritas? Lévinas and Marion on Individuation of the Other," *Philosophy Today* 49.1 (2005): 70–87.

4. He does make one attempt in a recent article, "The Banality of Saturation," where he considers the possibility that "common" phenomena might turn into "saturated" ones (and the reverse), depending on how we receive them. See CE, 383–418; VR, 143–82.

5. Marion employs this term in several senses. He uses it as a translation of *der Angesprochene* and takes it in the meanings of "being summoned by a claim" or "submitted to an interlocutory judgment." See also his article "L'interloqué," 243f.

6. "L'Interloqué," 236. All page references within the next few paragraphs refer to this text, unless indicated otherwise.

7. Both of these terms translate the German *Entschlossenheit* in Heidegger.

8. "L'Interloqué," 242.

9. Rolf Kühn, "Langeweile und Anruf: Eine Heidegger- und Husserl-Revision mit dem Problemhintergrund 'absoluter Phänomene' bei Jean-Luc Marion," *Philosophisches Jahrbuch* 102 (1995): 148.

10. Although Marion later distinguishes his talk of the self that appears in the dative from that of Lévinas (which plays in the accusative), he does not identify the use of the accusative here with Lévinas. The relationship of this self with what Lévinas has suggested about a dislocation of the metaphysical subject remains unexplored in *Reduction and Givenness.*

11. "Thus I experience — or: the I is experienced — as claimed, assigned, and convoked in the accusative, deprived of its right to the nominative that names every thing in the manner of an accused; interpellated in the accusative, dispossessed of the nominative by the appeal lodged against it, the me manifests phenomenally the absence of

any *I*. Under the in this sense absolute hold of the claim, the me that it provokes attests to the relegation of any transcendental or constituting *I*" (RG, 199; RD, 298).

12. RG, 201; RD, 300.

13. "Sketch of the Saturated Phenomenon: I" (§22, ED, 296–309; BG, 212–21).

14. Kosky, "Philosophy of Religion," 635. Emphasis his.

15. ED, 357; BG, 259.

16. Horner, "Betrayal of Transcendence," 61.

17. Ibid., 63.

18. Ibid., 64.

19. Kosky, "Philosophy of Religion," 639.

20. *Ruf und Gabe*, 64.

21. Ibid., 65.

22. Ibid., 66.

23. Ibid., 68.

24. Ibid., 68.

25. In my article on Marion's "phenomenologies of prayer" I suggested that his notion of the self remained solipsistic, and I still think that is true for *Being Given* to some degree, since a painting can constitute me fully and I thus have apparently no need of the human other. His subsequent account of the erotic phenomenon, however, alleviates that charge to a large extent.

26. Olivier Mathieu, review of Jean-Luc Marion, *De surcroît*, in *Philosophiques* 30.1 (2003): 282.

27. ED, 374–89; BG, 271–82.

28. ED, 394; BG, 286.

29. Again, Marion uses several biblical passages in order to illustrate this claim that calls to me in anonymous fashion and overwhelms me by its seduction, first the story of the calling of Matthew, especially as illustrated in a painting by Caravaggio, second the calling of Samuel. In both cases an invisible call is being made visible through the response. Despite these biblical examples Marion wants to insists that this is not essentially a divine calling, but that it always remains anonymous.

30. ED, 396–400; BG, 287–90.

31. ED, 400–405; BG, 290–94.

32. Thomas Carlson highlights these connotations by interpreting the response to the phenomenon as a type of belief which does not mean "that belief ensues from the force of evidence seen but rather, indeed, that I must first believe, thanks to a decision made in darkness, in order to see at all" (CE, 161). Even more emphatically, Falque finds that what "founds the whole project of *Being Given*" is the idea that "another intentionality, as absolute as essential to humanity, determines mine in me, and consecrates it as place and act of true sacramentality" (CE, 194).

33. ED, 409; BG, 296.

34. Carlson points out that the *adonné* becomes a sort of Christ-figure for Marion (CE, 170).

35. Kosky, "Philosophy of Religion," 640.

36. Ricard, "Question de la donation," 92.

37. Ibid.

38. Ibid., 94.

39. Horner, "Betrayal of Transcendence," 67.

40. Ibid., 74.
41. Ibid., 75.
42. PE, 19; EP, 8.
43. PE, 71–72; EP, 41–42.
44. PE, 138–40; EP, 85–87.
45. John Milbank, "The Soul of Reciprocity (Part One)," *Modern Theology* 17.3 (2001): 344.
46. Idem, "Can a Gift be Given?" 141–42.
47. Idem, "Reciprocity (Part One)," 345.
48. Ibid., 349.
49. Ibid., 350. He continues by claiming that Marion's "devoted" cannot exercise love and is entirely solipsistic.
50. Milbank, "The Gift and the Mirror," in CE, 252–317.

9. Charity and Eros

1. CQ, 112; QCI, 179.
2. CQ, 131; QCI, 208.
3. CQ, 135; QCI, 212.
4. CQ, 132ff; QCI, 208ff.
5. Milbank concurs with this (although he condemns it) by calling Marion's account of love a "bleakly Pascalian" one (CE, 254). Claude Romano also points to the importance of Pascal for Marion's work on love (CE, 325).
6. Marion suggests that Pascal actually employs the notion of the "super-" or "hyper-code" here that he uncovered in Descartes' early works. This principle of "overencoding," Descartes first formulated but later rejected. "Pascal tries to overencode thought (already the code of extension) only by submitting it to another parameter than its own. He will do this by no longer exposing it to the natural light of evidence, but to the invisible radiance of charity. The third order will thus be revealed indirectly, by the distorting effects that its radiance — the luminosity of charity — will have on the elements of the second order" (MP, 319; PM, 340).
7. In Milbank's view this division means that "knowledge is dismissed from the field of love" and is therefore "sent off on a lonely and comfortless ride, without the consort of *eros*" (CE, 256).
8. In Pascal's text, as Marion indicates, the language of love often seems to degenerate into a kind of self-loathing. He insists, however, that this is not a modern sense of self-hatred (which he thinks is really perverted self-love). Rather, it is a "hatred of self" that actually means "love for God." Pascal seems to return to an Augustinian division between love of self and love of God as opposed. Although we were created with love for both God and the self, since the fall love of self takes the only place in us and therefore must be replaced. He suggests that "the ego of metaphysics becomes idolatrous only when taken up by charity become self-love, to the exclusion of the love of God. The authentic status reserved for the metaphysical ego in the order of charity can ultimately be determined only in terms of the requirements proper to this order and to charity" (MP, 329; PM, 351). God is the appropriate object (or goal) of this love which is patterned upon the example of Christ: "If Jesus Christ offers himself as universal 'object' for the love of all, he discloses the universal self for the sake of all men, and does so as a consequence of his playing the role of a self 'thrice holy to God' and 'in the eyes of

the heart.' In the Christ, charity can recognize a self—no longer 'unjust,' 'incommodious,' and 'tyrannical,' but holy. Therefore it must love him" (MP, 331; PM, 353). Christ can assume the "I," the center, because he becomes the true self. Thus the term "ego" is applied to the human or the divine ego, depending on whether one speaks of second or third order. Christ has perfect knowledge of us (which does not refer to clear and distinct certainty) in terms of and through charity. Thus we can receive our self back (although we remain unworthy) because we are named by Christ, the original authority. These themes of naming, reception, and imitation of Christ of course all return in Marion's theology.

9. "'Christian Philosophy': Hermeneutic or Heuristic?" In *The Question of Christian Philosophy Today*, ed. Francis J. Ambrosio (New York: Fordham University Press, 1999), reprinted as VR, 99–117.

10. "Heuristic," 261; VR, 114.

11. "The Intentionality of Love" (PC, 71–101; PaC, 89–120).

12. Thus, "I do not reach the other by means of the consciousness I have of him; he forces himself upon me by means of the unconsciousness to which he reduces my consciousness" (PC, 83; PaC, 103).

13. In my view this is a misinterpretation of Lévinas. I have argued as much in my aforementioned article "Ethics, Eros, or Caritas?"

14. "Freed from intentionality, love in the end would be defined, still within the field of phenomenology, as the act of a gaze that renders itself back to another gaze in a common unsubstitutability. To render oneself back to a gaze means, for another gaze, to return there, as to a place for a rendez-vous, but above all to render oneself there in an unconditional surrender: to render oneself to the unsubstitutable other, as to a summons to my own unsubstitutablity—no other than me will be able to play the other that the other requires, no other gaze than my own must respond to the ecstasy of this particular other exposed in his gaze. But to render oneself other, to surrender this gaze to the gaze of the other who crosses me, requires faith" (PC, 100–101; PaC, 120).

15. I have argued this in detail in my "Praise—Pure and Personal?" 168–81.

16. This is especially evident in the final chapter, which was included only in the English translation: "What Love Knows" (PC, 153–69). Marion here posits phenomenology as limited in its thought about love and interprets charity throughout as a theological contribution to the philosophical discussion.

17. "Heuristic," 261.

18. He claims in the beginning that theology knows love "too well" and interprets it too directly in terms of Christ's passion (PE, 10; EP, 1).

19. The lover allows the other to emerge: "The lover, and he alone, sees something else, a thing that nobody except him sees—precisely no longer a thing, but, for the first time, this other, unique, individualized, furthermore cut off from economy, disengaged from objectity, unveiled by the initiative of love, surging up as a phenomenon so far unseen" (PE, 131; EP, 80). Marion's language throughout *The Erotic Phenomenon* is very masculine. I have retained this in quotations from his text, but attempted to paraphrase more inclusively. Stephen Lewis actually employs the feminine pronoun quite frequently in his translation of the text. See his note regarding this in EP, 24.

20. "The instability of loving phenomena thus never derives from a penury of intuition, but, on the contrary, from my incapacity of assigning him a precise, individualized, and stable signification" (PE, 154; EP, 96).

21. PE, 167; EP, 105.

22. Pain, on the other hand, is the refusal of the other's flesh to allow me entrance, its resistance to me which diminishes my flesh back into an object. Marion therefore condemns the discussion of the caress in several contemporary writers as much too superficial, because simple touch cannot really distinguish between body and flesh. Caress does not really make possible the contact of flesh with flesh. Only the full erotization of the flesh turns the lover into a devoted: "the one who receives himself from what he receives and who gives that which he does not have" (PE, 190; EP, 120).

23. John Milbank does not think this is true. He calls Marion's account "demonizing" and "sinister": "The irony, however, of Marion's perspective is that his somewhat Manichean demonization of the shaped and apparent is sustained also into the fleshly realm and in such a manner that the invisible and uncontrollable, which constitutes for him in the spiritual the most exalted, here becomes sinister and ambiguous and yet unavoidable" (CE, 266). He interprets this as being due to a dualism between body and flesh which returns Marion to a firm Cartesianism. The "descent into the flesh" is a "descent into darkness" characterized by "fatalism" and "a certain Gnosticism" (CE, 268). Milbank suggests that this is grounded in Marion's desire to defend a very conservative Catholic position: "One curious feature of Marion's exposition of the flesh is the way he in certain ways abandons the path of a traditional Catholic metaphysic, yet defends in terms of a strictly modern philosophy most of the strictures of current Catholic sexual teaching—indeed sometimes in an exaggeratedly rigorous form" (CE, 273). Marion's account results in "the dire situation of a sterile redemption" (CE, 275).

24. PE, 218; EP, 139.

25. Marion here plays on the French words *saturer* and *raturer*, which mean to saturate and to eliminate, erase, or scratch out, respectively. Unfortunately, the play on words is impossible to render into English.

26. In this context Marion engages in an extended analysis of the child which at first witnesses to the mutual love of the lovers and makes it visible in some fashion, but ultimately is unable to sustain such a witness, but goes on to live its own life. Marion also again deals with the issue of reciprocity here.

27. "The lovers thus do not promise each other eternity, they provoke it and give it to each other from now on" (PE, 322; EP, 209).

28. Marion maintains that this eschatological anticipation is needed for the erotic reduction in a three-fold manner because it answers three essential questions of the lovers. It is the "final judgment of love" which finally gives the assurance we have searched for from the beginning. First, it answers the question of who I truly love by loving fully that one as if it was the final and only possibility to love: "For only eternity responds to the need of erotic reason concerning *the assurance of the present*—knowing definitely whom I love" (PE, 323; EP, 210). Second, it answers the question of whether I am able to love without remainder or regret as a saturated phenomenon, because the other's face requires infinite hermeneutics and thus demands eternity: "In this way, only eternity responds to the need of erotic reason concerning *the assurance of a future*—to be able without end to tell me that I love and to teach it to him, because without me, he would not know it" (PE, 324; EP, 210). Finally it also responds to the question of how a separation and loss of love could have become possible, because most loves do indeed stop just like the suspension of the erotic moment always does. "In this way, eternity satisfies the need of erotic reason for *an assurance of a past*—to be able to tell us in the end how, despite everything, we still love each other" (PE, 325; EP, 211). Loving thus always happens in a moment that comprises all other moments, that envelops all of

eternity in that instant. "Loving demands that the first moment already coincide with the last moment" (PE, 326; EP, 211).

29. Robin Horner sees this "logic of love" as operative in both Marion's theology and his phenomenology (CE, 236, 238, 244).

30. He outlines this need for univocity already in the introduction (PE, 14–15; EP, 4–5) and concludes the book by insisting on it again.

31. Horner says, "the apparently phenomenological study of love has, in fact, been completed by the reassertion of the theological" (CE, 244). She suggests that we read this (against Marion) as a pragmatic reference where "the appeal to God as first lover could also find itself diverted to the other person" (CE, 246).

32. Milbank, however, thinks that "Marion offers no phenomenology of love after all, but only another metaphysics of nothingness and absence" because he refuses ontology and "analogical participation" (CE, 276).

33. Kevin Hart says, "We see Marion in sharpest focus when we perceive that he can be grasped in his totality as a philosopher of love" (CE, 3).

Conclusion

1. *Avec ou sans Dieu*, 16.

2. Ibid., 23.

3. "Although all the things that are important — aesthetic experience, the experience of love and even the experience of a decision I make (and I am not even speaking of God) — can be reduced to the domain of proof, it is precisely that in them that cannot be reduced to the domain of proof that has a determining influence on me" (Ibid., 35). See also ibid., 38.

4. Ibid., 30.

5. Ibid., 59.

6. "If, on the one hand, the horizon of being does not allow us to stage what is properly at stake in the knowledge we have of God's name; if, on the other hand, nothing appears within this horizon that is not a certificate-bearing entity, must we not conclude that there is no possible phenomenalization of God and, moreover, that this very impossibility defines God? Are we not, in the era of nihilism, led by our inner fidelity and devotion to thought to admit God in philosophy strictly as what is empirically impossible and lies outside phenomenalization as a matter of principle?" ("Impossible for Man," 5).

7. "God begins where the possible for us ends, where what human reason comprehends as possible for it comes to a halt, at the precise limit where our thought can no longer advance, to see, or speak — where the inaccessible domain of the impossible bursts open. What is impossible to human reason does not place the question of God under interdict, but rather indicates the threshold beyond which the question can be posed and actually be about God, transcending, by the same token, what does not concern him in the least. In God's case, and in God's case alone, impossibility does not abolish the question but actually makes it possible" ("Impossible for Man," 10).

8. Ibid., 21–27.

9. *Avec ou sans Dieu*, 13.

10. "'Christian Philosophy': Hermeneutic or Heuristic?" 255.

11. Ibid.

12. Ibid., 261.

13. PC, 57; PaC, 75.

14. "The irreducible irruption of the will marks the inconceivable and discontinuous passage from evidence to love. Between the evidence of reasons and the will of faith, the passage leads from one order to another. If then we know the truth not only by reason but also by the heart . . . it is because only the heart can reach the ultimate truth, that alone which is not a figure of something else, that alone which symbolizes itself: charity" (PC, 59; PaC, 78).

15. "In knowing God by the loving act of the will, man imitates God in his highest name . . . and becomes, by the grace of love, himself God. God is approached only by he who jettisons all that does not befit love; God, who gives himself as Love only through love, can be reached only so long as one receives him by love, and to receive him by love becomes possible only for he who gives himself to him. Surrendering oneself to love, not surrendering oneself to evidence." (PC, 61)

16. Kearney, *Debates*, 24–25.

17. The "excess of overlap" that Marion's commentators criticize so frequently thus is neither unconscious nor accidental. The relationship between philosophy and theology in Marion's work can be clearly delineated if one considers its rootedness in his analysis of Descartes and Pascal. It is therefore a relationship that functions in both positive and negative ways, proves itself both fruitful and problematic for Marion. Whether this is ultimately an appropriate way of relating philosophy and theology will probably always remain up to whoever does the evaluating. Yet it is neither a haphazard nor an unarticulated one.

18. Again in light of Pascal, Marion insists that one must make an ultimate choice between metaphysics and love: "To represent or to love — one must choose. Did Descartes in the end detect this?" (CQ, 138; QCI, 219). Of course, as I have pointed out above, this does not mean that we should dispense with all scientific endeavor or never seek for any kind of evidence or rationality. When Marion says that we must choose between love or metaphysics, he does not mean that the discourse or experience of love is the only discourse available or the only experience we have. But the language of metaphysics, rationality, scientific proof, etc. is inappropriate for describing the experiences with which Marion is concerned. They require another kind of evidence or knowing. One cannot "represent" the experience of love with the tools of metaphysics.

19. Tanner evokes similar Patristic Trinitarian images in her criticism of Marion: "The persons of the Trinity do not empty themselves to fill one another, but spill over into one another out of their fullness, as light or an ever-bubbling fountain would, without self-evacuation or self-loss, so as to mirror one another in what they all have and not in what they have lost to one another, in ways that never produce any sort of gap between them" (CE, 220). While she thinks that such shared givenness is lacking in Marion, I think this imagery captures well what is Marion's ultimate concern, even when he does acknowledge the existence of gaps or stresses the importance of self-emptying.

BIBLIOGRAPHY

Primary Sources (Marion)

Monographs

Marion, Jean-Luc. *Le visible et le révélé*. Paris: Éditions de CERF, 2005.
——. *Le phénomène érotique: Six méditations*. Paris: Grasset, 2003.
——. *De surcroît: Études sur les phénomènes saturés*. Paris: Presses Universitaires de France, 2001.
——. *Étant donné: Essai d'une phénoménologie de la donation*. Paris: Presses Universitaires de France, 1997; 2nd. ed. 1998.
——. *Index des "Meditationes de prima Philosophia" de R. Descartes*. En collaboration avec J.-P. Massonet, P. Monat, et L. Ucciani. Paris: Les Belle Lettres, 1995.
——. *Hergé: Tintin le terrible et l'alphabet des richesses*. En collaboration avec A. Bonfand. Paris: Hachette, 1996.
——. *Questions cartésiennes II: L'ego et Dieu*. Paris: Presses Universitaires de France, 1996.
——. *Questions cartésiennes: Méthode et métaphysique*. Paris: Presses Universitaires de France, 1991.
——. *La croisée du visible*. Paris: Éd. de la Différence, 1991; 2nd ed. 1994; 3rd ed. Presses Universitaires de France, 1996.
——. *Réduction et donation: Recherches sur Husserl, Heidgger et la phénoménologie*. Paris: Presses Universitaires de France, 1989.
——. *Prolégomènes à la charité*. Paris: Éd. de la Différence, 1986; 2nd ed. 1991.
——. *Sur le prisme métaphysique de Descartes*. Paris: Presses Universitaires de France, 1986.
——. *Dieu sans l'être*. Paris: Fayard, 1982; 2nd ed. Presses Universitaires de France, 1991; 3rd ed. 2002.
——. *Sur la théologie blanche de Descartes*. Paris: Presses Universitaires de France, 1981; 2nd ed. 1991.
——. *L'idole et la distance: cinq études*. Paris: Grasset, 1977.
——. *René Descartes: Règles utiles et claires pour la direction de l'esprit en la recherche de la vérité*. LaHaye: M. Nijhoff, 1977.
——. *Sur l'ontologie grise de Descartes*. Paris: Vrin, 1975; 2nd ed. 1981; 3rd ed. 1993; 4th ed. 2000.
Marion, Jean-Luc, and Alain de Benoist. *Avec ou sans Dieu? L'avenir des valeurs chrétiennes*. Paris: Beauchesne, 1970.

Translations

Marion, Jean-Luc. *On the Ego and on God: Further Cartesian Questions*. Trans. Christina M. Gschwandtner. New York: Fordham University Press, 2007.
——. *Descartes' Grey Ontology*. Trans. S. Donahue. South Bend, Ind.: St. Augustine's Press, 2007.

Bibliography

———. *The Erotic Phenomenon.* Trans. Stephen Lewis. Chicago: University of Chicago Press, 2007.

———. *The Crossing of the Visible.* Trans. James K. A. Smith. Stanford: Stanford University Press, 2004.

———. *In Excess: Studies of Saturated Phenomena.* Trans. Robyn Horner and Vincent Berraud. New York: Fordham University Press, 2002.

———. *Being Given: Toward a Phenomenology of Givenness.* Trans. Jeffrey L. Kosky. Stanford: Stanford University Press, 2002.

———. *Prolegomena to Charity.* Trans. Stephen Lewis. New York: Fordham University Press, 2002.

———. *The Idol and Distance: Five Studies.* Trans. and introduced by Thomas A. Carlson. New York: Fordham University Press, 2001.

———. *On Descartes' Metaphysical Prism: The Constitution and the Limits of Onto-theo-logy in Cartesian Thought.* Trans. Jeffrey L. Kosky. Chicago: University of Chicago Press, 1999.

———. *Cartesian Questions: Method and Metaphysics.* Chicago: University of Chicago Press, 1999.

———. *Reduction and Givenness.* Trans. Thomas A. Carlson. Evanston, Ill.: Northwestern University Press, 1998.

———. *God without Being.* Trans. Thomas A. Carlson. Chicago: University of Chicago Press, 1991.

Journal Articles

Marion, Jean-Luc. "Phenomenon and Event." *Graduate Faculty Philosophy Journal* 26.1 (2005): 147–59.

———. "La raison du don." *Tijdschrift voor Filosofie en Theologie* 65.1 (2004): 79–96.

———. "The Unspoken: Apophasis and the Discourse of Love." *Proceedings of the American Catholic Philosophical Association* 76 (2002): 39–56.

———. "They Recognized Him; and He Became Invisible to Them." *Modern Theology* 18.2 (2002): 145–52.

———. "Au nom: Comment ne pas parler de «théologie negative»." *Laval Théologique et Philosophique* 55.3 (1999): 339–63.

———. "The Other First Philosophy and the Question of Givenness." *Critical Inquiry* 25.4 (1999): 784–800.

———. "A Note Concerning the Ontological Indifference." *Graduate Faculty Philosophy Journal* 20–21.1–2 (1998): 25–40.

———. "A propos de Suarez et Descartes." *Revue Internationale de Philosophie* 195.1 (1996): 109–31.

———. "The Saturated Phenomenon." *Philosophy Today* 40.1–4 (1996): 103–124.

———. "La doble idolatria: Observaciones sobre la diferencia ontológica y el pensamiento de Dios." *Nombres* 6.8–9 (1996): 105–130.

———. "Saint Thomas d'Aquin et l'onto-théo-logie." *Revue Thomiste* 95.1 (1995): 31–66.

———. "Metaphysics and Phenomenology: A Relief for Theology." *Critical Inquiry* 20.4 (1994): 572–91.

———. "The End of the End of Metaphysics." *Epoche* 2.2 (1994): 1–22.

———. "The Exactitude of the 'Ego.'" *American Catholic Philosophical Quarterly* 67.4 (1993): 561–68.

———. "Is the Ontological Argument Ontological? The Argument according to Anselm and Its Metaphysical Interpretation according to Kant." *Journal of the History of Philosophy* 30.2 (1992): 201–18.

———. "Le sujet en dernier appel." *Revue de Métaphysique et de Morale* 96.1 (1991): 77–95.

———. "Réponses à quelques questions." *Revue de Métaphysique et de Morale* 96.1 (1991): 65–76.

———. "L'interloqué." *Topoi* 7 (1988): 175–80.

———. "Différence ontologique ou question de l'être: un indécidé de 'Sein und Zeit.'" *Tijdschrift voor Filosofie* 49 (1987): 602–45.

———. "L'*ego* et le *Dasein*, Heidegger et la 'destruction' de Descartes dans 'Sein und Zeit.'" *Revue de Métaphysique et de Morale* 92 (1987): 25–53.

———. "La conversion de la volonté selon «L'Action»." *Revue Philosophique de la France et de l'Etranger* 177 (1987): 33–46.

———. "La fin de la fin de la métaphysique." *Laval Théologique et Philosophique* 42.1 (1986): 23–33.

———. "On Descartes' Constitution of Metaphysics." *Graduate Faculty Philosophy Journal* 11 (1986): 21–33.

———. "De la «mort de Dieu» aux noms divins: L'itinéraire théologique de la métaphysique." *Laval Théologique et Philosophique* 41.1 (1985): 25–42.

———. "Die cartesianische Onto-Theo-logie." *Zeitschrift für philosophische Forschung* 38 (1984): 349–80.

———. "Le système ou l'étoile." *Archives de Philosophie* 46 (1983): 429–43.

———. "Descartes et l'onto-théologie." *Bulletin de la Societé Française de Philosophie* 76 (1982): 117–58.

———. "L'angoisse et l'ennui: Pour interpréter 'Was ist Metaphysik?'" *Archives de Philosophie* 43 (1980): 121–46.

———. "L'être et l'affection." *Archives de Philosophie* 43 (1980): 433–42.

———. "L'idole et l'icône." *Revue de Métaphysique et de Morale* 84 (1979): 433–45.

———. "De connaître à aimer: l'éblouissement." *Revue Catholique Internationale Communio* III (1978): 17–28.

———. "De la divinisation à la domination: Étude sur la sémantique de capable/capax chez Descartes." *Revue Philosophique de Louvain* 73 (1975): 262–93.

———. "Ordre et relation: Sur la situation Aristotelicienne de la théorie cartésienne de l'ordre selon les 'regulae V' et 'VI.'" *Archives de Philosophie* 37 (1974): 273–74.

———. "A propos de la sémantique de la méthode." *Revue Internationale de Philosophie* 27 (1973): 37–48.

Contributions

Marion, Jean-Luc. "The Impossible for Man — God." Trans. Anne Davenport. In *Transcendence and Beyond: A Postmodern Inquiry*. Ed. John D. Caputo and Michael S. Scanlon. Bloomington: Indiana University Press, 2007.

———. "From the Other to the Individual." Trans. Robyn Horner. In *Transcendence: Philosophy, Literature, and Theology Approach the Beyond*. Ed. Regina Schwartz. New York: Routledge, 2004.

———. "Saint Thomas Aquinas and Onto-theo-logy." Trans. B. Gendreau, R. Rethty, and M. Sweeney. In *Mystic: Presence and Aporia*. Ed. M. Kessler and C. Sheppard. Chicago: Chicago University Press, 2003.

——. "The 'End of Metaphysics' as a Possibility." In *Religion after Metaphysics*. Ed. Mark A. Wrathall. Cambridge: Cambridge University Press, 2003.

——. "The Final Appeal of the Subject." In *The Religious*. Ed. John D. Caputo. Oxford: Blackwell, 2002.

——. "The Formal Reasons for the Infinite." In *Blackwell Companion to Postmodern Theology*. Ed. Graham Ward. London: Blackwell, 2001.

——. "D'autrui à l'individu." In *Positivité et transcendance; suivi de Lévinas et la phénoménologie*, by Emmanuel Lévinas. Paris: Presses Universitaires de France, 2000.

——. "The Voice without Name: Homage to Levinas." In *The Face of the Other and the Trace of God: Essays on the Philosophy of Emmanuel Levinas*. Ed. Jeffrey Bloechl. New York: Fordham University Press, 2000.

——. "The Saturated Phenomenon." In *Phenomenology and the "Theological Turn": The French Debate*. Trans. Thomas A. Carlson. New York: Fordham University Press, 2000.

——. "'Christian Philosophy': Hermeneutic or Heuristic?" In *The Question of Christian Philosophy Today*. Ed. Francis J. Ambrosio. New York: Fordham University Press, 1999.

——. "In the Name: How to Avoid Speaking of 'Negative Theology.'" In *God, the Gift, and Postmodernism*. Ed. John D. Caputo and Michael Scanlon. Bloomington: Indiana University Press, 1999.

——. "Sketch of a Phenomenological Concept of Gift." In *Postmodern Philosophy and Christian Thought*. Ed. Merold Westphal. Bloomington: Indiana University Press, 1999.

——. "Descartes and Onto-Theology." Trans. B. Bergo. In *Post-secular Philosophy: Between Philosophy and Theology*. Ed. Phillip Blond. New York: Routledge, 1998.

——. "The Idea of God." In *The Cambridge History of Seventeenth-Century Philosophy*. Ed. Daniel Garber. New York: Cambridge University Press, 1998.

——. "Metaphysics and Phenomenology: A Summary for Theologians." In *The Postmodern God: A Theological Reader*. Ed. Graham Ward. London: Blackwell, 1997.

——. "Phénoménologie et philosophie première: La question de la donation." In *Le Statut Contemporain de la Philosophie première*. Philosophie 17. Paris: Beauchesne, 1996.

——. "Nothing and Nothing Else." In *The Ancients and the Moderns*. Ed. Reginald Lilly. Bloomington: Indiana University Press, 1996.

——. "The Place of the Objections in the Development of Cartesian Metaphysics." In *Descartes and His Contemporaries: Meditations, Objections, and Replies*. Ed. Roger Ariew and Marjorie G. Grene. Chicago: University of Chicago Press, 1995.

——. "'Aporias' and the Origins of Spinoza's Theory of Adequate Ideas." In *Spinoza on Knowledge and the Human Mind*. Vol. II. Ed. Yovel Yirmiyahu. Leiden: Brill, 1994.

——. "L'Interloqué." In *Who Comes after the Subject?* Ed. Eduardo Cadava, Peter Connor, and Jean-Luc Nancy. New York: Routledge, 1991.

——. "Aspekte der Religionsphänomenologie: Grund, Horizont und Offenbarung." In *Religionsphilosophie heute: Chancen und Bedeutung in Philosophie und Theologie*. Ed. Alois Halder, Klaus Kienzler, and Joseph Möller. Düsseldorf: Patmos Verlag, 1988.

——. "The Essential Incoherence of Descartes' Definition of Divinity." In *Essays on

Descartes' Meditations. Ed. Amélie Rorty. Berkeley: University of California Press, 1986.

——. "La double idolâtrie — Remarques sur la différence ontologique et la pensée de Dieu." In *Heidegger et la question de Dieu*. Ed. Richard Kearney and J. Stephen O'Leary. Paris: Grasset, 1980.

——. "La rigueur de la louange." In *La Confession de la foi chrétienne*. Ed. Claude Bruaire. Paris: Fayard, 1977.

Secondary Sources (Marion)

Alliez, Éric. *De l'impossibilité de la phénoménologie: Sur la philosophie française contemporaine*. Paris: Vrin, 1995.

Ambrosio, Francis J., ed. *The Question of Christian Philosophy Today*. New York: Fordham University Press, 1999.

Armour, Leslie. "The Idealist Philosophers' God." *Laval Theologique et Philosophique* 58.3 (2002): 443–55.

Barber, Michael D. "Theory and Alterity: Dussel's Marx and Marion on Idolatry." In *Thinking from the Underside of History: Enrique Dussel's Philosophy of Liberation*. Ed. Linda Martín Alcoff and Eduardo Mendieta. Lanham: Rowman and Littlefield, 2000.

Beards, Andrew. "Christianity, 'Interculturality,' and Salvation: Some Perspectives from Lonergan." *Thomist* 64.2 (2000): 161–210.

Bell, Jeffrey A. Review of Jean-Luc Marion, *Reduction and Givenness. International Studies in Philosophy* 35 (2003): 356–57.

Benoist, Jocelyn. "L'écart plutôt que l'excédent." *Philosophie: Jean-Luc Marion* 78 (2003): 77–93.

——. "Qu'est-ce qui est donné? La pensée et l'événement." *Archives de Philosophie* 59 (1996): 629–57.

Benson, Bruce Ellis. *Graven Ideologies: Nietzsche, Derrida and Marion on Modern Idolatry*. Downers Grove, Ill.: InterVarsity Press, 2002.

——. "Love Is a Given." *Christian Century*, 8 Feb. 2003, 22–25.

Bloechl, Jeffrey. "Dialectical Approaches to Retrieving God after Heidegger: Premises and Consequences (Lacoste and Marion)." *Pacifica* 13 (2000): 288–98.

Blond, Phillip. "Theology and Perception." *Modern Theology* 14.4 (1998): 523–34.

Bossche, Stijn van den. "God Does Appear in Immanence after All: Jean-Luc Marion's Phenomenology as a New First Philosophy for Theology." In *Sacramental Presence in a Postmodern Context*. Ed. L. Boeve and L. Leijssen. Leuven: Leuven University Press, 2001.

Boynton, Eric. "Enigmatic Sites and Continental Philosophy of Religion: Must Philosophy Once Again Yield to Theology?" In *Explorations in Contemporary Continental Philosophy of Religion*. Ed. Deane-Peter Baker and Patrick Maxwell. New York: Rodopi, 2003.

Bradley, Arthur. "God *sans* Being: Derrida, Marion and 'A Paradoxical Writing of the Word *without*.'" *Literature and Theology* 14.3 (2000): 299–312.

Brès, Yvon. "L'avenir du judéo-christianisme (suite et fin)." *Revue Philosophique de la France et de l'Etranger* 192.1 (2002): 55–83.

Brito, Emilio. "La réception de la pensée de Heidegger dans la théologie catholique." *Nouvelle Revue Théologique* 119.3 (1997): 352–74.

Caldarone, Rosaria. Review of Jean-Luc Marion, *De surcroît. Giornale di metafisica* 25 (2003): 424–27.

Caputo, John D. "God Is Wholly Other — Almost: 'Difference' and the Hyperbolic Alterity of God." In *The Otherness of God*. Ed. Orrin F. Summerell. Charlottesville: University Press of Virginia, 1998.

———. "How to Avoid Speaking of God: The Violence of Natural Theology." In *Prospects for Natural Theology*. Ed. Eugene Thomas Long. Washington, D.C.: The Catholic University of America Press, 1992.

———. "The Poetics of the Impossible and the Kingdom of God." In *Rethinking Philosophy of Religion: Approaches from Continental Philosophy*. Ed. Philip Goodchild. New York: Fordham University Press, 2002.

Caputo, John D., and Michael J. Scanlon, eds. *God, the Gift, and Postmodernism*. Bloomington: Indiana University Press, 1999.

Carlson, Thomas A. *Indiscretion: Finitude and the Naming of God*. Chicago: University of Chicago Press, 1999.

Clark, David L. "Otherwise than God: Schelling, Marion." In *Trajectories of Mysticism in Theory and Literature*. Ed. Philip Leonard. Houndsmills, Basingstoke, Hants.: Palgrave Macmillan, 2000.

Clayton, Philip. "Descartes and Infinite Perfection." *Proceedings of the American Catholic Philosophical Association* 66 (1992): 137–47.

Colette, Jacques. "Phénoménologie et métaphysique." Review of Dominique Janicaud, *Le tournant théologique. Critique: Revue générale des publications françaises et étrangères* 548–49 (1993): 56–73.

DeHart, Paul. "The Ambiguous Infinite: Jüngel, Marion, and the God of Descartes." *The Journal of Religion* 82.1 (2002): 75–96.

Del-Barco, Oscar. "La filosofia como pensamiento del don." *Nombres* 10 (2000): 101–53.

Depraz, Natalie. "Gibt es eine Gebung des Unendlichen?" In *Perspektiven der Philosophie*. Ed. Rudolph Berlinger. Amsterdam: Rodopi, 1997.

———. "The Return of Phenomenology in Recent French Moral Philosophy." In *Phenomenological Approaches to Moral Philosophy*. Ed. John J. Drummond and I. Embree. Dordrecht: Kluwer Academic Publishers, 2002.

Dodd, James. "Marion and Phenomenology." Review of Jean-Luc Marion, *Being Given. Graduate Faculty Philosophy Journal* 25.1 (2004): 161–84.

Drabinski, John E. "Sense and Icon: The Problem of *Sinngebung* in Levinas and Marion." *Philosophy Today* 42 Suppl. (1998): 47–58.

Duquesne, Marcel. "A propos d'un livre récent: Jean-Luc Marion «Dieu sans l'être»." *Mélanges de Science religieuse* 42.2 (1985): 57–75; 42.3 (1985): 127–39.

Ewbank, Michael B. "Of Idols, Icons, and Aquinas's Esse: Reflections on Jean-Luc Marion." *International Philosophical Quarterly* 42.2 (2002): 161–75.

Falque, Emmanuel. "Phénoménologie de l'extraordinaire." *Philosophie: Jean-Luc Marion* 78 (2003): 52–76.

Faulconer, James E., ed. *Transcendence in Philosophy and Religion*. Bloomington: Indiana University Press, 2003.

Gabellieri, Emmanuel. "De la métaphysique à la phénoménology: une «relève»?" *Revue Philosophique de Louvain* 94.4 (1996): 625–45.

Gagnon, Martin. "La phénoménologie à la limite." *Eidos* 11.1–2 (1993): 111–30.

Gilbert, Paul. "Substance et présence: Derrida et Marion, critiques de Husserl." *Gregorianum* 75.1 (1994): 95–133.

Godzieba, Anthony J. "Ontotheology to Excess: Imagining God without Being." *Theological Studies* 56.1 (1995): 3–20.

Greisch, Jean. "L'herméneutique dans la «phénoménologie comme telle»: Trois questions à propos de Réduction et Donation." *Revue de Métaphysique et de Morale* 96.1 (1991): 43–63.

Grimwood, Steven. "Iconography and Postmodernity." *Literature and Theology* 17.1 (2003): 76–97.

Grondin, Jean. "La tension de la donation ultime et de la pensée herméneutique de l'application chez Jean-Luc Marion." *Dialogue* 38.3 (1999): 547–59.

Gschwandtner, Christina M. "Ethics, Eros, or Caritas? Levinas and Marion on Individuation of the Other." *Philosophy Today* 49.1 (2005): 70–87.

———. "Love as a Declaration of War? On the Absolute Character of Love in Jean-Luc Marion's Phenomenology of Eros." In *Transforming Philosophy and Religion: Love's Wisdom*. Ed. Norman Wirzba and Bruce Ellis Benson. Bloomington: Indiana University Press, 2008.

———. "A new 'Apologia': The Relationship between Theology and Philosophy in the Work of Jean-Luc Marion." *Heythrop Journal* 46 (2005): 299–313.

———. "Praise — Pure and Personal? Jean-Luc Marion's Phenomenologies of Prayer." In *The Phenomenology of Prayer*. Ed. Bruce Ellis Benson and Norman Wirzba. New York: Fordham University Press, 2005.

Guarino, Thomas. "Postmodernity and Five Fundamental Theological Issues." *Theological Studies* 57.4 (1996): 654–89.

Han, Béatrice. "Transcendence and the Hermeneutic Circle: Some Thoughts on Marion and Heidegger." In *Transcendence in Philosophy and Religion*. Ed. James Faulconer. Bloomington: Indiana University Press, 2003.

Hankey, Wayne J. "Between and Beyond Augustine and Descartes: More than a Source of the Self." *Augustinian Studies* 32.1 (2001): 65–88.

———. "ReChristianizing Augustine Postmodern Style: Readings by Jacques Derrida, Robert Dodaro, Jean-Luc Marion, Rowan Williams, Lewis Ayres and John Milbank." *Animus* 2 (1997): 33–69.

———. "'Theoria versus Poesis': Neoplatonism and Trinitarian Difference in Aquinas, John Milbank, Jean-Luc Marion and John Zizioulas." *Modern Theology* 15.4 (1999): 387–415.

———. "Why Philosophy Abides for Aquinas." *Heythrop Journal* 42 (2001): 329–48.

Hanson, J. A. "Jean-Luc Marion and the Possibility of a Post-Modern Theology." *Mars Hill Review* 12 (1998): 93–104.

Hart, Kevin, ed. *Counter-Experiences: Reading Jean-Luc Marion*. Notre Dame, Ind.: University of Notre Dame Press, 2007.

Henry, Michel. "Quatre Principes de la phénoménolgie: A propos de *Réduction et donation* de Jean-Luc Marion." *Revue de Métaphysique et de Morale* 96.1 (1991): 3–26.

Höhn, Gerhard. "Suche nach Ursprünglichkeit: Die Wiedergeburt der Metaphysik aus dem Erbe der Phänomenologie." *Frankfurter Rundschau*, 29 November 1994, n.p.

Holzer, Vincent. "Phénoménologie radicale et phénomène de révélation." Review of

Jean-Luc Marion, *Étant donné. Transversalités: Revue de l'institut catholique de Paris* (1999): 55–68.

Horner, Robyn. "The Betrayal of Transcendence." In Regina Schwartz, ed. *Transcendence: Philosophy, Literature, and Theology Approach the Beyond.* New York: Routledge, 2004.

———. "The Face as Icon: A Phenomenology of the Invisible." *The Australasian Catholic Record* 82 (2005): 19–28.

———. *Jean-Luc Marion: A Theo-logical Introduction.* Hants: Ashgate, 2005.

———. "Problème du mal et péché des origines." *Recherches de science religieuse* 90.1 (2002): 63–86.

———. *Rethinking God as Gift: Derrida, Marion, and the Limits of Phenomenology.* New York: Fordham University Press, 2001.

Janicaud, Dominique. *La phénoménologie éclatée.* Combas: Édition de l'Éclat, 1998.

———. *Phenomenology "Wide Open": After the French Debate.* Trans. Charles N. Cabral. New York: Fordham University Press, 2005.

———. *Le Tournant thélogique de la phénoménologie française.* Combas: Éditions de l'Éclat, 1991.

Janicaud, Dominique, Jean-François Courtine, Jean-Louis Chrétien, Michel Henry, Jean-Luc Marion, and Paul Ricœur. *Phenomenology and the "Theological Turn": The French Debate.* New York: Fordham University Press, 2000.

Jones, L. Gregory, and Stephen E. Fowl, eds. *Rethinking Metaphysics.* Cambridge: Blackwell, 1995.

Kal, Victor. "Being Unable to Speak, Seen as a Period: Difference and Distance in Jean-Luc Marion." In *Flight of the Gods.* Ed. Ilse N. Bulhof and Laurens ten Kate. New York: Fordham University Press, 2000.

Kalinowski, Georges. "Discours de louange et discours métaphysique: Denys l'aréopagite et Thomas d'Aquin." *Rivista di Filosofia Neo Scolastica* 73 (1981): 399–404.

Kerr, Fergus. "Aquinas after Marion." *New Blackfriars* 78 (1995): 354–64.

Klein, Vincent. Review of Jean-Luc Marion, *De surcroît. Revue Thomiste* 103 (2003): 328–30.

Kosky, Jeffrey L. "Philosophy of Religion and Return to Phenomenology in Jean-Luc Marion: From *God without Being* to *Being Given.*" *American Catholic Philosophical Quarterly* 78.4 (2004): 629–47.

Kraftson-Hogue, Mike. "Predication Turning to Praise: Marion and Augustine on God and Hermeneutics — (Giver, Giving, Gift, Giving)." *Literature and Theology* 14.4 (2000): 399–411.

Kühn, Rolf. "Intentionale und Materiale Phänomenologie." *Tijdschift voor Filosofie* 54.4 (1992): 693–714.

———. "Langeweile und Anruf: Eine Heidegger- und Husserl-Revision mit dem Problemhintergrund 'absoluter Phänomene' bei Jean-Luc Marion." *Philosophisches Jahrbuch* 102 (1995): 144–55.

———. *Radikalisierte Phänomenologie.* Frankfurt am Main: Peter Lang/Europäischer Verlag der Wissenschaften, 2003.

Lacoste, Jean-Yves. "Penser à Dieu en l'aimant: Philosophie et théologie de J.-L. Marion." *Archives de Philosophie* 50 (1987): 245–70.

———. Review of Jean-Luc Marion, *L'idole et la distance. Résurrection* 56 (1977): 78–83.

Laird, Martin. "'Whereof We Speak': Gregory of Nyssa, Jean-Luc Marion and the Current Apophatic Rage." *Heythrop Journal* 42 (2001): 1–12.

Lakeland, Paul. "Is the Holy Wholly Other, and is the Wholly Other Really Holy? Reflections on the Postmodern Doctrine of God." In *Divine Aporia: Postmodern Conversations about the Other*. Ed. John C. Hawley. Lewisburg, Pa.: Bucknell University Press, 2000.

Larulle, François. "L'Appel et le Phénomène." *Revue de Métaphysique et de Morale* 96.1 (1991): 27–41.

Leask, Ian, and Eoin Cassidy, eds. *Givenness and God: Questions of Jean-Luc Marion.* New York: Fordham University Press, 2005.

Llewelyn, John. "Meanings Reserved, Re-served, and Reduced." *Southern Journal of Philosophy* 32 Suppl. (1994): 27–54.

Lock, Charles. "Against Being: An Introduction to the Thought of Jean-Luc Marion." *St. Vladimir's Theological Quarterly* 37.4 (1993): 370–80.

Longhitano, Tiziana. Review of Jean-Luc Marion, *Étant donné. Alpha omega: Rivista di filosofia e teologia dell'Ateneo Pontificio Regina* 4 (2001): 190–93.

Look, Brandon. Review of Jean-Luc Marion, *Cartesian Questions. Review of Metaphysics* 54.1 (2000): 160–61.

Loparic, Zeljko. "A propos du Cartesianisme gris de Marion." *Manuscrito* 11 (1988): 129–33.

MacKinlay, Shane. "Eyes Wide Shut: A Response to Jean-Luc Marion's Account of the Journey to Emmaus." *Modern Theology* 20.3 (2004): 447–56.

Macquarrie, John. "Postmodernism in Philosophy of Religion and Theology." *International Journal for Philosophy of Religion* 50 (2001): 9–27.

Manoussakis, John P. "The Phenomenon of God: From Husserl to Marion." *American Catholic Philosophical Quarterly* 78.1 (2004): 53–68.

——. "Thinking at the Limits: Jacques Derrida and Jean-Luc Marion in Dialogue with Richard Kearney." *Philosophy Today* 48.1 (2004): 3–26.

Marshall, David J., Jr. Review of Jean-Luc Marion, *Ontologie grise* and *Théologie blanche. Philosophische Rundschau* 31 (1984): 126–39.

Martis, John. "Thomistic Esse — Idol or Icon? Jean-Luc Marion's *God without Being.*" *Pacifica* 9 (1996): 55–68.

Mathieu, Olivier. Review of Jean-Luc Marion, *De surcroît. Philosophiques* 30.1 (2003): 280–85.

Milbank, John. "Can a Gift be Given? Prolegomena to a Future Trinitarian Metaphysic." *Modern Theology* 11.1 (1995): 119–58.

——. "Only Theology Overcomes Metaphysics." In *The Word Made Strange: Theology, Language, Culture.* Oxford: Blackwell, 1997.

——. "The Soul of Reciprocity, Part One: Reciprocity Refused." *Modern Theology* 17.3 (2001): 335–91.

——. "The Soul of Reciprocity, Part Two: Reciprocity Granted." *Modern Theology* 17.4 (2001): 485–507.

Morrow, Derek J. "The Love 'without Being' That Opens (To) Distance, Part One: Exploring the Givenness of the Erotic Phenomenon with Jean-Luc Marion." *Heythrop Journal* 46.3 (2005): 281–98.

——. "The Love 'without Being' That Opens (To) Distance, Part Two: From the Icon of Distance to the Distance of the Icon in Marion's Phenomenology of Love." *Heythrop Journal* 46.4 (2005): 493–511.

Narbonne, Jean-Marc. "Plotin, Descartes et la notion de 'causa sui.'" *Archives de Philosophie* 56.2 (1993): 177–95.

Neamtu, Mihail. Review of Jean-Luc Marion, *De surcroît. Studia phaenomenologica: Romanian Journal for Phenomenology* 1 (2001): 419–25.

——. Review of Jean-Luc Marion, *Étant donné. Studia phaenomenologica: Romanian Journal for Phenomenology* 1 (2001): 407–14.

Olivetti, Marco M. "L'argomento ontologico." *Archivio di Filosofia* 58.1–3 (1990): 711–64.

Piché, Claude. Review of Jean-Luc Marion, *Réduction et donation. Philosophiques* 20 (1993): 222–24.

Prouvost, Géry. "La tension irrésolue: Les *Questions cartésiennes, II* de Jean-Luc Marion." *Revue Thomiste* 98.1 (1998): 95–102.

Purcell, Michael. "The Ethical Signification of the Sacraments." *Gregorianum* 79.2 (1998): 323–43.

Ricard, Marie-Andrée. "La question de la donation chez Jean-Luc Marion." *Laval théologique et philosophique* 57 (2001): 83–94.

Robbins, Jeffrey W. "Overcoming Overcoming: In Praise of Ontotheology." In *Explorations in Contemporary Continental Philosophy of Religion*. Ed. Deane-Peter Baker and Patrick Maxwell. New York: Rodopi, 2003.

——. "The Problem of Ontotheology: Complicating the Divide between Philosophy and Theology." *Heythrop Journal* 43 (2002): 139–51.

Röd, Wolfgang. Review of Jean-Luc Marion, *Sur le prisme métaphysique de Descartes. Archiv für Geschichte der Philosophie* 75 (1993): 229–32.

Rosemann, Philipp W. "Der Melancholiker sieht wie Gott aber weil er das Andere verweigert, blickt er ins Nichts: Jean-Luc Marions negative Theologie." *Frankfurter Allgemeine Zeitung* 82, 4 April 1993, N5.

Sanders, Theresa. "The Gift of Prayer." In *Secular Theology: American Radical Theological Thought*. Ed. Clayton Crockett. New York: Routledge, 2001.

Schmitz, Kenneth L. "The God of Love." *Thomist* 57.3 (1993): 495–508.

Smit, Peter-Ben. "The Bishop and His/Her Eucharistic Community: A Critique of Jean-Luc Marion's Eucharistic Hermeneutic." *Modern Theology* 19.1 (2003): 29–40.

Smith, James K. A. "Between Predication and Silence: Augustine on How (Not) to Speak of God." *Heythrop Journal* 41.1 (2000): 66–86.

——. "The Call as Gift: The Subject's Donation in Marion and Levinas." In *The Hermeneutics of Charity: Interpretation, Selfhood, and Postmodern Faith*. Ed. James K. A. Smith and Henry Venema. Grand Rapids, Mich.: Brazos Press, 2004.

——. "How (Not) to Tell a Secret: Interiority and the Strategy of 'Confession.'" *American Catholic Philosophical Quarterly* 74.1 (2000): 135–51.

——. "Liberating Religion from Theology: Marion and Heidegger on the Possibility of a Phenomenology of Religion." *International Journal for Philosophy of Religion* 46.1 (1999): 17–33.

——. "Respect and Donation: A Critique of Marion's Critique of Husserl." *American Catholic Philosophical Quarterly* 71.4 (1997): 523–38.

Specker, Tobias. *Einen Anderen Gott denken? Zum Verständnis der Alterität Gottes bei Jean-Luc Marion*. Frankfurt am Main: Verlag Josef Knecht, 2002.

Stapleton, Charles Matthew. "The Derrida-Marion Debate: Performative Language and Mystical Theology." *Kinesis* 31.2 (2004): 4–17.

Verhack, I. Review of Ruud Welten, *Fenomenologie en beeldverbod bij Emmanuel Levinas en Jean-Luc Marion. Tijdschrift voor Filosofie* 64.3 (2002): 601–602.

Vogel, Arthur A. "Catching Up with Jean-Luc Marion." *Anglican Theological Review* 82.4 (2000): 803–11.

Ward, Graham. "The Theological Project of Jean-Luc Marion." In *Post-secular Philosophy: Between Philosophy and Theology.* Ed. Phillip Blond. New York: Routledge, 1998.

Welten, Ruud. *Fenomenologie en beeldverbod bij Emmanuel Levinas en Jean-Luc Marion.* Damon: Budel, 2001.

——. "Het andere ego van Descartes." *Tijdschrift voor Filosofie* 60.3 (1998): 572–79.

——. "The Paradox of God's Appearance: On Jean-Luc Marion." In *God in France: Eight Contemporary French Thinkers on God.* Ed. Peter Jonkers and Ruud Welten. Leuven: Peeters, 2005.

——. "Saturation and Disappointment: Marion according to Husserl." *Tijdschrift voor Filosofie en Theologie/International Journal in Philosophy and Theology* 65.1 (2004): 79–96.

Welten, Ruud, ed. *God en het Denken: Over de filosofie van Jean-Luc Marion.* Nijmegen: Valkhof Pers, 2000.

Westphal, Merold. "Continental Philosophy of Religion." In *The Oxford Handbook of Philosophy of Religion.* Ed. William J. Wainwright. Oxford: Oxford University Press, 2005.

——. "Transfiguration as Saturated Phenomenon." *Philosophy and Scripture* 1.1 (2003): 1–10.

Westphal, Merold, ed. *Postmodern Philosophy and Christian Thought.* Bloomington: Indiana University Press, 1999.

Winkler, Kenneth. "Descartes and the Names of God." *American Catholic Philosophical Quarterly* 67.4 (1993): 451–65.

Wohlmuth, Josef, ed. *Ruf und Gabe: Zum Verhältnis von Phänomenologie und Theologie.* Bonn: Borengässer, 2000.

Wolf, Kurt. *Religionsphilosophie in Frankreich: Der 'ganz Andere' und die personale Struktur der Welt.* München: Wilhelm Fink Verlag, 1999.

Zarader, Marlène. "Phenomenality and Transcendence." In *Transcendence in Philosophy and Religion.* Ed. James Faulconer. Bloomington: Indiana University Press, 2003.

Other Secondary Sources

Alliez, Éric. *De l'impossibilité de la phénoménologie: Sur la philosophie française contemporaine.* Paris: Librairie philosophique J. Vrin, 1995.

Balthasar, Hans Urs von. *Glaubhaft ist nur Liebe.* Einsiedeln: Johannes Verlag, 1963.

——. *The Glory of the Lord: A Theological Aesthetics.* Trans. Andrew Louth, Francis McDonagh, and Brian McNeil. San Francisco: Ignatius Press, 1982.

——. *The God Question and Modern Man.* Trans. Hilda Graef. New York: Seabury Press, 1967.

——. *Herrlichkeit.* Einsiedeln: Johannes Verlag, 1965.

——. *Im Raum der Metaphysik.* Einsiedeln: Johannes Verlag, 1965.

——. *Love Alone.* Trans. Alexander Dru. New York: Herder and Herder, 1969.

———. *The von Balthasar Reader.* Ed. Medard Kehl and Werner Loser. Trans. Robert J. Daly and Fred Lawrence. New York: Crossroads, 1982.

———. *Word and Redemption.* Trans. A. V. Littledale. New York: Herder and Herder, 1965.

Bloechl, Jeffrey, ed. *The Face of the Other and the Trace of God: Essays on the Philosophy of Emmanuel Levinas.* New York: Fordham University Press, 2000.

———. *Liturgy of the Neighbor: Emmanuel Levinas and the Religion of Responsibility.* Pittsburgh: Duquesne University Press, 2000.

Blond, Phillip, ed. *Post-secular Philosophy: Between Philosophy and Theology.* New York: Routledge, 1998.

Bruaire, Claude. *La Confession de la foi chrétienne.* Paris: Fayard, 1977.

Bulhof, Ilse N., and Laurens ten Kate, eds. *Flight of the Gods: Philosophical Perspectives on Negative Theology.* New York: Fordham University Press, 2000.

Cadava, Eduardo, Peter Connors, and Jean-Luc Nancy, eds. *Who Comes after the Subject?* New York: Routledge, 1991.

Caputo, John D. *On Religion.* London: Routledge, 2001.

———. *The Prayers and Tears of Jacques Derrida: Religion without Religion.* Bloomington: Indiana University Press, 1997.

———, ed. *The Religious.* Oxford: Blackwell, 2002.

Caputo, John D., Mark Dooley, and Michael J. Scanlon, eds. *Questioning God.* Bloomington: Indiana University Press, 2001.

Carraud, Vincent. *Pascal et la philosophie.* Paris: Presses Universitaires de France, 1992.

Coward, Harold, and Toby Foshay, eds. *Derrida and Negative Theology.* Albany: State University of New York Press, 1992.

Crockett, Clayton. *A Theology of the Sublime.* London: Routledge, 2001.

Derrida, Jacques. *Acts of Religion.* New York: Routledge, 2002.

———. *Adieu: To Emmanuel Levinas.* Trans. Pascale-Anne Brault and Michael Naas. Stanford: Stanford University Press, 1999.

———. *Aporias.* Trans. Thomas Dutoit. Stanford: Stanford University Press, 1993.

———. *Dissemination.* Trans. Barbara Johnson. Chicago: University of Chicago Press, 1981.

———. *Foi et Savoir.* Paris: Éditions de Seuil, 2000.

———. *The Gift of Death.* Trans. David Wills. Chicago: University of Chicago Press, 1999.

———. *Given Time: I. Counterfeit Money.* Trans. Peggy Kamuf. Chicago: University of Chicago Press, 1992.

———. *Khôra.* Paris: Galilée. 1993.

———. *Margins of Philosophy.* Trans. Alan Bass. Chicago: University of Chicago Press, 1982.

———. *Sauf le Nom.* Paris: Galilée, 1993.

———. *Speech and Phenomena and Other Essays on Husserl's Theory of Signs.* Trans. David B. Allison and Newton Garver. Evanston, Ill.: Northwestern University Press, 1973.

———. *Sur Parole: Instantanés philosophiques.* Saint Étienne: Éditions de l'Aube, 1999.

Descartes, René. *Oeuvres de Descartes.* Ed. Charles Adam and Paul Tannery. 12 vols. Paris: Vrin, 1964–76.

———. *The Philosophical Writings of Descartes*. Trans. John Cottingham, Robert Stoothoff, and Donald Murdoch (and Anthony Kenny for vol. 3). 3 vols. Cambridge: Cambridge University Press, 1984–91.

Duméry, Henry. *Phenomenology of Religion*. Trans. Paul Barrett. Berkeley: University of California Press, 1975.

Flanagan, Kieran, and Peter C. Jupp, eds. *Postmodernity, Sociology and Religion*. London: Macmillan, 1996.

Goodchild, Philip, ed. *Rethinking Philosophy of Religion: Approaches from Continental Philosophy*. New York: Fordham University Press, 2002.

Guerrière, Daniel, ed. *Phenomenology of the Truth Proper to Religion*. Albany: SUNY Press, 1990.

Hart, David Bentley. *The Beauty of the Infinite: The Aesthetics of Christian Truth*. Grand Rapids, Mich.: William B. Eerdmans Publishing Company, 2003.

Hart, Kevin. *The Trespass of the Sign: Deconstruction, Theology and Philosophy*. Cambridge: Cambridge University Press, 1989.

Heidegger, Martin. *The Basic Problems of Phenomenology*. Trans. Albert Hofstadter. Bloomington: Indiana University Press, 1982.

———. *Die Grundprobleme der Phänomenologie*. Frankfurt/M: Vittorio Klostermann Verlag, 1957, 1989, 1997.

———. *Holzwege*. Frankfurt/M: Vittorio Klostermann Verlag, 1957.

———. *Identität und Differenz*. Pfullingen: Günther Neske Verlag, 1957.

———. *On Time and Being*. Trans. Joan Stambaugh. New York: Harper and Row, 1972.

———. *Sein und Zeit*. Tübingen: Max Niemeyer Verlag, 1926, 1993.

———. *Wegmarken*. Frankfurt/M: Vittorio Klostermann Verlag, 1967, 1978, 1996.

Henry, Michel. *C'est moi la vérité: Pour une philosophie du christianisme*. Paris: Éditions du Seuil, 1996.

———. *The Essence of Manifestation*. Trans. Girard Etzkorn. The Hague: Martinus Nijhoff, 1973.

———. *Incarnation: Une phénoménolgie de la chair*. Paris: Éditions de Seuil, 2000.

———. *Paroles du Christ*. Paris: Éditions de Seuil, 2002.

———. *Philosophy and Phenomenology of the Body*. Trans. Girard Etzkorn. The Hague: Martinus Nijhoff, 1975.

Husserl, Edmund. *Cartesian Meditations: An Introduction to Phenomenology*. Trans. Dorion Cairns. The Hague: Martinus Nijhoff, 1960.

———. *Die Idee der Phänomenologie: Fünf Vorlesungen*. Haag: Martinus Nijhoff, 1973.

———. *Ideen zu einer reinen Phänomenologie und phänomenologischen Philosophie*. Den Haag: Martinus Nijhoff, 1976.

———. *Logische Untersuchungen*. Tübingen: Max Niemeyer Verlag, 1968.

———. *Phenomenology and the Crisis of Philosophy*. Trans. Quentin Lauer. New York: Harper and Row, 1965.

Kearney, Richard. *Debates in Continental Philosophy: Conversations with Contemporary Thinkers*. New York: Fordham University Press, 2004.

———. *The God Who May Be: A Hermeneutics of Religion*. Bloomington: Indiana University Press, 2001.

———. *On Stories*. London: Routledge, 2002.

———. *On Strangers, Gods and Monsters*. London: Routledge, 2002.

Kearney, Richard, and J. Stephen O'Leary, eds. *Heidegger et la question de Dieu*. Paris: Grasset, 1980.

Kosky, Jeffrey L. *Levinas and the Philosophy of Religion*. Bloomington: Indiana University Press, 2001.

Laycock, Steven William. *Foundations for a Phenomenological Theology*. Lewiston: Edwin Mellen Press, 1988.

Laycock, Steven W., and James G. Hart, eds. *Essays in Phenomenological Theology*. Albany, N.Y.: SUNY Press, 1986.

Lévinas, Emmanuel. *Alterity and Transcendence*. Trans. Michael B. Smith. New York: Columbia University Press, 1999.

——. *Autrement qu'être ou au-delà de l'essence*. Paris: Kluwer Academic, 1978.

——. *Basic Philosophical Writings*. Ed. Adriaan T. Peperzak, Simon Critchley, and Robert Bernasconi. Bloomington: Indiana University Press, 1996.

——. *De Dieu qui vient à l'idée*. Paris: Vrin, 1982.

——. *De l'existence à l'existant*. Paris: Vrin, 1963.

——. *Dieu, la mort, et le temps*. Paris: Grasset, 1993.

——. *Difficile liberté: Essais sur le judaïsme*. Paris: Albin Michel, 1963.

——. *Entre nous: Essais sur le penser-à-l'autre*. Paris: Grasset, 1991.

——. *Entre nous: On Thinking-of-the-Other*. Trans. Michael B. Smith and Barbara Harshav. New York: Columbia University Press, 1998.

——. *Éthique et infini: Dialogues avec Philippe Nemo*. Paris: Fayard, 1982.

——. *God, Death, and Time*. Trans. Bettina Bergo. Stanford: Stanford University Press, 2000.

——. *Humanisme de l'autre homme*. Paris: Fata Morgana, 1972.

——. *Otherwise Than Being or Beyond Essence*. Trans. Alphonso Lingis. The Hague: Martinus Nijhoff Publishers, 1981.

——. *Le temps et l'autre*. Paris: Presses Universitaires de France, 1979.

——. *Totalité et infini: essai sur l'extériorité*. Paris: Kluwer Academic, 1971.

——. *Totality and Infinity: An Essay on Exteriority*. Trans. Alphonso Lingis. Pittsburgh: Duquesne University Press, 1969.

Llewelyn, John. *Appositions of Jacques Derrida and Emmanuel Levinas*. Bloomington: Indiana University Press, 2002.

——. *Emmanuel Levinas: The Genealogy of Ethics*. New York: Routledge, 1995.

Lowe, Walter. *Theology and Difference: The Wound of Reason*. Bloomington: Indiana University Press, 1993.

Milbank, John. *Being Reconciled: Ontology and Pardon*. New York: Routledge, 2003.

——. *The Word Made Strange: Theology, Language, Culture*. Oxford: Blackwell, 1997.

Olthuis, James H. *The Beautiful Risk*. Grand Rapids, Mich.: Zondervan, 2001.

Pascal, Blaise. *Thoughts*. Trans. W. F. Trotter. Danbury, Ct.: Grolier Enterprises Corp., 1988.

Peperzak, Adriaan T. *Beyond: The Philosophy of Emmanuel Levinas*. Evanston, Ill.: Northwestern University Press, 1997.

——, ed. *Ethics as First Philosophy: The Significance of Emmanuel Levinas for Philosophy, Literature and Religion*. New York: Routledge, 1995.

Pickstock, Catherine. *After Writing: On the Liturgical Consummation of Philosophy*. Oxford: Blackwell, 1998.

Pseudo-Dionysisus. *The Complete Works*. Trans. Colm Luibheid. In *The Classics of Western Spirituality*. New York: Paulist Press, 1987.

Schrag, Calvin O. *God as Otherwise Than Being: Toward a Semantics of the Gift*. Evanston, Ill.: Northwestern University Press, 2002.

Schrift, Alan D., ed. *The Logic of the Gift: Toward an Ethic of Generosity*. New York: Routledge, 1997.

Smith, James K. A. *The Fall of Interpretation: Philosophical Foundations for a Creational Hermeneutic*. Downers Grove, Ill.: InterVarsity, 2000.

———. *Speech and Theology: Language and the Logic of Incarnation*. New York: Routledge, 2002.

Smith, Steven G. *The Argument to the Other: Reason beyond Reason in the Thought of Karl Barth and Emmanuel Levinas*. Chico, Calif.: Scholars Press, 1983.

Sokolowski, Robert. *Eucharistic Presence: A Study in the Theology of Disclosure*. Washington, D.C.: Catholic University of America Press, 1994.

———. *The God of Faith and Reason: Foundations of Christian Theology*. Washington, D.C.: Catholic University of America Press, 1995, 1982.

———. *Husserlian Meditations: How Words Present Things*. Evanston, Ill.: Northwestern University Press, 1974.

Summerell, Orrin F., ed. *The Otherness of God*. Charlottesville: University Press of Virginia, 1998.

Vries, Hent de. *Philosophy and the Turn to Religion*. Baltimore: John Hopkins Press, 1999.

Ward, Graham. *Barth, Derrida and the Language of Theology*. Cambridge: Cambridge University Press, 1995.

———, ed. *The Postmodern God: A Theological Reader*. Malden, Mass.: Blackwell, 1997.

Webb, Stephen H. *The Gifting God: A Trinitarian Ethics of Excess*. New York: Oxford University Press, 1996.

INDEX

l'adonné. See devoted

affection, 77, 82, 199–200, 216, 217, 225, 246, 293n29

analogy, doctrine of, xvi, 101, 105, 106, 109, 110, 112, 113–118, 122–123, 127–129, 130, 131, 133–138, 143, 150, 154, 174, 188, 229, 243, 273n7, 274n17, 276nn23,24,27,31, 277n34, 279n75, 280n9, 289n46

anamorphosis, 69–70, 76, 85

Aquinas, St. Thomas, xvii, 4, 5, 13–16, 23, 46, 57, 103, 113–115, 122–123, 128, 166, 202, 245, 251n4, 254n3, 256n22, 276nn27,31, 278n64, 280n9

Aristotle, xv, 11, 15–21, 26, 74, 185, 186, 187, 203, 254n3, 255n9

Augustine, 112, 186, 201–202, 253n20, 269n6

Balthasar, Hans Urs von, xii, xvii, 168, 282n26

Barth, Karl, xii, xvii, 4, 177

Benson, Bruce, xvi, 3, 65, 77, 160, 171–172, 173, 174, 251nPart 1:1, 261n16, 265n50, 290nn62–65

Caputo, John, xvi, xix, 73, 78, 95–98, 100, 157, 160–162, 163, 164, 165, 166, 167, 169, 174, 176, 264n42, 265n49, 269nn11–14, 284nn6,12, 286nn23,24, 287nn25–32

Carlson, Thomas, xiii, xvi, 102, 157, 160, 163–166, 167, 169, 174, 183, 217, 251nPreface:3, 271nn25–30, 287n38, 288nn39–44, 295nn32–34

causa sui, 3, 9, 22, 24–28, 37, 40, 46, 47, 50, 53, 64, 71, 90, 117, 121–124, 143, 187, 194, 202, 206, 256n24, 278nn52–54,64

charity, xiii, xvi, 4, 13, 31–38, 53, 56–57, 85, 126, 127, 128, 131, 137, 140–149, 158, 160, 177, 182, 184, 194, 223, 225–242, 243–250, 257n52, 269n4, 271n29, 279n74, 296nn6,8, 297n16, 300n14

code, 15, 17–19, 24–28, 62, 70, 79, 81, 115–116, 187, 194–195, 293n27, 296n6

constitution, 182; by intuitus, 20; onto-theo-logical, 9, 21–27, 30, 41–45, 51, 187, 188, 196, 199; phenomenological, 60–71, 77, 79, 81–83, 205, 206, 208, 209, 219, 231, 252n9, 253n19, 266n58

Dasein, xviii, 8–9, 49–50, 52, 53, 62, 63, 67, 71, 81, 83, 186, 189, 194–199, 206, 208–209, 211, 219, 263n28, 264n37, 293n18

death of God, 3, 8, 41, 45–47, 136, 146, 159

Derrida, Jacques, xii, xvii, xviii, 28, 29, 30, 34, 36, 41, 43, 45, 53–55, 58, 61, 72–75, 78, 96–98, 125, 136, 138, 151, 155, 160–162, 164–168, 171–172, 191, 192, 194, 222, 251n7, 257nn34,35, 260n4, 261n5, 262n19, 264n38, 265n49, 268n3, 270nn18,22, 280n15, 284n2, 285nn12,16, 286n24, 288n38, 290n62, 292n10

devoted, 206, 207, 211, 212–220, 221, 223, 296n49, 298n22

différance, 54–55, 136, 161, 259n31, 269n11, 287n28

Dionysius the Areopagite, xvii, 98, 114, 118, 125, 128, 131, 137–138, 144, 155–157, 165, 166, 169, 202, 251n9, 277n42, 280n15, 281nn16–19, 285n16

distance, xiii, xvi, 35, 36, 38, 42, 43, 49, 53, 55, 67, 69, 70, 74, 80, 101, 102, 107, 109, 111, 115, 128, 129, 131–149, 154, 166, 221, 227, 233, 234, 238, 249, 260n34, 264n36, 273n8, 276n30, 280nn9,11, 286n24

Ereignis, 63–65, 67, 83, 263n28

eternal truth, 71, 105–113, 115, 116, 119, 127, 147, 188, 195, 273nn4,6,8, 274n22, 279n70

317

CHRISTINA M. GSCHWANDTNER is an assistant professor in the philosophy department at the University of Scranton. She has published several essays on Marion and the philosophy of religion in edited collections and jour-
nals. She has translated Jean-Luc Marion's *Questions cartésiennes II* and is
currently editing a translation of *Le Visible et le révélé*.

Printed and bound by CPI Group (UK) Ltd, Croydon, CR0 4YY

13/04/2025

14656544-0005